BSA
TWINS - A7 & A10
Gold Portfolio
1946-1962

Compiled by
R.M.Clarke

ISBN 1 85520 3367

BROOKLANDS BOOKS LTD.
P.O. BOX 146, COBHAM,
SURREY, KT11 1LG. UK

A-BS46BGP

ACKNOWLEDGEMENTS

Brooklands Books have specialised for more than 30 years in producing books for car enthusiasts and over this period they have become an unparalleled source of reference on the worlds most sought after cars. Motorcycle enthusiasts have noted the success of the Gold Portfolio series and have repeatedly asked for a similar series to cover motorcycles. This book is one of four in answer to those requests, and more are planned for the future.

We have asked Jeff Clew, author and leading authority on vintage and classic motorcycles, to write an introduction to each of the motorcycle titles. He brings a specialised knowledge to us, not only as an historian, but also as an active rider who has ridden both on and off road, and is still doing so today.

Like the many other titles in the Brooklands Books library, this book could not have been compiled without the generous help of the world's leading magazine publishers. We are greatly indebted to the owners of *Cycle, Classic Bike, The Classic Motor Cycle, The Motor Cycle, Motor Cycling* and *Motorcycle Mechanics* for permission to reissue their copyright material.

R.M. Clarke

Although BSA were latecomers to the motorcycle market - they did not make their first complete machine until 1910 - they soon became a market leader. Vast numbers of good reliable motorcycles left their Birmingham factory in ever-increasing numbers and with such an extensive range of models there was something to meet almost every requirement. Their familiar slogan 'The most popular motorcycle in the world' was widely recognised, so much so that letters from overseas bearing only this slogan were invariably delivered to Armoury Road in Small Heath.

The company began making vee twins in 1920, but it was not until the early post-World War 2 period that vertical twins became a key feature of their model range. If everything had gone according to plan, they expected to launch two such models at the 1940 Motor Cycle Show. Well aware of the potential of Edward Turner's Speed Twin Triumph which broke new ground in 1937, they lost little time in producing prototype designs that would match the Triumph, and had them running in 1939. Sadly, World War 2 curtailed further development and when the production of civilian models resumed after the war, two entirely new models had taken their place.

The first was a 495cc vertical twin designed by Herbert Perkins, the A7 model. It was subsequently redesigned in 1949, after Bert Hopwood had joined BSA as Forward Product Designer. Hopwood also took the opportunity to introduce a 646cc variant in 1950, the renowned A10 Golden Flash model, which became BSA's most popular twin in the fifties. It is these models and their later variants with which this book concerns itself, all of which have a separate engine and gearbox.

Many memorable feats have been accomplished by BSA twins, but none more so than their Maudes Trophy attempt in 1952. An A.C.U. Certified Test , it began when an A.C.U. official selected three 497cc Star Twins from the production line and had them sealed and locked up until the test commenced. Three BSA 'works' riders then rode them from Birmingham to Oslo, competing on the way in the gruelling International Six Days Trial held that year in Austria. All three machines covered 4,958 miles in 24 days and completed the trial without losing a single mark, to make it one of the most outstanding feats of all time for standard production models. BSA were awarded the Maudes Trophy for the first time since 1939 and all three riders a Gold Medal from the trial.

Jeff Clew

CONTENTS

B.S.A.s ANNOUNCE

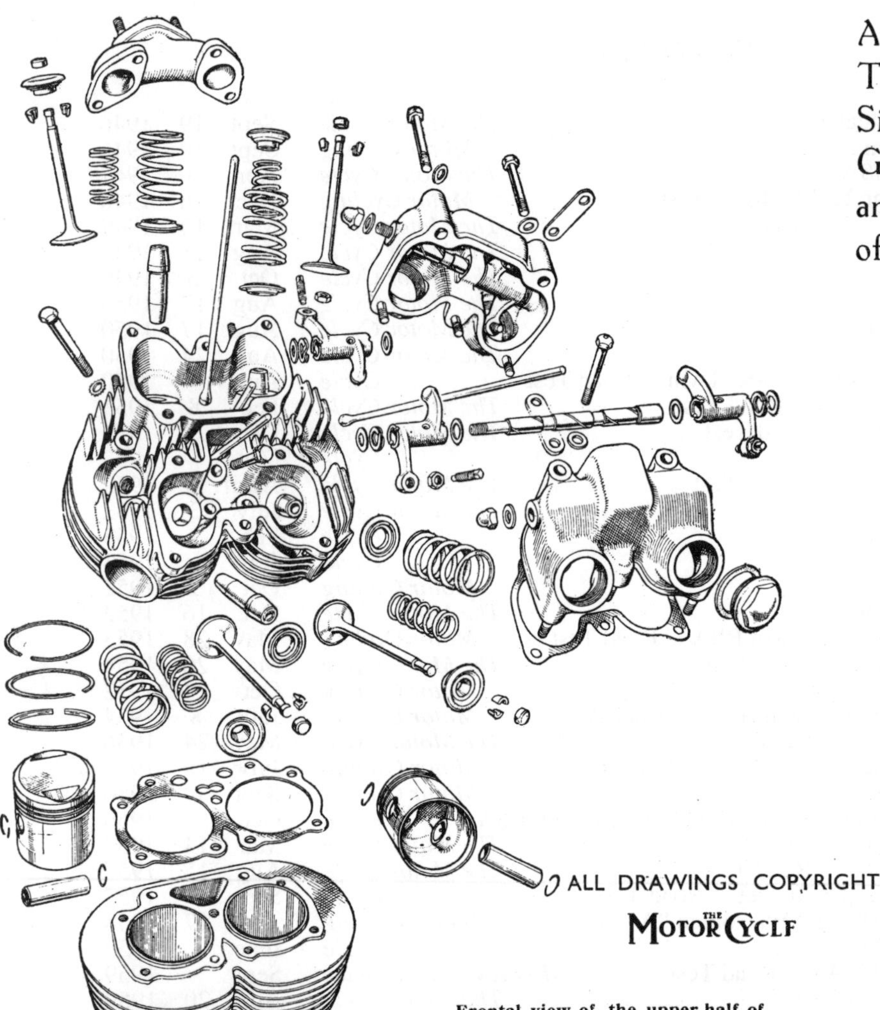

Frontal view of the upper half of the engine. A special drawing by "The Motor Cycle" laying bare the detail design and revealing how the parts go together. Note the way the inlet- and exhaust-valve chambers are separated

The heart of the engine—the crankcas Steel-backed lead-bronze bearings ar the engine is that ther

A Most Attractive 495 c.c. Twin=cylinder Mount with a Single Camshaft, Engine and Gear Box Built Up as a Unit, and an Extraordinary Number of Ingenious and Appealing Features

SELDOM has there been such an interesting new motor cycle as the overhead-valve vertical-twin B.S.A. The machine incorporates literally dozens of appealing features in its design—real "riders' features"—and is a motor cycle for both soloist and sidecarist, whether tourist or sportsman. The performance is of a Jekyll and Hyde variety: soft and genteel when the rider is in pottering mood and exhilaratingly lively when the throttle is used anything like to the full.

The overhead-valve 495 c.c. vertical-twin B.S.A., rather prosaically termed the "A7," has its engine and gear box built into a single unit, which is mounted in a duplex cradle frame. A full cradle frame is employed, with the 1in diameter front-down tubes running right from the nicely scarfed steering-head lug to the steel forgings which form the rear fork ends—fork ends which carry accessible screw-type rear chain adjusters. The frame is of brazed construction. The only welded item is a cross-member on the front-down tubes which provides a lug for the cylinder-head steady. Both side-car lugs and pillion-footrest lugs are incorporated.

A somewhat unusual feature is the vertical seat tube. It is vertical so that it also acts as the outer member of the ingenious telescopic stand. Press down the foot of this spring-controlled central stand and automatically, without any effort, the machine is supported on the bottom T-shaped member; keep the foot there and raise the rear of the machine—the back wheel is then held off the ground. For the stand to spring upwards it is only necessary to operate a little hand control, which releases the ratchet lock.

Hydraulically controlled telescopic front forks are fitted. These are of the patented B.S.A. type fitted to the other models in the B.S.A. range, but are slightly longer and wider than on the 350 c.c. overhead-valve models. They are wider to suit the wider front mudguard and will accommodate a 3.50in section front tyre and not merely the standard 3.25in. The gauge of wire in the springs and the diameter are the same as for the front forks fitted to the 350 c.c. machines, but the length is greater and the initial

A VERTICAL TWIN

spring poundage per leg is some 87lb per in as against 83lb per in. Incidentally, the amount of oil per leg remains the standard $\frac{1}{4}$ pint. A drain plug is fitted so that the rider can drain out the old oil, fill up with a quarter of a pint, and know that the level is then correct.

On the cycle side there are many other interesting points and detail fittings. These range from the employment of a single bolt for holding the cover plate of the front brake, the front stand and, therefore, the front mudguard. The wheels are both quickly detachable and interchangeable. They are really quick to detach. It is only necessary to insert a tommy bar in the hole at the end of the rear spindle, unscrew and pull out the spindle, remove the distance piece and the wheel comes out. A special form of tooth has been developed for engagement purposes; this is a cross between a spline and a gear tooth.

Strength With Resilience

The hub-shell steel pressings are crimped at their outer diameter so that the spokes run in a dead straight line from hub to rim. Double-butted spokes are employed; that is, they are thicker at the hub and nipple ends than towards the middle, so there is a combination of great strength with resilience. Deep-groove journal bearings are fitted in both wheels; thus no adjustments are required. A dome or "bead" runs along the middle of the mudguards for strength and freedom from vibration. The back mudguard is hinged at the rear end to facilitate wheel removal. A $\frac{3}{8}$in diameter tube forms the rear mudguard stay and lifting handle. Provision is made for a carrier or pillion seat, which are offered to special order.

A nice slow taper is employed for the footrest mountings. Since the exhaust pipes of the vertical-twin engine are com-mendably well tucked in, the footrests are fully adjustable. There is no adjustment for the brake pedal, but this, as is the invariable rule with B.S.A. machines, is well placed. The footrest rubbers are of oval section.

Handlebar controls are arranged neatly in "clusters." There are merely the twistgrip throttle control, a "cluster" comprising the clutch lever with the dip-switch bolted on the clutch-lever forging—the whole assembly fixed by a single pinch-bolt—and another "cluster" consisting of the front-brake lever and the horn push. A lever-type air control is fitted beneath the saddle. The handlebars could hardly be cleaner. The lighting switch and ammeter are mounted in the rear of the 8in diameter head lamp. The voltage control unit is carried on the rear mudguard beneath the saddle. With its bolted on "U"-shaped member at the front and the $\frac{3}{8}$in diameter mudguard stay cum lifting handle, the rear mudguard is unusually well supported. The saddle is a Terry, adjustable for angle by means of screw-type saddle-spring mountings. A specially large bolt is fitted at the saddle nose to ensure the maintenance of lateral rigidity. Handlebars are also adjustable for angle.

Until the special small electric horn becomes available—a horn which will be mounted inconspicuously on the seat tube behind the gear box—it is necessary to employ a standard type of horn fixed on the near side just below the saddle spring.

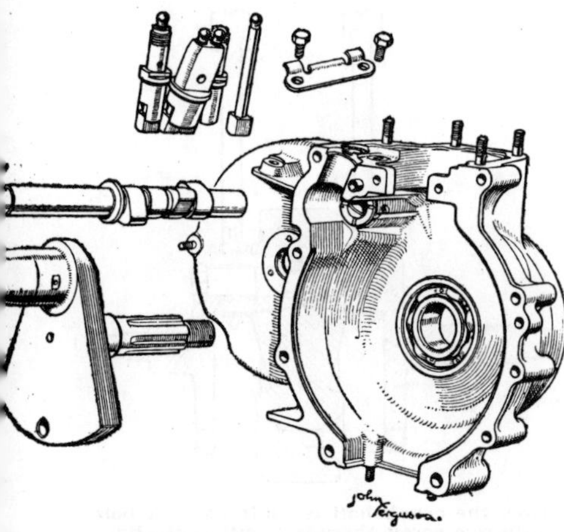

...d the ingenious built-up crankshaft. ...ployed for the big-ends. A feature of ...e no external oil pipes

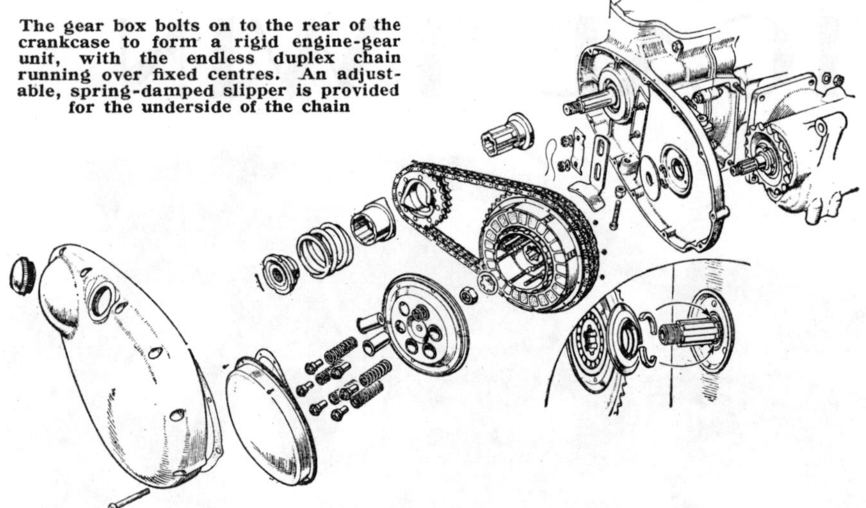

The gear box bolts on to the rear of the crankcase to form a rigid engine-gear unit, with the endless duplex chain running over fixed centres. An adjustable, spring-damped slipper is provided for the underside of the chain

The Smiths' speedometer head is mounted in the forward end of the 3-gallon petrol tank and matches up with the filler cap. An aim has been to obviate flexing of the driving cable, which runs neatly from the gear box along the off side of the front-down tube. The drive could, of course, have been taken from the rear wheel, but this would complicate the detachment of the rear wheel; also, there are the questions of dirt and ease of cleaning.

In order to facilitate removal of the tank, the wiring harness is not fixed to the tank and there are two petrol taps, which means that no draining is needed. The use of twin taps also results in the rider having a "reserve." The machine is finished in "Devon Red" and chromium or in black and chromium, with the black lined with gold.

A special feature of the ½-gallon oil tank, which is mounted on the seat tube, is that there is no drain hole; when the banjo union is removed for oil draining the strainer is automatically removed ready for cleaning and if the strainer is withdrawn the oil is automatically drained! Another interesting point is that the oil-tank breather pipe is carried down the inside of the tank instead of emerging from the top—yet another little feature of design which helps to ensure neatness and ease of cleaning.

Mating with the lines of the oil tank and on the other side of the seat tube, immediately between this tube and the battery, is a Vokes felt-type air cleaner. This has an area of approximately 80 sq in and is coupled to the air intake of the Amal carburettor by means of a short rubber sleeve. In addition to preventing the ingress of grit into the engine it acts as an induction silencer.

A point which will commend itself to experienced riders is the narrowness of the machine. The neat manner in which the exhaust pipes are carried close in has already been touched upon; the width over the footrests is also unusually small—22¾in overall, or a mere 14in if the length of the footrest rubbers is deducted. Saddle height is 29½in and the ground clearance 6½. The bars are 29in wide. The weight of 365 lb includes tools, but not petrol and oil.

Unit Construction

Other features on the "cycle" side are 7in diameter brakes—1⅛in wide in both cases—and Dunlop Universal studded tyres (3.25 × 19 front and 3.50 × 19 rear).

A bolted-up form of unit construction is employed for the engine and gear box. The new four-speed foot-controlled gear box has a flat machined face on the forward side which is bolted against a similar machined face on the rear of the crankcase. Thus there is, in effect, one rigid unit with a fixed centre distance between the engine shaft and the gear-box mainshaft. The drive from engine to gear box is by an endless ⅜in pitch flat-backed duplex chain which, should it ever call for adjustment, is tensioned, not by the often difficult task of resetting the position of the gear box in the frame—which also involves adjustment of the rear chain—but by a special case-hardened slipper fitted in the primary chain case immediately below the bottom run of the chain. The contact surface of this slipper is hard chromium, a deposit which offers both an outstandingly low frictional resistance and extreme durability. Adjustment is effected by a single screw locked by a Simmonds nut. A spring-loaded damper for the slipper is mounted on the inner half of the chain case. On the engine shaft there is a new two-cam, spring-loaded cush drive. Machines are despatched with a special mixture of grease and oil in the chain case, and all the owner has to do is to replenish occasionally with ordinary engine oil.

Ratios of 5.1, 6.2, 9 and 13.2 to 1 are provided for solo work, and 5.4, 6.6, 9.5 and 14 to 1 where a sidecar is employed. The new gear box is lighter and more compact and provides a lighter and sweeter gear change. A delightfully simple form of change-speed mechanism has been devised. The gear box is arranged with the layshaft submerged

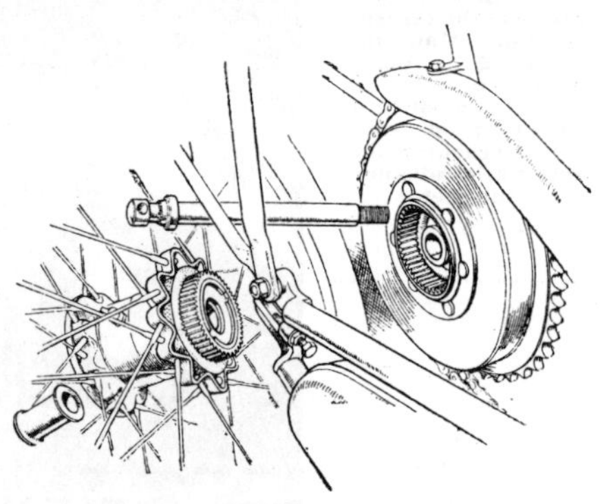

Quickly detachable, interchangeable wheels are fitted. Note how easily the rear wheel is detached and the clever arrangement that permits the use of straight spokes. The rear chain wheel and brake remain rigidly mounted in the frame

and is lubricated by oil, not grease. At the gear-box mainshaft there is a rubberized-fabric, knife-edge oil seal. There is also a shroud over the five-plate Ferodo-lined clutch, and an oil flinger on the back. The clutch mechanism is within the gear box. Access is gained

Front view of the machine revealing how the neat exhaust pipes are brought well into the design. The machine has been fined down with a marked gain in riding comfort

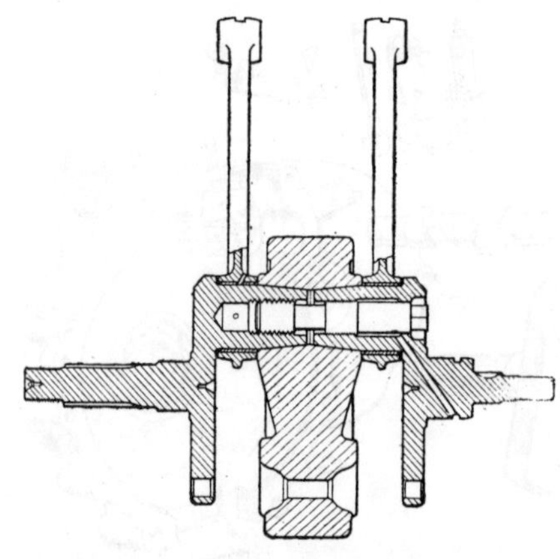

How the crankshaft is built up. A bolt with two screw threads of different pitch, and thus a differential action, "welds" the whole crankshaft into a single, rigid unit. Note the holes for alignment purposes

via a neat end-plate, which also acts as the gear-box filling orifice. A drain plug is provided; also, at the rear of the gear box, there is a level plug.

Most interesting of all is the construction of the vertical-twin engine with its four push-rods operated by a single camshaft carried in the rear of the crankcase. The engine is arranged with the crankpins in line, that is, the pistons rise and descend together and there is thus even firing, with one power stroke every revolution of the crankshaft. The bore and stroke are 62 mm×82 mm (2.440 ×3.228in), which give a total capacity of 495 c.c. or 30.2 cu in. Maximum power is stated to be 26 b.h.p. at 6,000 r.p.m., which is equivalent to 90 m.p.h. with the solo top gear of 5.1 to 1.

A most ingenious form of crankshaft assembly is employed. There are three main parts: the 7in diameter, 2in wide high-tensile steel central flywheel-cum-bobweight and two forged-steel members, each comprising a mainshaft, crank cheek and crankpin. Tapered holes are provided in the central flywheel and there are equivalent case-hardened tapered portions extending from the crankpins. But the crankshaft is of no ordinary built-up construction. The tapers are pulled up by the differential action of

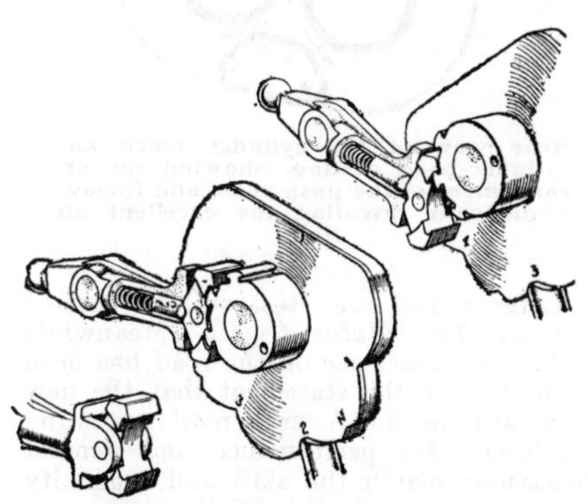

A delightfully simple form of foot-change mechanism is employed. In the above drawing the gears are shown marked on the cam plate for ease of reference.

two different-pitch screw threads cut on the single central securing bolt or, as it is proposed to term it, the "differential thread locking bolt." The thread in the near-side crank cheek member is 12 per inch, and that in the other 20 per inch. An ordinary box spanner is used for locking purposes, and the whole assembly can be built up by even a novice, since there are $\frac{7}{16}$in diameter alignment holes in all three parts—the central flywheel and the crank cheeks. The procedure is as follows: After being smeared with heavy grease, the securing bolt is screwed into the off-side crank cheek until the head of the bolt stands proud of the cheek by $\frac{1}{2}$in to 33/64in. Next the whole assembly is fitted together and a $\frac{7}{16}$in rod passed through the three holes. Finally, the bolt is screwed into the second crank cheek, the operator making certain that the thread starts immediately. Naturally, after tightening it is necessary to check that there is the required

A general view of the complete machine, actually the particular production model which " Torrens " tried on the road.

0.015in clearance laterally at the big-ends and that the overall dimension is 5.492in maximum, which results in the assembly fitting in the crankcase with 0.005in clearance after the appropriate shim has been fitted.

About the only points to watch are cleanliness and the position of the oil hole in the near-side big-end—a bleed which throws oil inwards to lubricate the inner cylinder wall. How satisfactory the arrangement is has been shown by pulling down a crankshaft and reassembling it again some 60 times. The crank cheeks come together a total of 0.033in for each revolution of the securing bolt.

This sturdy crankshaft assembly is located by the near-side main bearing, a deep-groove ball bearing. On the off side there is a steel white-metal-lined main bearing. The big-end bearings, which, it will be noted, thanks to the built-up construction, are not split, are steel-backed lead-bronze—1½in diameter and $\frac{13}{16}$in wide. A rib runs round the big-end eye of the steel connecting rods.

Pistons are of silicon alloy, oval ground from the bottom ring down to the full skirt. Two Brico tin-plated

compression rings and one Brico " Maxi-groove " scraper ring are fitted per piston. As usual, the taper-bored $\frac{11}{16}$in diameter gudgeon pins are fully floating and retained by circlips.

The flat-topped pistons, which are slightly cut away for valve clearance, give a compression ratio of 7 to 1. There is a small rib inside the piston skirts for stiffening purposes.

Combustion Head Shape

The combustion head is slightly less than a hemisphere—in other words, a hemisphere with a slice removed from the bottom. The inlet valve is inclined at 43 deg and the exhaust at 38 deg. Austenitic steel is employed for the exhaust valves and 3 per cent nickel for the inlets. Incidentally, the arrangement of the valves permits straight-line operation of the rockers and space between the inlet and exhaust rocker boxes. Nickel-chrome iron is used for the valve guides. Washers are provided beneath the twin valve springs for heat insulation.

Great pains have been taken to secure the maximum advantage of the opportunity the single rearwardly mounted

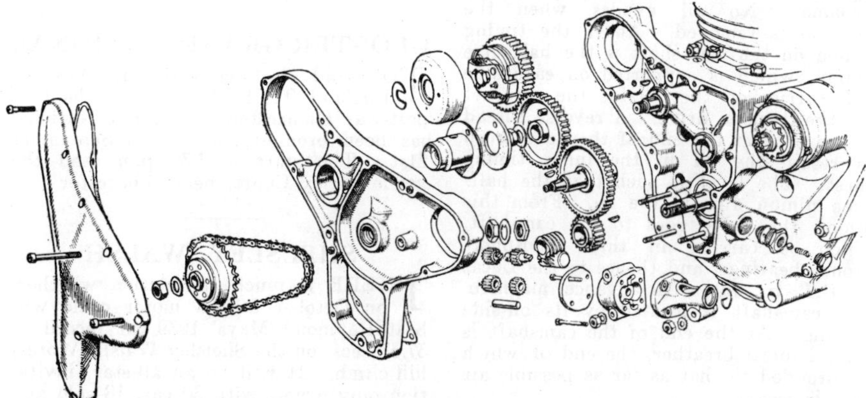

A timing chest within a timing chest. Arrangement of the gear drive, the mechanical breather, the gear-type oil pump and the chain drive to the separate forwardly mounted dynamo. A reverse thread prevents oil passing along the half-time shaft to the dynamo chain case

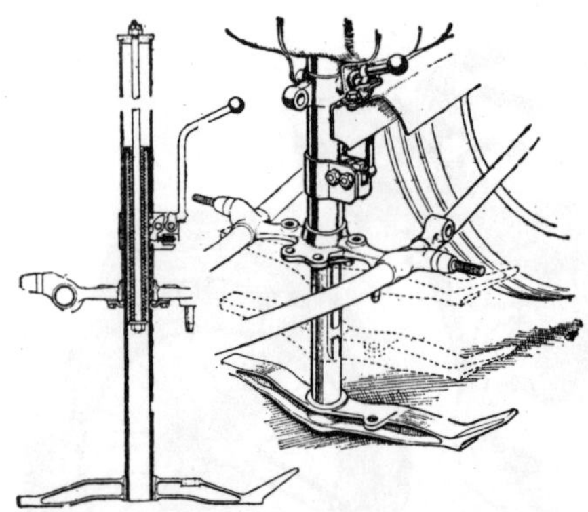

The clever ratchet-type prop-stand and central stand, housed in the vertical seat-pillar tube. The full line shows the position of the stand when the rear wheel is off the ground; the other two positions are those of " prop-stand " and " normal running "

camshaft offers in outstandingly efficient engine cooling and freedom from distortion. The monobloc cylinder head is designed so that there is an excellent air passage between the inlet and exhaust sides; there is also a good flow between the cylinders. Seven bolts and two studs provide the fixing for the cylinder-head casting, which is of spigoted type with a single copper-asbestos washer. The bolt in the middle of the head, which is slackened first and tightened last is set at an angle for ease of access. No cylinder-head bolts pass through the aluminium rocker boxes, so tightening of the cylinder heads is a plain, straightforward task, made particularly easy by the care taken over accessibility. An example of this is the employment of the two studs. These are at the rear and have the surrounding cooling fins cut away for ready access to the nuts.

The rocker boxes are held down by five bolts each and have large screwed light-alloy plugs for access to the valve-clearance adjusters carried in the ends of the valve rockers.

Automatic-advance Magneto

Both inner and outer timing-gear covers are employed, so there is no flooding of the chain drive to the separate dynamo. No oil exudes when the dynamo is removed. Above the timing pinion on the mainshaft is the half-time pinion, which is supported on each side and carries on the outside the sprocket for the dynamo drive. A reverse thread is provided at the end of the outer bush to retain the oil in the inner timing chest. The level is such that the half-time pinion dips in the oil. From this pinion the drive goes to the camshaft, which is carried in three phosphor-bronze bearings, and thence to the Lucas or B.T.-H. automatic-advance magneto. The camshaft is located by its off-side bearing. At the end of the camshaft is a mechanical breather, the end of which is shrouded so that as far as possible air only is passed.

Chain adjustment for the dynamo, which has a neat domed casing over the commutator end, involves slackening a single nut.

Attention to detail is emphasized once again by the arrangement of the tappets and tappet guides. The case-hardened tappets have a deposit of hard chromium on their feet, and the outer tappet guides, which are not of split construction like the middle pair, are provided with an external screw thread for ease of extraction. There is a single locking strip for all four tappet guides. The tappets are drilled so that oil passing down the push-rod housing lubricates the cams; in addition, the direction of rotation of the engine results in oil mist being driven upwards.

Lubrication Details

A submerged twin gear pump is employed for the force-feed lubrication. This is driven by skew gearing from the end of the crankshaft. A ball valve with a knife-edge seating prevents lubricant syphoning into the engine. From the pump the oil passes through a release valve working at 50 lb/sq in when the oil is hot. This, too, has a knife-edge type of seating to prevent trouble owing to grit; it is accessible from the front side of the timing chest. Oil is fed by the timing-side main bearing to the big-end bearings and passes on, in the form of oil mist, to lubricate the remainder of the engine. There are no external oil pipes other than the delivery and return pipes linking the oil tank to the timing chest. The oil pump has a delivery of $3\frac{1}{2}$ gallons an hour and on the scavenge side a capacity of some five gallons an hour.

Other features of the machine are the polished valve ports, provision of a central rocker-shaft bearing and hardened steel thrust washers for the nickel-steel overhead rockers, spring-loading of the rockers laterally to prevent tap owing to side-float, and the fitting of absorption-type silencers, which have a small-diameter middle tube with a spiral baffle around it and, between the spiral and the casing, a series of annular chambers. The bulk of the exhaust gas passes around the spiral and a small quantity through the middle tube. The purpose of the annuli is to absorb the high frequencies. Test on the road reveals that the exhaust is mellow in tone and inoffensive.

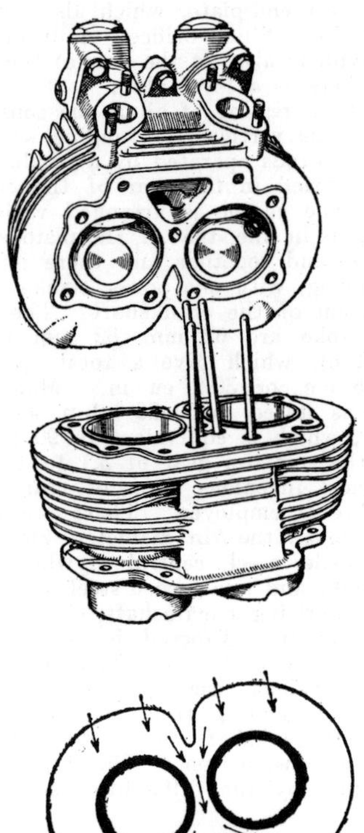

Rear view of the cylinder block and cylinder-head casting, showing the arrangement of the push rods and (below) a diagram revealing the excellent air flow

Later a full road test will be carried out by *The Motor Cycle*. Meanwhile sufficient experience on the road has been obtained for the statement that the new vertical-twin B.S.A. is a most appealing machine. Its performance and general behaviour match the skill and ingenuity that are such a feature of the design.

The price of the machine has been fixed at £135, plus, in Britain, £36 9s Purchase Tax. Speedometer costs £4; Purchase Tax £1 1s 7d. Production is going ahead well and deliveries, it is expected, will start towards the end of November.

GLOSTER GRAND NATIONAL

TO avoid clashing with the West of England Trial, the date of the first post-war Gloucestershire Grand National has been brought forward to September 21st. The start is 3.30 p.m. and the venue Tirley Court, near Gloucester.

SHELSLEY WALSH

THERE is much speculation whether, on October 5th, a motor cycle will beat Raymond Mays' 1939 car record of 37.37 secs. on the Shelsley Walsh (Worcs) hill-climb. It will be an all-star, invitation only event, with 30 car, 18 solo and five sidecar entries. Motor cycle entries include Freddie Frith, Noel Pope, Bob Berry, Kenneth Bills, H. L. Daniell, and J. Lockett.

CADWELL PARK

FOR next Sunday's final meeting organized by the Louth and D.M.C.C. at Cadwell Park, there are 84 entries. This meeting will decide the winner of the Folbigg Trophy for the fastest eight laps of the season. Racing starts at noon. The Park is five miles from Louth, Lincs.

HAGUE NATIONAL CHAMPIONSHIPS

THE first important road race for seven years was held in Holland last Sunday. This was the National Championship meeting, held in place of the famous international Dutch T.T., and, according to Reuter, it resulted in wins for British machines in each class.

Results.—250 c.c. class.—Bredjik (Royal Enfield). **350 c.c. class.—**Heeres (Excelsior). **500 c.c. class.** —Schilders (Triumph).

MANY outstanding design features put this B.S.A. Vertical Twin right at the top of its class . . . for performance, economy, reliability! See it with the other models of the complete B.S.A. range at Earls Court on STAND No. 32 — the centre of the Show and the centre of attraction!

LEAVE IT TO YOUR BSA

FREE!
Send now for Catalogue

TO B.S.A. Cycles Ltd.,
47 Armoury Road,
Birmingham, 11
England.

Please send me *free* the new B.S.A. Motor Cycle Catalogue :

NAME

ADDRESS

GRAHAM WALKER

Here's a smart Combination!

NOW'S THE TIME to prepare for those delightful summer runs. With the new B.S.A. de luxe Tourer Sidecar attached to your machine, your passenger enjoys well-sprung and roomy comfort—while your luggage is easily accommodated in the spacious rear boot. And with the quickly erected, close-fitting hood your passenger is given complete protection. In its smart cellulose finish and long-lasting leather upholstery, this superbly designed sidecar makes a perfect match for B.S.A. models A7 Vertical Twin, M20 500 s.v., M21 600 s.v., M33 500 o.h.v. See your local B.S.A. dealer *now* to be sure of early delivery.

B.S.A. de Luxe Tourer Sidecar

In black cellulose **£59. 5s.**
(*Tax £15. 16s. Total £75. 1s.*)
Finished in Devon Red
(*£2. 10s. extra, plus 13/6d. tax.*)

LEAVE IT TO YOUR BSA

LEADER OF BRITAIN'S
LEADING MOTOR CYCLE RANGE—

BSA
500 OHV TWIN
with these 8 outstanding features...

1 Enclosed clutch operation
2 Automatic ignition advance
3 Induction silencer cum air cleaner
4 Bolted-up unit construction
5 Single camshaft giving cooler running
6 Hydraulically damped telescopic forks
7 Instantly detachable wheels
8 Straight spokes (hub pat. 576457)

Price £140 plus purchase tax £37.16.0

LEAVE IT TO YOUR BSA

1 Enclosed clutch operation
2 Automatic ignition advance
3 Induction silencer cum air cleaner
4 Bolted-up unit construction
5 Single camshaft giving cooler running
6 Hydraulically damped telescopic forks
7 Instantly detachable wheels
8 Straight spokes (hub pat. 576457)

Model A7 Price £140 plus pur. tax £37.16.0

LEAVE IT TO YOUR BSA

THI

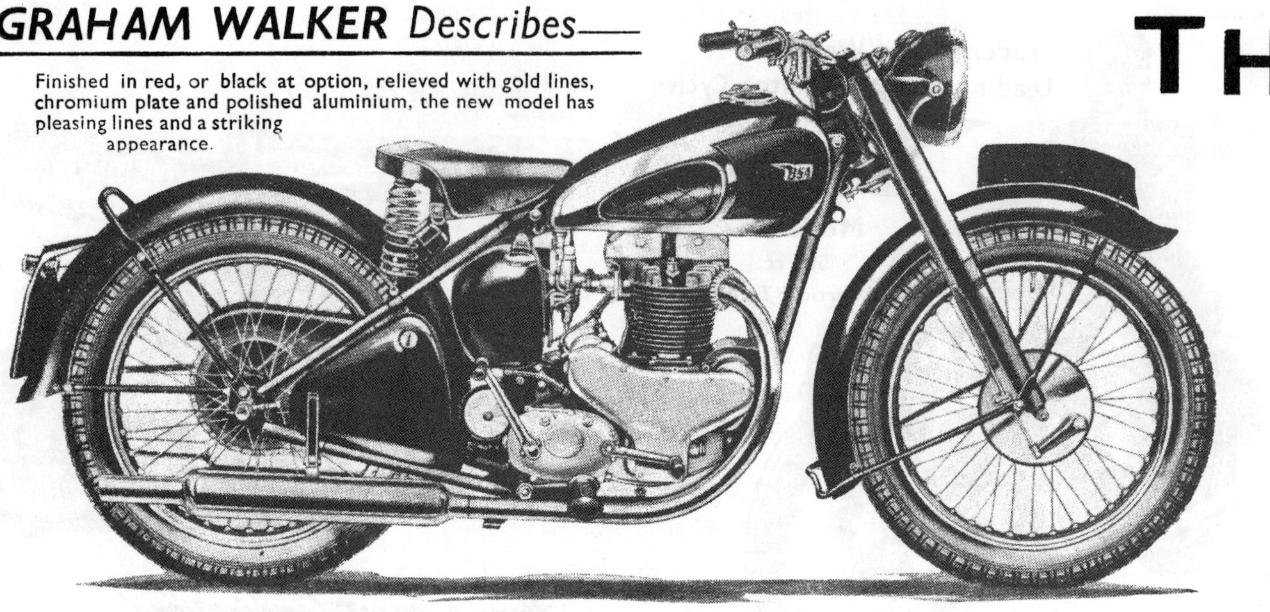

Finished in red, or black at option, relieved with gold lines, chromium plate and polished aluminium, the new model has pleasing lines and a striking appearance.

WAY back in August, 1939, a 500 c.c. vertical twin B.S.A. motorcycle was in process of development for 1940 delivery. Then came the war. The whole resources of the enormous Small Heath, Birmingham, factories were immediately diverted to the production of guns, rifles, intricate predictors and other military equipment in astronomical quantities, including the largest number of military motorcycles manufactured by any one British firm—no fewer than 125,000 of the solid and very reliable 500 c.c. sidevalve M.20 model being delivered to the Allied Forces before hostilities ceased.

But if practical development of new civilian types had to cease abruptly in September, 1939, mental planning for the post-war period went on uninterruptedly. The results of this " midnight oil " were to be seen in a succession of patents granted to B.S.A. Cycles, Ltd., some of which indicated to hawk-eyed enthusiasts that something particularly good in the way of twins could be expected from Armoury Road in due course.

At the first opportunity those plans were translated into metal. Thus it was that some 15 months back I had the pleasure of taking the prototype Model A.7 o.h.v. vertical twin B.S.A. for a test run. And a very pleasant model it proved to be. But, for the time being, I had to keep my findings to myself, because the company didn't want to be inundated with inquiries at a time when it had to concentrate on exporting thousands of its famous single-cylinder 250, 350 and 500 c.c. models in a Herculean effort to satisfy the overseas demand and to ensure the maximum importation of foreign currency.

Now, however, the time has come to disclose the full details of this " new throughout " model which is already in production. Considerations of space demand that wordage should be kept to the minimum, so I would ask the reader to study carefully the drawings which amplify much of the necessarily brief description.

Of the semi-unit construction type, the 62 mm. by 82 mm. (495 c.c.) engine produces 26 b.h.p. at 6,000 r.p.m. on a 7-to-1 compression ratio and is notable for its robust construction combined with an ingenious simplicity in design.

An excellent example of this ingenuity is to be seen in the unique case-hardened, built-up crankshaft which enables 1½-in. bore by 13/16-in. wide non-split ring-type lead-bronze lined big-ends to be employed. The inner end of each crankpin—forged in one piece with its appropriate web and mainshaft—is tapered. These tapers are drawn into mating tapers turned in the heavy central flywheel by a transverse bolt on which are cut two threads, one fine, the other coarse, a method which ensures an absolutely foolproof locking system.

The stamped steel connecting rods carry fully floating circlip-retained gudgeon pins in phosphor-bronze bushes, the flat top silicon alloy, full skirt, .010-in. taperturned pistons each being fitted with two pressure and one scraper rings. The crankshaft assembly is supported in a drive side 1⅛-in. bore by 13/16-in. wide locating ball journal and on the timing side by a plain steel-backed white metal 1⅛-in. bore by 1 3/32-in. wide bush. The light-alloy crankcase is formed integrally with the inner half of the primary drive oilbath case and carries the special gear-driven Lucas magneto at the rear. Fitted with automatic advance and a cut-out button in the contact-breaker cap, this instrument is spigoted and flange-fitted to the timing case.

The chain-driven Lucas 6-volt A.V.C. dynamo is carried in a semi-circular cradle at the front of the crankcase, being retained in position by a half-strap and bolt. The dynamo and its chain can be removed without disturbing the timing gear and chain adjustment is made by rotating the instrument bodily.

An outstanding feature of the A.7 is the single rearwardly placed camshaft (Patent No. 567,029), which operates both inlet and exhaust valves by inclined pushrods passing through a separate tunnel, formed in the nickel-molybdenum iron one-piece cylinder casting and passages cored in the cast-iron one-piece head. Supported in three long phosphor-bronze bushes, it is ¾-in. in diameter and driven by an idler wheel mating with the half-time pinion. The direction of flywheel rotation ensures that the cams are flooded with oil.

The cylinder block is deeply spigoted into the crankcase and held down by eight ⅜-in. bolts. The absence of a forward camshaft and pushrods permits the free passage of air between the barrels which makes its exit to either side of the pushrod tunnel at the rear. The cylinder head mates with a register formed in the barrel casting and seats on a copper-asbestos gasket, being held down by nine ⅜-in. bolts.

The inlet valves (1¼-in. diameter at throat) are inclined at 43 degrees and fed with mixture by a 15/16-in. choke Amal needle-type carburetter via an aluminium manifold. The 1 3/16-in. diameter exhaust

(Right) In this semi-exploded drawing by a "Motor Cycling" artist, the single camshaft, with its timed breather sleeve, the push-rod tunnel, bolted - on gearbox, ingenious foot-change, mechanism and crankpin construction are clearly shown.

(Left) The simple spring-loaded pawl—which operates direct on to a ratchet member attached to the cam-track plate.

New Vertical Twin B.S.A.

The Model A.7—A Semi-unit Construction 495 c.c. o.h.v. with a Single High Camshaft

valves are inclined at 38 degrees in the hemispherical combustion chambers. All valves have 5/16-in. stems, working in cast-iron guides, and are equipped with duplex coil springs and detachable hardened steel end caps. The four individual forged steel rockers and their hardened thrust washers are mounted on stationary case-hardened shafts, each supported in three bearings formed in the detachable die-cast light-alloy rocker boxes, which are secured to the cylinder head by two ⅜-in. and three 5/16-in. studs. This construction allows of the free passage of air to the centre of the head casting.

The four steel tappets, Monochromed on their working faces, are in direct contact with the cams. They slide in three steel blocks—one for each inlet tappet and a duplex one in the centre for the exhausts—pressed into the crankcase and secured by a keeper plate. The solid ¼-in. diameter pushrods have spherical bottom-end cups and ball ends at the top, whilst valve clearances are adjusted by the normal stud and locknut on the rocker ends, accessible via detachable caps in the rocker boxes. The valve timing is an excellent compromise between maximum performance and flexibility—inlet opens 24 degrees B.T.C., closes 65 degrees A.B.C.; exhaust opens 60 degrees B.B.C., closes 21½ degrees A.T.C.

Driven by a worm gear on the timing-side engine shaft, the double spur gear-type oil pump feeds lubricant through passages in the crankshaft to the big-ends, whence it is distributed by splash. Typical of the thought given to detail is the hole drilled in the shoulder of the drive-side connecting rod, which ensures equality of supply to both cylinder bores. A release valve controls the pressure at 50 lb. per sq. in. (hot oil), excess lubricant escaping into the timing gear chest.

The drilled overhead rockers rely on oil mist, sloping " floors " in the head casting returning the oil to the cam faces via the pushrod tunnel. A non-return ball valve on the pressure side of the pump and a gravity ball valve on the scavenge side prevent siphoning when stationary and ensure that the pump is always primed. Crankcase cleanliness is encouraged by a mechanically timed breather—a ported sleeve, mating with passages in the timing chest, being driven by the camshaft wheel. Surplus oil mist is diverted on to the final-drive sprocket.

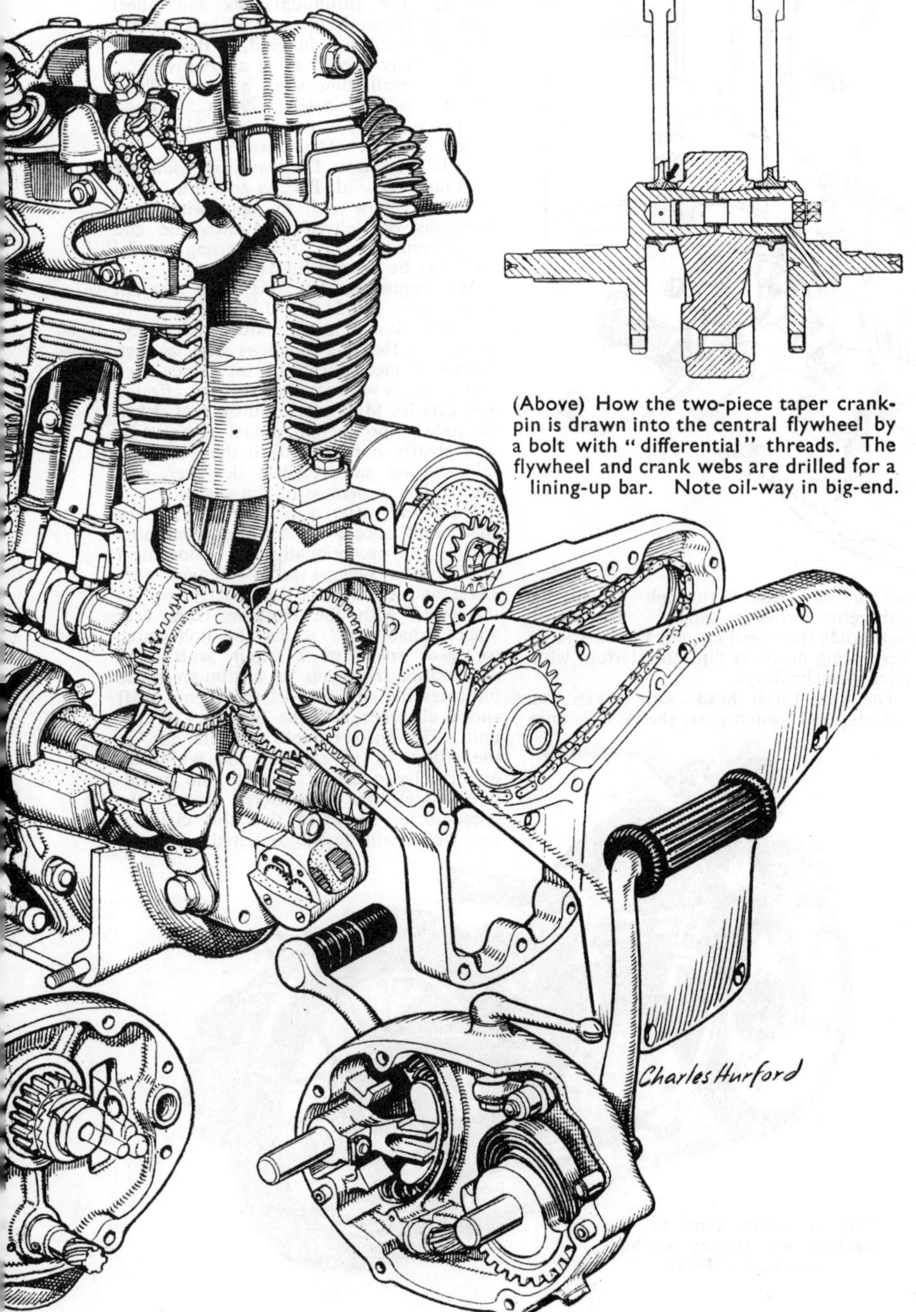

(Above) How the two-piece taper crank-pin is drawn into the central flywheel by a bolt with "differential" threads. The flywheel and crank webs are drilled for a lining-up bar. Note oil-way in big-end.

The Transmission

The primary drive is by an endless flat-backed ⅜-in. pitch duplex chain, tensioned by an externally adjustable spring-loaded slipper with a Monochromed working face. An improved two-cam spring-loaded engine shaft cush drive, working on a splined sleeve, eliminates driving snatch. Incidentally, the exceptionally large engine sprocket has no fewer than 27 teeth, whilst the case-hardened clutch sprocket, carrying a five-plate Ferodo-lined totally enclosed clutch, runs on a roller bearing.

The four-speed gearbox, with driving shaft vertically above the layshaft and with all operating mechanism totally enclosed, is attached to a machined face on the crankcase by four ⅜-in. studs. The sliding gears have rounded ends on their teeth to ensure easy engagement in the recesses fermed in the mating wheels. The positive-stop change mechanism is the subject of another patent (No. 569,742) and is a classic example of ingenuity. The method by which the movement of the foot pedal is translated through a spring-loaded ratchet member to the selector cam track is made clear in the sketches.

The mainshaft runs on two heavy duty deep-groove ball journals, whilst the worm gear on an extension of the layshaft drives the Smith's speedometer mounted in the fuel tank. Solo ratios are 5.1, 6.1, 8.9 and 13.1 and sidecar ratios 5.4, 6.5, 9.5 and 13.9—a surprisingly small difference which indicates the flexibility and " flat " power curve of the engine. Final drive is by ⅝-in. by ⅜-in. chain with two guards.

The frame is an all-brazed structure with single large-diameter top and saddle tubes. duplex down tubes running from the sturdy steering head right through to the rear fork ends, whilst the saddle stays are brazed into the seat lug. Sidecar lugs are incorporated. The engine-gear unit is attached to the frame at four points—two

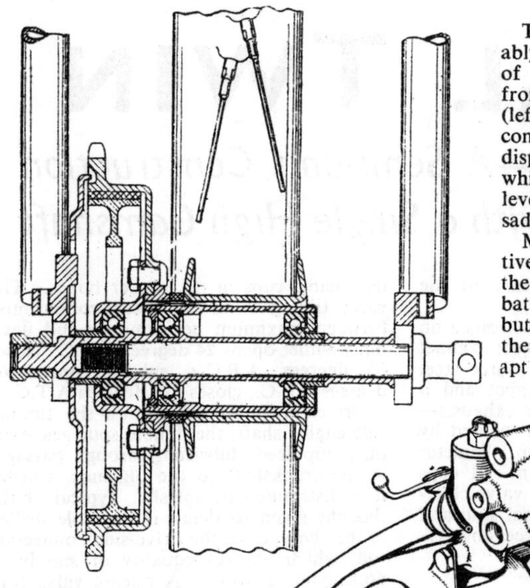

(Above) The quickly detachable, interchangeable rear wheel with straight-pull spokes. Splines on the hub engage with splines in the ball bearing-supported brake drum.

(Right) The oil tank, air filter and battery assembly. Note air lever behind seat lug. (Inset) The ingenious spring-loaded, ratchet controlled central stand concealed in the seat tube.

in front of the crankcase and one each above and below the gearbox.

The hydraulically damped telescopic spring forks are identical in design with those fitted to the 1946 B.S.A. single-cylinder models already fully described in this journal, but are slightly longer. They are notable for their sensitivity and sweet action. The steering head adjustment, subject of yet another B.S.A. patent, overcomes in a very simple manner the fundamental difficulty encountered where the fork attachment centres are fixed. An internally threaded sleeve can be screwed up or down the steering column to vary the bearing clearance and is then locked in position by a cap nut and the split clamp of the upper fork member.

Front and rear wheels are of the quickly detachable and interchangeable type, although the tyre sizes differ—front 26 by 3.25-in., rear 26 by 3.50-in., with pressures respectively of 17 and 22 lb. per square inch. The hubs run on deep groove non-adjustable ball journal bearings mounted on shouldered hollow spindles, through which pass the solid knock-out spindles. The 7-in. by 1⅛-in. front brakedrum is mounted on a sleeve, pressed into the fork end, which also carries the brake plate with its cast light alloy shoes.

The rear brakedrum-cum-sprocket is similar in size and principle, although carrying a bolted-on steel splined member. The rear fork ends are slotted to permit of chain adjustment. Brake reaction is taken through a lug on the front forks and an " ear " formed on the rear fork-end lug. Special " crinkled " hub flanges accommodate the straight-pull spoke heads, subject of yet one more B.S.A. patent.

The ⅞-in. handlebars are remarkably clean. The controls consist of (right) quick-action twistgrip, front brake lever and horn button, (left) clutch lever and lamp dipper control. Automatic advance has dispensed with the ignition lever, whilst the seldom-used air slide lever is mounted beneath the saddle.

Mounted in pannier, respectively on the near and off side of the saddle tube, are a 12 A.P.H. battery and a four-pint oil tank, but skilfully sandwiched between them—and therefore a good thing apt to be missed!—is a Vokes pattern air cleaner through which the carburetter draws its supply. The petrol tank holds three gallons and has two taps, there being no cross pipe to interfere with quick detachability.

The 8-in. Lucas head lamp carries the ammeter and switch gear, the A.V.C. unit being mounted beneath the saddle. The electric horn is mounted near the off side rear engine plates just abaft the gearbox. The standard equipment includes an exceptionally large capacity triangular metal toolbox and rubber kneegrips, whilst provision is made for pillion rests and seat (or tubular carrier) to order.

The twin silencers are a combination of the internal spiral baffle and absorption types, the exhaust pipes being a push fit in the cylinder head and decorated with finned ring nuts. Mudguards are of the ribbed " helmet " pattern.

A novel and excellent feature is found in the central stand. Pressure of the foot brings the stand base into contact with the road—a touch of the small hand lever releases the ratchet, whereupon the device disappears up the saddle tube!

The standard of finish is extremely high. Light alloy parts such as timing case, chaincase and gearbox end cover are buffed, whilst ferrous metal parts are enamelled in a rich and most attractive shade of red where they are not chromium plated. The chromium tank and wheel rims are respectively panelled and centred red and lined out in gold. Black with chromium is offered as an alternative.

The overall dimensions are: wheelbase 54½-in., saddle height 29½-in., ground clearance 6½-in., width of bars 29-in., dry weight 365 lb. The price is £135, plus £36 9s. Purchase Tax, with speedometer £4, plus £1 1s. 7d. P.T. as an extra. Production is now well in hand with good prospects of deliveries towards the end of November. A rear sprung model will also be announced later.

My impressions of this very pleasant model when I rode it in June, '45, were of a comfortable 80 m.p.h. mount with exceptional roadholding qualities and a high degree of mechanical silence. Since then many improvements have been effected and Charles Markham confirms that, when he rode a production model recently he was greatly impressed with the dead certain starting and excellent tick-over, plus the extreme quietness of the engine.

He found, after a few minutes on the road, that once he had accustomed himself to the exceptionally short movement of the gear change pedal changes were sweet and effortless. Particularly was he impressed with the freedom from rear wheel " hammer," whilst the non-snatch top gear speed of 7 m.p.h. with clean acceleration right up to maximum speed indicates the efficiency of the engine shaft shock absorber and the flexibility of the unit. The makers quote a maximum " in the region of 90 m.p.h." and whilst no opportunity occurred to time the brand-new model over a measured stretch, the speedometer suggested that this claim is one which will be substantiated.

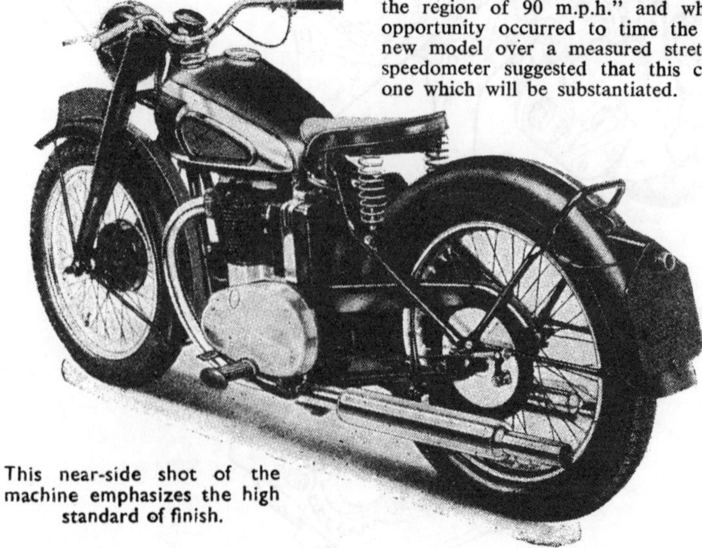

This near-side shot of the machine emphasizes the high standard of finish.

Seventy - Seven Percent!

BSA "STAR TWIN"

And at Daytona! SEVENTY SEVEN PER CENT—or ten out of the thirteen BSA "Star Twins" entered in the 200 mile National Championship race finished—six of them among the twenty boys who took home the folding money. Sixty-one of the one hundred and two machines of nine different American and European makes failed to finish, which indicates the severity of the test.

BSA "Star Twins" thus proved conclusively the ruggedness of their construction and the high degree of their speed and reliability. Truly "The World's Best Vertical Twin."

★ LEAVE IT TO YOUR BSA! ★

East Coast Distributor
RICH CHILD CYCLE CO., INC.
639 Passaic Ave.
Nutley, N. J.   NU 2-5600

West Coast Distributor
HAP ALZINA
3074 Broadway
Oakland, California

Profitable BSA-SUNBEAM franchise available. Write for full details.

East Coast BSA-SUNBEAM Distributor:
RICH CHILD CYCLE CO., INC., 639 Passaic Ave., Nutley, N. J.

West Coast BSA-SUNBEAM Distributor:
HAP ALZINA — 3074 Broadway, Oakland, Calif.

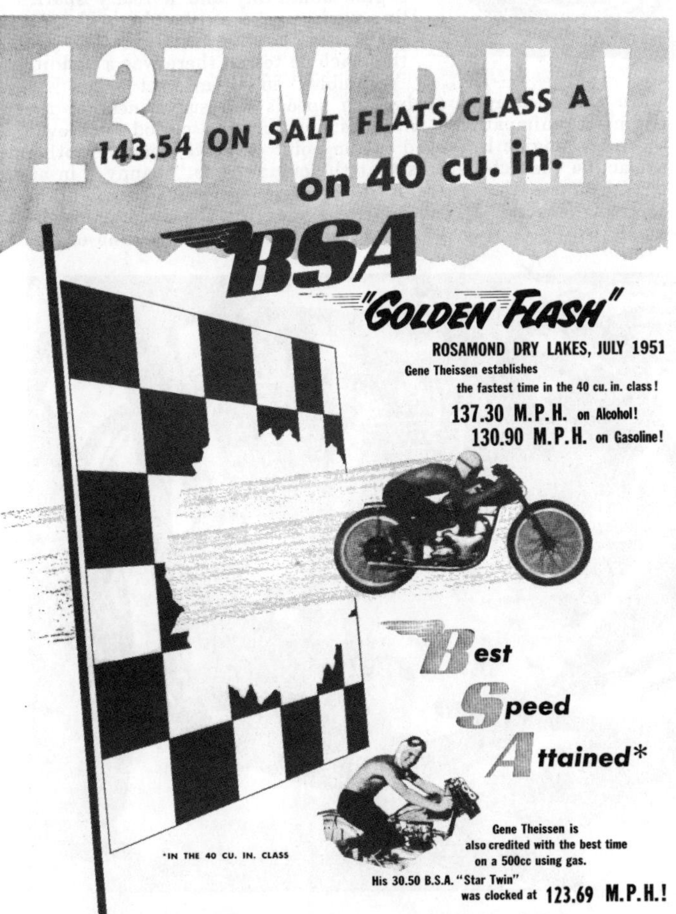

Profitable BSA-SUNBEAM franchise available. Write for full details.

East Coast BSA-SUNBEAM Distributor:
RICH CHILD CYCLE CO., INC., 639 Passaic Ave., Nutley, N. J.

West Coast BSA-SUNBEAM Distributor:
HAP ALZINA — 3074 Broadway, Oakland, Calif.

East Coast B.S.A.—Sunbeam Distributor RICH CHILD CYCLE CO., INC., 639 Passaic Av., Nutley, N. J.

West Coast B.S.A.—Sunbeam Distributor HAP ALZINA, 3074 Broadway, Oakland, California

495 c.c. Vertical

ABSOLUTELY new post-war models are as yet rare. Of those announced, the B.S.A. model A.7 proves on test to vindicate the promise of its design features. The 495 c.c. engine is a good example of the vertical-twin type. The straightforward duplex cradle frame, in conjunction with the hydraulically damped telescopic forks, endows the machine with first-class steering and road-holding qualities, and the compactness of the whole machine means more than a trim, business-like appearance; it means a five-hundred which has the feel of a three-fifty—until the grip is twisted.

The last is perhaps the greatest charm of the new B.S.A. In appearance and in feel on first acquaintance, it gives the impression of smallness. When manœuvred in the garage or when

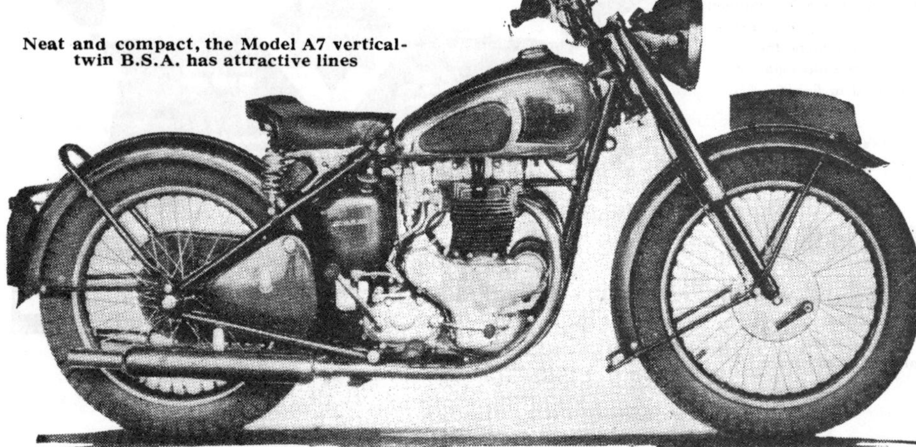

Neat and compact, the Model A7 vertical-twin B.S.A. has attractive lines

ridden at walking-pace speeds there is the inescapable sensation of handling a small, light machine with sedate performance. But when the vivacious engine is given its head the machine becomes a full-blooded five-hundred in the best sense of the term.

Starting the engine is very easy indeed. Such is the kick-starter leverage and gearing that it might be thought the engine has poor compression—so light is the weight necessary to depress the pedal. Whether the engine was hot or cold, no more than two gentle depressions of the kickstarter were required. Of course, for cold starting it was necessary to close the air lever —mounted unobtrusively under the saddle—and to flood the carburettor; the latter without the slightest compunction, for the magneto is protected, by a neat deflector, from the overflow petrol. Though the air lever might appear to be inaccessible it can, in fact, be operated when on the move.

Concealed Air Filter

With a warm engine, the tick-over was commendably slow, regular, and reliable, and the pick-up clean and certain. Mechanically the engine was quiet; at idling speeds the valve gear was audible, but there was a noticeable absence of intake hiss thanks to the Vokes air filter concealed between the oil-tank and the battery. Exhaust noise was subdued enough for the nippy performance of the machine to be used in towns without embarrassment.

The riding position is of the "sit up and beg" style, with the handlebars well upswept and wider than average—29in from tip to tip. Flatter handle-

The power unit; air spaces between the cylinders and through the head fins ensure even cooling

bars might be preferred by some riders, but it must be recorded that the combination of saddle position, close-in footrests, and the upswept, wide handlebars proved satisfactory in every way, except if the rider wished to crouch in the interests of sheer maximum speed. All controls are well positioned. The brake pedal comes immediately under the ball of the foot and the gear-change pedal can readily be operated in both directions without moving the foot from the rest. Handlebar controls are in keeping with the high standard of neatness of the whole machine. On the left is the clutch lever, with the dipper switch mounted on the lever clip, and on the right is the twistgrip throttle and the front-brake lever, with the horn button on its clip. Both clutch and brake assemblies are each clamped by a single pinch-bolt.

In all-round performance the A.7 approaches ideal. At low speeds it is as smooth and tractable as only good even-firing twins can be. The engine-shaft shock-absorber is up to its job, and the clutch is light to operate and sure in action. The clutch frees perfectly, and bottom gear can be engaged from neutral without noise. Gear-changing with the new positive-stop mechanism is absolutely positive, but a slowish movement of the pedal is required to obtain clean engagement. The gear ratios suit the characteristics of the engine admirably and a really sparkling performance can be obtained from the A.7 in the intermediate ratios. On the machine tested there was a definite "grumble" in all indirect gears.

On the open road at highish speeds the smoothness of the engine is unimpaired. There is no vibration period—not even when the engine is revved to the point of valve float. Another attractive characteristic is that the engine is so "happy" in all circumstances that there is no cruising speed which might be termed the best. If one aimed to keep the speedometer needle at 50, 60, 70 or even 80 m.p.h. as often as possible, the engine

Twin B.S.A.

responded without flagging and without fuss. Incidentally, all performance figures were obtained in boisterous wind and rain, and with the rider in bulky, all-weather garb.

Bends and corners can be swung stylishly, the B.S.A. holding its line without pitching or tail wag. The telescopic forks have a soft, long action, but were never bottomed throughout the test; they seem admirably suited to the frame, and steering is first class. The steering damper was never required.

Really good averages can be maintained without effort and zestful mile-gobbling and acceleration achieved in undulating country by making good use of the close third gear, which would be used less for equally good results if a higher octane fuel were available and the slight pinking sometimes experienced thus eliminated. The brakes are in keeping with this high performance, particularly the rear brake, which is light and spongy in operation yet powerfully arresting.

Throughout the test no adjustments were necessary and the engine retained its tune; if anything, it improved with the miles. Apart from a slight leak from one rocker box the engine and gear box remained oil-free externally.

There are so many commonsense riders' points on the A.7 that only a long list would include them all. But mention must be made of the really good lock, which would be envied on a

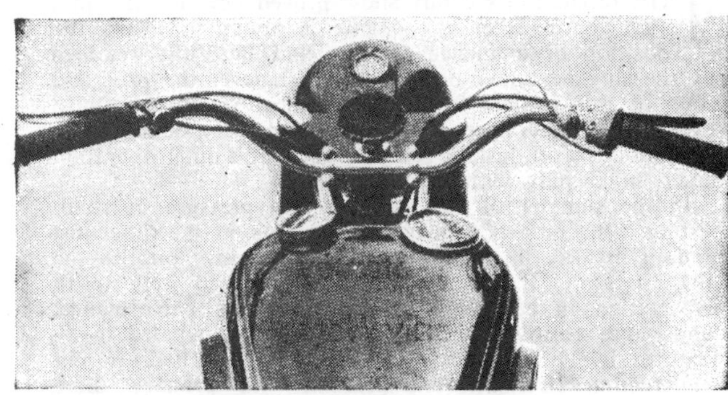

Really clean handlebars; the levers are retained by a single clamp bolt and have the dipper switch and horn bottom mounted on them

specially prepared trials machine—in point of fact, the machine will turn a circle of less than 12 feet diameter; of the filter-cum-drain plug in the base of the oil-tank, with plenty of air around it so that a spanner can easily be used on the hexagon and a funnel placed underneath; of the really quickly detachable wheels; of the well-tucked-in exhaust system; and of the stand telescoped into the vertical seat pillar—a boon for normal parking though not the complete answer because a fair amount of effort is required to get the wheel clear of the ground.

The B.S.A. model A.7 is an outstandingly attractive machine. It is assured of a brilliant future among discriminating riders—those who can evaluate genuine, worthwhile features.

Information Panel

495 c.c. Vertical-Twin B.S.A.

SPECIFICATION

TYPE : B.S.A. Model A.7.

ENGINE : 495 c.c. (62 x 82 mm.) vertical-twin o.h.v. Fully enclosed valve gear operated by single camshaft. Plain bearings at big-end and timing side mainshaft ; ball bearing on driving side. Dry-sump lubrication.

CARBURETTOR : Amal ; twist-grip throttle control and air lever mounted under saddle. Built-in Vokes air cleaner mounted on saddle pillar.

GEAR BOX : B.S.A. of bolted-up unit construction with engine ; positive-stop foot control. Bottom, 13.2 to I. Second, 9 to I. Third, 6.2 to I. Top, 5.1 to I. Five-plate clutch with Ferodo friction material.

TRANSMISSION : Chain. Primary 3/8in pitch duplex roller with manually adjusted slipper-type tensioner ; oil-bath chaincase. Secondary 5/8 x 3/8in lubricated by oil tank breather and with guards over top and bottom runs.

IGNITION : Lucas magneto, auto-advance.

LIGHTING : Lucas dynamo ; 8in head lamp.

FUEL CAPACITY : 3 gallons.

OIL CAPACITY : 4 pints.

TYRES : Front 3.25 x 19in ; Rear 3.50 x 19in ; both Dunlop Universal. Wheels quickly detachable and interchangeable.

BRAKES : 7 x 1⅛in ; hand adjusters.

SUSPENSION : B.S.A. telescopic forks with hydraulic damping.

WHEELBASE : 54½in.

GROUND CLEARANCE : 6½in unladen.

SADDLE : Terry.

WEIGHT : 385 lb (with I gallon of fuel and fully equipped).

PRICE : £135, plus Purchase Tax (in Britain) of £36 9s. Speedometer, extra £4 plus £I Is. 8d. P.T.

MAKERS : B.S.A. Cycles, Ltd., Birmingham, II.

PERFORMANCE DATA

MAXIMUM SPEED : Bottom : 38 m.p.h.*
Second : 59 m.p.h.
Third : 75 m.p.h.
Top : 82 m.p.h.

* Valve float just starting.

ACCELERATION :

	10-30 m.p.h.	20-40 m.p.h.	30-50 m.p.h.
Bottom … …	2⅘ secs.	3⅓ secs.	— secs.
Second … …	4 secs.	3⅘ secs.	4 secs.
Third … …	— secs.	5⅖ secs.	6⅙ secs.

Speed at end of quarter mile from rest 69 m.p.h.

PETROL CONSUMPTION : At 30 m.p.h., 92.8 m.p.g. At 40 m.p.h., 76.8 m.p.g. At 50 m.p.h., 70.6 m.p.g.

BRAKING : From 30 m.p.h. to rest, 31ft. (Surface : wet granite chippings).

MINIMUM NON-SNATCH SPEED : 12 m.p.h. in top gear.

WEIGHT PER C.C. : 0.78 lb.

THE recent Earls Court Show proved beyond all doubt that the parallel-twin engine is about to usurp the position of eminence so long and faithfully retained by the single-cylinder power unit. Whatever the pros and cons of this subject from the technical standpoint, most experienced riders agree that the twin supplies a combination of smooth travel, instant responsiveness and quiet operation much in keeping with modern ideas.

In the summer of 1947 we had the pleasure of road-testing a machine of this type which was, at the time, just finding its way into the hands of a receptive public—the 495 c.c. o.h.v. B.S.A. Model A7. It proved well up to expectations in the matter of speed and general performance, whilst the sensible layout and specification included many features likely to appeal to hard riders. Bolted-up unit construction of engine and gearbox with primary drive supplied by a duplex roller chain of $\frac{3}{8}$-in. pitch operating on fixed centres is a worth-while feature of the A7 and eliminates the necessity for adjustment. Maintenance of correct chain tension is achieved by the simple setting of a monochrome-faced slipper operating on the lower run of the chain. An inbuilt air-cleaner, duplex cradle frame and the ability to cruise easily in the region of 68-70 m.p.h. with reasonable fuel consumption were all points which evoked favourable comment in the course of the solo test.

Since the introduction of this machine certain modifications have been carried out with the object of improving further high-speed reliability and the opportunity for sampling the latest version, in sidecar form, was accepted with anticipation of some pretty lively motoring. Our correspondence files show that riders are displaying a keen interest in 500 c.c. twins as passenger machines and it was decided to extend the test over 2,000 miles to gain a thorough knowledge of general behaviour and to give the brand-new engine a reasonable chance to settle down.

Passenger accommodation was supplied by the now well-known B.S.A. 22/47 de luxe touring sidecar —a well-proportioned and handsome conveyance, scaling 178 lb. A regular passenger's personal views on this product are included in this report.

The test began with a little over 200 miles recorded on the fork-bridge mounted speedometer and the engine required careful treatment for the next 500 miles, with a progressive increase in cruising speeds. From this stage onwards—and following an oil change accompanied by a thorough check-over — the outfit was given little respite from every kind of usage. This varied from

The 495 c.c. o.h.v. Model A7 Vertical Twin

B.S.A.
AND SIDECAR

round-the-town business journeys to 250 miles in the day, high-speed runs against the clock with nothing spared and a total sidecar load of 15 stone.

Due allowance having been made for a speedometer slightly on the optimistic side, it was found that 222 miles in the day could be accomplished at a checked running average of 39.2 m.p.h. Although it was a pleasant feeling to be able to maintain a cruising speed of 50-60 m.p.h. on the 5.4 to 1 top gear, there was clearly audible evidence on frequent occasions that this ratio was too high

A capacious and readily reached locker is a feature of the Model 22/47 B.S.A. sidecar which commends itself to the tourist.

The A7 pulls its load comfortably at a cruising speed of 58 m.p.h. which can be reached in less than 25 seconds from a standstill. Cleanliness of the power - unit after a strenuous test was rated as one of the machine's cardinal virtues.

A Long-distance Test of a
Well-established "Multi"
in Combination Form
Equipped with a Model
22/47 Sidecar

Weighing 178 lb. the B.S.A. sidecar used in the test is a handsome vehicle equipped with a well-sprung body carried on a robust chassis. Note the folded hood and neat envelope containing it.

The "chair" accommodates a 15-stone passenger with ease whilst a lifting dash facilitates entry and exit.

for "lazy" driving in conjunction with a 7 to 1 compression ratio. Such a blending of high gearing and high-efficiency engine caused the tester to bemoan the presence of automatic ignition control because it was felt that here was an individual instance where a manually operated lever would have proved an undoubted advantage. At all times it was kinder to use the 6.6 third gear for acceleration from speeds below 30 m.p.h. if a quick getaway was desired.

Minimum non-snatch gait in top gear with a laden sidecar was 14 m.p.h., and, by *careful* use of the throttle, it was possible to get away gently from this low speed. Normal changing-up speeds on the open road were 20 m.p.h., 28 m.p.h. and 52 m.p.h. in the respective gears, figures which indicate clearly that the unit liked to "spin." Once accustomed to the outfit and its mannerisms we found it to possess an excellent rate of acceleration and the 58 m.p.h. cruising speed could be reached in less than 25 seconds without fuss.

The clutch was smooth, immediately responsive and was light enough for two-finger operation, but the gear change was a little heavy, despite a commendably short lever-travel, and it was necessary to judge engine revolutions in accordance with road speed if clashing was to be avoided. This is simply a matter of gaining familiarity with the particular machine and, in point of fact, "clutchless" changes were often made without a vestige of noise—although such driving habits are not advised! With the intermediate ratios in use there was a just perceptible hum from the gearbox.

Mechanical noise from the engine was in evidence only at low speeds when it was possible to hear a faint clicking from the tappet gear just above tickover. This was accompanied by a "whining" from the primary chaincase—no doubt attributable to the tensioner in action. Above 30 m.p.h. there was nothing to be heard above the deep-toned exhaust note which was prominent without being annoying. Vibration hardly existed and the only time the engine could be "felt" was between 52-56 m.p.h. in top gear, when a faint tremor could be detected through the bars.

Fuel consumption was outstandingly good and, with a little care in driving, it was possible to achieve 65 m.p.g. at a cruising speed maximum of 40-45 m.p.h. The test sheet "country" figure of 56 m.p.g. was taken over an average main road route with 55-58 m.p.h. maintained whenever possible. Oil consumption was very light and this was certainly one of the "cleanest" engines tested in our post-war series. After 800 miles without a wipe-over, there was no external evidence of oil at any point of the engine unit or chaincase.

Starting was always easy and the drill, even after all-night parking without cover was simple and effective. Closing the air lever, a fairly generous flooding, and a full-eighth throttle opening proved to be the correct tactics, and no more than three kicks were required under the worst conditions experienced. Use of the air lever and flooding were not necessary with the unit warmed up; the tickover was slow and reliable. The front brake did not seem up to the usual B.S.A. standard and there was a certain amount of "squealing" in action—with insufficient "bite." No complaint could be levelled at the rear "anchor," which was powerful enough to lock the wheel if used too heartily.

Non-stop runs in excess of a round hundred miles were accomplished without fatigue—thanks, largely, to a fork action almost ideal in its soft responsiveness. The wide bars and somewhat low saddle position proved exactly right for comfortable sidecar driving and the general handling, with the steering damper just biting, proved very good indeed.

To possess a headlight of sufficient strength to enable day-time averages to be maintained is a great asset, and the A7's 8-in. Lucas lamp, with the bulbous fluted glass, was well up to its job. Unfortunately, perhaps, the setting of its penetrating "flat" beam is critical and it was found

Brief Specification of the 495 c.c. Twin Model A7 B.S.A. and 22/47 Sidecar.

Engine: Vertical twin o.h.v.; 62 mm. bore by 82 mm. stroke=495 c.c.; compression ratio 7 to 1; single camshaft operating duralumin push-rods through chamber cast in cylinder and head blocks; camshaft incorporates timed mechanical breather. Forged steel crankshaft with central bob-weight and flywheel; induction-hardened journals; plain big-end bearings; plain bearing on timing side mainshaft and ball bearing on drive side. Gear-driven camshaft and magneto. Dry-sump lubrication; force feed to timing side mainshaft and big-end bearings, with direct feed to rocker spindles. Amal carburetter with built-in air cleaner forming a unit with oil tank. High-efficiency absorption-type tubular silencers.

Transmission: Four-speed gearbox in bolted-up unit construction with engine; built-in foot-change mechanism; ratios (sidecar), 5.4, 6.6, 9.5 and 14.0 to 1; ratios (solo), 5.1, 6.2, 9.0 and 13.2 to 1; endless primary chain $\frac{3}{8}$-in. pitch, duplex roller, operating on fixed centres with monochrome-faced adjustable-type slipper tensioner in oilbath case. Five-plate clutch, with Ferodo inserts, on roller-bearing centre. Rear chain $\frac{5}{8}$ in. by $\frac{3}{8}$ in. with top and bottom run chain guards.

Frame: Duplex cradle type with built-in sidecar lugs; telescopic forks with automatically controlled hydraulic damping; spring-up central and clip-up front stands.

Wheels: Quickly detachable with patented hub flange design to accommodate straight spokes. Dunlop Universal tyres. 26-in. by 3.25-in. section front, and 26-in. by 3.50-in. section rear; 7-in. by 1⅛-in. brakes with finger adjustment.

Tanks: Petrol tank. 3¼ gallons' capacity; saddle-tube mounted oil tank of 5 pints capacity.

Dimensions: Saddle height, 28¼ ins.; wheelbase, 54½ ins.; overall length, 85 ins.; overall width, 29 ins.; ground clearance, 6½ ins.; weight, 375 lb. (dry).

Finish: Black and chromium petrol tank, gold lined; polished timing, gearbox and primary chaincase covers; chromium wheel rims, black centres with gold lining; chromium brake cover plates; black frame, mudguards. Alternative Devon red finish available at option.

Equipment: Gear-driven Lucas magneto with automatic ignition advance and retard; separate Lucas 6-volt dynamo lighting with voltage control; large-diameter head lamp and electric horn; Smith 120 m.p.h. speedometer (internally illuminated), mounted on top fork bridge and gearbox driven.

Sidecar: B.S.A. de luxe tourer Model 22/47; triangular construction chassis with four-point attachment; body suspended by quarter-elliptic leaf springs at rear with phosphor-bronze bushed shackles; double helical springs at front; hinged scuttle; wide door; Rexine upholstery; pneumatic seat cushion; full enclosure hood with protective envelope cover; streamlined boot cover with metal strap retainer and lock; black finish; 3.25-in. section tyre on 19-in. rim; chassis assembly incorporates easily operated jack. Weight, 178 lb.

Price: A7 solo, £177 16s. (including £37 16s. purchase tax), plus £4 (plus £1 1s. 8d. purchase tax) for speedometer. Sidecar, £75 1s. (including £15 16s. purchase tax). Price complete as tested, £257 18s. 8d.

Other Extras: Spring frame, £12 14s. (including £2 14s. purchase tax); luggage carrier or pillion seat, £1 6s. 8d. (including 5s. 8d. purchase tax); pillion footrests, 12s. 9d. (including 2s. 9d. purchase tax).

Manufacturer's Address: B.S.A. Cycles, Ltd., Armoury Road, Small Heath, Birmingham.

---

that accurate adjustment, with a laden sidecar, was all wrong for travelling empty. Normally, it should be set so that the centre beam strikes the road 80-100 yards ahead.

Twin petrol taps are fitted to the 3¼-gallon fuel tank so that a reserve supply may be " trapped," and the best figure obtained on reserve—until a partial blockage caused trouble—was nine miles. Both wheels are quickly detachable, removal of the rear being facilitated by a hinged rear guard, the sprocket, driving chain and brake remaining *in situ*. The drive is taken through coupling splines on the hub and brake drum assembly. Dismantling the carburetter is not easy, due to the close proximity of the drip shield to the jet-well, having regard to the fact that, with a sidecar fitted, it is usual to work from the off side.

Summing up general impressions, it must be said that this vertical-twin B.S.A., in combination form, can provide a sparkling performance above the average pace for the driver who is willing and able to use a gearbox as it is intended, i.e., in the most intelligent manner. At the conclusion of the test it was performing better than ever and there was not a single, solitary blemish or sign of " blueing " on either exhaust pipe in spite of a deliberately hard " towsing " over four busy weeks.

A lady passenger's comments on the B.S.A. 22/47 de luxe sidecar are as follow:—

" This is the second time I have experienced the pleasure of travel in this handsome sidecar. It manages to combine a sporting line with an unusual extent of roominess (actually 20 ins. at normal elbow level), while a squab depth of 26 ins. gives good support for natural seating. Back-draughts are almost eliminated by the sensibly shaped deep windscreen and the hood which is contained in an envelope when out of use can be erected in a matter of seconds to give complete enclosure by stud side-fastenings and a wing-nut screen attachment. Fast travel in heavy rain caused odd drops to enter over the screen, but the hinged dash was leakproof. The side-opening door might have been wider for graceful entry and exit, but this, in my experience, is a common fault among sidecars.

" The amount of leg room is worth good mention—there's lots of it and no need to adopt a cramped position, and when I compared notes with a 6-ft. male, who tried a brief trip, he had no complaints to make on this score. A 200-mile journey with a five-year-old youngster sharing the sidecar was covered twice with only minor discomfort—and swapping from knee to knee provided a measure of ease. The point is that there was sufficient room for me—10 stone and 5 ft. 6 ins.—and the youngster.

" Body-springing is quite satisfactory—the front being helped in every way by the soft front fork action on the machine. It is odd that so few riders study passenger comfort when discussing telescopic forks—because they make an enormous difference. The seat cushioning might have been softer with all-round advantage, I thought. The room available in the rear locker may be judged by the fact that I could have a suitcase measuring 22 ins. by 14 ins. by 6½ ins. just fitting on the floor and still have room for picnic basket, rucksack and two spare coats.

" I am quite convinced that this is one of the nicest touring outfits of the post-war ranges."

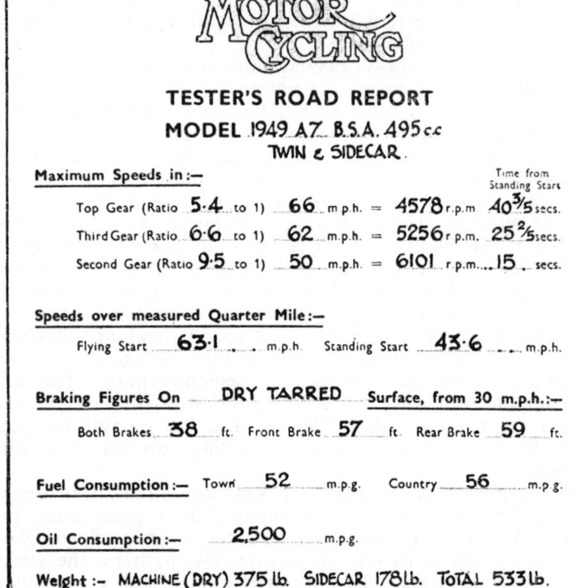

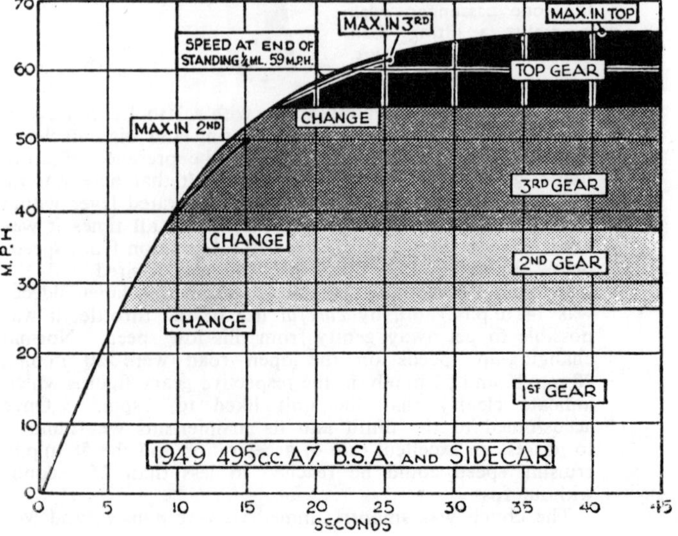

495 c.c. B.S.A.

High Performance Sports Mount with

WITH its full-blooded engine performance and first-class steering and road-holding, the new 495 c.c. B.S.A. Star Twin fully justifies the promise behind the general lay-out. It is a machine to thrill the man with a penchant for packing a large number of miles into each hour. In Britain, at least, cruising speed is limited only by road conditions.

The combination of sturdy, full duplex cradle frame, oil-damped telescopic fork and plunger-type rear-springing, endows the machine with steering and road-holding second to none. Indeed, the general handling properties of the B..S.A., and the compact feel of the model, are among its especially appealing features. It is a five-hundred that can be swept round corners and bends with the facility of a racing mount.

Fast, spirited cornering could be indulged in with the utmost confidence. The B.S.A. fork has a very long, soft movement (approx. 7 in.) which, whether the model is upright or heeled over almost to the limit of tyre adhesion, smooths out road irregularities in the most satisfactory manner. Round the static load position, the movement of the fork is extremely light so that care is taken of even the most minor of road ripples. Even at high speed there was never at any time any trace of jarring, and the fork never bottomed.

Of the rear suspension, it can be said that it was unobtrusive —apparent only by the marked absence of wheel hop. One of the most telling tests for suspension systems lies in riding the machine over the regularly placed, tram-track inspection covers, set in cobbles. Even in these circumstances the suspension earned full marks.

Docile in Traffic

As for cruising speed, 60, 70 or 75-80 m.p.h., it made no difference. There was never the slightest indication that the machine was being over-driven, not even to the extent of slightly discoloured exhaust pipes. In traffic, the engine was extremely docile and gave no indication of the high power output available. The all-round engine performance of the Star Twin is definitely above average in the 500 c.c. class. At low traffic speeds the engine is as quiet and tractable as that of almost any twin of to-day. The two carburettors, in delivery tune, were perfectly synchronized to give a clean, rapid pick-up from idling speeds to full throttle. A tickover that was slow, smooth, and 100 per cent reliable was, however, never achieved.

Engine balance is exceptionally good and, except for a slight "period" at exactly 50 m.p.h. in top gear, unimpaired up to speeds in the region of 70 m.p.h. Above 70 m.p.h. vibration could be felt at the handlebars and footrests.

It is, of course, when an engine has been driven very hard that any oil leaks begin to manifest themselves. The B.S.A. was ridden just as hard as it possibly could be over much of the 500-mile test, yet not the slightest oil stain appeared on any part of the engine or gear box. The only trace of oil that showed externally was a little that was flung from the chain on to the rear tyre and rim.

The clutch took up the drive smoothly. The gear ratios are admirably suited to the engine characteristics and, if the full engine performance is used, acceleration is rapid in the extreme. All the indirect ratios, and third gear especially, were audible, and clean, sweet gear changes were not too certain. Although the clutch appeared to free perfectly, it was not possible to select bottom gear with the machine stationary and the engine idling without a distinct "scrunch."

Easy Engine Starting

Engine starting is very easy indeed, and because of the leverage of the kick-starter pedal and its gearing, only slight physical effort is required. Flooding of both carburettors was, of course, necessary when the engine was cold and the handlebar-lever-operated air slides had to be closed. There is a separate feed to each carbu-

The plunger-type rear springing has a total movement of approximately 2⅛ in. Note the neat lifting handle for use when operating the central stand

A machine for the sporting rider, the Star Twin has a separate carburettor for each cylinder and plunger-type rear-springing. Saddle height is 31 in. The riding position is very good —one which ensures absolute control at all speeds. The tank is finished in silver and chromium and the frame and mudguards are black

Star Twin

First-class Steering and Road-holding

rettor, and both petrol taps and ticklers are easily accessible. Provided that the throttle was opened only the merest fraction, starting was certain at the second kick if the engine was cold, and first kick if it was hot. After a cold start, the air lever required to be left in the closed position for a mile or so; then it could be opened fully and forgotten until the next cold start was necessary.

Mechanically, the engine was reasonably quiet. After a cold start there was a fair amount of piston slap and noise from the valve gear. These decreased, of course, after the engine was hot. The exhaust was a pleasant, unobtrusive hum—so unobtrusive that it in no way interfered with using to the full the machine's nippy acceleration. On "Pool" petrol the twistgrip had to be handled carefully to avoid pinking during hard acceleration.

What was especially appreciated about the Star Twin was the excellence of the riding position. In delivery trim it was of the sit-up-and-beg variety so popular with many riders. An even better and more individual position was obtained after a few minutes' work with the tools. With the footrests raised so that the hangers were in a higher-than-horizontal position, and the bars turned slightly in their split clamps so that the grips were approximately horizontal, the riding position became one that allowed the rider to sit over the machine in a way that assured absolute control at all speeds. The saddle height of 31 in. is one that is "just right" for the majority of riders.

Excellent Steering Lock

All the controls are well placed and, with the exception of the throttle, which was slightly heavy, light in operation. The horn button and dipper are carried on the front brake and clutch lever clamps respectively and are easily reached by thumb. Both brakes were smooth and progressive in action, but with advantage could have been more powerful.

The steering lock (which gives a 12-foot turning circle) is worthy of employment on a works' trials mount, and is a most useful feature. Several other points of the Star Twin merit special mention. There is the deeply valanced front mudguard, which has the registration numbers painted on the sides. The wheels are really quickly detachable and interchangeable. Centre and front stands are provided, and a special lifting handle is fitted above the

Throughout the test the engine remained completely free from oil leaks. The twin carburettors are unobtrusive and the petrol taps and ticklers easily accessible

nearside seat stay to facilitate operating the centre stand. The exhaust pipes are neatly tucked in under the primary chain case and timing chest. Of black, silver and chromium, and with the primary chaincase, timing chest and gear-box end cover all highly polished, the general finish is very attractive.

Driving light from the 7 in head lamp is adequate at speeds up to 60-65 m.p.h. The tool-box, mounted below the offside seat stay, is of ample dimensions to carry comfortably the tool-kit, spare plugs, and a repair outfit. Both petrol and oil filler caps were liquid-tight, the former to the extent that there was no fear of spilling even when the tank was filled absolutely brim-full. Carried on the top fork bridge, the speedometer is mounted at such an angle that it can be easily read from the saddle. There are so many genuinely worth-while features about the B.S.A. that the list could go on almost indefinitely.

The Star Twin is a machine to make a wide appeal to the sporting fraternity—to all who want a high cruising speed and handling that is as good as the best available to-day.

Information Panel

SPECIFICATION

ENGINE: 495 c.c. (62 x 82 mm) vertical-twin o.h.v. Fully enclosed valve-gear operated by single camshaft. Plain bearings at big-ends and timing-side mainshaft; ball bearing on driving side. Dry-sump lubrication.

CARBURETTORS: Twin Amal; twistgrip throttle control; air lever on right handlebar.

GEAR BOX: B.S.A. of bolted-up unit construction with engine; positive foot control. Bottom, 13.2 to 1. Second, 9 to 1. Third, 6.2 to 1. Top, 5.1 to 1. Five-plate clutch with Ferodo friction material.

TRANSMISSION: Chain. Primary ⅜in pitch duplex roller with manually adjusted slipper-type tensioner; oil-bath chaincase. Secondary, ⅝ x ¼in lubricated by oil-tank breather and with guards over top and bottom runs.

IGNITION: Lucas magneto, auto-advance.

LIGHTING: Lucas dynamo; 7in head lamp.

FUEL CAPACITY: 3 gallons.

OIL CAPACITY: 4 pints.

TYRES: Front, 3.25 x 19in; rear, 3.50 x 19in; both Dunlop Universal. Wheels quickly detachable and interchangeable.

BRAKES: 7in x 1⅛in; hand adjusters.

SUSPENSION: B.S.A. telescopic front fork with hydraulic damping. Plunger-type rear-springing, with springs for shock and rebound.

WHEELBASE: 55in.

GROUND CLEARANCE: 5in unladen.

SADDLE: Terry, unladen height, 31in.

WEIGHT: 385 lb (with no fuel and fully equipped).

PRICE: £160—plus Purchase Tax (in Britain), £43 4s. Speedometer, extra £4, plus £1 1s 8d P.T.

MAKERS: B.S.A. Cycles, Ltd., Birmingham, 11.

DESCRIPTION: *The Motor Cycle, November 4th, 1948.*

PERFORMANCE DATA

MAXIMUM SPEED: Bottom: 37 m.p.h.
Second: 57 m.p.h.
Third: 75 m.p.h.
Top: 84 m.p.h.

ACCELERATION:				10-30 m.p.h.	20-40 m.p.h.	30-50 m.p.h.
Bottom	...	...	...	2.2 secs	—	—
Second	...	...	...	4 secs	2.8 secs	3.4 secs
Third	...	...	...	—	5.2 secs	5.8 secs
Top	...	...	...	—	9.2 secs	9 secs

Speed at end of quarter-mile from rest: 77 m.p.h.
Time to cover standing quarter-mile: 17.2 secs.

PETROL CONSUMPTION: At 30 m.p.h., 92.8 m.p.g. At 40 m.p.h., 83.2 m.p.g. At 50 m.p.h., 73.6 m.p.g. At 60 m.p.h., 65.5 m.p.g.

BRAKING: From 30 m.p.h. to rest: 32ft (surface, dry tar macadam).

MINIMUM NON-SNATCH SPEED: 19 m.p.h. in top gear.

WEIGHT PER C.C.: 0.78 lb.

A Catechism On an Established Power

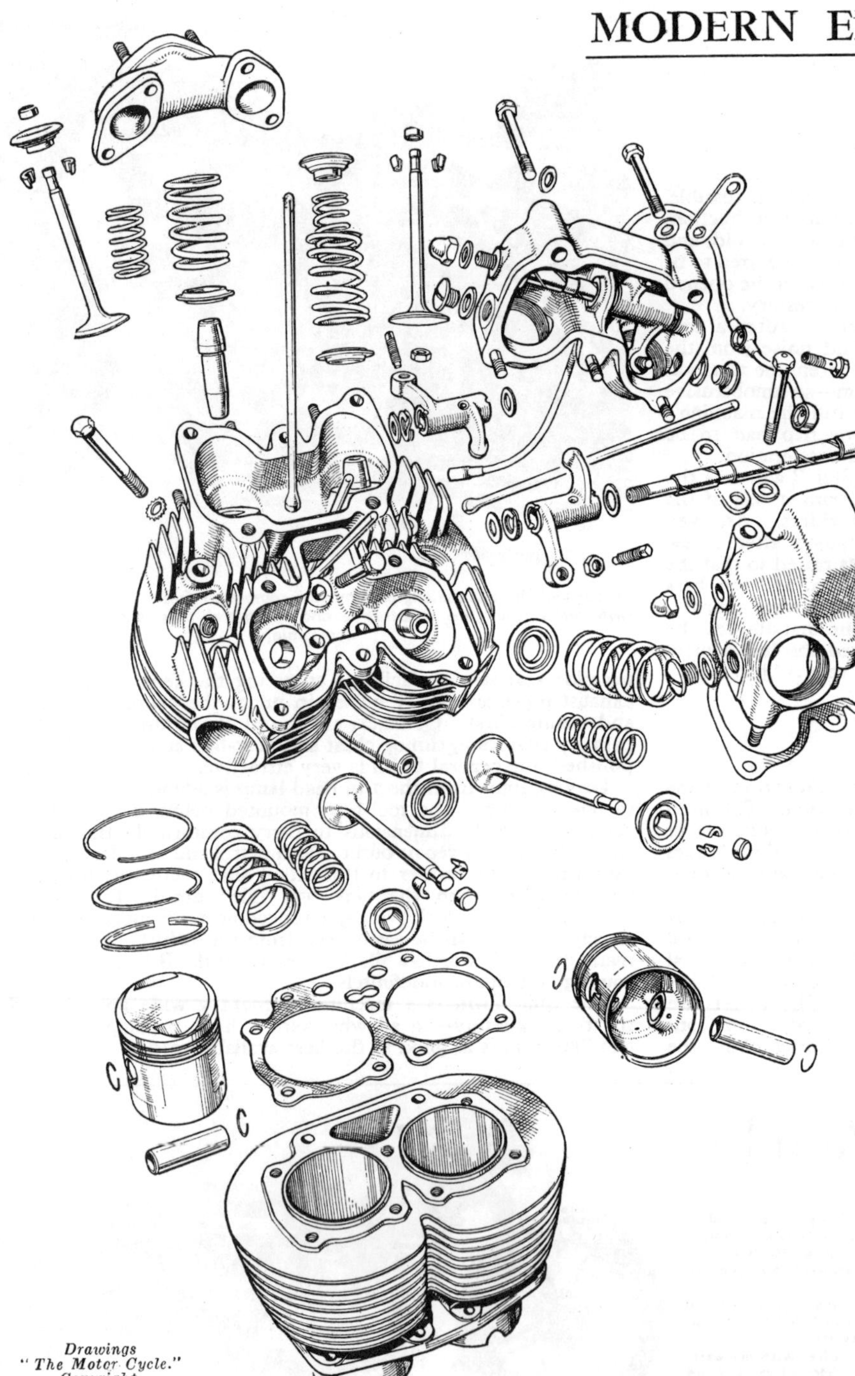

*Drawings
"The Motor Cycle."
Copyright.*

Two separate valve-spring wells, with an air space between them, are formed in the cylinder-head casting. The head is retained by nine bolts, one of which is in the middle to prevent distortion and give a good joint seal. Light-alloy rocker boxes are bolted independently to the head. Rockers operate direct on the steel spindles

crankshaft revolution; with a single there is one firing stroke every *other* revolution. Hence a graph curve about a neutral datum showing the unbalanced forces in a single-cylinder machine would show a hump indicating each exhaust stroke, whereas in a vertical twin the exhaust strokes would, by comparison, be shown as a lesser variation from a straight line."

We reached that stimulating observation at the tail-end of a list of reasons for the adoption of a vertical-twin engine. It was pointed out by Mr. Perkins that B.S.A.s had been following closely the development of multi-cylinder engines; the factory had had much experience with twins, and engines of that type were in production during the first World War. It was foreseen that while the single-cylinder engine was far from on its way out in public favour, there was increasing demand for engines that were smoother and quieter in operation. The vertical-twin has those merits. "And," added Mr. Hopwood, "it is neat and compact and will fit comfortably in a conventional frame; it can be cooled adequately and gives good accessibility for maintenance."

Then emerged another consideration connected with inertia loading. Mr. Hopwood pointed out: "Though the actual weight of the two pistons complete with rings and gudgeon pins, plus that part of the connecting rods assessed as reciprocating motion, might be higher than with a single-cylinder engine of similar capacity, the inertia loading will be lower by reason of the shorter stroke of the twin."

THE afternoon's discussion promised well. In the airy B.S.A. office was a wealth of technical experience. At the head of the table was Mr. H. Hopwood, Chief Designer (Motor Cycles), who was "in" on the designing of the highly successful vertical-twin that started the trend in 1938. And it was a vertical-twin —the B.S.A. Model A7, introduced in 1946—I had journeyed to the Small Heath works to discuss. Supporting Mr. Hopwood was Mr. H. Perkins, Assistant Chief Designer; he laid down the A7 engine and it was, in Mr. Hopwood's words, "Mr. Perkins' baby." Further support came from Mr. D. W. Munro,

M.I.Mech.E., of the Technical Department, who has a reputation for his technical writings and his predilection for technical chit-chat.

Mr. Munro was not long in propounding a theory that deserved a verbatim note. "I maintain," said D.W.M., with eyes a-twinkle, "that the balance of a vertical-twin is better than that of a single. True, the two types of power unit are identical in *dynamic* balance. But in a four-stroke cycle, the inertia loading on the compression stroke is minimized or may be completely opposed by the combustion pressures. Now with a vertical-twin there is a firing stroke for every

Model A7 Twin

Unit, With Answers from B.S.A. Technicians   By HARRY LOUIS

Next, I asked the reason for the semi-unit construction achieved by bolting the gear box to the rear of the crankcase. "That arrangement gives a compact unit," said Mr. Perkins, "and makes for the utmost rigidity. Hence there are lower mechanical losses in the primary drive." Mr. Hopwood pushed the point further: "There is also the attraction of weight saving by the elimination of engine plates between crankcase and gear box and by the reduction in the frame member lugs." Maintenance was easier because a primary chain adjustment could be made very quickly by resetting a slipper, which did not mean the rear chain had afterwards to be readjusted as with a separate gear box design.

"Did you encounter any snags with this bolted-up arrangement during the development stages? For instance, did any bother arise in connection with heat transference to the clutch; did you find that the engine and transmission noises were accentuated?" The answer was, "No, trouble with heat transference never arose and, on the subject of noise, well, the A7 has gained a high reputation for quietness."

Superfine Finish

The crankshaft is a one-piece forging in 65-ton, 3½ per cent nickel, toughened steel. The crankshaft has integral bob-weights and a flange in the middle to which the flywheel is bolted. Formed with the flywheel are additional bob-weights. On the drive side at the main bearing, the shaft measures 1¼in diameter, the timing-side bearing journal measures 1⅜in diameter, and the big-end journals are 1.46in diameter. Each crankshaft assembly is individually balanced within narrow limits; the big-end journals and the timing-side crankshaft journal are induction hardened, and ground and polished to a superfine finish.

Oil hardening, high-carbon, nickel-steel, H-section connecting rods, with conventional split big-end eyes, are employed. Big-end bolts are in high-tensile nickel-chrome steel. Bearing liners are steel-back, lead-bronze with indium flash. At this point Mr. Munro chipped in. "We shouldn't overlook the importance of the indium flash—indium is nearly as expensive as gold, by the way—which is diffused into the surface of the lead bronze. It provides an amazingly high resistance to instantaneous overloading and it is therefore particularly advantageous during running-in of a new engine."

Gudgeon pins measure 1-1/16in diameter, are taper bored, and are in nickel-chrome steel case hardened and tempered; they are of the fully floating type retained by wire circlips. Pistons are of B.S.A. design and are cast in silicon-alloy, which has a very low coefficient of expansion. Each piston has two compression rings and one slotted scraper ring. Compression ratio is 7 to 1. On the Star twin it is 7.5 to 1.

"This monobloc cylinder casting is unusual in the arrangement of the push-rod tunnel," I observed. "Would you give me the considerations that led up to that layout being adopted?"

"Oh, yes," volunteered Mr. Perkins. "The idea of the push-rod tunnel at the rear was to obviate any obstruction to cooling air impinging on the cylinders. There is adequate air flow between the two bores with outlets round the sides of the push-rod tunnel. The one-piece casting gives rigidity and is eminently sound practice providing the design allows good cooling. Incidentally, the material used is iron, as you can see, and the bores are hone finished."

"And arising from this layout, is the attraction to be able to employ a single camshaft with a resulting simplification of the timing gear?" I queried. "Agreed," came the reply.

The iron cylinder-head casting includes the valve-spring wells on which fit the light-alloy rocker boxes. Mr. Munro added, "You will note that those wells are distinct and separate from each other with a lateral air space between them. That is important; the air space ensures proper cooling, and since one well is for the exhaust valves and the other for the inlets, the temperatures of the wells will be vastly different in normal running conditions. By keeping the wells separate, there is no chance of one well 'pulling' the other owing to the different temperatures and hence different amounts of expansion."

Nickel-chrome iron valve guides are a press fit in the cylinder head. The shallow cups to receive the valve-springs have each a narrow collar underneath making contact with the head. "Thus," said Mr. Perkins, "the cups are clear of the head and less heat is conducted to the valve-springs."

90 lb Pressure

Inlet valves are in 3½ per cent nickel-steel with a high carbon content. Jessop G2 nickel-chrome austenitic steel is employed for exhaust valves. The coil valve-springs exert 90lb pressure with the valves fully open—that is, with 5/16in lift. Springs are retained by a collar and split, taper collets. Valve stems are fitted with hardened steel end-caps on which the adjustable rocker ball-ends bear.

"You will have seen," said Mr. Perkins, "that the head is held down by nine bolts. The rocker boxes are independently bolted to the head so that the nine bolts have one job — to hold the head firmly and squarely on the cylinder block." Then Mr. Munro added, "And one of the bolts is plumb in the middle of the head; it is an important bolt because it prevents the chance of distortion and plays a big part in making a good joint."

"You employ separate light-alloy rocker boxes," I observed. "Why not

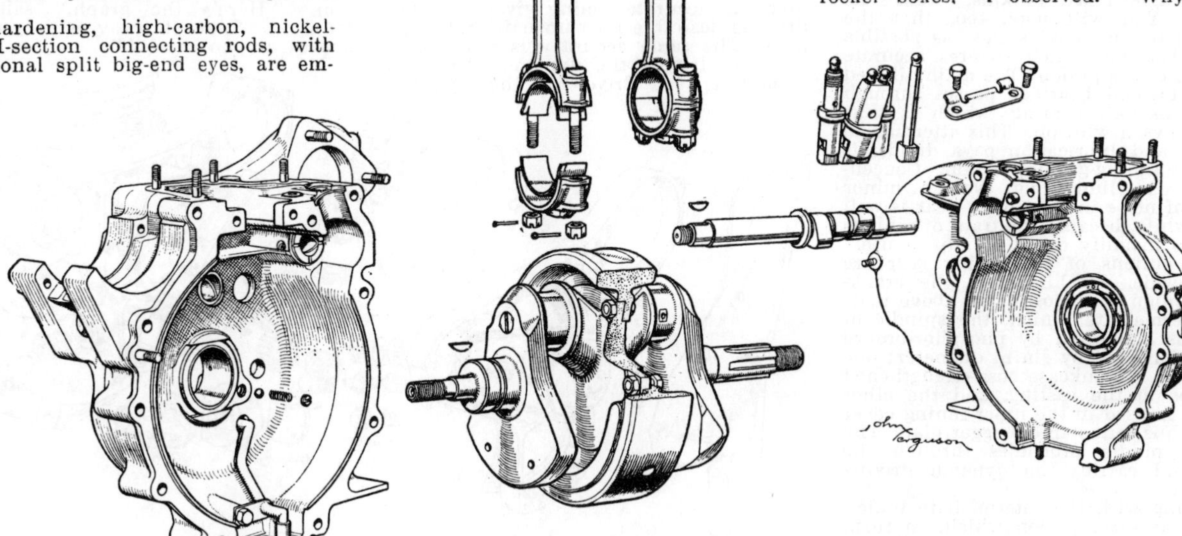

A sturdy, one-piece crankshaft has a bolted-on flywheel. The shaft is supported by a journal ball bearing on the drive side and a long, large-diameter plain bearing on the timing side

B.S.A. MODEL A7 TWIN

rocker boxes integral with the cylinder head, so eliminating joints between boxes and head and also, possibly, obtaining a stiffer ensemble?"

"Integral rocker boxes may seem an attractive proposition," said Mr. Perkins, "but adequate cooling can be difficult to achieve; furthermore, the differences in thicknesses of metal inevitable in such a casting might encourage distortion."

Manganese - carbon, case - hardening steel is used for the ½in diameter rocker spindles; each spindle is supported not only at the ends, but also in the middle by a ribbed boss in the casting; the boss separates the two rockers. Very stiff, yet light in weight, the 3 per cent nickel case-hardening steel rockers operate directly on the spindles (in other words, there are no rocker bushes). "The best possible bearing," said Mr. Hopwood.

Ends of the rocker arms are cupped to receive the solid steel push-rods. "Is there no difficulty with lubrication of those 'upside down' cups?" I queried. "No. The contact surface gets adequate lubrication and an advantage is that the cups will not hold water that might arise from condensation; hence there is no chance of sludge—or even rust—formation," said Mr. Perkins. He went on to mention that the absence of a cup on the push-rod and a ball end on the rocker meant a saving in weight.

A specially interesting point is that in the sides of the rocker boxes are detachable duralumin plugs—one for each valve—to allow a feeler gauge to be inserted between adjuster and valve-stem end cup. There are, of course, screw caps to give access to the lock nuts and adjuster heads.

Long Bearing

The crankcase is an extremely robust aluminium-alloy casting. The crankshaft is carried and located by a large deep-groove, ball journal bearing on the drive side. On the timing side there is a steel white-metal-lined bearing, 1¼in in length; the bearing area is thus 1¼in long by 1⅜in diameter.

"That long, plain bearing gives good support to the crankshaft," I observed. "Yes," agreed Mr. Perkins, "that's its charm. You will note, too, that the crankshaft pinion is as close as possible to the bearing, which ensures accurate running of the pinion. The main oil feed to the big-end bearings passes through this crankshaft bearing, which is thus almost awash with oil. This attention to rigidity and lubrication pays dividends in quiet timing-gear operation. Concentration on eliminating even a minor source of noise in the timing gear is well worth while, because the train of pinions tends to magnify or 'throw up' noise."

Spur pinions of the timing gear are 7/16in wide. Meshing with the crankshaft pinion, and positioned above it, is the intermediate pinion, the spindle of which is supported by phosphor-bronze bushes ⅜in long by ⅜in in diameter; one bush is in a crankcase boss strengthened by webs in the casting, and the other bush is housed in the inner timing cover which thus forms an outrigger plate. The pinion spindle protrudes through the bush and carries the dynamo driving sprocket.

Meshing with the intermediate pinion is the camshaft pinion which, in turn, drives the magneto with its auto-advance mechanism.

"Special attention has been given to obtaining a rigid camshaft," mentioned Mr. Hopwood. Then Mr. Perkins added,

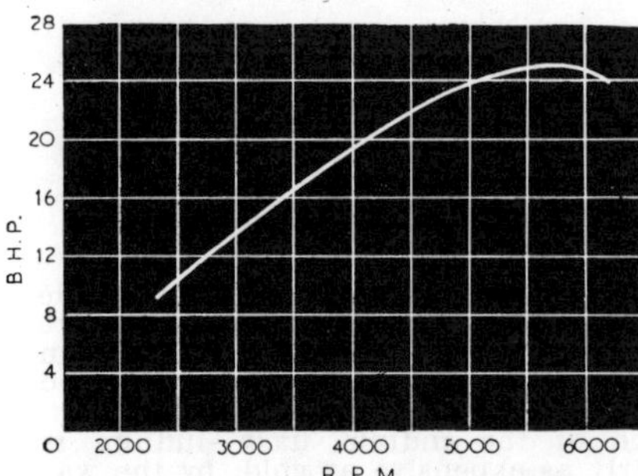

Power curve of the 495 c.c. A7 twin.

"The material is manganese case-hardening steel and the shaft and cams are in one piece. There are three ¾in × ¾in phosphor-bronze bushes supporting the camshaft. The tappets and guides are in similar material to the camshaft. A ball-end is formed at the top of each tappet, which operates in the cup forged in the lower end of the solid push rod."

Fitted on the outer face of the camshaft pinion and turning with it is a breather valve which operates in a boss in the inner end cover of the timing chest. "This looks a rather more elaborate breather than on many engines," I suggested. "Why?"

"We wanted a really effective breather and were prepared to go to some trouble to get it," said Mr. Perkins. "Not only was the A7 to be a smooth, quiet engine, but also it was to be clean, which means oil tightness. How far we succeeded with this breather can be gauged from the fact that even at maximum crankshaft revolutions, there is still a depression in the crankcase—something of an achievement. The engine has gained a reputation for oil-tightness."

Then we started to discuss the chain dynamo drive; this drive is enclosed by the outer timing chest cover and is remote from the timing chest proper with its camshaft and magneto driving pinions.

"Why the separately enclosed drive and why chain drive?" was my next question.

Mr. Perkins replied: "With a high-performance engine such as the A7, the precisely accurate timing given by gear drive is desirable for camshaft and magneto. The same accuracy is not necessary for driving the dynamo. To have employed gear drive for the dynamo

would have increased the chance of operating noise in a design on which considerable pains to secure silence had been expended. Another point is that the chain is lubricated by grease, and thus the possibility of oil from a timing chest reaching the dynamo is eliminated."

"This layout makes it necessary to have both inner and outer timing covers," I observed. "Presumably the added cost and complication are worth while?"

"Certainly. The outrigger support that the inner cover gives to the intermediate pinion is, in our view, essential for quiet operation. The outer cover takes no load; in fact, the engine can be run without the cover."

"And now for the lubrication system," I suggested to Mr. Perkins. "You mentioned earlier that the oil feed to the big-ends passed first through the timing-side crankshaft bearing. I take it that from the big-ends, the oil is flung out to lubricate the pistons, small ends, and so on?" "Quite right," concurred Mr. Perkins. "At the same time the cams and tappets are lubricated because these components are not in a separate compartment—they are exposed to the crankcase as in car practice."

"What pressure is maintained for the main and big-end bearings?" I inquired.

Lubrication

"The pressure release valve—detachable, by the way—at the front of the timing chest is set to pass oil at 55lb sq in when the oil is hot. As you might expect, the gear pump creates a far higher pressure than 55lb, and the oil by-passing the valve flows into the timing chest."

"What is the capacity of the pump?"

"At 5,000 r.p.m., the pump passes 126.6 pints an hour," said Mr. Munro, after consulting a chart. "And the return pump will pass 177 pints an hour at a similar crankshaft speed."

The rockers and valve gear are lubricated from a tapping off the return pipe to the tank. Oil is fed along the rocker spindles and emerges through a hole under each rocker arm to lubricate the valve guides. Surplus oil drains down the push-rod tunnel past the tappet guides into the crankcase.

When examining this arrangement, I said, "Would one not obtain a more positive supply of oil by taking a by-pass off the feed side of the pump?"

"Theoretically, yes," agreed Mr. Munro, "but the amount of oil required 'upstairs' is not very great and the present system does the job admirably with the utmost simplicity. Can one ask for more?"

"What does the power curve of this engine look like?" was my final question. "Here's the graph," said Mr. Munro. "Take it away with you—the figures are no secret!"

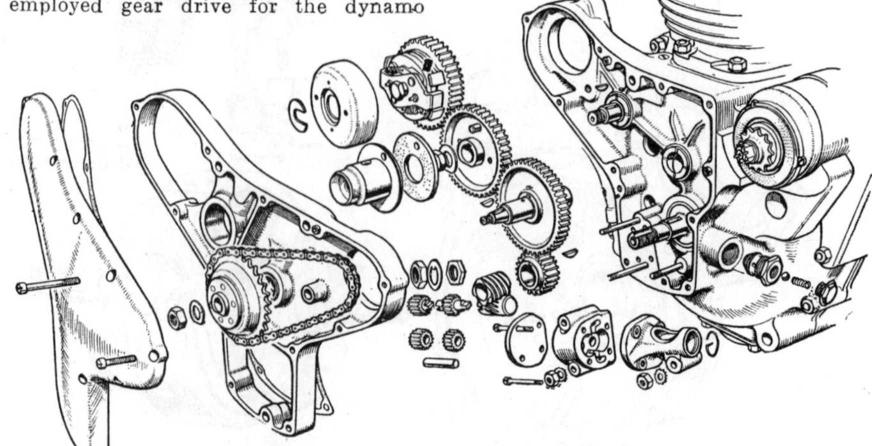

A train of pinions drives the camshaft and the magneto. The inner timing-chest cover provides an outrigger bearing for the intermediate pinion. Fitted to the camshaft pinion is the breather operating in the inner cover boss. Chain drive to the dynamo is in a separate compartment

New B.S.A. 650 c.c. Twin

A Side-by-side Twin Based on the Design of the Popular A7 : The 125 c.c. Bantam available with Rear-springing, Coil Ignition, and Battery and Rectifier Lighting, and also in Competition Form

BY the end of the year, it is anticipated, a new B.S.A. will be in production. What will it be? Nothing less than a 650 c.c. vertical-twin! Though the new twin bears strong resemblance to the firmly established 495 c.c. A7, and many of the same parts are employed in its manufacture, the engine has numerous wide departures from current A7 practice. The frame of the "Golden Flash," as the new model is called, will be of the duplex cradle type identical to that of the A7. Dimensions, such as wheelbase and saddle height (55in and 31in respectively), are as on the A7.

Wheel and tyre dimensions will be 3.25 × 19in front and 3.50 × 19in rear. To cope with the greater performance of the 650 c.c. engine, a new front brake measuring 8in × 1⅜in will be employed. The drum is to be a Millenite casting (Millenite is a high-grade iron alloy which offers a high degree of rigidity and great fatigue resistance). Aluminium alloy will be used for the shoe plate and shoes; the latter will be webbed and heavily ribbed.

Total weight is expected to be roughly equal to that of the A7. The gear box will be of the semi unit-construction design used on the A7, but the ratios to be finally employed have not yet been fixed. It is certain, of course, that they will be higher than those employed on the A7. High gearing, in conjunction with the power obtainable from the 650 c.c engine, will ensure an easy, fast cruising speed and, a complement of "effortlessness," low inertia stresses in the engine and longer life. As on the A7, primary drive is by means of a duplex chain with an adjustable tensioner. Ignition and lighting are also as for the A7.

Bore and stroke of the new engine are 70 × 84mm, as opposed to the 62 × 82mm of the A7. Crankcases of the A10 and A7 are not interchangeable, but engine units are. Dimensions of the A10 crankcase are naturally greater since, in order to cope with the increase in width between the centres of the cylinder bores, the crankshaft is longer.

Like the A7, the crankshaft of the A10 is of one-piece design with a bolted-on central flywheel. It is a high-grade steel forging comprising the two mainshafts, two crank webs, the big-end journals, and the central flywheel flange. Six bolts hold the forged steel flywheel to the crankshaft flange. Bob-weights for balancing are incorporated in the flywheel and crank webs. Supporting the crankshafts are a ball journal bearing on the driveside and a plain bearing on the timing-side. The journals of the plain bearing are induction-hardened, ground, and polished.

Wider Cams

Light-alloy connecting rods with conventional split big-ends are employed; the big-end bolts are of high-tensile nickel-chrome steel. The bearing linings of the big-ends are steel-backed, indium-flashed, lead bronze—a material which has a high load capacity. Con-rods are of H-section and measure 6½in between the centres.

Timing gear design is on A7 lines, but the camshafts are not interchangeable. Cams will be wider than on the 495 c.c. engine, and car-type barrel tappets with chilled rubbing surfaces will be used. The timing cover will be of similar design to that on the A7, but more neatly proportioned.

A normal cast-iron is used for the cylinder casting. As in the case of the five-hundred, the push-rod tunnel is cast integrally in the block. The cylinder head is of an entirely new design. It has narrower angle valves (58 deg) than the five-hundred, and a "flatter," shallower combustion chamber, which goes nearer to the ideal since the ratio of combustion space to surface area should always be as high as possible. It is anticipated that the compression ratio will be 6.5 to 1. The cylinder head also has a new finning arrangement designed to give improved cooling.

Instead of the A7's pair of rocker boxes, there is a single rocker box on the A10. Access to the valve-clearance adjusters is gained by removing aluminium-alloy plates: one for the exhaust valves and one for the inlets. Each will be held in position by four ¼in nuts. Valve sizes, incidentally, are not yet fixed. As on the A7, duplicated, helical valve-springs will be used. Oil drainage of the rocker gear will be via internal oilways in the head and block castings.

Rocker spindles are of the fixed design, drilled axially and radially for lubrication purposes. The rockers themselves are of case-hardened, unbushed steel, bearing directly on the rocker spindles. The new head, incidentally, has the induction manifold cast integrally with it. It is probable that a 1in choke Amal carburettor will be employed.

Like most other machines in the B.S.A. range, the A10 will be available with spring or solid frame, and it is anticipated that there will be one of each on display at Earls Court. At the time of this issue's going to press, a colour scheme for the

The new 650 c.c. Golden Flash will have higher gearing than the 495 c.c. A7, thus ensuring effortless, fast cruising speeds. The spring-frame is an optional extra.

new model had not definitely been decided.

Another B.S.A. pre-Show surprise is that the very popular 125 c.c. two-stroke Bantam will be available for 1950 with plunger-type rear-springing of straightforward design, battery and rectifier lighting, and coil ignition. The Bantam will also, of course, be obtainable in its 1949 guise as well as in Competition form.

Total movement of the rear-springing is said to be $2\frac{1}{4}$in ($1\frac{1}{2}$in on depression and $\frac{3}{4}$in on rebound). "A" quality steel tubing, $\frac{3}{4}$in in diameter and of 10 s.w.g., forms the main stanchion in the plunger

A new 8in front brake is fitted to the 350 c.c. B32 " Gold Star " model

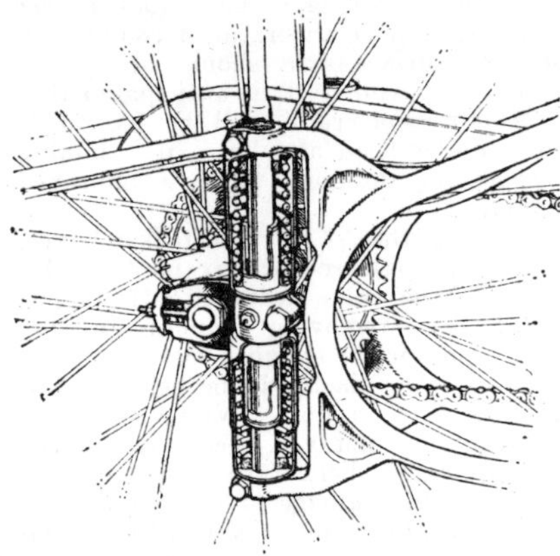

Rear-springing will be available on the 125 c.c. Bantam model

units. Bushes are of M.P.C. high-duty bronze and as much as $1\frac{1}{4}$in long. Wall thickness of the bushes is 0.1in. The single helical spring is of 4 s.w.g. and has a free length of $5\frac{5}{16}$in. Outside diameter of the spring is 1.729in.

The employment of the Lucas 45-watt A.C. generator (as optional equipment) has allowed the near side of the timing case to be considerably "cleaned up." Carried side by side with the tool-box, the battery is a small-size Lucas 6v. type with a capacity of 5 ampere-hours. The coil is carried on the top frame tube and is hidden by the fuel tank. A lightweight electric horn is fitted to one of the saddle bolts. The ignition and lighting switch is mounted in the head lamp. On all 1950 Bantams, incidentally, the exhaust pipe passes above the footrest instead of below

it—a detail modification which considerably improves the general appearance. On all three versions of the model, rubber sleeves will be fitted to the bottom of the fork legs to prevent the ingress of grit and water to the sliding members.

On the competition Bantam, the exhaust pipe is turned up at the rear and a wide-clearance light-alloy front mudguard is fitted. The front tyre is as standard: the rear measures 3.25 × 19in. A larger-than-standard chain sprocket on the rear wheel gives overall gear ratios of 8.65, 14.5 and 27.10 to 1.

A model that is already well-known among sporting riders, the B34 500 c.c. Gold Star, will also be in full production in 1950. It follows the better-known 350 c.c. Gold Star engine design except, of course, in engine size and in gear ratios.

Bore and stroke of the engine are 85 × 88mm. As in the case of the three-fifty, an aluminium-alloy cylinder barrel and head are used. Four sets of gear ratios—for touring, trials, scrambles and road racing—are available. The new 8in front brake to be used on the A10 will also be fitted to the B32 and B34 Gold Star models.

All other models in the B.S.A. range are unaltered in every way from last year. It is the widest range of machines produced by any motor cycle manufacturer in the world and provides for almost every conceivable class of rider. The makers are B.S.A. Cycles, Ltd., Small Heath, Birmingham, 11. Prices are as follows:—

	Basic Price			Total Price		
125 c.c. D1 Bantam	63	3	6	80	4	8
125 c.c. D1 Competition	68	3	6	86	11	8
250 c.c. s.v. C10	89	0	0	113	0	9

Right : Detail drawing of the rear stand of the Bantam

Below : The Bantam is now listed in competition as well as standard form

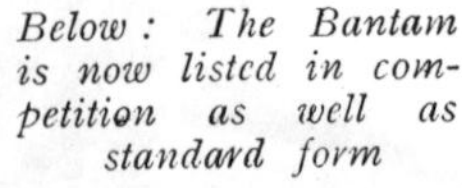

	Basic Price			Total Price		
250 c.c. o.h.v. C11	94	0	0	119	7	8
250 c.c. o.h.v. C11 de luxe	96	0	0	121	18	6
350 c.c. o.h.v. B31	116	0	0	147	6	6
350 c.c. o.h.v. B32 Competition with magneto and bulb horn	120	10	0	153	0	10
with Magdyno	128	0	0	162	11	3
350 c.c. o.h.v. B32 Gold Star	170	10	0	216	10	9
500 c.c. o.h.v. B33	126	0	0	160	0	6
500 c.c. o.h.v. B34 with magneto and bulb horn	130	10	0	165	14	8
with Magdyno	138	0	0	175	5	3
500 c.c. o.h.v. B34 Gold Star	180	10	0	229	4	9
500 c.c. s.v. M20	118	0	0	149	17	4
600 c.c. s.v. M21	121	0	0	153	13	6
500 c.c. o.h.v. M33	128	0	0	162	11	4
500 c.c. o.h.v. Twin A7	144	0	0	182	17	8
500 c.c. o.h.v. A7 Star Twin	164	0	0	208	5	8
650 c.c. o.h.v. Twin A10	152	0	0	193	0	10
Spring-frame for A10	10	0	0	12	14	0
Sidecar 22/47	59	5	0	75	1	0
Chassis No. 22 only	22	10	0	28	10	0
Spring-frame for D1 Bantam	5	0	0	6	7	0
Lucas ignition and lighting for D1	6	0	0	7	12	5
Electric horn for standard D1 (operated by a dry battery)		18	6	1	3	6
Gold Star light-alloy engines for standard B32 and B34	10	0	0	12	14	0

All prices include speedometer.

From a Berchtesgaden balcony

The Hagen Gebirge from the road near Galling

A7 to Austria

Tale of a Tour for Two
to the Tyrol and Beyond

By "EX-TYKE"

THE tour really began as we stood in the cramped square before the cathedral at Strasbourg, straining our necks to peer up at the famous spire, which pointed its 470 beautiful feet into a perfect summer sky. The rays of the lowering sun struck obliquely across the red, west façade of the cathedral, throwing into strong relief the carved intricacies of the steeple, which has a grace and delicacy rarely achieved in stone.

In half a thousand years the surrounding buildings can have changed but little, and later, having secured our lodging, Margaret and I explored the old part of the town. We wandered at random among the centuries-old buildings, crazily roofed and with steep, fantastic gables, their timbers carved from street level to eaves.

Next morning we headed for the Pont du Rhin, and at Kehl faced the tedious procedure necessary to enter Occupied Germany. The formalities were completed with commendable speed, and soon we were swinging steadily along a pleasant road through a succession of bright half-timbered villages, clean and attractive in the strong sunshine. Haymaking was in full swing, and the

27

The Steiner's Meer from the Eagle's Nest

the war—we saw many long-haired and bewhiskered players going about their normal business. A few miles farther on we passed the picturesque castles of Hohenschwangau and Neuschwanstein, perched on their rocky pinnacles. Mittenwald provided shelter for the night. Famed for centuries for its fiddles (musical), the town is now apparently notorious for "fiddles" of another kind, to judge from the many anti-smuggling warnings prominently displayed!

After a perfunctory Customs examination and another currency quiz, the red-and-white barrier was lifted at Scharnitz and we passed into Austria. The first few villages had a strangely dejected air; but the writer, at least, soon forgot that as he picked his way down the hair-raising, loose-surfaced Scharnitz Pass, which plunges wildly to the wide valley of the Inn. From Zirl we turned along the fine road flanking the river and followed the turbulent grey-green waters to Innsbruck, capital of the Tyrol.

After spending a few hours exploring the town, once more we took the road by the Inn, and ran into the only rain of the tour. It seemed wise to carry on, so, waterproofs donned, we continued to Zell-am-see. With more than a thousand miles behind us, next day was ordained a day of rest so far as our more tender parts were concerned. The time was very pleasantly divided between a stroll along the shore of the Zellersee in the cool of the morning and a ride by funicular to the 6,300 ft. summit of the Schmittenhöhe in the heat of the afternoon.

The following morning promised well for our run up the Glocknerstrasse, but by the time we reached Fuschertörl heavy cloud had mustered and the views proved disappointing. It was here that we encountered the jet-propelled gentleman from Manchester. He volleyed round a bend and decelerated like a hard-pressed T.T. leader making a pit stop. He leapt from his Trophy Triumph, with its rainbow-coloured yard of exhaust pipe.

Brief Encounter

In ten seconds he had introduced himself, produced and set a camera, asked a passing native to make the exposure, and posed alongside Margaret and me. Twelve hours later he was due on the docks at Calais; he had made the outward ride from Calais to Villach within 24 hours! He said he found it quicker to use the bike (It was an oft-made business trip) than to fly to Zurich and to use auxiliary land services to reach Villach! Three minutes after his arrival, he was rocketing away down the pass—surely the briefest of brief encounters!

To the south, black clouds enveloped the peaks and rain swirled through the valleys, so we decided not to descend that side of the pass. Instead, we turned and made towards the valley of the Salzach, which we followed to Bishopshofen for our night's lodging.

Salzburg was reached early on a Sunday morning and, lodging gained, we looked round the town and spent the afternoon in the Festung, whence spreading views of the town are obtained. Our information again proved false, and attempts to change cheques on the Sunday were unavailing. However, an obliging chambermaid loaned us 50 schillings, with which to ward off starvation and visit a theatre. After dark, the beauty of Salzburg's principal buildings was emphasized by flood-lighting, and we spent a pleasant half-hour strolling along the Rudolfskai.

Leaving Salzburg, we made the short ascent of the Gaisberg. From the summit we enjoyed the wide panoramas over the Salzburg Lakes and across to the Alps in the south. Vainly we tried to follow the course of the autobahn to Munich, but its white ribbon rapidly dissolved into the heat haze.

Then our course was set once more for Germany and, the frontier crossed, we headed for Berchtesgaden. A glorious evening was passed in the exploration of Obersalzburg, where we scrambled among the bomb-blasted ruins of Hitler's Berghof. Gazing out through the enormous window of the one-time conference room, we agreed that Adolf, evil though he was, knew a "highly desirable building plot" when he saw one.

The Eagle's Nest, a sort of glorified summer house presented to Hitler as a 50th birthday present, may only be visited through the U.S. Army's Special Service trips; in spite of that drawback, it is definitely worth a visit. The building and approaches occupied 3,000 men for 18 months, and cost £2,500,000. Climbing steadily at about 1-in-6, the approach road is roughly five miles long. Leaving the bus on a wide car-park, we walked through a long tunnel and were then silently transported the last 400 feet through the heart of the mountain in a magnificently appointed bronze-lined lift which delivered us into the Eagle's Nest. The building is quite

peculiar, tall stooks, built on wooden frames, stood like paraded soldiers in the fields on each side. The crop seemed to demand the labour of the entire population, from knee-high nippers to bent old-timers. All eyes followed us as we bowled past and occasionally one of the sweating workers gave us an envious wave.

The route followed the River Kinzig along a broad valley which gradually narrowed as the road climbed and wriggled its way into the rolling pine-garbed hills of the Black Forest. For hours we rode through a dark-green countryside, the villages becoming ever more picturesque, until, at last, the day's mileage was deemed ample. The night was spent at a *gasthaus* overlooking the Alpsee, from the swampy shores of which a myriad frogs croaked their throaty chorus.

Our information being that petrol coupons could be obtained at any German bank against travel cheques, next day we halted at Immenstadt to get the necessary tickets. The bank cashier told us they were unobtainable there, but were unnecessary, anyway, as petrol was available (at extra cost) without the coupons. Thus assured, we carried on, only to be dismayed when eventually, requiring petrol, we were refused it because we had no coupons. However, on seeing our G.B. plate, the good lady who owned the pump relented to the extent of five litres.

By now we were well into the American Zone, and at a barracks near Füssen it seemed wise to inquire about the procedure for obtaining coupons. A sympathetic American Army officer knew nothing about "civilian gas," but obligingly filled the tank at a pump in the barracks, for which he provided his own "PX" coupons and refused all attempts at payment!

Passing through painted Oberammergau—famous for the Passion Play, which was being performed for the first time since

The Glocknergruppe from near Fusch

undamaged and commands wonderful views of the Bavarian and Austrian Alps.

Next we went to Königsee, where we were rowed on the lake in a picturesque boat reminiscent of a gondola by a boatman and his wife fully decked in the local costume. At one point where there is a famous echo, the "captain" suddenly produced a trumpet and treated us to a "duet."

By now our time was getting short, so next day good use was made of the autobahn, and the 330 miles between Berchtesgaden and Heidelberg were covered comfortably at a very satisfactory average. Again we relied on Shanks' pony for a day; we visited the castle, where we inspected the 50,000-gallon Great Tun; and later we philosophized along the Philosophen Weg. The four days our military permit allowed for crossing Germany had now expired. Our next hop was a bee-line for the Belgian border, which was eventually crossed at Wasserbilligerbrück.

In the Ardennes the vivid red of poppy patches on the intensively cultivated hillsides was challenged by the blaze of yellow from blossom-laden broom. Gladly we would have dawdled, but time did not allow, and we pressed on as far as possible, eventually halting at an isolated inn, freshly re-built after being demolished in the Battle of the Bulge.

One more day remained to us on the Continent. We started early, travelled rapidly where the road allowed, and threaded our way through the hectic, unpredictable traffic of Brussels. We continued through Ghent and Bruges. As we approached Ostend, the wide, flat road seemed to symbolize the 50 flat weeks of toil which lay between us and the next already anticipated tour.

* * *

What of the machine which made this grand holiday possible? The A7 B.S.A. twin carried us 2,700 miles on 27½ gallons of petrol. The only tool used was a tyre gauge !

On the lower slopes of the Glocknerstrasse

Jim Ferriday and George Wilson check-over their outfit before the start

LONG
WEEK-END

Tale of a Round-Britain Trip with a B.S.A. Golden Flash and Sidecar: 2,212 miles Covered Between Thursday Morning and Monday Evening

By George Wilson

IT was 9.30 p.m. in the gathering darkness when a travel-stained B.S.A. Golden Flash and sidecar slipped into Birmingham on the road from Llangollen, in North Wales. Arriving at Feridax House in Frederick Street, where a small group of friends was waiting to welcome the équipe, two tired but cheerful travellers dismounted. Since 7.30 a.m. on the previous Thursday, 2,212 miles had been covered in England, Scotland and Wales—and the only regret felt by the crew, Jim Ferriday, managing director of Feridax accessories and myself, was that the trip was at an end.

Now, 2,212 is a lot of miles: it is a fifth of the total covered by my personal mount in fifteen months and it is roughly twice the distance involved in a Scottish or International Six Days' Trial. Why so many miles in so few days? In Jim Ferriday's words, "Just for the devil of it!"

It all began a few weeks earlier when a group of us was discussing long-distance rallies and their incomparable value in "improving the breed." Ferriday wanted to prove to his own satisfaction that a new Dualseat he was experimenting with was really as good as he thought it was; he had a prototype of a new screen he wanted testing and he had also what he called a "Sidecar Comfort Set." He would also like my opinion of them, so what about our riding in a rally? However, because of my week-end commitments and one thing and another, the idea of a Continental rally was scrapped and we decided instead on a rally of our own. A route was planned which would take us round Britain, the total time allowance being five days and the average daily mileage in the region of 450.

The machine we chose was a 650 c.c., for obvious reasons, and also because I wanted to know how the B.S.A. Golden Flash performed when fitted with a sidecar. Ferriday "organized" an outfit. It was, in fact, the machine used by Colin Edge in the Monte Carlo Rally, and Ferriday collected it a day or so before we were due to leave. Though a new engine and gear box had been fitted, we were told that they were run-in, so we had no compunction about setting out on such a trip as that envisaged. We were armed against nearly every contingency—or so we felt. We carried a spare wheel on the sidecar locker door and an air bottle held by elastic ropes to the side-screen which forms part of the proposed sidecar set; we had spare cables fitted all round; and spare chains, bulbs and inner tubes in the sidecar. The new Dualseat felt comfortable and so did the foam rubber sidecar cushions, the toe-rest, and floor cushion.

To suit my personal preference I had asked that the machine be fitted with a manual ignition control, a special handlebar bend, pillion rests of the type supplied to oversea police forces—the last so that should one of us feel bored or tired in the sidecar we could both ride on the machine; and, lastly, that the outfit be lined up with something like 2in of toe-in on the sidecar wheel. The prototype screen looked good on paper and I had high hopes for it; but it proved most disappointing and, as a result of our experiences, will not go into production.

Theoretically, our first day's route, which lay over an estimated 470 miles, should have been one of our easiest days. The itinerary included starting from Birmingham at 7.30 a.m., and travelling south by south-west to Worcester, Gloucester, Bristol, Bridgwater and Taunton, where we decided on a coffee stop. Lunch, we said, would be at Plymouth and tea in Bournemouth. We anticipated arriving at our hotel in London at round 9 p.m. that evening.

The weather when we set out was perfect. Ferriday drove and I, in the sidecar, felt at peace with the world. Heavy, going-to-factory traffic was encountered in the city streets and progress was slow for the first 20-odd miles. A38 is a good road, however—wide and with clear bends. When the built-up area had been left behind we pressed on smartly. The sun grew warmer and bathed the Malvern Hills in brilliant light. The air was crisp and fresh. It was with an elated feeling that I traced the route on the map spread out on my knees.

Then, suddenly, panic! As we rounded a second-gear left-hand corner, in a traffic stream, there came a screech from the gear box—a screech that intensified with every second! The brakes were applied and we swung off the road on to the grass verge. We stopped the engine immediately and with the gear in neutral pushed the machine forward a few feet. No sound. I was out of the chair by this time and started the engine. Screech—S-c-r-e-e-c-h—S-C-R-E-E-C-H!! I diagnosed picking-up of the layshaft bushes and quickly earthed the magneto. We decided to let the tight bearings cool for a few minutes and try again.

Ten minutes later all appeared to be well and, I driving, we set off—quite slowly and ready to stop quickly should the screaming recur. Six miles on, recur it did and we stopped again. Our projected tour seemed merely a pipe dream! After another brief halt, however, we set off once more, driving slowly at first and gradually increasing the speed as the miles totted up and all went well.

Twenty miles farther on, nothing else had happened. I had the outfit tramping along very smartly in the upper sixties, driving it up to that speed quite hard each time after a turn or traffic conditions demanded caution. Then, suddenly, a piston dried up, and Ferriday mentioned that maybe I'd been driving just a bit too hard? It was no more than a partial seizure. I had the clutch out

Plymouth: A detour was made to visit the Mayflower Steps

before the engine became solid and the engine turned quite freely immediately we stopped. The cylinders and heads and the oil tank were very, very hot.

This time realization dawned ! The engine-gear unit had obviously not been sufficiently run-in ! So when the job had cooled off a shade, we set off again, keeping the speed in the region of 50-55 m.p.h. on the straights, working up to that fairly quietly, and letting the engine turn over easily. With these tactics the miles sped by. Coffee in Taunton, lunch in battle-scarred Plymouth; and this being my first visit to the heroic city, I took time off to have a look at the historic Mayflower Steps whence the Pilgrim Fathers sailed for the New World over 300 years ago.

The afternoon passed uneventfully and pleasantly. Already I felt that the new Luxury Dualseat was the best I had ever experienced and that the sidecar was very comfortable. Though as a rule I am not a happy passenger, I was quite content to lounge in the sidecar. Ferriday's driving was not over-fast, he was one-hundred per cent courteous, and completely safe. The scenery along the South Coast was new to me. There were beautiful panoramas of rolling hills and fresh green fields with neatly trimmed hedges. I made a mental note to holiday Lyme Regis way, or thereabouts, at some future date. We had tea in Bournemouth with Joy Foster, wife of the famous racing man. Bob, unfortunately, had not yet returned from the Continent.

I was again at the controls after tea and increased the speed slightly as we rode up A31 towards London. We made a brief stop to have a word with Len Heath in Farnham, and by the time we reached the Kingston By-pass lights were required. At the Esher roundabout, known locally as the Silly Isles, I saw on the left a Royal Enfield Flea I recognized. Sitting under the trees waiting to have a cheery word with us, was friend "Torrens." By this time both Ferriday and I were quite convinced that we should have no recurrence of our troubles of the morning. "Torrens" confirmed that we would be wise to leave well alone. Knowing of our project he mentioned a real round-Britain trip he had taken part in when, as official observer, he accompanied Hugh Gibson on his memorable trip in 1924. The complete coastline was followed and 3,429 miles were covered in 11½ days.

London was reached. The Golden Flash was running beautifully. Next morning we set off again at 7.30 and had little traffic to bother us as we headed for Stevenage. The tank was full and Jim mentioned that he thought the top of the tank was split. I didn't think so, believing that the filler-cap was leaking and that eddies from below the screen were sending the leaking petrol swirling. But I was wrong. As the petrol level dropped the swirling on top of the tank continued. It was not very serious, however, and we decided that we would have the tank repaired in Edinburgh

"Torrens" has a night meeting with the équipe on the Kingston By-pass

that night. The welding on the battery carrier broke before lunch-time. We decided we were having fun and no mistake ! One of Ferriday's aero-elastic ropes was pressed into use and held the battery securely for the remainder of the trip.

It was a grey, beautifully fresh morning. Cambridgeshire was a mass of delightful greens and browns. The roads were excellent. We cut inland to Sleaford, Lincoln, which revived memories of Dunholme, and then took A15 to Brigg—a magnificent road with long straights, few side-turnings and little traffic. From Brigg we went to Goole, and from Goole to Hull. I don't know much about that part of the trip because, in the sidecar, I fell asleep entering Goole and woke up in Hull !

In Hull we stopped for lunch. When I went into the hotel dining-room Jim was already seated and standing talking to him was a tall, bespectacled, studious-looking young man, dressed in immaculate morning clothes. He was hotel manager and very interested to learn where we were going. Was he a motor cyclist ? Why yes !—he rode a 596 c.c. Panther !

After lunch I drove to Middlesbrough by way of Bridlington, Filey, Scarborough, Whitby and then across a moorland road—

Down South—rolling scenery near Sidmouth

bleak, lonely, sinuous and undulating—to Middlesbrough. The moors looked majestically vast and then forbidding as the clouds darkened. The sky closed down on us. Rain began to fall in large drops and with rapidly increasing intensity.

When we stopped for fuel at Guisborough it was as though the very heavens had burst. Rain sheeted down, transforming the gutters into miniature torrents. We paused in the garage for ten minutes and soon the rain eased as the storm passed out to sea. I replaced my ordinary gloves with P.V.C. ones and we restarted. So long as my hands remain dry, riding in the rain does not bother me in the slightest. And these P.V.C. gloves are one-hundred per cent waterproof. They were a boon on this trip, as I have found them to be in the past.

The outfit had not seemed to be handling too well over the last rain-washed miles and I decided to have a look over the sidecar connections at Middlesbrough. There was nothing wrong, but I was astonished to find that the rear tyre was as bald of tread as an egg is of hair. We changed the wheel with the spare and had a replacement tyre fitted to the old wheel at Edinburgh. The Golden Flash engine develops a deal of power and the rear tyre, of course, had had to transmit a fair amount of "bang." I know also, of course, that while the 2in of sidecar toe-in we were using provides excellent handling, it also tends to be rather hard on rear tyres.

Jim had the honour of driving the outfit over the Scottish border at Carter Bar, and, looking down at me, he patted my head and said, "Welcome home, George." And what a welcome it was! Well may the traveller to the north rub his eyes at Carter Bar and wonder at the magic that has taken place in the last few miles. We Scots, I know, are all birds of a feather. But I say in all sincerity that the panorama of the southern uplands of Scotland as seen from the summit of Carter Fell, 1,815 feet above sea-level, is one that is in my experience incomparable anywhere. Long shadows reached over the distant green and brown hills. There was an impression of everlasting loneliness and quiet. Contour and colour—*and smell*—were immediately and intimately those of Scotland.

We arrived in Roxburgh in the gathering gloom, and I took the controls to drive the final 48 miles or so to Edinburgh. As the light faded further I switched on the pilot light—and the ammeter showed a discharge. I switched on to "head"—and an even greater discharge showed itself. I drove all the way into Edinburgh using only the pilot bulb and we had the dynamo replaced when we arrived.

In the capital both Jim and I have numerous friends. We were welcomed by Jimmy Alexander, grand old man of Scottish motor cycling who in his day rode in the T.T., and Bill Smith, pre-war trials and scrambles champion. One of my proudest possessions now is a copy of "Alexanders the Great," a history of the Alexander family; inscribed on the flyleaf, by Jimmy himself, are the words, "To George of the wild Wilson blood—from another of the same clan," for Jimmy's mother was a Wilson.

(To be concluded).

Top: On the Firth of Forth ferry—the famous bridge towers in the background

Above: George Wilson No. 2 peers upward at relative George Wilson No. 1. Jim Ferriday looks suitably serious

Huntingdon left, Cambridge right—a riverside halt on the way north

Round-Britain Journey

GEORGE WILSON Concludes the story of a Long-distance Journey with a 650 c.c. Sidecar Outfit

The Golden Flash sidecar outfit by Loch Lochy, Inverness-shire

EDINBURGH was left the next morning—the city looking her very best. There is no errant Scot who is not moved to the core by the sight of the castle in sunlight—almost as if it is forming the very crown of Midlothian. However, there was little time to be lost if we were to catch the 8 o'clock ferry—we were bound to press on if we were to be at John o' Groats by nightfall.

The ferry over the Forth passes under the famous 8,000 ft cantilever bridge. On the north side, as a native of Fife, I was on my own territory. I know every bump in Inverkeithing's not-too-perfectly surfaced main streets. The sun shone and I pointed out proudly to Jimmy scenes that brought back to me memories of my youth. On through Glenfarg to Perth, home of the glorious Black Watch. We were there comfortably in the hour. Then to Dundee. The scenery was completely enchanting and our progress was punctuated by cries of, "Oh, I say, look at that . . .!" from Jim. At Dundee we were met by George Wilson No. 1, giant brother of my father, and one of the country's earliest motor cyclists, and by George McLean, veteran trials rider.

After a brief stop for a chat, we left for the north, taking the coast road to Aberdeen. The road surface is perfect and the B.S.A. went like a song. The running-in process was now complete, and the engine running more coolly with every mile. It was going so well, and producing so much power, in fact, that Jim christened it "The Tramper!" It was a brilliantly sunny day and I could feel my face tingling with the heat of the sun. By mid-day Aberdeen lay basking beneath us as we dropped down to sea-level.

Wealthiest Men

Lunch was excellent and was provided with true Scottish hospitality and charm. A young enthusiast we met, who owned a single-cylinder B.S.A., and rode it impeccably, offered to guide us through the city and out on the road to Huntly and Keith. In Morayshire and Nairn we saw such scenery as made us literally gasp. Scenery of this type really *can* take one's breath away. The fields of oats, wheat and barley were more golden than gold itself. The hills rose and fell in glorious splendour. Visibility was a thousand miles. Between Keith and Elgin we felt that it would be sacrilegious to carry on, and stopped to take photographs and feast our eyes to the full on Caledonia's beauty. As Jim said, we were at this moment the wealthiest men on earth. No part of Italy, Austria or Switzerland that we have seen could equal this.

We pottered into Elgin to find the town liberally beflagged and basking in glorious sunshine. The whole of the town's population appeared to be parading the streets. It looked as though Royalty was expected. Glancing down at Jim—who was in the sidecar—to gauge his reaction, I was astonished to see him straightening his tie, smoothing his hair, and hear him murmuring something about wondering how they knew we were coming! Couldn't he have seen the board displaying the sign "Gala Week" a few yards back? Came Forres and Nairn and the tremendously long, fast, well-surfaced straight into Inverness, where we stopped for tea.

When we started off again after Inverness, we took the road round Beauly Firth, cutting north to Dingwall, then to Ardgay and Bonarbridge. And it was on this section of road that we were to experience our last bit of trouble. I was in the sidecar and Jim was motoring very swiftly over the rather bumpily surfaced road that is cut in the lower slopes of Ben Dearg and overlooks the beautiful Dornoch Firth. I was just about to suggest that he should perhaps ease up to give the sidecar springs a chance, when, glancing down, I saw that the top leaf of the left-hand spring was already broken !

It was not terribly serious, of course, but it meant that we should have to go easy on the rougher surfaces we had been led to expect in what Jim termed the "Far North." In order to help matters I left the chair and rode on the pillion. And I liked that so much—as Jim did when I was driving—that we never used the sidecar again for more than a brief spell until we reached Glasgow the next night !

It was near Ousdale, in Caithness, that we experienced an odd coincidence. We were climbing steadily when below us we saw a trim, white-washed cottage, one gable of which was festooned with dozens of pairs of stags' antlers. I wanted to take a photograph, so we turned off the road and dropped down the steep three-ply track. The sound of our arrival brought the tenant to the door. We asked for permission to take the photograph and Jim introduced me. Though I know this sounds too fantastic to be true, it is a fact that Mr. Meller, in this Highland fastness, had just laid down the current copy of *The Motor Cycle* to come to the door ! Before we left, a few minutes were spent inspecting Mr. Meller's 600 c.c. Levis, and bemoaning the fact that the make is no longer available.

North of Wick the scenery changed. The roads were no longer sinuous, but comprised long, fast, well-surfaced straights. John o' Groats, or rather the huge pylons used by one of the military services thereabouts during the war, could be seen from nearly 20 miles away. Though the light was fading, distant landmarks stood out in fine detail.

The air was clear as crystal, and held an invigorating, salty flavour. The country is flat, but ringed to the west by lofty ranges of craggy peaks. Crofts, some derelict, formed the only signs of habitation. The sky was a blaze of gold and scarlet.

I doubt if we met a single car or saw a single person until just before reaching John o' Groats. We drove hard in this vastness, keeping the needle on the 70 m.p.h. mark. As we neared the northern coast the smell of tangle, that thick, musty seaweed that litters the rocky shore when the tide is on the ebb, became quite pronounced. It seemed almost as though, since leaving Wick, we had entered some strange, dead world.

A Danish student hiker to whom we gave a lift amused us by saying that since encountering us he had become certain that the British were indeed mad. Here we had a perfectly comfortable sidecar yet insisted on both riding on the machine—and after having covered nearly 400 miles we laughed continuously, rather like schoolboys, when we should have been tired and weary ! It was with difficulty that I restrained the light-hearted Ferriday from signing the hotel register as James Oliver Ferriday and George Tozer Wilson ! The outfit when we arrived that night was at its best. The total mileage completed to date was 1,380. All we did that evening was to top up the petrol tank in readiness for leaving the next day.

Since we were uncertain of the type of roads we should encounter to the west, we made an early start next morning, breakfasting at 6.30 a.m. and leaving soon after seven. It was a dull and rather dismal morning—typical of that part of the country. A stiff wind blew from the east, swishing through the whins and rocks and sounding like the moaning of a lost soul. Peewits and curlews wheeled and swooped above the foam-flecked sea, which broke

into white, angry surf at the foot of the rocks. There is always wind at John o' Groats, I was told. Few trees grow there. Summer and winter the wind sweeps over the bare hills to the sea or back to the land with the scent of the tangle. As I watched, away on the horizon a ship steamed away on some magic adventure. I scrambled down the rough, winding track leading to the beach to have a final look at Stroma, standing like a sentinel in the Pentland Firth.

As we left we rode past the white-washed church, in the graveyard of which lie the remains of the Groats family. The sun came up and the prospect brightened. In the next 85 miles we met two cars, saw very few houses after leaving Thurso, but enjoyed to the full miles and miles of magnificent scenery. We also saw hundreds of rabbits—flaunting their white tails as they scampered neatly from rock to warren at the sound of our passing.

The road to Tongue is quite good—narrow, it is true, but with a moderately good surface. Farther west, we were told, the surface deteriorates into a three-ply track; so we turned south at Tongue and headed for Loch Loyal, the tail of Loch Naver, and Lairg, which nestles at the south of Loch Slin. The road all the way is no wider than the track of a sidecar outfit and the surface, though tarred, is broken in places. We kept the speed down, and were pleased to do so, for the scenery was enchantingly beautiful. On my pointing out a scene to Jim, he fatuously replied that he couldn't see the scenery for hills and valleys! The sole vegetation hereabouts is in the form of a dryish, brown-looking grass, only fit for sheep feeding. We saw no trees for mile after mile.

As we progressed south we rejoined our route of yesterday. We passed the beautiful ancestral home of the Sutherlands, now a Youth Hostel, standing majestically poignant in a beautiful wood of firs and pines. At Bonarbridge rain began to fall, and it developed into a downpour by the time we reached Inverness, where we had decided to stop for lunch.

The rain continued with unabated intensity and we left Inverness in a downpour. We had to stop at the swingbridge over the Caledonian Canal to let a beautiful pleasure craft pass southwards. The bridge was the most pleasing I have seen, opening quickly, smoothly and quietly—the epitome of mechanical perfection. Perhaps I was too loud in my praises of Scottish engineering, because for all I know the bridge is still open! We had to make a detour and cross another bridge when all efforts to close our one had failed!

Our route took us to Drumnadrochit, with beautiful Glen Urquhart to the west; Invermoriston; Fort Augustus; Loch Ness; Loch Oich; Loch Lochy; Loch Eil; Loch Linnhe; and then to Fort William : scenes of more magnificent natural splendour cannot be imagined. No longer did we see whins and rocks and brownish grass. Here was lush, green verdure, beautiful, coniferous-wooded slopes, and towering heights, capped by magnificent cloud formations. The surface of the Canal shimmered under the teeming rain. No road in Britain is better-surfaced than the Canal Road. We remained two-up on the B.S.A. and pottered, gloriously happy to be awheel, and acknowledging cheerfully the hand-waves from enthusiasts camping on the sites bordering the road and Canal.

We crossed Loch Leven by the Ballachulish Ferry; the rain teemed down harder than ever. A stop was made for tea, at the foot of Glencoe, but when we emerged from the café there had been no easing of the storm. I was driving at the time and I begged Jim to go in the chair; he refused point-blank, saying that he was determined to sit on his Dualseat all day and in any case he was enjoying the rain !

Glencoe was deserted and in her grimmest and most forbidding mood. The wind howled down through the Grampians, driving the rain horizontally into us. The hills on each side of the Glen were shrouded in thick,impenetrable clouds. Distances and heights seemed tremendous, making us feel very small and, against the wrath of Nature, quite insignificant. So we pressed on and I gave the B.S.A. all the throttle. We covered 28 miles to Tyndrum in 33 minutes and topped the Glen at 70 m.p.h. The power developed by the engine by this time seemed to be colossal and it was quite impossible to overdrive it.

In that dismal Glen of Weeping we saw only one vehicle—an old Norton and sidecar driven by a cheerful enthusiast who waved as we sped past. By way of Crianlarich and Loch Lomond we carried on to Balloch and Glasgow. The rain ceased and the grass and leaves glistened with a million lights. I spent a short time in the sidecar to see what it was like inside with the hood raised—the first time it was used that day !

Glasgow was inhospitable and, though we were staying at a good hotel, we were unable to obtain a dinner and had to be content instead with a few delicately cut sandwiches—hardly sufficient for a pair who had spent a day in the open ! The second rear tyre was by now showing signs of wear so we replaced the rear wheel with the spare "just in case." When we left at 7.30 a.m. the next day—the last day of our memorable *voyage*—the sky was clear, though the roads were wet and slimy. Ahead we were faced with nearly 500 miles, half of which lay in Wales and included the famous Bwlch-y-Groes Pass, which rises 1,250 feet and has an average gradient of 1 in 7.

Journey to Wales

As the morning aged the sun strengthened, brightening the countryside. We intended that the morning run be completed quickly so that we should have as much time in Wales as possible. Jim drove for the first 118 miles to Penrith, a run which was completed at an average of something like 45 m.p.h. without the speed ever exceeding 65 m.p.h. anywhere. There was very little traffic and the journey proved quite exhilarating. After refuelling, I took over the reins and drove to Liverpool.

Over the Shap the B.S.A.'s performance was completely devastating. I had to stop at the foot because of traffic conditions, yet we topped the first part of the rise in top gear using a shade of ignition retard, with the speed never dropping below 45 m.p.h. Over the second gradient, I had to drop into second for traffic and completed the climb very comfortably in third gear. Heavy holiday traffic was encountered between Lancaster and Preston, and the standard of courtesy and the degree of road sense possessed by the majority of these drivers was appalling.

A man ahead of us driving a small car, cut out into a blind right-hand turn to overtake a lorry we were trailing. On another occasion, a bus driver overtaking on a blind corner while coming towards us, had his off-side wheels practically in our gutter, and I was forced to lift the sidecar wheel up on to the grass verge. There was nothing for it but to proceed cautiously.

After lunching in Liverpool's Adelphi, we left the city by way of the Mersey Tunnel and Queensferry. The road to Colwyn Bay, Conway and Bettws-y-Coed is quite good. From the road south

Magnificent panorama over Dornoch Firth

we could see Snowdon in the distance, towering—all 3,560 ft of it —into an azure sky. Farther south the road deteriorated, becoming narrower and with a surface of the type that really made the chassis flex and tired my arms. In the two hours I drove from Conway to Festiniog I covered only 50 miles—which were for me, anyway, the most tiring of the trip so far.

We shared the honour of driving the machine up Bwlch-y-Groes. It was an easy climb for the six-fifty, accomplished carefully in bottom and second gear; had we been in a hurry we could easily have used third most of the way—and still have had power on tap. From the top of the Bwlch we took the road to Bala and joined A5 to Corwen. From here on, the road back to Birmingham was wide and fast and the B.S.A. was given the gun. During the final 50 miles, in fact, I did my utmost to blow it up. I drove it flat out, on top or in third as required. On one occasion we clocked "80" and, according to Jim's timing, we covered nine miles in eight-and-a-half minutes on one section of that route. Everywhere that speed could be safely used I thrashed the job really hard—harder by far than we had ever done before.

Memorable Days

It gave no signs of being overdriven and, indeed, when we stopped, the engine and oil-tank were much, much cooler than they had been during our first day's run. I am convinced that had we realized we were starting with a new engine, or had we started with the engine in the condition in which it was in at the finish, the entire trip would have been accomplished without those early bothers. Vibration apparent in the early stages was considerably less noticeable after the third day, though, of course, there remained the "period" between 50 and 55 m.p.h. The brakes provided the best stopping power I have ever experienced with a sidecar outfit. The front brake was adjusted twice and the rear once, and both were in first-class condition when I drove the machine home that final Monday evening.

What do I feel about the Golden Flash in general? I think that it is a wonderful motor cycle, developing all the power I could possibly want even with a sidecar and certainly far more than I could ever aspire to use with the machine in solo form. The Dualseat, the Sidecar Comfort Set? Both were really excellent and in each case they proved entirely comfortable. On arriving at any one of our night stops, either of us could quite easily have carried on for as far as was wanted. The Dualseat is definitely by far the best Feridax seat yet. As I mentioned earlier, the screen we were testing proved inadequate since, by virtue of its shape, it set up annoying eddies and draughts.

In conclusion, I should like to pay a tribute to one, James R. Ferriday. Throughout the tour he proved to be a delightful companion. I was, as I have said, completely comfortable to be his passenger and grateful for the way in which, when being given a signal to overtake, he would acknowledge the courtesy by a wave of the left hand, a smile, and a polite "Thank you." All things considered, I would say that my "business man's long week-end," —Thursday to Monday!—in the company of the Golden Flash and Ferriday to be among the most memorable few days I have ever spent. It made me decide definitely not to spend my holidays riding abroad, but to go back to Scotland—and I'm doing just that later this month!

Bwlch-y-Groes . . . "an easy climb for the six-fifty"

Fine mountain scenery near Bettws-y-Coed, in Wales

BSA 650 c.c.
"GOLDEN FLASH" VERTICAL TWIN

By Officer H. Filker, Alhambra P. D.

PRELIMINARY arrangements to secure a 650 cc Golden Flash BSA for this road test met with a series of unending obstacles. Shipments of new models were received steadily by local Los Angeles dealers who delivered them to "waiting list" customers almost at once. Several dealers promised a bike would become available only to have to countermand this statement. Finally Caspary Bros., Los Angeles, authorized BSA dealers, provided me with their shop demonstrator.

Before leaving the shop I looked the bike over quite closely to see new and advanced features about the whole machine. The most noticeable thing was the fact that the intake manifold was cast as an integral part of the cylinder head. This design feature seemed like a very good idea. Also, the one-piece rocker box, with small inspection covers removable for valve adjustment, suggested rigidity and an absence of possible oil leaks.

Internally, the 650 cc engine is somewhat similar to a 500 cc "star twin." A central flywheel with bolted-on crankthrows, supported between a large roller bearing on the sprocket side of the cases and a plain phosphor bronze bearing in the cam case side, plus replaceable con rod bearing inserts, added up to a really different type of machine than I had ever ridden before.

Before reaching the area selected, about nine miles, both gasoline taps under the tank showed slight leakage. Tightening with tools from the tool kit did not stop the leakage, the taps had to be screwed further up into the tank. A stop at a gas station for a cresent wrench did the trick. The leakage did not return.

Several times the plunger rear springing could be made to hit bottom in really rough, plowed ground, and especially when running off a 9" curb at 40 mph! Such usage is not met with in everyday operation, however!! Under normal riding, the rear springing and telescopic front forks rode swell.

The speedometer was 4 mph fast at 50 mph, 2 mph fast at 85 mph. The steering damper was never needed and except for sidecar use could probably be omitted by the factory.

The clutch had a tendency to slip during fast "drag outs" and may have kept the machine from turning a higher top speed. At 101 mph I wasn't interested in much more top speed but the clutch slippage, if not present, perhaps would have added 2 to 3 miles an hour more.

Tire pressures most suitable for my weight were: front—25 lbs., rear—23 lbs. Turning circle was: to left—11 ft. 9 in., to right—12 ft. 5 in. Weight proved very well distributed; without rider, front wheel load—190 lbs., rear wheel load—230 lbs., with rider, front —240 lbs., rear—370 lbs. Total weight of machine, without rider, 420 lbs.

Both brakes measure 8" diameter. These proved ideal as revealed by the figures in the Performance Summary.

Gas mileage worked out at 61.3 mpg, very good considering the amount of low gear revving done in the sandy spots and the climbing of several rather steep hills.

The machine suggested an ideal road cruising bike with lots of riding comfort, good economy, and a terrific amount of acceleration in high gear, even at 80 mph.

ENGINE. Even-firing Vertical Twin Cylinder ohv 70 mm bore by 84 mm stroke; 646 cc (40 cu. in.). One-piece forged steel crankshaft with integral bobweights and bolted-on central flywheel also incorporating a bobweight. Roller journal bearing on drive-side mainshaft. Plain bearing big-ends with replaceable indium-flashed lead-bronze liners. Plain bearing for mainshaft timing side. Forged light alloy connecting rods with phosphor-bronze bushes for small-end bearings; low expansion aluminum silicon alloy pistons, with two compression rings, and slotted scraper ring in special duplex oil control groove. Twin cylinders cast in single unit with specially cored air passages. Unit cylinder head-casting with narrow angle valves, two per cylinder, operating in shallow combustion chambers specially developed for maximum efficiency. Separate exhaust rocker box for each cylinder with twin inlet rocker box at rear; special cylinder fin arrangement ensures maximum air flow between ports and over the combustion heads. Valves operated by overhead rockers and push rods actuated by a single camshaft at rear through large car-type tappets with specially generous bearing surfaces. Camshaft gear-driven from engine-shaft through idler pinion, and incorporating timed mechanical breather. Twin exhaust pipes with cylindrical absorption type silencers.

LUBRICATION SYSTEM. Engine lubricated by dry-sump system with twin gear-type pump, driven by skew gear from engine shaft; pressure feed to timing-side main bearing and big-ends, with by-pass oil pressure release. Metered pressure oil feed to overhead rocker spindles, with return to crankcase. Camshaft operates in specially designed oil trough. Other moving parts lubricated by oil mist. Capacity of oil tank—four Imperial pints.

INDUCTION SYSTEM. Bifurcated inlet manifold cast in cylinder head, ensuring correct gas flow from Amal carburetor specially adapted to accommodate large capacity built-in air cleaner, mounted on seat tube between oil tank and tool box.

IGNITION. Lucas magneto, gear driven from camshaft with centrifugal type automatic advance.

TRANSMISSION. Primary drive from engine by ⅜" duplex roller chain, running in cast aluminum oil-bath chaincase, inner portion forming part of crankcase. Chain tension correctly maintained by adjustable slipper-type tensioner with hard-chrome bearing surface and external adjustment. Twin cam-type spring-loaded engine shaft cush drive. Rear chain ⅝" x ⅜" roller, lubricated by special breather-pipe from oil tank. Five-plate clutch with oil-proof fabric inserts; six radially disposed springs designed for uniform pressure distribution; clutch center mounted on roller bearing to ensure correct alignment when disengaged. Clutch operation by hardened steel push-rod through center of hollow gearbox mainshaft.

GEARBOX. B.S.A. four-speed constant mesh gearbox with built-in positive stop foot change. Gearbox mainshaft mounted on ball journal bearings.

FRAME. Duplex triangulated cradle of ample strength for solo or sidecar work. All frame lugs including those for sidecar and pillion footrests are of forged steel. B.S.A. telescopic front forks with automatic progressive hydraulic damping, and special oil seals at sliding members. Wheels quickly detachable, front with the 8" brake incorporating duplex type ribbed shoes of great strength operating in high MOLYBDENUM cast iron drum; rear of straight spoke type with 7" brake; Dunlop tires, front 3.25-19, rear 3.50-19. Welded pressed steel petrol tank—capacity 4¼ Imperial gallons (5 U.S. gallons); adjustable handlebar; generous mudguards; tail portion of rear guard detachable for easy wheel removal; spring-up central stand; adjustable footrests.

EQUIPMENT. Adjustable spring-seat saddle; Lucas 6-volt cvc lighting set with sealed-beam headlamp and high frequency electric horn; metal toolbox under seat tube with complete toolkit; tire pump; rubber knee-grips.

CONTROLS. On left of handlebar, clutch lever and headlamp dim-switch; on right of handlebar, front brake, air lever and horn button; damper knob on steering head; ignition cut-out button on nearside back stay; rear brake operated by left toe pedal; kickstarter and gear-change pedals on right, both provided with rubber sleeves. Twin petrol taps at rear of tank, both with reserve levers and fine mesh gauze filters. Finger adjustment for brakes and clutch controls.

FINISH. All bright parts including the exhaust system heavily chromium plated; frame, mudguards, etc., lustrous black enamel; petrol tank, black and chrome with distinctive motif; wheel rims chrome with black centers; polished front chain case, gearbox cover, timing cover.

PERFORMANCE SUMMARY

Acceleration

* Standing start to 59 mph—6.1 secs.
** Standing start to 79 mph—13 secs.
*** Standing start to 91 mph—22.1 secs.

     * Low only
    ** Low and second
   *** Three gears used

Braking

From 25 mph to stopped, rear brake only—
    47 ft. 3 in.

From 25 mph to stopped, front brake only—
    27 ft. 1 in.

From 25 mph to stopped, both brakes—
    22 ft. 1 in.

Slow Running

High gear without chain jerk—15 to 16 mph

Speed

Maximum in low—59 mph
Maximum in second—79 mph
Maximum in third—91 mph
Maximum in High—101 mph

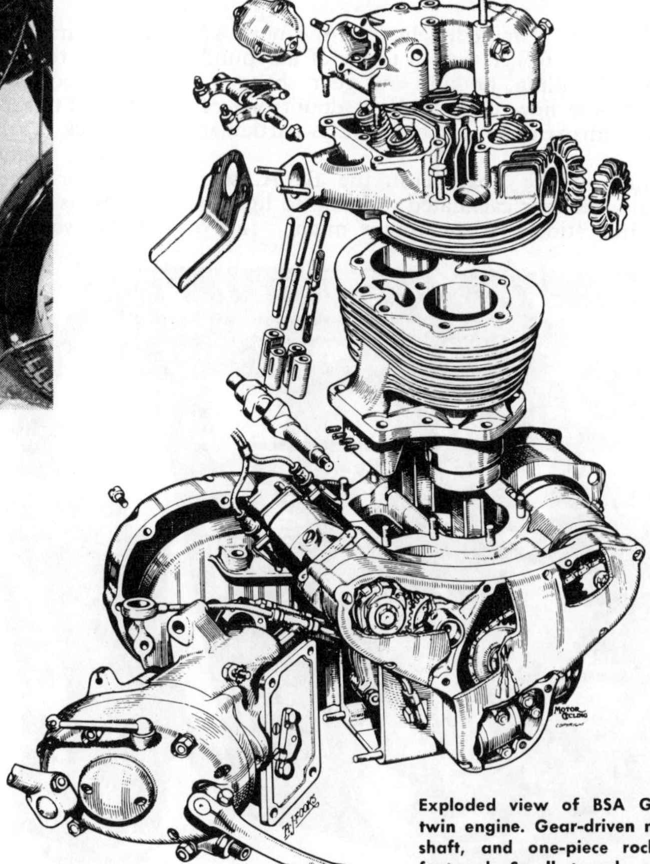

Exploded view of BSA Golden Flash vertical twin engine. Gear-driven magneto, single camshaft, and one-piece rockerbox housing are featured. Small trough near intake port insulates Amal carburetor from heat, provides drip scoop when flooding carburetor to start

495 c.c. B.S.A. Model

Latest Edition of an Established High-performance Five-hundred

THE original 495 c.c. A7 B.S.A. was introduced to an eager, war-weary market in 1946 and retained its basic and detail design features almost without change until the end of last year. Though even to an experienced eye the 1951 engine and gear box exteriors are largely unchanged, both units are, in fact, new and almost identical in internal detail design with those of the already illustrious Golden Flash model. The result of the change-

The 1951 A7 is a cobby, neat, businesslike mount

over is such that many will immediately class the new A7 as being the best 500 c.c. B.S.A. yet; in terms of all-round engine performance, handling, braking and gear change—particularly the last—the new A7 is without doubt one of the best of two, or perhaps three, machines in its particular capacity class.

During the course of the Road Test, the B.S.A. was generally driven in a manner calculated to bring to light—and quickly—any indication that the engine might "fuss" or tire. In other words, the engine was revved very hard in the indirect ratios, and speeds wherever possible were just as high as road conditions permitted. On one particular occasion a run of 150 miles in Warwickshire and Shropshire was completed in a few minutes over three hours.

Speeds on the main roads were regularly in the 70-75 m.p.h. region, and 80 m.p.h. was maintained and held effortlessly on several occasions—this by a heavily garbed rider sitting in an orthodox position. When the machine was stopped after several miles on full bore, a hand could be placed on the cylinder finning. The exhaust pipes had not even discoloured near the ports; they later became slightly straw coloured, but never blue. Throughout the entire test the engine and gear box remained absolutely oil-tight. Transmission smoothness was of a high order. The rear chain, however, tended to run dry.

When motor cycling, there are naturally occasions when one begins a run with some fixed idea, such as: "I am going to potter," or, "I am out for a whang." Such were the A7's characteristics that, irrespective of the state of one's mind at the beginning of a run, speeds generally rose and rose throughout the run's duration. Reasons for this are not hard to seek; for instance, at 70 m.p.h. there is as complete lack of fuss as there is at 50-55 m.p.h. From 50 m.p.h. onwards, high-frequency vibration could be felt at the handlebar, but it was slight and would not worry even fastidious riders. Vibration was marked only when the engine was revved to the point of valve float.

A slow, reliable tick-over was one of the A7's most attractive features. At idling speeds, the engine was beautifully quiet mechanically, the only certainly identified noises being piston slap and slight "rustling" from the valve-gear. The built-in air cleaner completely eliminates induction hiss. Performance figures, incidentally, were taken with the filter in use. Pick-up throughout the entire throttle range was clean and brisk, and there was no undue tendency to pinking.

Slightly heavy in operation, the clutch freed perfectly at all times, required no adjustment even after the high stresses imposed when performance figures were being taken, and was delightfully smooth in its take-up. Bottom gear could be engaged noiselessly and certainly when the machine was stationary with the engine idling. Clean and entirely positive upward gear changes were accomplished by moving

New twin-cylinder power unit follows closely the design of the 650 c.c. A10

A7 Twin

An Enthralling Machine

the pedal without due attention to making a deliberate lag in pedal movement. Snap racing-type changes could be made with certainty and with or without freeing the clutch. When snap changes were made, the pinions engaged with the merest suggestion of a "clonk." In the indirect ratios, notably in third gear, there was considerable gear whine. Clean, sweet, downward changes could be accomplished just as quickly as the controls could be operated. Pedal movement was short and light, and the pedal could be moved up or down by lightly pivoting the right foot on the footrest. The combination of positive gear change, clean pick-up and reliable idling made the B.S.A. particularly useful for safe, effortless traffic threading.

The front fork has a long, soft movement, allowing the front wheel to follow the road surface accurately, be it bumpy or smooth, be the speed high or low. Greasy cobbles and wet tramlines could be traversed with complete confidence. The rear suspension (which on the A7 is an extra) provided reasonable comfort, though slightly more travel, it was felt, would have been appreciated.

Light Brake Operation

Both brakes were smooth and progressive in operation, and provided adequate stopping power. Fade was never experienced under hard-driving conditions on the road, but it did occur when the braking figures were being taken —a quick succession of crash stops in this instance being made from 30 m.p.h. Both brakes were light in operation.

The only point of criticism applying to the riding position was that the top corners of the knee pads were slightly sharp and caused discomfort towards the end of a day in the saddle. Relationship between saddle, footrests and handlebar provided a comfortable knee angle and arm reach, and the angle of the grips allowed a natural position for the

Primary drive is by a duplex chain with a slipper for adjustment. Gear box is bolted to the rear of the crankcase

wrists. Both footrests and handlebar are, of course, adjustable. All controls were delightfully sweet in operation.

An intense and commendably wide driving beam was furnished by the 7in Lucas head lamp. In its position on the fork bridge, the speedometer was easily read by a normally seated rider. The instrument read approximately seven per cent fast. Mudguarding provided above-average protection for rider and machine. The centre stand could be operated without undue muscular effort, but required knack. The prop stand (which is an extra) was easily operated and held the machine safely.

Engine starting from cold (during some of the coldest weather experienced this winter) was certain at the third or fourth dig on the kick-starter. Kick-starting required commendably little physical effort or knack, and engendered the thought: "A child could do it." Finish of the A7 is black and chromium, with the tank finished in red and chromium.

Information Panel

SPECIFICATION

ENGINE : 495 c.c. (66 x 72.6 mm) o.h.v. vertical twin. Fully enclosed valve gear operated by push rods from a single camshaft. Plain-bearing big-ends. Mainshaft supported by roller and plain bearings. Compression ratio, 6.7 to 1. Dry-sump lubrication ; tank capacity, 4 pints.

CARBURETTOR : Amal ; twistgrip throttle control ; air-slide operated by handlebar lever. Built-in air cleaner.

IGNITION AND LIGHTING : Lucas magneto with auto-advance. Separate 45w Lucas dynamo. 7in. head lamp. 30/24w head lamp bulb.

TRANSMISSION : B.S.A. four-speed gear box with positive-stop foot control. Bottom, 13.2 to 1. Second, 9.0 to 1. Third, 6.2 to 1. Top, 5.1 to 1. Multi-plate clutch with fabric inserts. Primary chain, ⅜in duplex in cast-aluminium, light-alloy case. Secondary chain, ⅝ x ⅜in. R.p.m at 30 m.p.h. in top gear, 1,990 approx.

FUEL CAPACITY : 3½ gallons.

TYRES : Dunlop, Front 3.25 x 19in. Rear 3.50 x 19in. Both studded tread.

BRAKES : 7 x 1⅛in front and rear.

SUSPENSION : B.S.A. telescopic front fork with hydraulic damping. Plunger-type rear springing.

WHEELBASE : 54¾in. Ground clearance, 4½in unladen.

SADDLE : Lycett. Unladen height, 30in

WEIGHT : 436lb with fuel and oil tanks full and machine fully equipped.

PRICE : £144 plus Purchase Tax (in Britain only), £38 17s 8d. Spring frame extra, £10, plus P.T. £2 14s.

ROAD TAX : £3 15s a year ; £1 0s 8d a quarter.

MAKERS : B.S.A. Cycles, Ltd., Small Heath, Birmingham, 11.

DESCRIPTION : *The Motor Cycle,* 19 October, 1950.

PERFORMANCE DATA

MEAN MAXIMUM SPEED : Bottom : 36 m.p.h.*
Second : 54 m.p.h.*
Third : 78 m.p.h.
Top : 88 m.p.h.
*Valve floating starting

MEAN ACCELERATION :

	10-30 m.p.h.	20-40 m.p.h.	30-50 m p.h.
Bottom	2.4 secs	—	—
Second	4 secs	3 secs	3.2 secs
Third	—	5.4 secs	5 secs
Top	—	8.2 secs	7.4 secs

Mean speed at end of quarter mile from rest : 76 m.p.h
Mean time to cover standing quarter mile : 17.6 secs.

PETROL CONSUMPTION : At 30 m.p.h., 92 m.p.g. At 40 m.p.h., 81 m.p.g. At 50 m.p.h., 72 m.p.g. At 60 m.p.h., 64 m.p.g.

BRAKING : From 30 m.p.h. to rest, 29ft 6in (surface, wet tar macadam).

TURNING CIRCLE : 13ft 6in.

MINIMUM NON-SNATCH SPEED : 18-19 m.p.h. in top gear.

WEIGHT PER C.C. : 0.88lb.

646 c.c. B.S.A. Golden

AFTER the war a spate of vertical twins appeared on the British market. These at first were limited to 500 c.c. capacity and there ensued a widespread demand for larger engines, especially from oversea riders and from those requiring machines for sidecar work. The 646 c.c. B.S.A. A10, or Golden Flash, was introduced to meet this demand. It was an immediate success, and in terms of all-round engine performance generally, and in its good torque at medium engine r.p.m. particularly, it far exceeded popular expectations.

The compactness of the engine and gear box—which are wedded on semi-unit-construction lines—makes it difficult to realize that the capacity is as much as 646 c.c. Indeed, the entire machine is clean and trim and, bearing in mind its 425 lb weight, it presents no special difficulties in wheeling it in and out of garages. An idea of its degree of compactness may be judged from the wheelbase, which is less than 55in.

An admirable riding position is provided by the relation-ship between the seat, footrests and handlebar. The new B.S.A. dual-seat is of ample dimensions and nicely shaped for the maximum comfort of both rider and pillion passenger. Well judged for persons of average stature, the height of the seat furnishes a comfortable knee angle and does not prove unduly high on the occasions when the machine is straddled while at rest, or is being kick-started. Handlebar angle and the height of the footrests are adjustable.

Starting, so far as the test machine was concerned, was not at first as easy as could be desired. Considerable muscular effort was required to rotate the engine, and the mixture strength was weak at smallish throttle openings. The impression was that a throttle slide with rather less cut-away was desirable.

When the engine was cold the starting drill was to flood the carburettor, close the air lever and open the throttle fractionally. Four digs on the kick-starter were the maximum required during the test. When the engine had been running for perhaps a minute, or when, say, a quarter of a mile had been covered, the air slide could be opened fully. Idling had to be on the fast side to be satisfactorily reliable, this because of the patchiness of the carburation mentioned earlier.

Mechanical Quietness

With the engine idling, mechanical noises were all but absent. Piston slap was just audible when the engine was cold, and slight rustling from the overhead-valve rockers could also be heard. In short, however, mechanical quietness is of an extremely high order. Exhaust silencing is most effective and commendably subdued throughout the entire speed range. It is good enough, indeed, to place the Golden Flash right in the front rank in this respect. Induction hiss is completely eliminated by the built-in air filter.

Bottom gear could be engaged noiselessly with the engine idling and the machine stationary. Slightly heavy in operation, the clutch freed perfectly on all occasions, and it was smooth and sweet in taking up the drive. The gear change was well-nigh perfect. Clean and entirely positive upward changes could be made with an easy movement of the right toes. Pedal movement is light and creditably short, and no deliberate slowness in pedal travel was necessary to ensure noiseless gear engagement.

A criticism is that there was considerable gear whine in the indirect ratios, particularly in third. Clean, sweet downward changes could be executed between any pairs of gears just as rapidly as the controls could be operated.

Generally speaking, a small, light machine possessing nippy acceleration forms the most attractive type

Although driven at high speeds throughout the test, the engine unit remained entirely free from oil leaks

The 646 c.c. Golden Flash is a compact machine—its wheelbase is less than 55in. Riding position and dual-seat comfort were both found to be excellent

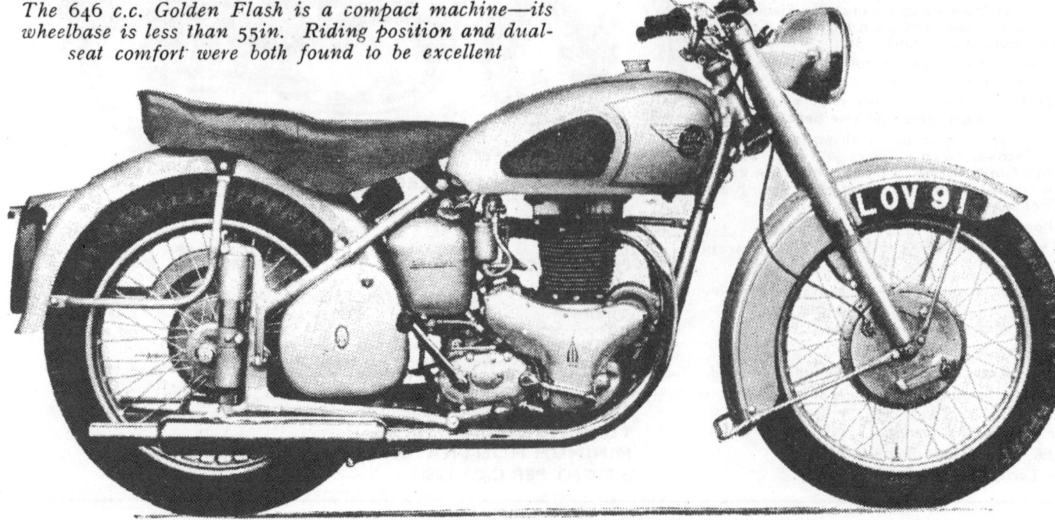

Flash

and with Sidecar

for use in towns and cities. But the A10, though no lightweight, has perfect city manners. Low-speed handling and manœuvrability are first class; so good, in fact, as to make one forget that the machine is a six-fifty. Low-speed torque is exceptional and the transmission is smooth at low r.p.m. The tendency to pinking was not unduly pronounced, and the response to opening the throttle was full-blooded. Not least important is that the full performance in the indirect gears could be used without fuss from the engine, transmission or exhaust.

But if the Golden Flash has traits which make it attractive in towns and cities, it really comes into its own when being ridden at speed on the open road. Exceptionally high average speeds could be achieved with the minimum of effort on the part of the rider. This was so, not so much because of the machine's over-95 m.p.h. maximum speed, but because of the engine's high mechanical efficiency, even at speeds in excess of those normally used, and its excellent torque at medium revs.

At speeds over 70 m.p.h. there was no marked impression of deliberate hard riding. Only slight increase in throttle opening was necessary to compensate for head-winds or up-gradients. With such colossal engine performance the rider's chosen cruising speed was almost instantaneously regained after a slow-up made necessary by adverse road

Best cruising speed with the B.S.A. single-seat sidecar fitted was judged to be between 55 and 65 m.p.h.

conditions or traffic. Although consistently high speeds were used throughout the test, the engine remained free from the slightest oil leak. Further, though Pool petrol was used, "running-on" after really hard riding was never experienced. The timing-side exhaust pipe discoloured only faintly, the drive-side one considerably, betraying some degree of carburettor bias.

Handling was very good indeed under all conditions, and the degree of comfort afforded was distinctly outstanding, even judged by the highest present-day standards. The B.S.A. telescopic fork has a long, soft movement which not only absorbs road shocks satisfactorily but, in conjunction with the duplex frame, furnishes, in addition, precise, hair-

---

Information Panel

SPECIFICATION

ENGINE : 646 c.c. (70 x 84 mm) o.h.v. vertical twin. Fully enclosed valve gear operated by push rods from a single camshaft. . Plain bearing big-ends. Mainshafts supported by roller and plain bearings. Compression ratio, 6.5 to 1. Dry-sump lubrication ; oil-tank capacity, 4 pints.

CARBURETTOR : Amal ; twistgrip throttle control ; air-slide operated by handlebar lever. Built-in air-cleaner.

IGNITION AND LIGHTING : Lucas magneto with auto-advance. Separate 45w Lucas dynamo. 7in head lamp. 30/30w head lamp bulb.

TRANSMISSION : B.S.A. four-speed gear box with positive-stop foot control. Solo ratios : Bottom, 11.41 to 1. Second, 7.77 to 1. Third, 5.36 to 1. Top, 4.42 to 1. Sidecar ratios : Bottom, 13.3 to 1. Second, 9.06 to 1. Third, 6.26 to 1. Top, 5.16 to 1. Multi-plate clutch with fabric inserts. Primary chain, $\frac{3}{8}$in duplex in cast-aluminium case. Secondary chain, $\frac{5}{8}$ x $\frac{3}{8}$in. R.p.m. at 30 m.p.h. on solo top gear, 1,723 ; sidecar, 2,012 approx.

FUEL CAPACITY : 4$\frac{1}{4}$ gallons.

TYRES : Dunlop. Front, 3.25 x 19in. Rear, 3.50 x 19in., both studded tread.

BRAKES : 7 x 1$\frac{1}{8}$in rear ; 8 x 1$\frac{1}{8}$in front ; finger adjusters.

SUSPENSION : B.S.A. telescopic front fork with hydraulic damping. B.S.A. plunger-type rear springing.

WHEELBASE : 54$\frac{3}{4}$in. Ground clearance, 4$\frac{1}{2}$in unladen.

SEAT : B.S.A. dual-seat.

WEIGHT : 425 lb fully equipped and with one gallon of fuel. Complete outfit, 660 lb fully equipped and with one gallon of fuel.

PRICE : Machine only, £175, with Purchase Tax (in Britain only), £223 12s 3d. Extras : Dual-seat, £3 ; beige finish, £3 (P.T., 16s 8d extra in each case) ; prop-stand, 15s (P.T., 4s 2d).

ROAD TAX : Solo, £3 15s a year ; £1 0s 8d a quarter. Sidecar, £5 a year, £1 7s 7d a quarter.

MAKERS : B.S.A. Cycles, Ltd., Small Heath, Birmingham, 11.

DESCRIPTION : *The Motor Cycle,* 6 October, 1949, and 19 October, 1950.

SIDECAR

MODEL : B.S.A. 22/47.

CHASSIS : Triangular, with quarter-elliptic springs at rear and twin compression coil springs at front. Four-point attachment.

BODY : Coachbuilt (timber frame, steel panels). Celluloid screen. Folding twill hood. Locker at rear.

PRICE : £61, with Purchase Tax (in Britain only), £77 18s. Beige finish, £3 extra (P.T., 16s 8d extra).

646 c.c. B.S.A. Golden Flash.

PERFORMANCE DATA

(Sidecar figures in brackets)

MEAN MAXIMUM SPEED : Bottom : *42 (*36) m.p.h.
Second : *61 (*51) m.p.h.
Third : 89 (69) m.p.h.
Top : 96 (70) m.p.h.
* Valve float starting.

MEAN ACCELERATION :

	10-30 m.p.h.	20-40 m.p.h.	30-50 m.p.h.
Bottom	2.6 (3.5) secs	3 (—) secs	—
Second	4 (4.8) secs	3.2 (4.2) secs	3.6 (4.1) secs
Third	—	5.2 (6.8) secs	5 (6.4) secs
Top	—	— (9.3) secs	6.8 (9) secs

Mean speed at end of quarter-mile from rest : 84 (64) m.p.h.
Mean time to cover standing quarter-mile : 16.8 (20) secs.

PETROL CONSUMPTION : At 30 m.p.h., 72 (50) m.p.g. At 40 m.p.h., 69 (47) m.p.g. At 50 m.p.h., 65 (42) m.p.g. At 60 m.p.h., 59 (37) m.p.g.

BRAKING : From 30 m.p.h. to rest, 29ft (44ft 6in). Surface in each case, dry tar macadam.

TURNING CIRCLE : 12ft 9in.

MINIMUM NON-SNATCH SPEED : 21 (20) m.p.h. in top gear.

WEIGHT PER C.C. : 0.66 lb (1.02 lb).

line steering. Uncertainty was never felt, no matter how greasy the road surface or how tricky the conditions. On one occasion, indeed, when an attempt was made to take the maximum speed figures, the road was distinctly greasy and there was a strong, gusty cross-wind.

As will be seen from the information panel, the mean maximum speed is given as 96 m.p.h. That figure was obtained at the M.I.R.A. Proving Ground and represents a mean of runs in opposite directions. Average wind speed was 14 m.p.h., with gusts up to 20 m.p.h. The maximum speed recorded down wind—with the air filter connected—was 102.75 m.p.h. and, with it disconnected, 104.5 m.p.h. Maximum speeds up-wind were 86.7 and 87.5 m.p.h. respectively with, and without, the air filter.

Control Positions

When these figures were taken the steering damper was just biting, and the handling was exemplary. Light although the fork movement is, there was no pitching, and there remained a direct "tautness" about the steering that was most satisfying.

In delivery tune, the twistgrip was unduly heavy in operation and a replacement throttle cable and twistgrip had to be fitted to effect a cure. In the main, the controls were well placed for ease of operation, but a criticism in this respect is that it was not possible to set the brake pedal so that the pad lay in the desired position relative to the left footrest.

Used in unison, the brakes provided adequate stopping power even for a machine in the A10's performance class. During the course of the solo test, which included over 500 miles of hard riding, the brakes inevitably came in for severe usage, yet no adjustment was required throughout. Both brakes possessed just the right amount of sponginess to permit hard application. Braking from speed was smooth and

The 646 c.c. engine, neat and well-proportioned, appears to be no larger than the average five-hundred unit

progressive, and not the slightest indication of fade, nor any loss of power whatever, was experienced at any time.

At the end of the solo part of the test, the Golden Flash was returned to the factory, where it was fitted with a B.S.A. single-seat sidecar. Alterations to the machine included changing the 42-tooth rear wheel sprocket for one of 49 teeth, and fitting heavier fork springs. At this time, too, the standard 6/4 throttle slide was replaced by a 6/3 (which has $\frac{1}{16}$in less cutaway) in order to enrich the mixture at smallish throttle openings.

The result was that patchiness at low speeds disappeared entirely; starting became first-kick instead of third or fourth; acceleration was better than before; and the pick-up was as clean and brisk as could be desired by the most critical enthusiast.

Some 400 miles were covered during the sidecar test. For the greater part of this mileage a 10½-stone passenger was carried and for the remainder of the time the sidecar was empty. In either case the outfit handled magnificently, steering hands-off (with the steering damper just biting) and sweeping round corners with the utmost facility. No more than slight steering-damper friction was required at either high or low speeds. Owing in part to this, the steering was light enough for there to be no driving fatigue, even after a full day in the saddle.

Sidecar Cruising Speed

Best maximum cruising speed with the sidecar fitted appeared to be anything between 55 and 65 m.p.h. At the lower end of the scale the outfit would trickle along in top gear without snatch at speeds of just over 20 m.p.h. Careful handling of the throttle was necessary if, with Pool-quality fuel, pinking was to be avoided during acceleration from this speed. But, bearing in mind the excellent exhaust silencing and the effortless gear change, it was, of course, advisable to make use of the indirect ratios when accelerating from inordinately low speeds.

There was at no time any external indication of overdriving, even though on several occasions the outfit was driven for mile after mile with the throttle against the stop. The riding position for sidecar work was excellent, and no change was required either in footrest position or angle of the grips from the settings used earlier in the test.

Some high-powered machines of the past have been criticized when fitted with sidecars because the brakes have not provided adequate stopping power. No such criticism could be levelled at the B.S.A., however. On the contrary, the sidecar braking figure of 44ft 6in is well above average and would be difficult to better.

Polychromatic Beige

The sidecar itself earned all but full marks. The suspension absorbed road shocks satisfactorily and provided an extremely high degree of comfort for the passenger. Seat and squab are at comfortable angles to one another, and when the hood was raised the interior was cosy and unusually free from draughts. Of the folding type, with a pivoting frame, the hood stows away in a twill envelope when not in use but can be erected in a matter of seconds. A criticism is that during the unusually cold weather prevailing when the test was carried out, the screen provided rather insufficient side protection.

Both the machine and the sidecar were luxuriously finished in polychromatic beige. The tank finish was fully polychromatic, with no chromium plating, and with red lining on the top and side surfaces. The quality of the Golden Flash finish as a whole was unusually high for any class of road vehicle. It is a machine which will undoubtedly do as much to enhance the reputation of the marque as any other B.S.A. produced in the last 20 years.

STAR TWIN ECLIPSES SINGLE

sensational performing new half-mile job now offered in touring trim

Departing from their previous policy on competition machines, the 500 cc Star Twin for '52 tends to eclipse the grand old Gold Star single as "Star of the Family." This Daytona twin is trim looking and packs a surprising amount of power in its 30.50 cubic inches. Important to flat track riders is its torque characteristic at low rpm, reminiscent of a good single. At high revs, power and torque curves are much steeper than the single, and at 5,500 rpm the twin delivers the same brake horsepower as does the Gold Star single at its maximum of 6,500 rpm. From 5,500 rpm to 6,800 the twin power curve takes off in an almost straight line.

The engine is basically the same as in all road Star Twins except that a generator is not fitted and a racing magneto with manual spark advancement replaces the standard automatic advance magneto. A 1⅛th Amal TT carburetor with remote float-chamber permits the engine to breathe freely at any

A shapely yet slim model presents little frontal resistance. Equipped for the road, this speedster should cruise fast and easy. High performance is claimed on the track model with one downdraft TT carburetor. Other features are folding kickstarter, 8-in. front brake, alloy wheel rims, centrally mounted tachometer, racing magneto

throttle opening and gives a clean pick-up all through the range. Compression on the competition model is 7.9:1 as compared to 7.5:1 for the road version, and pistons are of the low expansion, split-skirt type. An assortment of quick change rear wheel sprockets bolt directly to rear hub. Engine sprockets come only in 27-tooth size and all ratio changes are made by variance of gear box or rear wheel sprockets. Top speed of the racer with a 4.45 high gear is given at 125-130 mph at approximately 7,000 rpm. The engine obtains its best horsepower near 6,800 rpm at which point it delivers about 1.5 bhp per cubic inch. Horsepower to weight ratio is eight pounds per horsepower. Speed and reliability of the machine have long since ceased to be a matter of speculation as witnessed by the fact that seven out of the first 20 bikes crossing the finish line in the Daytona "200-miler" this year were BSAs.

Polished and ported, the 30 cubic inch Star Twin is a hotted-up version of the more docile A-7 twin. In both models the crankcase and crankshaft have been redesigned. Rods, bearings and the whole flywheel assembly in general are now heavier. This is the half-mile competition model—its equivalent comes through in road touring trim; biggest difference being the cam

Built along the lines of their 40 in. twin, the new 30 in. Star Twin is a night and day improvement over the earlier A-7 twin. Most severe test of design was made at punishing Daytona 200 mile race, where no structural difficulties were encountered. Engine is claimed to be remarkable for lack of vibration. The A-7, incidentally, now embodies these same qualities of smoothness and durability

The 497 c.c. B.S.A.

A High-performance Model in the Best

ZESTFUL acceleration, excellent road holding, and the ability to devour the miles in unobtrusive fashion, are but a few of the attributes of the 497 c.c. B.S.A. Star Twin. Fitted with the compact, semi-unit construction B.S.A. engine and gear box, the machine is the sports version of the now celebrated A7. A redesigned engine was employed for 1951. Good as the pre-1951 Star Twin was, the present model is decidedly better. There is now only one carburettor instead

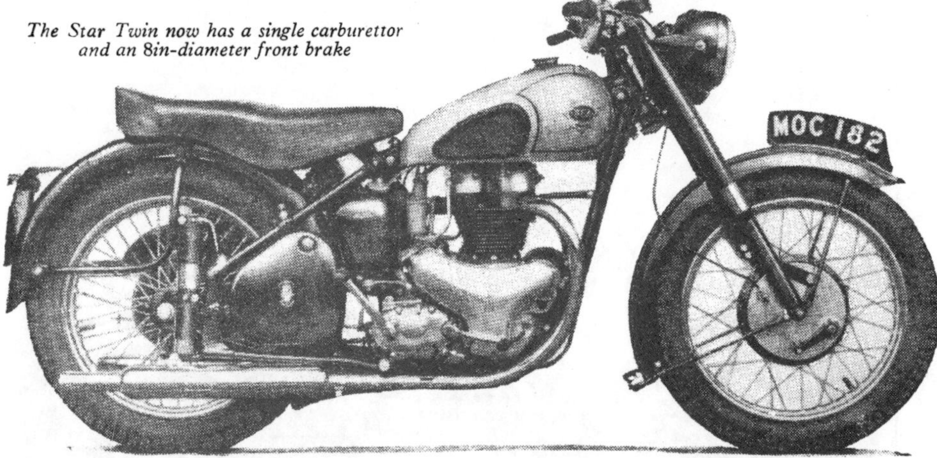

The Star Twin now has a single carburettor and an 8in-diameter front brake

of two; and carburation, once the engine is warm, is as clean as could be desired. With the present B.S.A. gear box, the gear-change is among the best encountered on present-day machines.

A sports machine in the true tradition, the Star Twin requires "knowing" if it is to give of its best on Pool-quality fuel. The throttle must be used intelligently in conjunction with the manual ignition control; engine revolutions must be maintained in the higher ranges; in short, there must be knowledgeable understanding of the engine's characteristics. These requirements fulfilled, the Star Twin has few equals as a machine for sustained, high-speed road work.

Used to the full in conjunction with the indirect gear ratios, the twin-cylinder engine provides acceleration of no mean order. In bottom and second gears the speed can be stepped up with exhilarating rapidity; and even in third or top gears the build-up from medium to peak r.p.m. is shatteringly quick. At 70 m.p.h. in top gear, the machine noticeably surged forward in response to a tweak of the twistgrip. Vibration was negligible. No matter how hard the engine was driven or for how long, there was at no time any indication that it was being over-driven.

During the test, cruising speeds in the seventies were used as often as road conditions permitted; 70 m.p.h., indeed, was felt to be the machine's happiest cruising speed. The engine turned over smoothly and sweetly, and with no more fuss than there was in the fifties. That it would cruise without being over-driven at higher speeds, say, 75-80 m.p.h., there is little doubt; but, at speeds of over 70 m.p.h., wind pressure became tiring to the rider's arms. At a true road speed of 65 m.p.h., the speedometer registered approximately 5 m.p.h. fast.

An idea of the Star Twin's performance may be gained from the fact that on several (admittedly favourable) occasions during the course of the 700-mile test, 20 miles were covered in as many minutes. Notwithstanding such usage, no engine oil leaks were apparent at the end of the test. A small seepage of oil appeared at the oil-tank filler-cap, and some messiness resulted through excessive oil issuing from the oil-tank breather if the tank was over-filled.

Engine performance is but one of the ultimate factors in the attainment of high road averages. Steering and road-holding are equally important; as far as the B.S.A. was concerned, these characteristics were fully up to desirable standards. The long, soft action of the B.S.A. telescopic front fork dealt adequately with every type of going encountered. Steering was of the hair-line variety. A steering damper is fitted; during most of the test it was set just barely biting.

The action of the plunger-type rear springing was pleasantly soft around the static-load position and it proved to be equally effective whether the machine was ridden one- or two-up. A criticism is that the suspension clashed on the occasions when deep road irregularities (such as sunken manhole covers) were encountered. Steering was good whether the machine was on greasy city surfaces, or ridden at speed on the open road.

For a person of average height, the riding position could hardly be bettered. Seat height is 30in—a height which permitted a comfortable knee angle while allowing easy straddling of the machine for kick-starting. The position of the brake-pedal pad was such that the brake could be applied without the foot being taken off the rest; an adjustable brake-pedal stop—a new feature—allows the pedal to be set in the optimum position relative to the footrest. Some discomfort to the rider's knees resulted from contact with the angular edge of the tank knee-grips.

That the Star Twin is a sports machine has been amply illustrated, and it might be thought

Though endowed with zestful performance characteristics, the 497 c.c. engine was found to be pleasantly flexible

Star Twin

Sporting Tradition

from this that the engine would prove intractable under slow-running conditions. Yet the reverse is true. During town riding the machine proved to be pleasantly flexible. As intimated earlier, knowledgeable handling of the ignition control was called for; the long ignition lever fitted to the left handlebar is pleasant to use and, because of its length, greatly facilitates accurate settings.

Upward or downward gear changes could be effortlessly achieved by lightly pivoting the right foot on the footrest. Pedal movement was short and feather-light, and clean, precise upward or downward gear changes called for no special care. Racing-type upward gear changes were accompanied by a slight click from the gear box as the pinions engaged—a click which could be heard rather than felt. Clean, noiseless downward changes could be made as rapidly as the clutch and gear pedal could be operated.

Both front and rear brakes were smooth and progressive and, applied in unison, provided satisfactory stopping power, even for a machine in the Star Twin's performance class. The 8in front brake was very good, yet did not provide quite all the power of which this type of brake is known to be capable. During the course of several hundred miles of fast road work, both brakes came in for hard usage. In spite of this, no fade was experienced, and only slight adjustment was called for.

Little effort was required to operate the kick-starter. With the temperature below freezing point, the engine would start from cold at the second or third kick—this provided that the carburettor was lightly flooded and normal cold-starting procedure followed. The air lever could be fully opened after the engine had been running for about a minute.

The degree of exhaust and mechanical quietness was commendably high. With the machine stationary and the engine idling on full retard, no individual source of mechanical noise could be indentified. Slight piston-slap could just be detected when the ignition was set at full advance. Induction hiss is eliminated by the built-in air-cleaner. Effective at all speeds,

A picture showing the compactness of the semi-unit construction of engine and gear box

the silencers produced a pleasant yet unobtrusive exhaust note.

Mudguarding on the Star Twin was only reasonably effective. Operation of the centre-stand called for a fair amount of muscular effort until the knack had been mastered. Its use is facilitated by the lifting handle on the left side and a curved, "roll-on" extension piece on the left leg of the stand. Adjustment of the primary chain is by moving the slipper-tensioner inside the chain case; the adjusting screw protrudes through the bottom of the case. Another commendable feature is that the guard for the rear chain has a deep back plate which effectively shields the chain from much of the road grit shed by the rear tyre. Other notable features are the B.S.A. really quickly detachable wheels; and the use of heavy-gauge clutch and front brake control cables. A comprehensive set of tools is provided.

The standard of finish on the Star Twin is extremely high. A general colour scheme of black and silver is employed; the tank is finished in matt-silver, lined in red, and it bears a handsome "Star Twin" insignia.

Information Panel

The 497 c.c. B.S.A. Star Twin

SPECIFICATION

ENGINE : 497 c.c. (66 x 72.6 mm) o.h.v. vertical twin. Fully enclosed valve gear operated by push-rods from a single camshaft. Plain-bearing big-ends. Mainshaft supported by roller and plain bearings. Compression ratio, 7.2 to 1. Dry-sump lubrication ; tank capacity, 4 pints.

CARBURETTOR : Amal ; twistgrip throttle control ; air-slide operated by handlebar lever. Built-in air cleaner.

IGNITION and LIGHTING : Lucas magneto with manual ignition control on left side of handlebar. Separate, 3in diameter Lucas dynamo ; 7in headlamp ; 30/24w headlamp bulb.

TRANSMISSION : B.S.A. four-speed gear box with positive-stop foot control. Bottom, 12.9 to 1. Second, 8.8 to 1. Third, 6.05 to 1. Top, 5.0 to 1. Multi-plate clutch with fabric inserts. Primary chain, $\frac{3}{8}$in duplex running in cast-aluminium, oil-bath case. Rear chain, $\frac{5}{8}$ x $\frac{3}{8}$in, lubricated by breather from oil tank. R.p.m. at 30 m.p.h. in top gear, approximately 1,950.

FUEL CAPACITY : 3½ gallons.

TYRES : Dunlop ; front 3.25 x 19in ; rear, 3.50 x 19in ; both studded tread.

BRAKES : 8in diameter front, 7in diameter rear ; finger-operated adjusters.

SUSPENSION : B.S.A. telescopic front fork with hydraulic damping ; plunger-type rear springing.

WHEELBASE : 54¾in. Ground clearance, 4½in. unladen.

SEAT : B.S.A. dual-seat. Unladen height, 30in.

WEIGHT : 423 lb fully equipped and with one gallon of fuel.

PRICE : £174, with Purchase Tax (in Great Britain only), £222 6s 8d. Extras : dual-seat in lieu of saddle, £3 (P.T., 16s 8d) ; prop-stand, 15s (P.T., 4s 2d).

ROAD TAX : £3 15s a year : £1 0s 8d a quarter.

DESCRIPTION : *The Motor Cycle*, 19 October, 1950.

MAKERS : B.S.A. Cycles, Ltd., Small Heath, Birmingham, 11.

PERFORMANCE DATA

MEAN MAXIMUM SPEED : Bottom : 37 m.p.h.*
Second : 55 m.p.h.*
Third : 86 m.p.h.
Top : 92 m.p.h.
* Valve float just starting.

MEAN ACCELERATION :

	10-30 m.p.h.	20-40 m.p.h.	30-50 m.p.h.
Bottom	3 secs	2.4 secs	—
Second	4.2 secs	3.2 secs	3.2 secs
Third	6 secs	5.4 secs	4.8 secs
Top	—	7.2 secs	6.8 secs

Mean speed at end of quarter-mile from rest : 84 m.p.h.
Mean time to cover standing, quarter-mile : 16.8 secs.

PETROL CONSUMPTION : At 30 m.p.h., 89 m.p.g. At 40 m.p.h., 75 m.p.g. At 50 m.p.h., 70 m.p.g. At 60 m.p.h., 64 m.p.g.

BRAKING : From 30 m.p.h. to rest, 30ft 6in (surface, dry tar macadam).

TURNING CIRCLE : 13ft 6in.

MINIMUM NON-SNATCH SPEED : 22 m.p.h. in top gear.

WEIGHT per C.C. : 0.73 lb.

The 646 c.c.

H. HOPWOOD, Chief Designer,
Design

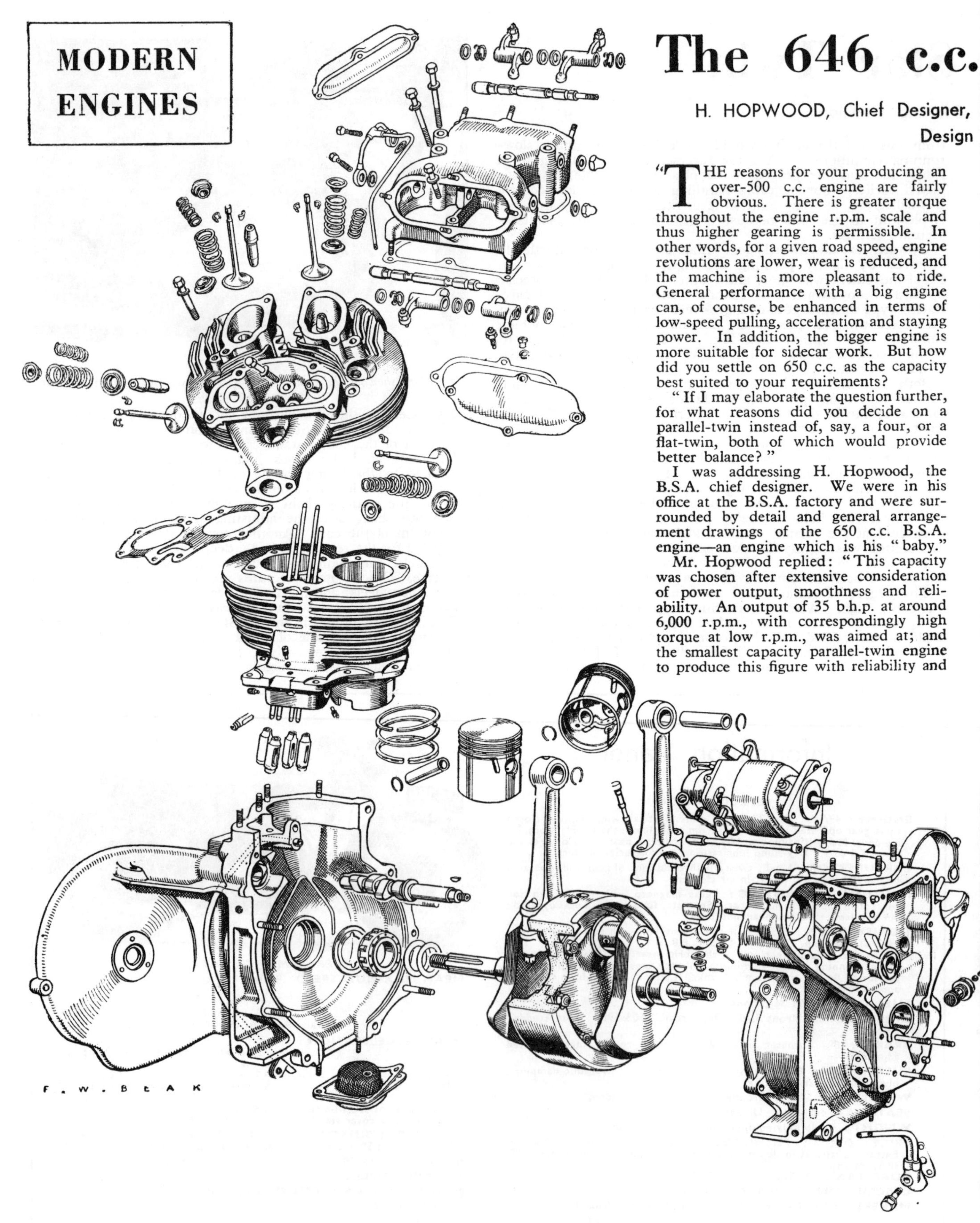

"THE reasons for your producing an over-500 c.c. engine are fairly obvious. There is greater torque throughout the engine r.p.m. scale and thus higher gearing is permissible. In other words, for a given road speed, engine revolutions are lower, wear is reduced, and the machine is more pleasant to ride. General performance with a big engine can, of course, be enhanced in terms of low-speed pulling, acceleration and staying power. In addition, the bigger engine is more suitable for sidecar work. But how did you settle on 650 c.c. as the capacity best suited to your requirements?

"If I may elaborate the question further, for what reasons did you decide on a parallel-twin instead of, say, a four, or a flat-twin, both of which would provide better balance?"

I was addressing H. Hopwood, the B.S.A. chief designer. We were in his office at the B.S.A. factory and were surrounded by detail and general arrangement drawings of the 650 c.c. B.S.A. engine—an engine which is his "baby."

Mr. Hopwood replied: "This capacity was chosen after extensive consideration of power output, smoothness and reliability. An output of 35 b.h.p. at around 6,000 r.p.m., with correspondingly high torque at low r.p.m., was aimed at; and the smallest capacity parallel-twin engine to produce this figure with reliability and

B.S.A. Golden Flash

B.S.A.s, Answers a Questionnaire by GEORGE WILSON on the
and Production of a Famous Engine

comparative smoothness was, I felt, a 650 c.c. The question of the four-cylinder or the flat-twin did not arise, as our target of power and reliability was most satisfactorily achieved with the present design."

Question: "But why did you want to use the *minimum* possible capacity? Would it not have been better to go to, say, 1,000 c.c., in which case you would have a greater reserve of power for the same r.p.m. figure? Would not a greater capacity have given even better torque at the bottom end? "

Answer: "We had, as I say, set ourselves a target of 35 b.h.p. But we also felt that a parallel-twin was the type of engine called for. I felt that anything over 650 c.c. in a parallel-twin design was out of the question—chiefly on the scores of reliability and smoothness."

Question: "Did weight considerations come into this particular question at all? "

Answer: "No, there would not be very much difference. For example, a six-fifty is only two or three pounds heavier than a five-hundred."

Exceptional Rigidity

Question: "What was the chief characteristic you aimed at with the A10? Was it that you concentrated on squeezing the highest possible b.h.p. from the engine at high r.p.m., or were your chief considerations to provide good torque in the middle ranges, or exceptional power at low revolutions? Were you at all influenced by striving for a high maximum speed? "

Answer: "The term 'squeezing' high b.h.p. certainly does not apply in this case. The chief characteristic aimed at and attained was exceptional rigidity in the 'bottom half.' This is achieved mainly because of the short and robust one-piece, forged crankshaft, and the unusually tall crankcase of conical cross-section. If a

crankcase has a weak point it is at the open end, i.e., at the large aperture through which the cylinders pass. And the farther from the crankcase centre line this joint face is positioned, the stronger is the construction. This feature also helps by shortening the cylinder barrel, so that the loading on the holding-down bolts is not great. As regards performance, certain of our markets demand high maximum speeds, and the A10 was designed with this requirement in mind. In addition, however, good pulling at comparatively low revolutions was desirable. Our use of very compact and shallow combustion chambers is a major factor in our achieving this last feature."

Question: "This engine is, I believe, a derivative of the original A7. But the bore/stroke ratio is very different. The original A7 had a bore and stroke of 62 × 82mm. When the A7 was redesigned last year, the dimensions were changed to 66 × 72.6mm. Bore and stroke of the A10 are 70 × 84mm. Will you explain, please, why you adopted these particular engine dimensions? "

Answer: "The A10 is a completely new engine and must not be confused or compared with the pre-1951 A7. The question of choice of bore size was somewhat involved, insofar as I decided upon a shallow combustion chamber and narrow valve angle, and an inlet valve size of 1.415in. These together with valve overlap and clearance considerations, fixed a minimum combustion-chamber diameter at around 70mm, assuming both valve seats to run out in a common sphere, thus obviating subsidiary machining operations.

"There were two other main considerations which more or less governed the maximum bore size. I had decided on a two-bearing crankshaft, the length (or shortness) of which fixed the cylinder centres. It is also, of course, necessary to have adequate air space between the cylin-

der walls. Thus, in the interests of achieving the right power, compactness, rigidity and cooling, 70mm was practically dictated as the bore size. And, of course, it was necessary to keep the weight of the con-rods and pistons down to a minimum in order to maintain the lowest possible inertia loadings."

Question: "Will you please comment upon your reasons for employing semi-unit construction of engine and gear box? "

Answer: "Unit or semi-unit construction (where the gear box is bolted direct to the engine) has the advantage of great rigidity, because connecting plates are dispensed with. If, as in the case of the A10, the primary drive is by chain, the periodic adjustment is easily made by a tensioner slipper bearing on the slack rim of the chain. The shorter chain centres enable us to cast the back half of the primary-chain cover integrally with the drive-side half crankcase, this without the casting becoming over bulky and difficult to handle in the machine shops. The layout saves weight, and appearance is undoubtedly enhanced."

Reduces Noise Problems

Question: "A prominent feature of the A10 design is that it employs only one camshaft, which is situated at the top-rear of the crankcase. Will you explain why you favour this arrangement? "

Answer: "Quite obviously a single camshaft requires a minimum of driving gears or sprockets, thus reducing noise problems. It is also obvious that a single camshaft, with four cam lobes, tends to operate less unevenly than one having half that number, and it therefore runs more quietly. The camshaft is situated at the rear of the engine because push-rod and rocker geometry dictates a common chamber in the cylinder head for the inlet valve springs, and the push-rods which operate at an angle to the vertical. The inlet 'side' of the engine is the obvious choice for the push-rod tunnel, since the exhaust 'side' is then free to be separated with cooling passages and fins."

Question: "The crankshaft is a one-piece design in 3½ per cent nickel steel, toughened to 65 tons tensile strength. I believe that, all things being equal, a one-piece shaft such as this should be more rigid than its built-up counterpart, but

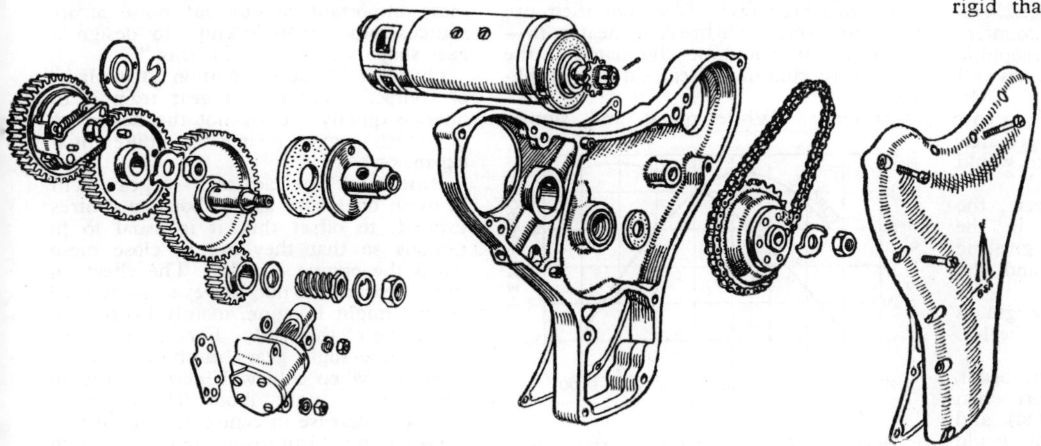

Golden Flash power unit employs a rigid one-piece crankshaft forged in 3½ per cent nickel steel, toughened to 65 tons tensile strength. The single flywheel is flange-bolted to the middle of the shaft. Other unusual features of the engine are the single, gear-driven camshaft at the rear of the crankcase, the separate compartment for the dynamo chain, and the use of silicon-alloy pistons, of ingenious flex-ible-skirt design

Modern Engines:
646 c.c. B.S.A. Golden Flash

a one-piece shaft is more difficult to forge and more complicated (and hence more expensive) to machine.

"Will you explain just why you adopted this type of shaft and this type of material? I have in mind that it is held in some quarters that the machining necessary with a one-piece shaft renders the use of steel uneconomical; moreover, that an alloy iron, a possible alternative, provides a good bearing surface *without* heat-treatment. Then, cast-iron shafts have proved in some cases to be superior in resistance to fatigue and in damping properties in respect of torsional oscillation. Appropriate heat treatment results in ultimate strength values comparable with medium-alloy steels."

Answer · "I cannot agree that a one-piece crank is more difficult to forge than a built-up one. Indeed, I can quote the instance of a designer going to great pains in designing a built-up crank, to have the forger remark that it was a pity the crankshaft was in two pieces! It is a question of the design and of the capacity of the forge. You will see that the A10 crankshaft has a circular flange in the middle to which is bolted the cast-iron flywheel. With a one-piece shaft of this design, it is not difficult to visualize the hot metal—during the forging operation—altering its shape from the straight billet to the rough crankshaft. There are no changes in section which present difficulty to the forger, and the two half dies have no over-deep draws. Proof of this is that one set of the dies will forge approximately 3,000 crankshafts.

Little or No Gain

"It is a fact that a cast shaft would require less metal to be removed during the machining stages to the finished article, but my experience is that the alloy iron necessary for the manufacture of a cast shaft requires a high degree of temperature and laboratory control. The separate cores which might be necessary in the production of a successful cast crankshaft would render little or no gain on the score of economy. It is also a fact that a cast shaft would require much closer inspection control than its forged counterpart, since the former is more susceptible to failure due to the presence of lines and nicks and variations of fillet radii. On the whole, I feel that if the saving in cost of a cast-iron crank over a forged-steel crank were really attractive, there would be much wider use of cast-iron."

Question: "Distance between the main-bearing centres must be in the region of $6\frac{3}{4}$in. Will you please give me the weight of the crankshaft and the weight of the wheel?"

Answer: "Total crankshaft weight is 12lb $12\frac{3}{4}$oz, and that of the flywheel is 8lb $7\frac{1}{2}$oz."

Question: "Total weight of the beam, therefore, is $21\frac{1}{4}$lb (and slightly more when nuts, bolts and washers are added), and with a crankcase of this width, some would consider the use of a middle bearing an advantage. Would you care to discuss the point?"

Answer: "To maintain the same flywheel inertia value and the same bearing loads, a centre bearing could not be accommodated without considerably increasing the length of the crankshaft. It would, for instance, be necessary to make room for the centre bearing. In my opinion there is just no substitute for the short, stiff shaft, which has little or no whip under load. If there were a centre bearing, the shaft would have to be reduced in diameter at the journal to a size giving a reasonable rubbing speed. This would make the shaft somewhat less rigid; and the three bearings would undoubtedly complicate production."

Question: "What are the reasons for the use of a roller bearing on the drive side and a plain bearing on the timing side?"

Answer: "On the drive side of the engine, a journal roller bearing is used to cater for the transmission loading as well as the load imposed by the inertia forces and gas pressure. Extra bending loads at this end of the engine are best carried by a ball or roller bearing, as plain bearings do not 'enjoy' this sort of work. The timing side of the crank is carried in a plain, white-metal bearing which plays no small part in the quietness of our timing-gear train. The bearing is the feeding station of all oil under pressure en route to the big-ends and, therefore, it operates in an excellent oil film at all times."

Rapid Heat Exchange

Question: "Have the light-alloy connecting rods any significance other than that the use of light-alloy keeps down reciprocating weight, thus reducing inertia loadings?"

Answer: "Light-alloy connecting rods are primarily specified for the purpose of weight reduction and consequent reduction of bearing loading due to inertia forces. Their use also tends, to some extent, to cool the gudgeon pin and piston by providing some capacity for rapid heat exchange."

Question: "The rods are light-alloy Hiduminium stampings in RR56, a material which forms a good bearing surface when used in conjunction with forged steel. Why, then, do you fit loose, thinwall, shell bearings? Does not their use mean that there is a break in heat path— a break that would be eliminated if the rods were running direct on the crankpins?"

Answer: "White metal and similar

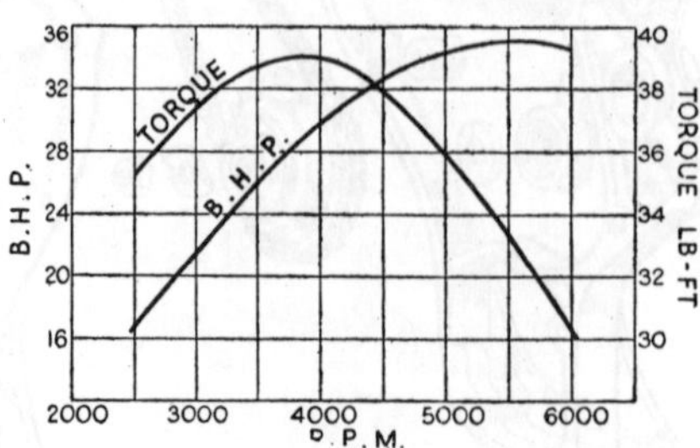

Torque and brake horse power curves of the A10 Golden Flash

bearing materials have the advantage of becoming semi-plastic and 'running' when subjected to overload. If a con-rod is lined with this material and for any unfortunate reason the metal runs, the user is given audible warning and he is able to make a replacement before damage is extended. If no lining is fitted in the big-end of an aluminium-alloy connecting rod, seizure and possibly even further damage could occur. Steel-backed shell bearings are used because they are easily replaceable. A break in the heat path? It is unlikely that the big-end bearings have an average running temperature higher than that of the upper part of the rod; therefore, a break in the heat path is really a desirable feature."

Question: "A10 timing gear is unusual in that gear drive is employed to the camshaft and magneto, and chain drive is utilized to the dynamo. While this system has obvious merits, it seems to be complicated in that an extra timing-case casting is called for. What were your reasons for adopting this system?"

Answer: "The 'sandwich case' or inner timing cover has three main features. It reduces the volume of casing around the timing gears, enables oil to follow their path more closely, and it forms an outrigger plate for the intermediate pinion spindle—thus divorcing the outer cover from load and noise transmission. It provides a good bearing housing for the mechanically timed breather and enables us to have a separate grease chamber for the dynamo drive chain, thus eliminating any danger of oil leaks into the dynamo."

Question: "Mechanical quietness is a feature that is receiving more and more attention these days. Do you find that the timing pinions 'ring'—or have you taken steps to prevent their magnifying or throwing up noise?"

Mechanical Quietness

Answer: "In a good engine, probably the greatest contribution to mechanical quietness is accuracy in manufacture: accurate line-reaming of gear centres, close attention to fits and the fine control of gear tooth shapes which is possible with gear shaving. Other things already discussed, such as the single camshaft and the submerged tappets and cams, play their parts in an equally important way. So far as gear ring is concerned, it is far more important to cut out noise at its source, rather than attempt to design a gear shape which does not ring."

Question: "Close attention to mesh is, of course, essential if a gear train is to operate quietly. Does not the degree of of mesh vary owing to differential expansion?"

Answer: "The clearance of gear teeth in mesh does vary as the housing centres expand; to offset this, it is usual to fit pinions so that they are in close mesh when the engine is cold. The effect on mesh clearance is not, however, so marked as one might imagine, mainly because of the shape of the teeth. For instance, two $14\frac{1}{2}$-degree-angle gears meshing with no clearance when cold will increase in tooth clearance by only about 0.001in for a 0.0021in increase in centre measurement."

Question: "Improved cooling is given as one of your reasons for employing a single, rearwardly mounted camshaft. Does not the position of the broad push-rod tunnel at the rear of the cylinder block prevent a straight-through flow of air?"

Answer: "No; the cast push-rod tunnel, for the greater part of its length, has generous air passages round it. You will notice, too, that the cylinder head is designed with adequate cooling spaces, and with fins between the exhaust and the inlet sides. The push-rod tunnel situated at the back of the engine means an unrestricted air passage at the front."

Question: "The pistons are in silicon-alloy and of flexible skirt design. An unusual feature is that, cut parallel to the internal webs which run from the base of the gudgeon pin bosses up to the crown, there are four 'heat gaps.' These are in the form of $\frac{3}{16}$in-wide × $\frac{7}{8}$in-long slots extending from the centre line through the gudgeon pin to just below the oil-control ring. Each pair of slots is joined by a $\frac{3}{16}$in-wide horizontal slot, cut across the piston thrust faces, parallel to the scraper ring. Will you please explain the reasons for this particular piston design and why silicon-alloy is used?"

Reduce Ring Year

Answer: "Yes, the piston design is unusual. There is a fully flexible skirt and yet the gudgeon-pin boss is very rigidly connected to the piston crown. The thrust faces of the skirt are, in fact, divorced from the gudgeon pin and crown by heat gaps. These trap the heat flow to the skirt, give great flexibility (enabling smaller clearance to be used), and thus improve smoothness and reduce noise and ring wear.

"I have often been asked whether, by preventing heat passing from crown to skirt and thus out through to the cooling fins of the barrel, any ill-effect such as piston over-heating results. The answer is that this does not happen, because most of the heat transference from the piston to the cylinder wall is made through the piston rings. Silicon-alloy of LO-ex type is used because of its high strength at elevated temperatures and its comparatively low thermal-expansion figure, which has a smaller disparity than other aluminium-alloys as against the material used for the cylinder barrel."

Question: "There is another feature of the piston which intrigues me. What is the reason for using a concave crown?"

Answer: "A concave crown is used because, for a given compression ratio, the rings may be positioned higher up the piston; thus more skirt length above the gudgeon pin is provided."

Question: "I note that the inlet port is semi-downdraught and that the manifold is of Y-shape, or bifurcated design. I believe that one school of thought holds that where a twin is fed by a single carburettor, any tendency to induction bias can be better overcome by using a T-shape manifold. Will you tell me whether your thermocouple readings give any indication of bias, and comment, please, on the manifold shape queries?"

Answer: "Temperature readings which have been taken on our engines from time to time do not indicate combustion or induction bias. Our inlet-port design was arrived at after lengthy tests on various shapes of manifold. It should be remembered that a variety of conditions must be satisfied—including that of good power at high revolutions. Our Y-shape manifold, you will notice, has quite a large radius at its branching point; machining of the carburettor flange is located at this point, thus bias due to poor alignment is ruled out."

Question: "Will you please explain why you have a 'floor' to the rocker box and why you prefer a separate rocker box? The use of an integral rocker box has many attractive advantages. Do you consider that a separate, bolted-on box is better?"

Answer: "The 'floor' enables us to pass air between the cylinder head and the rocker box. The single rocker box is an extremely rigid construction and a 'must' in this design because of the rocker and push-rod layout. In an engine of this type, the disadvantages of a rocker box cast integrally with the cylinder head far outweigh the advantages. For instance, the box, instead of being in light alloy, would have to be of the same material as the cylinder head, thus increasing the weight, and the cost of the cylinder-head casting would be increased enormously. Complicated coring operations, for example, would be necessary to maintain the air passages already mentioned."

Question: "The A10 combustion chambers are very shallow. Would you care to explain their shape?"

Answer: "The combustion chambers are shallow because I aimed at low surface area. The resulting combustion shape is very good, in that with higher compression ratios, particularly, the clearance volume is less attenuated. In addition, the ratio of available gas passage at the valve seats—for a given lift—is greater than that of a combustion chamber with a smaller hemispherical radius."

TECHNICAL DATA

CAPACITY : 646 c.c.

BORE : 70 mm.

STROKE : 84 mm.

COMPRESSION RATIO : 6.5 to 1

PISTON RING END-GAP : compression rings, 0.013-0.008in ; side-clearance, 0.003–0.001in ; scraper ring, 0.013–0.003in ; side-clearance, 0.003–0.001in.

VALVE-SPRING FREE LENGTH : outer, $1\frac{7}{8} \pm \frac{1}{64}$in ; inner, $1\frac{17}{32} \pm \frac{1}{64}$in.

ROCKER CLEARANCE : 0.010in inlet and exhaust when cold.

VALVE TIMING : inlet valve begins to open 30 degrees before top dead centre and closes 70 degrees after bottom dead centre ; exhaust valve begins to open 65 degrees before bottom dead centre and closes 25 degrees after top dead centre.

IGNITION TIMING : 34 degrees ($\frac{11}{32}$in) before top dead centre with points just opening.

ENGINE DIMENSIONS : crankshaft roller bearing, 30 mm bore, 62 mm outside diameter × 16 mm wide ; plain bearing, timing-side shaft diameter, 1.3750–1.3745 × 1.075–1.070in long ; crankpin diameter, 1.4600–1.4595in ; gudgeon-pin diameter 0.7502–0.7500in ; small-end bush bore diameter, 0.7506–0.7503in ; big-end to small-end centres, 6.469–6.467in ; inlet valve throat diameter, $1\frac{5}{16}$in ; exhaust valve throat diameter, $1\frac{1}{16}$in ; seat angle, 45 degrees ; valve lift, inlet 0.310in, exhaust, 0.300in.

CARBURETTOR : Amal, with $1\frac{1}{16}$in choke diameter, 6/4 throttle slide and 170 main jet.

Question: "What is the choke diameter, and the induction pipe length?"

Answer: "Choke diameter is $1\frac{1}{16}$in. Induction pipe length, to the middle of the mixing chamber, is $6\frac{9}{16}$in."

Question: "I note that you use a two-cam cush drive. What advantage has this type, in your opinion, over the three-cam type?"

Answer: "The two-cam type shock absorber gives a large rotational movement for small increase in spring pressure, and it is particularly suited to this engine. If a shock-absorber with a greater number of cams were used, much steeper cam flanks would be required. The shock-absorber would have entirely different characteristics."

Question: "The A10 lubrication system is one of the best to-day in that excess oil from the delivery side of the pump is fed direct to the camshaft and timing gear. From its trough under the camshaft, surplus oil overflows on to the big-ends from where it is flung on to the cylinder bores. Might this not lead to over-oiling and smoky exhausts?"

Answer: "One of the attributes of this lubrication system is that after surplus oil has passed through the camshaft tunnel, most of it gravitates directly to the sump. Cylinder lubrication bias, which might be apparent if oil release and consequent drainage to the sump were made in any other way is thus avoided. The amount of oil passed to the cylinder bores via the surfaces of the moving parts is governed largely by the position of the outlet from the camshaft trough, and also by the shape of the trough itself. This condition was arrived at after extensive motoring tests."

Why the A10 ?

Question: "How is such a high standard of valve-gear quietness achieved? Do the cams have quietening ramps to lower the valve gently on to its seat, and are there any other special features which contribute to the high degree of quietness?"

Answer: "Our cams have quietening ramps which give 0.001in lift for three degrees of crankshaft rotation. Not only do these ramps allow the valve to seat at low velocity, they also enable the 0.010in tappet clearances to be taken up on the lift side at an equally slow rate. The rigidity of the rocker housings, the ingenious lubrication system enabling the smallest possible working clearances to be used, and a very robust tappet arrangement, which means that the correct clearances are maintained over long periods, all help to this end."

Question: "A final question, and one which has always intrigued me. Why is this engine so prosaically designated 'A10'?"

Answer: "We prefer to know this model as the 'Golden Flash.' But having already decided that our vertical-twins should be known as the 'A' range, it was fairly reasonable to jump from A7, which is a 500 c.c., up to A10, which is a 650 c.c."

Which led me to think aloud: "Then may we expect an A8 and an A9 in the future?" Mr. Hopwood grinned and said: "Who knows?"

FRESHMAN ON A FLASH

BSA makes history— one horsepower per cubic inch in stock vertical twin

by Dick Day—Associate Editor

photos by Felix Zelenka

AROUND THE LONG banked curve, and down the straight country road a couple of miles awaited Frank Christian, official AMA timer, with his electric clocks all set to pick up the flat-out speed of the latest BSA Golden Flash. I grabbed a handful of throttle and felt the front end of the 40 cubic inch bike lighten with a terrific surge forward. Forty . . . five . . . eight . . . fifty, she lunged into second gear and once more came that big surge in the same direction. I was just now starting into the long curve, still accelerating fast when the Flash and I laid into the turn, right on the white line dividing the two lane road. The pavement was anything but smooth and, with front forks and the plunger-type rear suspension func-

tioning properly, there wasn't one instance when the bike seemed to walk or drift towards the outside of the curve. In fact, the more body-English applied to the Flash in the corner, the more traction it seemed to possess.

Pulling out of the corner and pointing the front wheel straight down the road. I dropped her into third at approximately 72 miles per hour and again she repeated her crazy surge forward. One shift later, I slid back on the rear fender and flattened out as low as possible, without the advantage of rear pegs. The road test crew, now in sight, was beginning to grow in size and the ground beneath was only a blur. One last peek at the speedometer revealed she was on her way. One hundred . . . one . . . one hundred and two . . . the Beezer now had reached that smooth gliding feeling, as if she were just barely touching the surface of the road. Vibration was nil and the steering, even in this position, seemed as easy as if sitting on its center stand in your own driveway. Whoom . . . the crew and the first timing clock went by. A few seconds later we flashed by the second light and were out of the traps. I feathered the throttle back.

climbed up into the saddle and began easing down through the gears. Cruising back past the trap, I could see by the expressions on the fellows' faces that the 40-incher hadn't done bad. Ray Bowles held up four fingers which meant the little bomb had turned 104 miles per hour.

This was e-a-s-y? Well, not quite. Let us go back a couple of hours to ten o'clock of that same morning, to where our road test crew had assembled on the speed strip anxiously waiting to put the Flash through its paces. First it should be mentioned that the cooperation and attention we received on this month's road test was class "A." For all but a couple of BSA shops in this area were represented. Frank Christian, of Modern Cycle Works, had generously brought out his flawless electric timing clocks to record the speeds. Jack Milne had brought along Gene Ryan, ace mechanic for Lammy Lamoreaux. Ray Venitozzi, San Gabriel BSA dealer, was also present to give a hand.

The biggest drawback to the whole test was the mileage factor: the bike had been ridden only 250 total miles when we lifted it out of the truck and warmed up for the first high speed run. It was obvious

Outstanding are the clean lines of styling that the forty-incher possesses. Chrome accessories and highly polished aluminum components are plentiful. Note the heavy duty braces that support the rear fender

Emphasis has been put on such fittings as: tail light assembly, toolbox, horn, oil tank, all tucked-in and molded to the overall contour of the machine. Full valanced front fender is also big feature for wet weather

Handling qualities of the Beezer were tops once you became acquainted with the sudden power the engine offers. Stiff barrel seat springs proved hard for maximum riding comfort

Added rear safety for the rider is apparent with this new designed tail light unit which includes an extra large tail light and reflector. While testing, one rear fender brace vibrated loose

Nacelle headlight unit has no bulkiness to its design and yet houses the speedometer, light switch, ammeter, and a seven-inch seal beam unit that may be replaced by any U.S. lamp

that this low mileage was going to play a large part in the final performance analysis. The bike was still tight and needed several hundred more miles of running-in before being able to roll free of excess friction. Although the machine was in our hands for a week before this test, we were unable to put on any further miles because of some freak weather conditions here in "sunny" Southern California—*rain*.

After the Flash was warmed up, Editor Bob Greene took it up the road on a practice run. Upon returning, at about 90, the machine began developing a sputter from both banks of the exhaust. Another run brought the same effect so Gene Ryan changed the jet size of the carburetor from 90 to 220 and installed KLG F80 plugs, thinking she needed more gas and a colder plug. Back down the road, acceleration in all gears revealed that it had apparently lost its cackle at high rpm's. But on the return trip through the traps, she began dropping beats once more. With the completion of several more runs, we changed back to a 180 jet and turned 99 miles per hour, which was a definite improvement over the previous tries. Checking the plugs on the next run revealed that the left barrel was running lean. Gene then went back up the scale to a 200 jet, still retaining the F80 plugs, and sent the Flash back for another try, only to have the top speed miss reappear. Upon returning to the pit area once again, the BSA stalwarts reached out and snapped the cap off of the petrol tank, cleaned a wad of polish out of the vent hole and sent us back to start for another run. Results: 103.44 miles per hour. I guess it's like the man said, "You're never too old to learn."

Two more runs brought the same reading from the clocks and the pit crew agreed that it had gone just about as fast as it was going to under the circumstances. The motor was still burdened with a slight splatter at high speeds and it was apparent that the low mileage definitely had a serious effect on top-end perform-

ance. We found out later that the sputtering at high rpm's could be attributed to the magneto's armature, which would break down when taking on the full load of fourth gear ratio at top speed. This trouble did not confront us in the acceleration test, although turning a much higher engine revolution, because the ratio through the gears is much lower and takes the heavy pulling load off the engine. On paper the 40 cubes figured out at 110 miles per hour for top speed, and I will go on to personally say the bike is good for another 5 mph over what we accomplished once it had benefit of further breaking-in.

I would like to bring out at this time a test point that, to my thinking, was of greater importance than if the twin had stormed 120 in high cog. For two solid hours we had been throwing shifts at this machine at top rpm's through all the gears. It is hardly necessary to relate the effect that this has on transmission, clutch, engine and chains. The usual shifting troubles found common in the BSA transmission seemed to have disappeared completely and there was no indication of tightening up, even after the most severe usage. Not once was there any indication of the motor slowing from over-heating. This gearbox offers a positive, easy shift that never seems to vary with a rise in running temperature. After coming to a stop in low gear it only took a light tap on the shifting lever to spot neutral. Another feature of the transmission was the ease with which low could be entered from neutral with the machine standing dead still. There was no need to rock the bike to or fro for, just like Grandpa's dentures, it would slip into place with a faint click.

Checking further into this transmission we learned that it will also be found on the B series of the single line, such as the Gold Star racer, the B-34 alloy, etc. There was no sign of clutch slippage or chains slacking throughout the test. In fact, after the high speed ordeal, I lined up for the standing start quarter-mile acceleration

test, turned on too much throttle and laid off a good 20 feet of Dunlop rubber. Believe me, this was self-explanatory as to any questions on clutch slippage.

The only demerit that was given at this point of the test was to the rear chain oiler. The lower left side of the bike was soused with oil that had been thrown off the chain. Checking further we found that the rear chain oiler was actually the oil tank breather and apparently the oil tank had been filled to excess and, slopping around in the tank, the oil had run out through the breather tube onto the chain.

While the test crew took off for chow, Ray Venitozzi and I stuck around to keep tab on the clocks and the timing equipment. This gave me a chance to get in a little free time at the various tests that were soon to come. Simulating a few Field Meet capers the Flash was first tried for balance with a one-man slow race. While it is neither a heavy nor a lightweight, the machine juggles perfectly, allowing motionless balance for seconds on end. In a spin and dig race it would be a constant threat, for with a slight turn of the front wheel and a twist of the throttle the bike whips around and you're off for the finish line in a double flash.

The next chore was an imaginary stake race. Here the bike gave quite a tussle for sharp turning was made nil by what many sports riders might consider exaggerated fork stops. But this is only of minor importance, nothing that a hack saw couldn't remedy. The proximity of the gas tank still leaves room for alteration.

With the road test crew back, we recommenced with a brake test. Here is the part that I found most difficult, with all fairness to the statistics of the machine. We approach a white line in fourth gear at 25 miles per hour and apply the brakes as viciously as possible just short of a slide. Just for kicks, in your spare time, chalk a line across the road, approach it at exactly 25 miles per hour,

The road test crew stands by while Frank Christian records the flat-out speeds of the Flash with his electric timing clocks which assures no errors in times. Frank's clocks will be used on all road tests from here on in. One last check revealed that the week-long test of fast acceleration, high speed and rugged cow-trailing had caused one oil tank hanger to spring a leak, the voltage regulator had worked loose, the battery strap lost a hinge pin

apply the binders as your front axle crosses the line and measure the distance. You might go farther than that if you wish, and dig out a back issue of CYCLE Magazine that contains a road test on your model and compare the braking distances. You will find, as I did, that three things enter into this test that can throw the recorded footage off.

First, it is very hard to maintain an even 25 miles per hour for any length of time because of the way the needle moves in jumps of two to three miles per hour. Unless you've practised this for quite some time you're apt to misjudge at the crucial moment and accuracy goes out the window. Fortunately, my first test was done under the critical eye of your editor, who has developed a remarkable faculty for catching any miscues in speed. Second, it is very difficult to watch the line in the road and the speedo at the same time while making your approach. Third, judging when the front wheel's axle is directly over the line isn't the easiest thing that ever happened, and applying the brakes a few inches before or after the mark will make quite a difference when the measuring tape is held down.

This being my first road test for CYCLE Magazine, I can assure you that while doing the brake test I was traveling at a generous 25 miles per hour before pulling the Flash to a halt. This machine is equipped with a large 8-inch front brake, while the rear measures 7 inches in diameter. With the application of these brakes you will find that the balance of power is such that there is no deviation from a straight line stop. The bike merely squats to a halt. Both front and rear brakes are fitted with a simple type method of adjustment. The rear is equipped with a spring-loaded rod and a large screw while the front has a long threaded bolt with two locking nuts, both of which may be adjusted easily by hand and saves a trip to the tool box.

Although the Flash was a bit short of our expectations regarding the high speed figures, it turned some very incredible acceleration times. Rearranging the clock to a quarter-mile distance, we fired up the 40 horses and made ready for the start. With the "OK" from Frank Christian I wound the job up, popped the clutch, and was off. Using low gear as just a starter I dropped it into second early to get the maximum speed out of this ratio. The front wheel came off the ground slightly (there's that clutch again) for an instant. Here I felt a large amount of vibration, caused by the high rpm's the engine was then turning. Easing it into third showed no pause or dropping of revs, only a continued higher buzz from the exhaust tips.

(*Continued on page* 53)

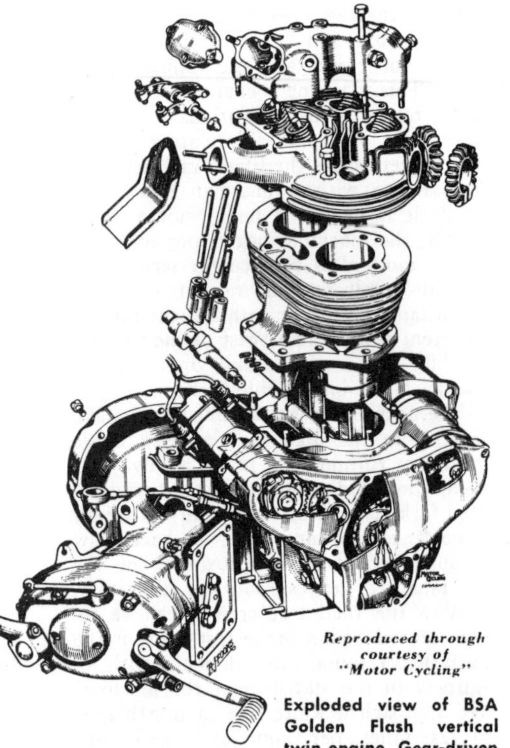

Reproduced through courtesy of "Motor Cycling"

Exploded view of BSA Golden Flash vertical twin engine. Gear-driven magneto, chain-driven generator and single camshaft. Rockerbox housing is one-piece, intake manifold is cast into head, oil lines are internal. Small trough near intake port insulates Amal carburetor from heat and provides a drip pan for gasoline if carburetor begins to overflow

Editor Bob Greene relates a few scabby experiences, recalling his first time out on road test. Removal of Volkes air cleaner yielded very little difference in speed, proving theory of removing the cleaner for better gas mixtures in competition events is not practical when riding this bike

Close-up photo shows splined rear hub assembly that locks rear wheel in place. This method has proven flawless over a period of years and a unique way of removing rear wheel, less brake

(Continued from page 52)

At the conclusion of the drag runs, we found the clock had recorded three very consistent times. not deviating as much as one mile per hour either way to average out a 60 miles per hour figure. Referring back to the top speed obtained in third gear; which was 98 miles per hour and practically peaked in third cog while running the quarter mile, we can assume the Flash was turning somewhere between 90 and 95 mph for the standing start quarter-mile acceleration test.

With a full day of very hard running under its belt and not one sign of trouble, not even as much as a clutch adjustment, we loaded the two-wheeled powerplant into the truck and headed back into town looking forward to one more day of testing this power-plus out on the good old "tierra firma."

Early next morning we rolled into Le-Bard and Underwood's BSA shop, where a brand, spanking new 1953 Flash sat on the showroom floor. It was to be used in conjunction with the late '52 model that we had actually been testing. We were unable to use this '53 model because of it being the only one in this area and already on the delivery list. By using the late '52 set-up with the Star Twin cam, which is the little goodie that gives this 40-incher its horsepower per inch, we could test performance without riding the new model.

From a cut-a-way engine we learned more of the inner workings. A central flywheel with bolted on crank throws, supported between a larger roller bearing on the sprocket side of the cases and a plain bearing for main-shaft timing side, plus replaceable con rod bearing inserts, added up to a real husky lower end. With $7\frac{1}{2}$:1 compression, thermoslot cam ground pistons made of silicon alloy, the motor is able to withstand quite a bit of heat without any worry of seizure, which was undoubtedly proven in yesterday's test. We also noticed the push rod's position inside and at the rear of the cylinder, which eliminates quite a few parts such as covers.

seals, etc. The transmission is bolted to the crank cases, making the two units practically one. In the primary we found a duplex roller chain running in a cast aluminum oil bath chain case. Chain tension is correctly maintained by an easy-to-get-to adjustable screw that moves a slipper-type tensioner with hard chromed bearing surface that will take up chain slack by moving up or down to the wanted position. The cam that is being adapted to the 1953 model is the same cam that is found in the new Star Twin 30.50 racer that has been really storming this year at national events around the country.

This four-lobed single stick is the one and only modification to the engine this year, but from just changing this cam from stock to the new Star Twin cam rejuvenated the horsepower from 37 to 40 horsepower in one jump. I might add here for the benefit of the owners of earlier model 40-inch jobs that for the price of $21 this accelerating cam can be bought to replace the stock stick. On hand also, for riders that are looking for little speed goodies, are factory-made pistons ranging from $7\frac{1}{4}$ compression ratio up to $9\frac{1}{2}$. By going deeper into the speed angle, you might refer to June, '52 CYCLE for an article by Russ Kelly, "More Dash for Your Flash," a how-to-do-it article on hopping up. But, believe me, the adaptation of the Star Twin cam alone will give you more suds than you could ever hope to use.

The most noticeable change of styling is the new nacelle headlight unit which offers several new advantages. The speedometer is mounted completely in a rubber seal which insures a longer life for the speedo by absorbing vibration impacts. A 7-inch diameter sealbeam headlight adorns the front of the unit and gives out a sufficient beam of light, either on low or high setting, operated by a dimmer switch mounted on the handlebars. The nacelle unit also houses the ammeter and the light switch on the sides to put the finishing touches on a cleverly designed instrument panel. The new Beezer tail light bracket

PERFORMANCE SUMMARY

Maximum in low	62:37 mph	**Acceleration**	
Maximum in second	81:63 mph	⅒ mile drag (8.31 sec.)	43.36 mph avg.
Maximum in third	98:63 mph	¼ mile drag (14 sec.)	64:28 mph avg.
Maximum in high	103:53 mph	**Turning Circle**	

Braking

Minimum diameter   11′9″

From 25 to stopped
rear brake only   40′10″

Slow Running

From 25 to stopped
front brake only   25′9″

High gear without snatch   15 mph

Mileage

From 25 to stopped, both brakes   18′1″

Town   55 mpg

Price, $892.42, plus local freight, set-up charges, tax and license.

GENERAL SPECIFICATIONS

ENGINE. Even-firing vertical twin cylinder overhead valve 70 mm bore by 84 mm stroke, 646 cc (40 cubic inch). One-piece forged steel crankshaft with integral bob weights and bolted-on central flywheel also incorporating a bob weight. Roller journal bearings on drive side main shaft, plain bearing big ends with replaceable Indium flashed lead-bronze liners, plain bearing for mainshaft timing side. Forged light alloy connecting rods with phosphor bronze bushes for small-end bearings, low expansion aluminum silicon alloy pistons, with two compression rings, and slotted scraper ring in special duplex oil control groove. Twin cylinders cast in single unit with specially cored air passages. Unit cylinder head casting with narrow angle valves, two per cylinder, operated in shallow combustion chamber specially developed for maximum efficiency. Separate exhaust rocker box for each cylinder with twin inlet rocker box at rear. Special cylinder fin arrangement insures maximum air flow between ports and over combustion heads. Valves operate by overhead rockers and push rods actuated by a single camshaft at rear through large car-type tappets with especially generous bearing surfaces. Camshaft gear driven from engine shaft through idler pinion and incorporating timed mechanical breather. Twin exhaust pipes with cylindrical absorption-type mufflers. Compression ratio 7¼-1.

LUBRICATION SYSTEM. Engine lubricated by dry sump system with twin gear-type pump, driven by skew gear from engine shaft. Pressure fed to timing-side main bearing and big ends with by-pass oil pressure release. Metered pressure oil fed to overhead rocker spindles with return to crankcase. Camshaft operated in specially designed oil trough. Other moving parts lubricated by oil mist. Capacity of oil tank: 2½ U.S. quarts.

INDUCTION SYSTEM. Forked inlet manifold cast in cylinder head, ensuring correct gas flow from Amal carburetor specially adapted to accommodate large capacity built-in air cleaner, mounted on seat tube between oil tank and tool box.

IGNITION. Lucas magneto gear driven from camshaft with centrifugal-type automatic advance.

TRANSMISSION. Primary drive from engine by ⅜″ multirow chain running in a cast aluminum oil bath chain case, inner portions forming part of crankcase. Chain tension directly maintained by adjustable slipper-type tensioner with hard chromed bearing surfaces and external adjustment. Twin cam-type spring

loaded engine shaft cush drive. Rear chain ⅝ inch by ⅜ inch roller. Lubricated by special breather pipe from oil tank. Five plate clutch with oil-proof fabric inserts, six radially disposed springs designed for uniform pressure distribution. Clutch center mounted on roller bearings to insure correct alignment when disengaged. Clutch operation by hardened steel push rod through center of hollow gear box main shaft.

GEAR BOX. BSA four speed constant mesh gear box with built-in positive stop foot change. Gear box main shaft mounted on ball journal bearing.

FRAME. Duplex triangulated cradle of ample strength for solo or side-car work. All frame lugs including those for sidecar and pillion foot rest are of forged steel. BSA telescopic front forks with automatic progressive hydraulic dampening and special oil seat at sliding members. Wheels quickly detachable; front wheel, 8-inch diameter brake incorporating duplex-type rib shoes of great strength operating in high molybdenum cast iron drums. Rear, of straight spoke type with 7-inch diameter brake. Dunlop tires; front, 3.25x19; rear, 3.50x19. Welded pressed steel petrol tank. Capacity: 4 U.S. gallons and one pint. Adjustable handlebars. Generous mudguards. Tail portion of rear guard detachable for easy wheel removal. Spring-up central stand, adjustable foot rest.

EQUIPMENT. Adjustable Lycett spring saddle. Lucas 6-volt cvc lighting set with 7-inch seal-beam headlight and high frequency electric horn. Metal tool box under seat tube with complete tool kit. Tire pump, rubber knee grips.

CONTROLS. On left handlebar, clutch lever, kill button and headlamp dim switch. On right handlebar, front brake, air lever and horn button. Damper knob on steering head. Rear brake operated by left foot pedal. Kick starter and gear change pedal on right, both provided with rubber sleeves. Twin gas outlets at rear of tank, both with reserve levers and fine mesh gauze filters. Finger adjustment for brakes and clutch control.

FINISH. All bright parts, including the exhaust system, heavily chromium plated. Frame, mudguards, etc. lustrous black enamel. Gas tank, dark maroon and chromed with distinctive motif. Wheel rims completely chromed. Polished front chain case, gear box cover and timing cover.

WEIGHT. Dry, 395 lbs.

WHEELBASE. 54¾ inches.

OVERALL WIDTH. 28 inches.

GROUND CLEARANCE. 4½ inches.

SADDLE HEIGHT. 30 inches.

supports a rear tail light which measures approximately 4 inches long and 2½ inches deep. When the rear brake is put on, the stoplight resembles that of a fishtail Cadillac, for brilliancy.

Two other changes were very dominant; one being the new tank design of deep maroon, while the centers of the rims were not painted as usual, but completely polished to add more over-all allure.

With a farewell to Jim and Aub, the photographer and I left for Baldwin Hills.

a perfect playground for bikes and a terrific area for testing, as it offers about every conceivable type of terrain. On the way through town, I noticed that when passing motorists there was no excessive noise from the mufflers and at times I had the feeling that the motorists were curious as to the fact that a bike had just passed them without blowing the window panes out of their cars. This effect can be laid to the efficient stock mufflers that the

Flash comes equipped with. The mellow, even tone is not in the least annoying to the rider and is especially easy on the next door neighbors about midnight.

Once out in the dirt, I looked for a suitable area that would simulate an English Trial hazard. I came upon a ditch that would be a toughy to negotiate. Easing down one side of the steep ravine with the engine idling and the clutch just barely engaged, the balance of the bike was again a definite advantage. Once the forks had absorbed the blunt impact of an 8-inch drop-off at the bottom of the gully, there was nothing to do but turn the throttle on, climb up over the tanks and, with a little body-English, scramble up the other steep side with a perfect score. Ground clearance was ample and the traction of the rear wheel sufficient. Finding a nice knoll to come bounding off of was easy, for this vast area was once a golf course and offered many varied small knolls. After numerous jumps from one of these deep banks, the left peg had loosened without my knowledge. The next jump, with my weight entirely on the foot pegs, it swung under, giving me a terrific surprise.

Investigating the peg, I found that it differs from the other BSA models. Singles of this line have a splined shaft that secures the pegs at the wanted position while the peg and shaft are secured with a large nut that holds the whole unit tight. The Flash has a tapered shaft and the foot peg has a beveled hole that allows it to be wedged tight onto the shaft. This is fine, but why not include a small key or a pin locking the peg in a position so that when, and if, this nut becomes loose the bracket will not swing under?

Another noticeable distraction while jumping was a terrific crash of the rear frame suspension. Several times I looked to the rear after the jump, expecting to see some devastating damages but nothing could be found wrong. Checking with Aub LeBard on this matter, I was amazed to learn that the crashing noise was not that of the frame bottoming, but actually the recoil action of the frame topping. Although this noise is irritable to the rider, no damage can be done to the spring mechanism.

One more test and I figured we had put the Flash through every conceivable shenanigan that could be thought of. Picking out one of the ruggedest paths a large hill could offer, the Beezer and I started up. It was no strain for this powerhouse to carry itself and the rider over in flying colors. Upon reaching the crest of the hill we concluded our analysis of the '53 Flash, its report card showing double "A's" all down the line.

Coming from an old die-hard single rider, the come-back "No, I don't want any" is going to be mighty difficult to say for those riders contemplating on buying a new machine this year. Here is a bike that contains ease of handling, speed and ruggedness all in one package.

Stars in your Eyes

HEADLIGHTS on the new models are much more bulbous, actually quite shapely once your eyes return to the bike. Ammeter, speedo and ignition switch are contained in the new nacelle of BSA 30.50 Star Twin. When attractive 20-year-old Merry Anders stopped Bob Hope in the N.B.C. parking lot for his autograph, Bob looked at her and said: "You shouldn't be asking for these. You ought to be giving them." Bob was right, in the opinion of 20th Century-Fox who has just signed Merry to a long-term contract. Too bad, fellows!

Photo by Felix Zelenka

B.S.A. TEST COMPLETED

Fred Rist, Brian Martin and Norman Vanhouse Bring Home the I.S.D.T. Gold-Medal-Winning "Star Twins" After 5,000-mile A.-C.U. Observed Continental Tour

INTO the port of Newcastle upon Tyne early last Friday morning steamed the vessel carrying the triumphantly proud B.S.A. team which not only achieved the splendid record of covering the recent International Six Days Trial without the loss of a single mark, but also made this strenuous event part of an extended Continental journey carried through from start to finish under strict observation by a representative of the Auto-Cycle Union.

As all readers will know now, the three riders were Fred Rist, Brian Martin and Norman Vanhouse, and their mounts were a trio of perfectly standard A.7 "Star Twin" B.S.A.s which had been selected from stock at the Small Heath factory by A.-C.U. observer John McNulty, who accompanied the party throughout the trip. This began on Sunday, September 7, when, after the riders had been allowed to make routine adjustments such as "tailoring" footrests, saddles and handlebars to suit their statures, the 4,900-mile adventure was embarked upon with London as the first scheduled stop. Here, at the headquarters

England. Holland, Belgium, France, Switzerland, Austria, Germany, Denmark, Sweden and Norway— through these ten European countries the B.S.A. test route took the trio of "Star Twins," and also included 1,200 miles of mark-free "Six Days" Competition.

of the R.A.C. at Pall Mall, A.-C.U. officials turned out to wish the party godspeed and the cavalcade, which in addition to the three machines included the car conveying the observer and George Savage, B.S.A. Cycle's sales manager, went on to Harwich where the night boat ferried them across the North Sea to the Hook of Holland.

After a reception at the Hague, a route was followed to include as many as possible of the principal West European cities, and in Antwerp, Brussels, Paris, Geneva, Zurich and Innsbruck the travellers were greeted

with great enthusiasm by local motor-cyclists and dealers. Wherever a stop was made for lunch or for the night, hospitality of an almost overwhelming magnitude was forthcoming. And at each of the night stops the three motorcycles were carefully locked up behind sealed doors by the observer, who had also made notes of any adjustments carried out during the day.

Only one unforeseen incident occurred when, on the outward trip, the photographer who was accompanying the party to make a film, was taken ill. He manfully carried on with his "Golden Flash" and sidecar until, at Tonnerre, in France, a local doctor ordered him instantly to hospital. An hour or two later he underwent an appendix operation, which was so successful that, when George Savage visited him on the way back, the patient was getting about again. In one way, he was extremely lucky, for the hospital's visiting surgeon calls only once a week and happened that day to be on duty!

Unfortunately weather conditions were not kind, but the B.S.A.s had no difficulty in making their way over the snow-slushed Arlberg Pass. At Bad Aussee, locale of the Six Days Trial, a halt was made to watch the preliminaries for the event, but the test schedule led on eastwards over the British zone frontier into the Russian zone of Austria, with Vienna as the destination. The Austrian capital delighted the party and traditional Viennese hospitality was not lacking. Russian authorities raised no difficulties but, while behind "the curtain," Russian petrol only was obtainable—the Esso spirit on which the machines ran everywhere else being unprocurable.

After a short stay, the route was retraced to Bad Aussee in time for Rist, Martin and Vanhouse to weigh-in their three already much-travelled mounts for the rigorous Six Days competition that began on September 17 and finished on September 23.

As is now history, the "Star Twins" carried their riders through in perfect style, all gaining gold medals and bringing honour

Continued on page 83

Unfavourable weather conditions were experienced throughout most of the journey, with snow-bound roads adding to the hazards, as this picture of Brian Martin, taken during the I.S.D.T., clearly shows.

B.S.A.s Win Maudes Trophy

Magnificent Achievement by F. M. Rist, N. E. Vanhouse, and B. W. Martin on Star Twins

AT its meeting last Thursday, the competitions committee of the Auto-Cycle Union awarded the Maudes Trophy to B.S.A.s. The award was in recognition of the A.C.U.-observed trip by F. M. Rist, N. E. Vanhouse and B. W. Martin on B.S.A. Star Twins, which embraced a 4,958-mile journey from England through Holland, Belgium, France, Switzerland, Austria, Germany, Denmark, Sweden and Norway. The trio, with A.C.U. observer John McNulty in attendance, left England on Sunday, September 7, on machines which had been selected off the production line by McNulty from a batch of 37.

Before the start, the following attention was given to each machine under the supervision of the A.C.U. observer.—(1) rear-wheel sprocket (and bearing) changed from 45 tooth (the usual solo size) to the sidecar size with 49 teeth; (2) appropriate rear chain fitted for the larger sprocket; (3) appropriate speedometer head fitted for the larger sprocket; (4) saddle removed and standard B.S.A. dual-seat fitted; (5) pillion footrests fitted; (6) clock fitted; (7) I.S.D.T.-type number plates fitted; (8) tank-top toolbag fitted; (9) oil tank, gearbox, and primary-chain case drained and refilled with Essolube 40 oil; (10) petrol tank drained and refilled with Esso fuel; (11) holes for I.S.D.T. sealing drilled in the cylinder head, cylinder barrel and crankcase.

After the initial stage of the journey—by way of the Netherlands, Belgium, France, Switzerland, and Austria, the machines were taken through the International Six Days' Trial which started on September 18. Before that date, the trio had visited Vienna, which was the easternmost city of their route.

Before the International Six Days' Trial, the machines were given special preparation. The tasks included the fitting of security bolts for the tyres, fitting of crankcase shields, nail catchers, touring-type handlebars, air bottles, and tommy bars to wheel spindles. In addition, normal adjustments such as the setting of magneto points, the checking of oil levels and battery-acid levels were carried out.

As already reported in these columns, no marks were lost in the trial, and each rider gained a gold medal; in fact, the three men, who were entered as representing the Birmingham M.C.C., were the only British team to come through without loss of marks.

After the trial was over, the test continued through Germany, Denmark, Sweden and Norway. Finally, the test was concluded by speed runs at Oslo aerodrome over a measured distance of 400m (nearly ¼ mile). Standing-start figures showed a mean speed of 49.99 m.p.h., 47.98 m.p.h., and 50.15 m.p.h. for the three machines respectively. Flying-start speeds were 82.12, 84.43, and 80.27 m.p.h. The best speed achieved from a standing start—one way speed— was 51.44, and the best flying-start speed—one way— was 85.23 m.p.h.

During the long run through Europe and Scandinavia, normal maintenance attention was given—that is to say, checks were made of tyres, chains, etc., as necessary, and grease-gun and oil-can lubrication was attended to. In the Six Days' Trial the machines were ridden under the normal rules appertaining to the trial, which means that components were marked and, therefore, could not be replaced. The only replacements required during the time the machines were under the jurisdiction of the A.C.U. observer were, according to the official report, two headlamp pilot bulbs, and three rear-lamp bulbs; two frayed rear-lamp lighting leads had to be replaced, and a new primary-chain case filler cap had to be fitted when one was lost *en route*. Two of the machines suffered from leaking petrol tanks; the leaks were remedied by welding. On one of the machines, a loose horn lead had to be refixed. During the final speed test at Oslo, the main jets of two of the machines were found to be choked; in both instances, the jets were cleaned and replaced.

The Maudes Trophy was presented in 1923 by Mr. Pettyt, of Maudes of Exeter, to be awarded in any year ended September 30 for the best performance in a test certified by the A.C.U. In that year, the winners were Nortons for a 12-hour high-speed test at Brooklands with a 490 c.c. Norton; the machine broke 18 world's records. Nortons were also successful in 1924, 1925 and 1926, until, in 1927, the sequence was broken by Ariels when a 557 c.c. Ariel sidecar outfit covered 5,000 miles without an engine stop. Ariels were successful again in 1928; Dunelt won in 1929 and in 1930.

Ambitious Undertaking

In later years (1938), B.S.A.s gained the Trophy for tests with a 500 c.c. Empire Star and a 600 c.c. side-valve sidecar outfit selected from retail stocks. Then, in 1939, the Trophy was awarded to Triumphs when Tiger 100 and Speed Twin models covered 1,800 miles on the roads at an average speed of 42 m.p.h. and lapped Brooklands for six hours at high speed—78.50 m.p.h. for the Tiger 100 and 75.02 m.p.h. for the Speed Twin. Final laps in the test showed a speed of 88.46 for the Tiger 100 and 84.41 for the Speed Twin.

Since 1939 no manufacturer has embarked on a test for the Maudes Trophy. Indeed, interest has varied throughout the years; for example, in 1924 there were 11 tests; in 1927, 8; in 1929, 6; and in 1936, 6.

The recent B.S.A. undertaking was novel and, before it started, was considered by knowledgeable observers to be most ambitious, for the reason that the three machines were to be taken through the International Six Days' Trial. Invariably the Trial is arduous and hard on machines. The successful conclusion of the 4,900 miles is a great credit to the manufacturers and the riders and, furthermore, provides a fillip to British prestige.

Fuel and oil were supplied by Esso and all filling-up was from Esso service stations in Great Britain and on the Continent, except that this brand of products was not available in Vienna; the mileage covered on the replenishments obtained in that town was about 230. During the International Six Days' Trial, Esso supplies were obtained from the official I.S.D.T. depots.

As intimated earlier, standard equipment and accessories were used on the B.S.A.s and included Dunlop tyres, Renold chains, Ferodo brake and clutch linings, Amal carburettors, Tecalemit grease nipples, Champion sparking plugs, Lucas lighting and ignition and Smiths speedometers.

The 646 c.c. Model A10 o.h.v. TWIN

B.S.A.

The Biggest Machine in the Extensive Small Heath Range Shows its Paces to "Motor Cycling"

Very "clean" lines characterize the "Golden Flash" B.S.A., with its big parallel twin o.h.v. engine capable of dealing with a heavy sidecar or of providing super-sporting solo performance.

BRIEF SPECIFICATION

Engine: Vertical twin-cylinder, push-rod o.h.v.; bore 70 mm. by stroke 84 mm. = 646 c.c.; cast-iron cylinder head and block; compression ratio 6.5 to 1; valve gear fully enclosed in light alloy housing; light-alloy connecting rods: V.P.2 lead-bronze big-end bearings; forged steel crankshaft; mainshaft carried on roller bearing on drive side and plain bearing on timing side: Amal type 276ER/1DB carburetter with twist-grip control; dry sump lubrication with twin gear-type pump.

Transmission: ⅜-in duplex primary drive chain in aluminium oilbath case; ⅝-in. by ⅜-in. final drive chain; engine shaft shock absorber; four-speed constant-mesh gearbox; ratios 4.42, 5.36, 7.77 and 11.41 to 1; five-plate clutch.

Frame: Duplex loop frame with plunger type coil-spring rear suspension; hydraulically controlled telescopic front forks; prop and centre stands.

Electrics: Lucas magneto, 60-watt dynamo, lighting with Lucas 7½-in. headlamp; electric horn.

Wheels: WM2-19 front and rear rims; Dunlop 3.25-in. by 19-in. front and 3.50-in. by 19-in. rear tyres; 8-in. front; 7-in. rear brakes.

Tanks: Welded steel fuel tank, capacity 4¼ gallons; oil container 4 pints.

Dimensions: Saddle height 30 in.; wheelbase 54¾ in.; ground clearance 4½ in.; overall width, 28 in.; overall length 84 in.; weight 408 lb.

Finish: As standard; black enamel, chrome plated tank with black panels; beige and chrome as tested, with B.S.A. embossed motif on fuel tank, extra £3 12s. 6d.

Equipment: Smiths 120 m.p.h. internally illuminated speedometer.

Price: £178 0s. 0d. plus £37 1s. 8d. P.T. = total £215 1s. 8d.

Manufacturers: B.S.A. Cycles Ltd., Small Heath, Birmingham, 11.

TESTER'S ROAD REPORT

Maximum Speeds in :—

Top Gear (Ratio 4·42 to 1) 98 m.p.h. = 5,600 r.p.m. Time from Standing Start 41 secs.

Third Gear (Ratio 5·36 to 1) 82 m.p.h. = 5800 r.p.m. 22 secs.

Second Gear (Ratio 7·77 to 1) 64 m.p.h. = 6200 r.p.m. 9⅗ secs.

Speeds over measured Quarter Mile :—

Flying Start 97 m.p.h. Standing Start 55·58 m.p.h.

Braking Figures On ASPHALT Surface, from 30 m.p.h. :—

Both Brakes 29 ft. Front Brake 39 ft. Rear Brake 59 ft.

Fuel Consumption :—

30 m.p.h. — 84 m.p.g. 40 m.p.h. — m.p.g. 50 m.p.h. — 58 m.p.g.

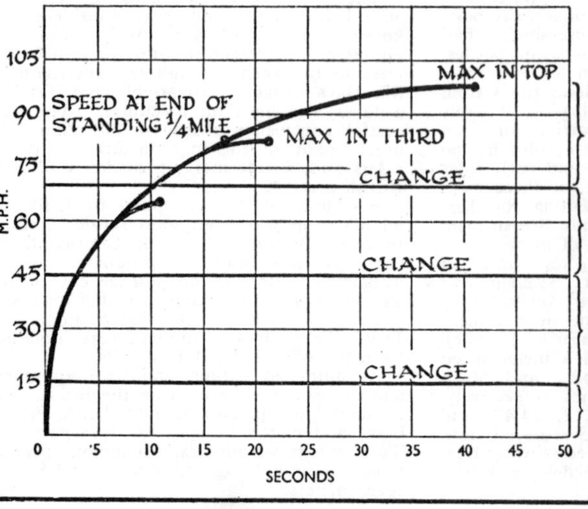

(Above) In the cowled headlamp is neatly fitted a 120 m.p.h. speedometer, the ammeter and the lighting switch.

(Right) The sturdy engine drives the gearbox through a chain enclosed in a massive cast alloy case. Note the method of cradling the forward-mounted dynamo.

"On any type of road surface, the handling and steering were excellent . . . on all main roads the suspension, aided by the comfortable dual seat, gave tireless riding."

ON an " m.p.h. per pound " basis, the B.S.A. " Golden Flash " must be one of the least expensive high-performance projects offered to the buying public in post-war years. In fact, every mile indicated on the speedometer at the machine's maximum speed, costs approximately forty-two shillings and sixpence: a standing " quarter-mile " in 16½ sec. is thrown in for good measure.

Such performance does give the fast-moving, long-distance rider an opportunity to cover daily mileages that are likely to remain proud boasts throughout his lifetime, and it is to this type of rider that the " Golden Flash " is most likely to appeal, for an outstanding feature of the machine is its ability to cruise at a speed dictated by traffic conditions rather than by the capability of the engine. In spite of this characteristic, the " bottom end " performance has not suffered and there is no low speed temperament to make traffic negotiation a niggling business of clutch slipping and throttle blipping.

Several efforts were made to get rid of a tendency to spit back through the carburetter when the throttle was opened quickly with the engine ticking over. This apparent weakness did not show at any other stage, and past experience has revealed that this slight fault can be cured by attention to the throttle slide. Starting was always effortless and the carburation was clean from low speed to maximum throttle. At the end of the test, the near-side exhaust pipe had blued slightly at the port, but this minor tendency toward induction bias had no apparent effect on the unit.

Comfortable Riding

Both the handlebars and the footrests are located well forward and this produced a straight-armed position well suited to " leaning on the breeze." Although mounted forwardly, the handlebars are not low and did not induce tired wrists when riding in thick traffic. All controls, both for foot and hand, are adjustable and a satisfactory stance can be quickly arranged. An adjustable stop is now fitted to the brake pedal which can be set comfortably below the ball of the left foot. Both footrests are set on tapers and the gear-change pedal is mounted on a splined spindle.

All hand controls were pleasantly smooth in operation and this, particularly where the clutch was concerned, assisted toward clean and noiseless gearchanges. Some pause was necessary when changing from second to third gear, but on this occasion only was any unusual delicacy needed. Changes were quite positive and could be made as fast as the pedal could be moved. First gear was selected from neutral without sign of clutch drag and no difficulty was experienced when finding neutral at traffic lights.

No doubt the high degree of acceleration was due as much to well-selected gear ratios as to the excellent power output of the engine. Power output of substantial proportions is, however, necessary to maintain acceleration at above 70 m.p.h. and the manner in which the speedometer needle would continue moving beyond the 70 m.p.h. figures on the dial was most exhilarating. In this country, at any rate, the cruising speed of this machine is hard to define: not so difficult to ascertain was the minimum top gear speed, which could be assessed at 25 m.p.h. Below this speed, third gear was advisable if roughness in the transmission was to be avoided. At any speed, pinking, with the better quality fuels now available, could only be induced by brutal use of the throttle.

On any type of road surface the handling and steering were excellent. The hydraulically-controlled telescopic front forks— now fitted with two-way damping—provided 6 inches of well-controlled movement. This softness of the front suspension tended to accentuate the firmness of the plunger units fitted to the rear wheel, particularly on bad surfaces, but on all main roads the springing, aided by the comfortable dual-seat, gave tireless riding.

Silent Power

There was little evidence of the engine when it was at work. In every department—pistons, valve gear and crankcase—nothing could be heard of the unit when the machine was under way and little indeed when the machine was stationary. The subdued exhaust note was undoubtedly assisted by a high top-gear ratio (4.4 to 1), which ensured that no offence was given. Some slight noise emanated from the intermediate ratios of the gearbox, but against the overall excellence, it was little to complain of.

Both brakes were well up to their job and would stop the machine from high speed in a most reassuring fashion. During the unusually extended test, and in spite of very thorough use, the front brake needed adjusting twice only and the rear brake not at all. Some squeal from the front drum was experienced in the early stages, but this disappeared as the unit bedded down. Those unused to a unit of 8 in. diameter might consider the application to be fierce, but on closer acquaintance and using two fingers on the lever only, such criticism would undoubtedly disappear.

No definable vibration period existed throughout the engine speed range until the unit was working at maximum throttle opening in the intermediate ratios.

Ease of Adjustment

Several routine adjustments were carried out prior to the maximum-speed tests. These involved a check on tappet adjustment, magneto points and, on one occasion, the removal of dirt from the main jet. It is advisable to remove the 4¼-gallon tank to adjust the tappets, and this can be done by removing two bolts. At this stage, a recent addition to the tank-attachment lug at the rear was noticed; the bolt now passes through rubber bushes held in lugs welded to the tank. The work on both carburetter and magneto was easily and quickly done.

Several troubles were experienced with the electrical equipment, all of them subsequent to the maximum speed runs. A considerable quantity of electrolyte escaped from the battery and, leaking over both carrier and primary chaincase, spoilt the appearance of the machine. Inevitably, the wiring faults were discovered late at night. The first consisted of a broken wire close to the battery, which was easily found. The cables that came away from the switch terminal posts were not so easily discovered. These faults did, however, give the tester an opportunity to discover the accessibility of the switch gear and ammeter in the nacelle; this is revealed by removing the two head lamp bolts and lowering the lamp. There is undoubtedly more room than would be available if the units were mounted inside the head lamp.

Two minor criticisms can be levelled at the machine itself. The first concerns the limited amount of " free space " in the oil tank. If several miles are covered at high speed, frothing oil tends to over-lubricate the rear chain which, in turn, flings a film of oil over the rear of the machine. This spoils an otherwise clean unit on which the only small leaks were at the filler caps of both oil tank and primary chaincase. The second point concerns the rubber cover to the gear-change pedal; in the duration of the test, in which 1,500 miles were covered, the rubber had worn sufficiently to show the metal of the lever, which finally chafed the toes of shoes and waders.

Small enough criticisms, both—and minor complaints when the general excellence of this good-looking machine is assessed as a whole.

646 c.c. Golden

A Flexible, Economical, Comfortable and Easily Managed

BY introducing, in 1950, the 646 c.c. Golden Flash model, B.S.A.s bridged the performance gap between the many popular five-hundreds and the specialized 1,000 c.c. machines. The choice of a vertical twin-cylinder layout for the new engine was popular, for vertical twins had gained wide approval among the riders of contemporary five-hundreds. In the four years which have passed since its introduction, the Golden Flash has amassed an enviable following among both soloists and sidecar drivers.

Little noticeable change in the design was made until last autumn, when the finning of the cylinder and cylinder head was considerably increased in depth. This markedly enhanced the appearance of the engine besides providing improved heat dissipation. For 1954, however, the Golden Flash became available, for solo use only, with the latest all-welded, duplex-cradle frame employing pivoted-fork rear springing with three-position adjustment for load. The merits of this frame layout had been amply demonstrated in competitions. As an alternative, however, the Golden Flash is still marketed, for solo and sidecar work, with the earlier-type frame incorporating plunger rear springing.

More Suitable Gear Ratios

Use of the pivoted-fork frame on the six-fifty twin has entailed a departure from the semi-unit construction of engine and gear box which was formerly a feature of the model. Advantage has been taken of the movable engine- and clutch-sprocket centres afforded by the separation of engine and gear box to effect a slight reduction in overall gearing. The new ratios are a trifle better suited to the engine's performance characteristics. Another corollary of the change of frame is that the footrests are farther rearward relative to the seat. The effect is to provide a riding position which, for a person of medium stature, is more conducive to reducing fatigue at sustained high cruising speeds, while sacrificing nothing in comfort at town speeds. The footrests and both control pedals are adjustable for height.

In its new guise, the Golden Flash must enhance the already high reputation which its precursor has built up. It is a machine of exemplary manners and versatile performance—comfortable, quiet and safe to ride. In spite of its thrilling road potential, the B.S.A. was remarkably economical on petrol. Moreover, the engine was outstanding for the wide speed range over which it produced high torque. In practice, this meant that whether the machine was travelling uphill or down, and irrespective of which gear was engaged, opening of the throttle was invariably accompanied by a smooth and lusty surge of pulling power, provided only that the engine r.p.m. were above the rate at which transmission snatch was perceptible. This engine speed, equivalent to 20 m.p.h. in top gear, was adequately low for all practical purposes; above it, the transmission was commendably sweet.

Smooth Power Delivery

In city traffic the Golden Flash proved tractable and easy to handle. All controls, both hand and foot, could be set for convenient use and all were smooth and light to operate. A rider with comparatively short legs experienced no difficulty in placing his feet on the ground at traffic halts. Once on the move, the machine was not noticeably heavier to handle than the average five-hundred; a generous steering lock aided manœuvrability. Added to those traits, the smooth nature of the power delivery made the Golden Flash a pleasure to ride at town speeds.

On the open road the performance available was most exhilarating. Because of the engine's excellent torque characteristics, surging acceleration could be effected either in top gear or by making use of the indirect ratios, according to the whim of the rider. In the higher speed ranges a tremor was perceptible through the handlebar, particularly between 65 and 75 m.p.h. in top gear. However, the vibration was not troublesome, and above and below the speed range mentioned the engine was considered to be smooth by contemporary standards. Power reserve was such as to minimize the effects of headwinds and adverse gradients; only a slight increase in throttle opening was required to compensate for such conditions.

However hard the Golden Flash was ridden, its exhaust note never gave cause for criticism. At low and moderate speeds it was a subdued burble; at the highest cruising speeds, or during hard acceleration, it became a pleasant hum. Open-road cruising at an indicated speed of 80-85 m.p.h. was not only possible but was perfectly comfortable and wholly delightful.

The Golden Flash is well proportioned. The valanced mudguards are noticeably effective

Flash B.S.A.

Touring Mount Capable of Very High Speeds

Notwithstanding many miles of such hard riding, the engine remained completely oiltight. Some seepage occurred from the oil-tank filler cap, however, and a slight smear of oil appeared on the gear box and blew back on to the silencer. The exhaust pipes blued for the first few inches of their length.

The engine's stimulating performance was not achieved at the expense of economy. The petrol-consumption figures listed in the information panel speak for themselves. The figures were obtained under standard test conditions and were confirmed by rough checks carried out over large mileages. On one occasion the B.S.A. was ridden from Liverpool to London, via Manchester, with a slightly favourable wind. A good deal of traffic was encountered and, on the open stretches of A6, speeds up to an indicated 85-90 m.p.h. were used where possible. The mileage was brought up to 225 by subsequent riding in London traffic. No more than 3¾ gallons of petrol were consumed in that mileage—an average of 60 m.p.g. The speedometer, checked by stop-watch over a measured distance, read fast by approximately 2 m.p.h. at 30 m.p.h. and by 3 m.p.h. at 40 m.p.h. From 50 m.p.h. to 100 m.p.h., the error was roughly constant at 5 m.p.h. fast.

Starting the engine was perfectly simple at all times. For a cold start it was necessary to close the air lever and flood the carburettor moderately, when a first-kick start could practically be guaranteed. In spite of good engine compression, the physical effort required on the kick-starter was not great, thanks to favourable gearing. With the engine warm, starting could be achieved without closing the air lever or flooding the carburettor. Once the engine was warm it would idle quite reliably, though slightly irregularly, when the throttle was closed. Mechanical quietness was good; only a slight clack from the timing gear was audible.

No doubt a contributory factor to the engine's outstand-

The rear wheel is readily detachable after unscrewing the spindle. A C-spanner is provided to adjust the rear shock absorbers

ing economy was that carburation was a shade lean at small throttle openings. As a result, it was necessary to leave the air lever partially closed for about 1½ miles after starting off from cold if the engine was to respond without hesitation to snap throttle openings.

There are those who criticize modern machines as being overgeared because peak-power r.p.m. cannot normally be achieved in top gear. Such criticism does not apply to the Golden Flash. On a top-gear ratio of 4.57 to 1, the engine's peak r.p.m. of 5,750 represents a road speed of 98 m.p.h. That figure was exceeded down wind and might have been equalled in both directions under windless conditions. The other three ratios are equally well chosen.

Engagement of bottom gear with the engine idling was practically noiseless, and neutral could be selected easily from either first or second gears. Upward gear changes, given a normal-pace movement of the pedal, were of the knife-into-butter variety. Rapid pedal movement produced a slight click of meshing dogs when changing from second

---

Information Panel—646 c.c. Golden Flash B.S.A.

SPECIFICATION

ENGINE : 646 c.c. (70 x 84 mm) o.h.v. vertical twin. Fully enclosed valve gear operated from a single camshaft. Light-alloy connecting rods ; plain-bearing big ends. Roller main bearing on drive side : plain bearing on timing side. Compression ratio, 6.5 to 1. Dry-sump lubrication ; oil-tank capacity, 5¼ pints.

CARBURETTOR : Amal with twistgrip throttle control ; air-slide operated by handlebar lever. Vokes air filter.

IGNITION and LIGHTING : Lucas magneto with auto-advance. Separate 60-watt Lucas dynamo. 7in-diameter headlamp with sealed-beam light unit.

TRANSMISSION : B.S.A. four-speed gear box with positive-stop foot control. Bottom, 11.67 to 1. Second, 7.95 to 1. Third, 5.47 to 1. Top, 4.52 to 1. Multi-plate clutch with fabric inserts. Primary chain, ½ x 0.305in, in oil-bath case. Rear chain, ⅝ x ⅜in, with guard over top run. Engine r.p.m. at 30 m.p.h. in top gear, 1,800.

FUEL CAPACITY : 4¼ gallons.

TYRES : Dunlop Universal. Front, 3.25 x 19in. Rear, 3.50 x 19in.

BRAKES : 7in-diameter rear ; 8in-diameter front. Finger adjusters.

SUSPENSION : B.S.A. telescopic front fork with hydraulic damping. Pivoted-fork rear springing employing coil springs and hydraulic damping ; three-position adjustment for load.

WHEELBASE : 56½in unladen. Ground clearance, 5in unladen.

SEAT : B.S.A. dual-seat. Unladen height, 31in.

WEIGHT : 443 lb fully equipped, with full oil tank and one gallon of petrol.

PRICE : £186. With purchase tax (in Great Britain only), £223 4s. Extras : prop stand, 15s. (p.t., 3s.) ; pillion footrests, 10s. (p.t., 2s.).

ROAD TAX : £3 15s a year ; £1 0s 8d a quarter.

MAKERS : B.S.A. Motor Cycles, Ltd., Small Heath, Birmingham, 11.

DESCRIPTION : *The Motor Cycle,* 22 October 1953.

PERFORMANCE DATA

MEAN MAXIMUM SPEED : Bottom : *43 m.p.h.
Second : *62 m.p.h.
Third : *90 m.p.h.
Top : 95 m.p.h.
* Valve float occurring.

HIGHEST ONE-WAY SPEED : 100 m.p.h. (Conditions : strong tail wind ; rider wearing two-piece suit and overboots).

MEAN ACCELERATION :

	10-30 m.p.h.	20-40 m.p.h.	30-50 m.p.h.
Bottom	.3 secs	2.8 secs	—
Second	4 secs	3.6 secs	3.6 secs
Third	—	5.6 secs	5.4 secs
Top	—	7.4 secs	7 secs

Mean speed at end of quarter-mile from rest : 80 m.p.h.
Mean time to cover standing quarter-mile : 16 secs.

PETROL CONSUMPTION : At 30 m.p.h., 100 m.p.g. At 40 m.p.h., 88 m.p.g. At 50 m.p.h., 70 m.p.g. At 60 m.p.h., 60 m.p.g.

BRAKING : From 30 m.p.h. to rest, 32ft (surface, dry tarmac).

TURNING CIRCLE : 13ft.

MINIMUM NON-SNATCH SPEED : 20 m.p.h. in top gear.

WEIGHT PER C.C. : 0.68 lb.

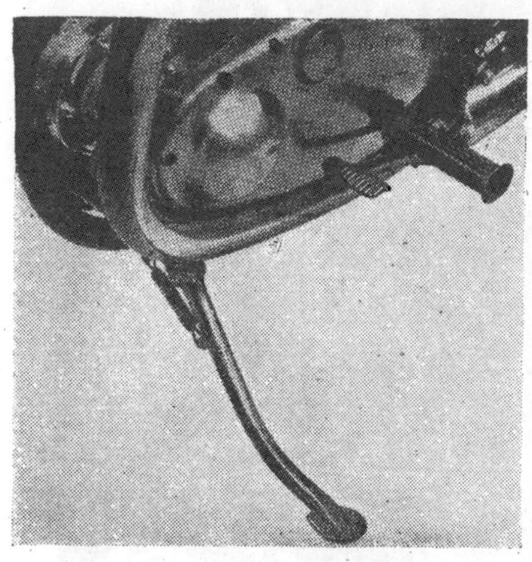

Deep cylinder and cylinder-head finning is employed

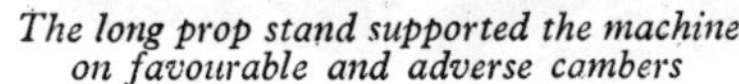

The long prop stand supported the machine on favourable and adverse cambers

Road Test—Golden Flash B.S.A.

to third. It was a simple matter to execute clean and rapid downward changes. The clutch was light to operate, and smooth yet positive in its take-up of the drive.

A criticism concerns the rear chain. No provision is made for its lubrication; consequently it ran dry and required frequent adjustment.

Front- and rear-wheel suspensions are extremely efficient, both as regards their effect on riding comfort and on road holding. The suspension units are sensitive to minor road irregularities and absorb major shocks in exemplary fashion. An extremely comfortable ride under all road conditions resulted. For solo riding, the softest of the three settings of the Girling rear-suspension units was employed by an 11-stone rider. When a pillion passenger was carried, the hardest setting gave excellent compensation for the added weight. The intermediate position is suitable for a heavy solo rider, and it was at times employed by a lighter rider to obviate fouling of the ground by the prop stand when the machine was well banked over to the left.

All three stands—front, centre and prop—are accessible and efficient in use. It was found imperative to turn off the petrol taps when the machine was supported on the prop stand; otherwise, carburettor flooding resulted owing to the relative dispositions of float chamber and mixing chamber.

The 32ft stopping distance given in the panel does not do full justice to the brakes. Both were reasonably light to operate and extremely powerful. Applied together, even from 100 m.p.h., they pinned the machine down firmly and without the slightest hesitation. At first, the front brake emitted a loud and annoying squeal whenever it was used. The defect was cured by dismantling and cleaning the brake and, at the same time, chamfering the ends of the linings.

A shade heavy at ultra-low speeds, the steering was really first class and rock steady; it responded to the slightest banking of the machine. The steering damper was treated purely as an ornament.

Before the headlamp beam could be correctly elevated, it was necessary to remove the rubber sealing strip from the front edge of the headlamp cowl. When correctly set, the main beam permitted safe cruising speeds in the 70s to be maintained on unlit main roads.

Of average motor-cycle quality, the tool-kit included several special tools for specific purposes, and was comprehensive except that none of the spanners was suitable for the rear-wheel spindle nut or for the chain-adjuster lock nuts. In filthy weather, the effectiveness of the mudguarding was appreciated.

The black and chromium finish of the Golden Flash is good and its appearance is distinctly impressive. It is a machine of which any owner may be justly proud.

Left : the very potent, 8in-diameter front brake with knurled finger adjusters.   Above : removal of a rubber grommet exposes the solitary tank-retaining bolt

FRED RIST'S 5,000 MILE MODEL

DENNIS HARDWICKE Enjoys an Autumn Afternoon on a Maudes Trophy-winning B.S.A. "Star Twin."

A BEAUTIFUL afternoon, coming as it did in the middle of October, made a fitting close to the "conker" season, and I recalled a paragraph concerning the winner of the Schoolboys' Conker Marathon. He, the proud possessor of a well-pickled, case-hardened piece of horse chestnut fruit, had remained undefeated, leaving a trail littered with sorry segments of broken challengers that had queued with their owners, 1,760 strong, to battle with him. His, therefore, was a "1760-er."

I was thinking of this as I went my way through Midland lanes on Fred Rist's I.S.D.T.-Maudes Trophy-winning B.S.A., which could well be described as a "5000-er" in view of the 5,000 hard miles to which it was put, in company with two of its kind, during the recent test.

Although, in truth, Fred's "Star Twin" was not battered—except for a dent or two in exhaust pipes and silencers—and there certainly weren't any broken segments, it was quite obvious that every one of those 5,000 miles registered on the speedometer had been in itself an individual battle. Dust and mud had caked on wheel rims, frame tubes and on the engine—and quite a cosmopolitan collection of soils it was, England, Holland, Belgium, France, Switzerland, Austria, Germany and Scandinavia had all contributed.

"International" Souvenirs

In spite of this "agricultural" exterior, it was quickly apparent that the internals were quite unaffected. The machine started remarkably easily and ticked over rather lumpily—until I remembered that a manual ignition control was provided. On half-retard the engine beat settled down smoothly and evenly.

Sidecar gear ratios were fitted to help the riders on the "rough stuff" encountered during the International Six Days Trial and they improved the docility of a machine that in standard form sometimes needs humouring with gearbox and ignition control if pinking is to be avoided entirely.

One non-standard rattle was traced to the nail catcher on the front tyre. At certain road speeds it induced a sympathetic vibration in the front mudguard. Except for this the machine was in as good a condition mechanically as it was on the day that A.-C.U. observer John McNulty chose it from the production line.

This is the second occasion on which I have ridden a machine that has been "tailored" by Fred Rist. He employs a "straight-arm" riding stance and his handlebars are set so that both arms are almost fully extended from wrist to shoulder. It wasn't until well out into the country that I noticed this; earlier I had been taking stock of brakes and controls.

Hardwicke goes lane-storming on the Fred Rist-Maudes Trophy I.S.D.T. as-you-can-buy "Star Twin" B.S.A.

A certain amount of slackness had developed in the hand levers, but otherwise things were working beautifully. The clutch operated smoothly and showed no sign of slip. The 8-in. front brake had lost none of its power and had obviously bedded down admirably. Light foot pressure indicated that a slight ovality existed in the rear drum, but it was insufficient to lock the wheel with normal pressures.

The third-gear ratio gave sparkling acceleration; over 70 m.p.h. could be obtained without difficulty, and in a very brief space of time. Sitting up and without effort, the speedometer needle could be pushed round to 80 m.p.h. as soon as top was engaged.

Satisfied that the engine and gearbox showed no more sign of their strenuous journey than would follow a mileage of this description accumulated by normal day-to-day riding, a diversionary trip was made across country. Of this there is little to say except that it was most enjoyable. A grey squirrel sitting in the middle of the road nearly departed this life when I rounded a sharp bend in a country lane, but his initial acceleration was, fortunately for him, slightly better than that of the "Star Twin."

Stopping for tea, I watched the sun change colour and the wisps of mist form up in the hollows; it would be foggy later, no doubt, and it was time to return to the big city. Back at the factory I handed the machine into the experimental shop and wondered how long it would be before the coagulated dust and mud was removed. Not for some time, I should think for, without the travel stains and the green plaque over the headlamp, you wouldn't know that the machine had been farther than Brighton!

THE NORTH-WESTERN SCRAMBLE CHAMPIONSHIP
Reg Pilling Wins for the Second Year in Succession.

A HIGH wind and persistent rain made the going very heavy at Pinfold Farm, Nangreaves, near Bury, last Sunday when the Bury and D. M.C. organized the North-Western Centre Championship Scramble on behalf of the A.-C.U. After a very exciting race, when the issue was not certain until the flag actually fell at the finish, R. K. Pilling, riding his 498 c.c. A.J.S., emerged as the 1952 champion, repeating his success of 12 months ago.

Two preliminary events preceded the championship proper and these were won by E. Myers (490 Norton) and Ted Ogden (348 B.S.A.).

At 4.0 p.m. 36 riders faced the starter for the big race and as the flag dropped J. D. Hughes (498 Triumph), Ted Ogden and F. Bentham (500 Ariel) headed the pack. Reg Pilling had a bad start and was almost last. At the end of the first circuit it was still Hughes and Ogden. Pilling was now in fifth place, but Bentham must have fallen somewhere, for he came round in 11th position. Next time round, Ogden passed Hughes, E. Myers (490 Norton) was third and Pilling fourth. Then Myers passed Hughes and led the latter for two laps, but at half distance Myers had dropped back to fourth place, Pilling had moved up to second position, making the order Ogden, Pilling, Hughes and Myers with Bentham no better than seventh. On the penultimate circuit the leaders could all have been covered by 25 yards, but at the finish Pilling was out on his own. Hughes led Ogden home and Myers filled the fourth berth. A rather tame finish after a grand race.

A six-lap non-winners race rounded off the proceedings, providing an easy win for Yorkshireman, Bentham.

Provisional Results

Unlimited c.c. machines (six laps): 1, E. Myers (490 Norton); **2,** E. Ogden (348 B.S.A.); **3,** D. Eaven (350 Royal Enfield). **Winner's time,** 8 mins. 48 secs.

Unlimited c.c. machines (six laps): 1, E. Ogden (348 B.S.A.); **2,** J. D. Hughes (498 Triumph); **3,** E. Myers (490 Norton). **Winner's time,** 9 mins. 52.2 secs.

Championship Race. The Lord Nelson Cup (ten laps): 1, R. K. Pilling (498 A.J.S.); **2,** J. D. Hughes (498 Triumph); **3,** E. Ogden (348 B.S.A.). **Winner's time,** 15 mins. 21.2 secs.

Previous non-winners race (six laps): 1, F. Bentham (500 Ariel); **2,** E. Pearson (499 B.S.A.); **3,** J. K. Hirst (499 B.S.A.). **Winner's time,** 9 mins. 29.2 secs.

The 497 c.c. o.h.v. MODEL A7 TWIN B.S.A.

A High-performance, Attractively-priced Twin, with De Luxe Specification and Suitable for Solo or Sidecar Duty

At £216 12s 0d. including P.T., tested as shown, the A7 B.S.A. represents one of the cheapest 500 c.c. twins on the British market. A criterion of its performance appears below.

CAPABLE of pushing the speedometer needle round to nearly 85 m.p.h.; of cruising comfortably in the region of 70 m.p.h., so long as road conditions permit. and, in give-and-take circumstances, of taking the rider nearly 70 miles for the price of a gallon of petrol, the 497 c.c. A7 B.S.A. commands high respect. It was one of the several vertical twins tested early in the post-war period, from which time the design has remained largely unaltered, although the machine in general has been progressively embellished season by season with various refinements. This development process has inevitably resulted in an increase in weight, a disadvantage offset by enhanced rider comfort and better road-holding owing to the swinging-fork, Girling-damped, rear frame structure, which is now an optional extra.

Initial impression was of the readiness, almost the eagerness, of the engine to start at first pressure on the kickstarter crank; the tick-over was good, subject to careful adjustment of the air control. Hasty pulling back of the lever revealed what appeared

TESTER'S ROAD REPORT

Maximum Speeds in :—

			Time from Standing Start.
Top Gear (Ratio 5·28 to 1)	84·5 m.p.h.	= 5700 r.p.m.	33/5 secs.
Third Gear (Ratio 6·38 to 1)	77·5 m.p.h.	= 6300 r.p.m.	22 secs.
Second Gear (Ratio 9·0 to 1)	60 m.p.h.	= 7000 r.p.m.	12 secs.

Speeds over measured Quarter Mile :—

Flying Start 82 m.p.h.   Standing Start 52·93 m.p.h.

Braking Figures On DRY CONCRETE Surface, from 30 m.p.h. :—

Both Brakes 30 ft.   Front Brake 40 ft.   Rear Brake 58 ft.

Fuel Consumption :—

30 m.p.h. 90 m.p.g.   40 m.p.h. 72 m.p.g.   50 m.p.h. 56 m.p.g.

(Above) Accessibility is an attractive feature. This view shows the large primary chain oil-bath filler, the valve tappet covers, contact-breaker, etc., and, safely out of sight in the toolbox, is the C.V.C. unit.

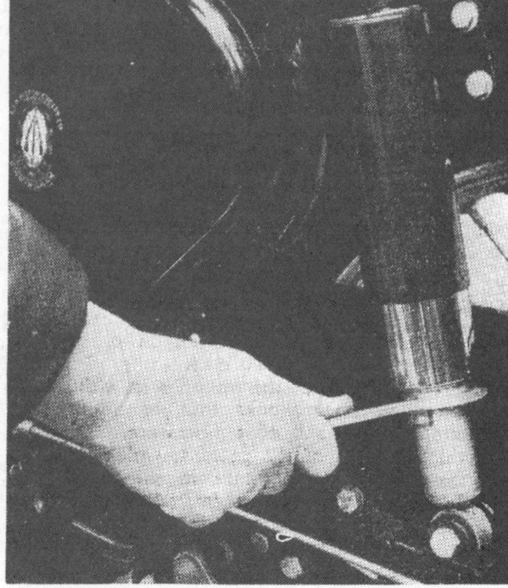

(Right) A special spanner in the tool-kit enables the adjustment of the rear suspension to be set to personal requirements, easily and quickly giving adequate damping to suit the load carried.

Personal comfort was a notable feature of the A7 enabling considerable mileages to be covered fast without fatigue and, consequently, in safety.

to be a weak spot at the cut-away phase when the engine was cold and it paid to keep the carburetter almost fully choked for the first mile or so. This point is mentioned because it is a feature of careful B.S.A. mixture control.

Once normal running temperature had been attained, the r.p.m. rate could be raised swiftly, or the throttle snapped shut, as and when traffic conditions called for swift acceleration or slowing down, and, throughout the speed range, the power output was exceedingly smooth and the machine a delight to handle. A slight tremor felt through the foot-rests when the engine was pulling really hard in top gear at about 38-40 m.p.h. must be recorded, but with the

reservation that the rider, of course, was diligently seeking such things. It was not in any way a pronounced vibration period.

Most pleasing was the speed pick-up from a 20 m.p.h. top-gear town crawl, and the absence of snatch, or back-lash from the chains. By reason of the now separate, instead of bolted-up-to-the-engine, gearbox, centres between the mainshaft of the box and the swinging-fork pivot, are reasonably close and the rear chain tension almost constant, this factor contributing further to the positive, snatch-free transmission characteristics. The primary and rear chains, although new, required no adjustment during the 500-mile test distance.

In essentials, the 1954 A7 gearbox is similar to that of its semi-unit type predecessor, save that since 1947 several improvements in foot-change and gear-selector mechanism have been effected. These modifications have made a good gearbox even better. Light clutch action and excellent, non-fade brakes give the rider an easy time from the point of view of personal energy and mental effort expended in driving the machine along the road.

The ratios of the swinging-fork model are slightly lower than those in the standard A7 specification, and they proved very suitable for the 27 b.h.p. power output available from the 1954 unit, with its compression ratio of 6.6 : 1, and the premium grade fuel used throughout the test. The rider did not try—as used to be the vogue—to make the engine pink. The practice seems pointless when, under conditions of normally hard usage, there is no sign of detonation.

Close to the top gear of 5.28, the 6.38 third ratio provided a most useful range and, although the graph shows an arbitrary 70 m.p.h. gear-change point, it is possible and, indeed, reasonable, in given circumstances, to hold on to third up to the mid-70s. This gear was particularly useful on long, main-road up-grades where one may be baulked by slower traffic and may wish to make a quick recovery afterwards.

During cross-country journeys through winding lanes, the occasional use of this "lower top" helped to maintain over-all

high averages and, thanks to the engine's flexibility, the 6.2 ratio was useful well below the 53 m.p.h. graphed as the average change point for second to third gears.

The steering of the A7 was good and the general behaviour of the machine inspired confidence. Main-road cornering could be carried out with hair-line precision and the model felt equally stable irrespective of wet or dry conditions. At one time, Birmingham's cobbled Bradford Street used to be regularly used by motorcycle testers. The writer feels that this test-piece is now fairly out-moded by Leopold Street, in the same city, for here is a quarter-mile stretch which contains cobbles, wood blocks and the now comparatively rare hazard of tram lines. The B.S.A. gave no cause for panic during its almost daily two-way journey throughout this thoroughfare.

It is, perhaps, a tribute to the good working of the well-designed and damped rear suspension that the B.S.A. dual seat is only of moderate resilience. While the seat, in itself, did not cause discomfort, its general design had a certain spartan character. A point noted by the tester was the standard angle of the seat, which, suiting the attractive lines of the machine, tends, nevertheless, to tip the rider towards the nose. This tendency may be accentuated by the forward position of the handlebars and the combined result, for an average-to-small stature man is that he is riding with his arms a little too outstretched for comfort on a long run.

For one-man solo work the dampers were left at the "soft" setting. Adjusted by means of a special spanner included in the tool-kit, their action can be stiffened, and this was found to be necessary when a pillion passenger was to be carried for any considerable distance. The job is done with the damper units in situ and the work takes no more than a few moments.

All major components, except the battery, which is housed beneath the seat, are accessible for maintenance. Wheel detachability, front and rear, is excellent, and for attention to the rocker box or cylinder head, the petrol tank, anchored centrally, can be removed in less than a minute. The very full range of kit, including a valve-grinding tool and template guide to assist in refitting the push-rods after an overhaul, is adequate for all running adjustments and general maintenance.

Listed as an extra at 18s., including P.T., the prop-stand fitted to the test model received full marks. Pivoting from the front of the lower rail of the duplex frame, the stand swings out and downwards and is held by spring tension in either the folded or operative position. It is a fitment which proved to be a real blessing, particularly during the many town journeys undertaken during the course of the test. In the garage, the model could be pulled on to the substantial, wide-angle, central stand without difficulty. The angled tube, acting as the stay to the deeply valanced rear mudguard, forms an ideally-positioned lifting handle.

All-in-all, high marks go to the latest A7 for its smooth, surging power output and the twin attribute of fine-quality brakes. Praise goes also to the first-class suspension, adequate Lucas lighting, high degree of silence and quality finish of this, the least expensive of the 500 c.c. twin, swinging-fork equipped models now on the home market.

BRIEF SPECIFICATION

Engine: Vertical twin o.h.v., 66 mm. bore by 72.6 mm. stroke=497 c.c.; compression ratio 6.6 : 1; single camshaft operating push-rods through chamber cast in cylinder and head blocks; camshaft incorporates timed mechanical breather. Forged steel crankshaft with central flywheel; induction-hardened journals; plain big-end bearings with indium-flash lead-bronze liners; plain bearing on timing side mainshaft and ball bearing on drive side. Gear-driven camshaft and Lucas K2F magneto with automatic advance. Dry sump lubrication; pressure feed to timing-side main bearings and big-ends; with feed to overhead rocker spindles. Amal carburetter type 276EU/IDB, with 140 jet, 6/4 slide and built-in air cleaner forming a unit with oil tank. High-efficiency absorption-type tubular silencers.

Transmission: Separate, four-speed, B.S.A. gearbox with positive-stop foot-change; ratios (solo) 5.28, 6.38, 9.0 and 13.6 : 1; ½-in. by .305 in. endless primary chain in oilbath case. Six-plate clutch with Ferodo inserts; rear chain ⅝-in. by ⅜-in. with deep top- and bottom-run chain guards.

Frame: Duplex-type, steel, all-welded, loop frame with swinging-fork rear structure, styled to accommodate flush-fitting pannier oil tank and tool container.

Ignition and Lighting: Gear-driven K2F Lucas magneto with automatic ignition advance; separate Lucas 6-volt dynamo lighting with voltage control; 7½-in. headlamp and 12 amp. hr. battery.

Suspension: Telescopic front forks and swinging-fork rear frame; hydraulic damping with quick adjustability for load on rear suspension.

Wheels and Tyres: Quickly detachable and interchangeable; patented hub-flange designed to accommodate straight spokes; fitted with WM2-19 front rim accommodating 3.25-in. by 19-in. Dunlop tyres; rear rim WM2-19 fitted with 3.50-in. by 19-in. tyre.

Brakes: 8-in. by 1⅜-in. front brake; 7-in. by 1⅝-in. rear brake with finger adjustment.

Equipment: 120-mile Smiths trip speedometer; high-frequency electric horn; metal toolbox; rubber kneegrips; brazed-on prop stand lugs.

Finish: Dark maroon enamel with bright parts chromium plated; maroon petrol tank with chrome panels and B.S.A. motif.

Tank: Welded steel petrol tank of 4-gal. capacity; oil tank 5½ pt. capacity.

Dimensions: Wheelbase 54¾-in.; ground clearance, 4½-in.; saddle height 30 in.; overall width, 28 in.; overall length, 84 in.; handlebar width 28⅛ in.; weight 416 lb.

Price: Basic Price, £180 10s., plus P.T. £36 2s.=total £216 12s.

Annual Tax: £3 15s. Quarterly, £1 0s. 8d.

Makers: B.S.A. Motor Cycles, Ltd., Small Heath, Birmingham, 11.

---

497 c.c. B.S.A. A7 Twin

A Smart, Tractable Touring Mount Capable of High-speed Cruising with Marked Comfort for Two People

MANY changes have been made in the specification of the B.S.A. A7 twin during the 10 years which have elapsed since the model made its début. The modifications have kept it abreast of modern trends in design but have not altered its basic character as an economical and flexible touring five-hundred with a well-blended engine performance. In its latest form the A7 furnishes first-class evidence of what can be achieved in terms of smoothness, tractability and quietness with a parallel twin when super-sports acceleration is not demanded. Yet it should not be concluded that the A7 is a sluggard, for its remarkable 90 m.p.h. maximum speed is more than adequate for normal requirements.

Features of the original B.S.A. parallel-twin were a solid frame, a long-stroke engine with comparatively shallow finning of the cylinders and cylinder heads, and semi-unit construction of power unit and gear box. In course of time rear springing of plunger type superseded the solid frame and was, in turn, replaced by the present pivoted-fork layout. Both engine and gear box have been extensively redesigned and form two separate units to suit the frame layout. Latest finning of the cylinder block and cylinder head is of above-average depth and enhances the appearance of the engine as well as making for more efficient cooling and greater rigidity.

Styling has been carried out on a minor scale as the model has been developed: the pannier-type oil tank matches the tool box; a cowl enshrouds the headlamp and houses the speedometer, lighting switch and ammeter; both mudguards are valanced and the dual-seat and rear number plate blend with the shape of the rear guard; capacity of the petrol tank has been increased from three to four gallons; the battery is concealed but accessible. For the current year smart, full-width hubs with 1½in wide brakes are standardized, while rear-chain enclosure is optional. The model tested was fitted with a rear chaincase which proved to be a boon.

Perhaps the outstanding and most likeable characteristic of the engine performance is the silky response to throttle opening. No matter how rapidly the twistgrip was rotated the resultant surge of power was always well graduated and progressive; there was never any suggestion of suddenness. As befits a touring five-hundred, top-gear acceleration was gentlemanly without being sluggish, brisk without being tigerish. Transmission was smooth and, except in the upper speed ranges, engine vibration was barely perceptible.

Top gear was used not only when riding at the legal maximum of 30 m.p.h. in built-up areas but also in the normal course of events when accelerating from as low a speed as 25 m.p.h. Pinking was never experienced. Away from speed restrictions, the A7 was equally pleasant to ride whether it was burbling along at 30 m.p.h. in top gear, humming at 45 to 50 m.p.h. on a mere whiff of throttle or proceeding at a purposeful 70 m.p.h. If and when required, a cruising speed of 80 m.p.h. could be sustained indefinitely for the engine was entirely untroubled by hard riding. Normally, however, 70 to 75 m.p.h. was the highest speed used for long periods; from that speed upward, engine vibration could be felt through the petrol tank and handlebar. When checked for accuracy the speedometer was found to read correctly up to 40 m.p.h.; it read fast by 1½ m.p.h. at an indicated 50 m.p.h., by 2 m.p.h. at 60 and 70 and by 3 m.p.h. at 80 and 90.

The exhaust note was reasonably well subdued, as was mechanical noise. A faint whine emanated from the timing gear

The rear wheel is retained by four nuts which can be turned by a box spanner passed through an orifice in the pressed-steel chaincase

Lines of the B.S.A. A7 are well proportioned. Both hubs are of light-alloy full-width design. Front and rear mudguards have deep valances

Left : Removal of two bolts enables the seat to be lifted away, thus giving access to the battery. Right : The voltage-control regulator is flexibly mounted in a separate compartment at the top of the pannier-type tool box

and there was a perceptible hiss from the air filter during acceleration. Engine starting drill was not critical. Provided the carburettor was flooded lightly, the air lever closed and the throttle set a fraction open, one sharp thrust on the kick-starter would bring the engine to life from cold. No pre-liminaries were required for a first-kick start when the engine was warm. Hot or cold, the engine would idle slowly, reliably and unobtrusively when the throttle was closed. But if the engine was allowed to tickover on a closed throttle for about half a minute or more, subsequent pick-up was hesitant as the result of a rich spot just off the pilot jet.

Riders of different stature found the A7's riding position comfortable at low and high speeds. The relative heights of footrests and dual-seat furnished a pleasantly wide knee angle, while the fore-and-aft siting of the footrests gave a slightly forward inclination to the rider's body, thus minimizing the tiring effects of wind pressure at high speeds without throwing too much weight on the wrists at low speeds. Both rider and pillion passenger found the padding of the dual-seat a little too firm on long runs. All controls were well placed for convenient operation save that the reach to the clutch and front-brake levers was too long for some riders' hands.

Both front and rear springing reacted with long, soft movements which took the sting out of all manner of road bumps and gave a comfortable ride. The range of adjustment for load provided on the rear shock absorbers was adequate for all normal passenger carrying. On the test model, the front fork, however, was insufficiently damped and the resultant pitching on bumpy or undulating surfaces tended to spoil the otherwise excellent steering and to render the machine lively when being braked heavily on bumps; in the latter circumstances the fork was prone to bottoming. On road surfaces which did not give rise to pitching the A7 could be heeled through fast or slow bends with zest and confidence. Straight-ahead steering was of the hands-off variety.

The speed of the twin was well matched by the efficiency of its brakes, both of which were smooth and powerful. Applied independently, they could easily be made to evoke squeals of protest from the tyres. When used together the brakes would arrest the model remarkably quickly from any speed of which

Information Panel — 497 c.c. B.S.A. A7 Twin

SPECIFICATION

ENGINE: 497 c.c. (66 x 72.6 mm) overhead-valve vertical twin. Fully enclosed valve gear operated from a single camshaft. Light-alloy connecting rods; plain big-end bearings. Crankshaft supported in roller bearing on drive side and plain bearing on timing side. Compression ratio, 6.6 to 1. Dry-sump lubrication; oil-tank capacity, $5\frac{1}{2}$ pints.

CARBURETTOR: Amal Monobloc with twistgrip throttle control; air-slide operated by handlebar lever. Air filter.

IGNITION and LIGHTING: Lucas magneto with auto-advance. Separate Lucas 60-watt dynamo. Lucas 6-volt, 12-ampere-hour battery. Lucas 7in-diameter headlamp with pre-focus light unit.

TRANSMISSION: B.S.A. four-speed gear box with positive-stop foot control. Gear ratios: bottom, 13.62 to 1; second, 9.28 to 1; third, 6.38 to 1; top, 5.28 to 1. Multi-plate clutch with fabric inserts. Primary chain, $\frac{1}{2}$ x 0.305in in oil-bath case. Rear chain, $\frac{5}{8}$ x $\frac{3}{8}$in enclosed in pressed-steel case. Engine r.p.m. at 30 m.p.h. in top gear, 2,040.

FUEL CAPACITY: 4 gallons.

TYRES: Dunlop: front, 3.25 x 19in with ribbed tread; rear, 3.50 x 19in Universal.

BRAKES: Both 7in diameter x $1\frac{1}{8}$in wide; fulcrum adjusters.

SUSPENSION: B.S.A. telescopic front fork with hydraulic damping. Pivoted-fork rear springing employing coil springs and hydraulic damping; three-position adjustment for load.

WHEELBASE: $56\frac{1}{2}$in unladen. Ground clearance, $5\frac{1}{2}$in unladen.

SEAT: B.S.A. dual-seat Unladen height, 32in.

WEIGHT: 427 lb fully equipped, with full oil tank and approximately one gallon of petrol.

PRICE: £192 10s. With purchase tax (in Great Britain only), £238 14s. Extras: rear chaincase, £2 10s (p.t., 12s); prop stand, 15s (p.t., 3s 8d).

ROAD TAX: £3 15s a year; £1 0s 8d a quarter.

MAKERS: B.S.A. Motor Cycles, Ltd., Small Heath, Birmingham, 11.

DESCRIPTION: *The Motor Cycle*, 13 October 1955.

PERFORMANCE DATA

MEAN MAXIMUM SPEED: Bottom: *38 m.p.h.
Second: *56 m.p.h.
Third: *83 m.p.h.
Top: 90 m.p.h.
*Valve float occuring.

HIGHEST ONE-WAY SPEED: 92 m.p.h. (conditions: light tail wind, rider wearing two-piece plastic suit and overboots).

MEAN ACCELERATION:

	10-30 m.p.h.	20-40 m.p.h.	30-50 m.p.h.
Bottom	3 sec	—	—
Second	4.2 sec	3.7 sec	4.1 sec
Third	—	6.3 sec	6.3 sec
Top	—	8 sec	8.1 sec

Mean speed at end of quarter-mile from rest: 75 m.p.h.
Mean time to cover standing quarter-mile: 17.4 sec.

PETROL CONSUMPTION: At 30 m.p.h., 98 m.p.g. At 40 m.p.h., 86 m.p.g. At 50 m.p.h., 76 m.p.g. At 60 m.p.h., 65 m.p.g.

BRAKING: From 30 m.p.h. to rest, 32ft (surface, dry tarmac)

TURNING CIRCLE: 14ft.

MINIMUM NON-SNATCH SPEED: 17 m.p.h. in top gear.

WEIGHT PER C.C.: 0.86 lb

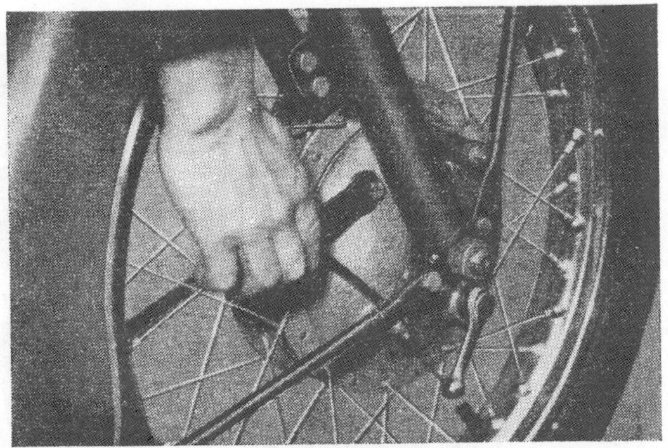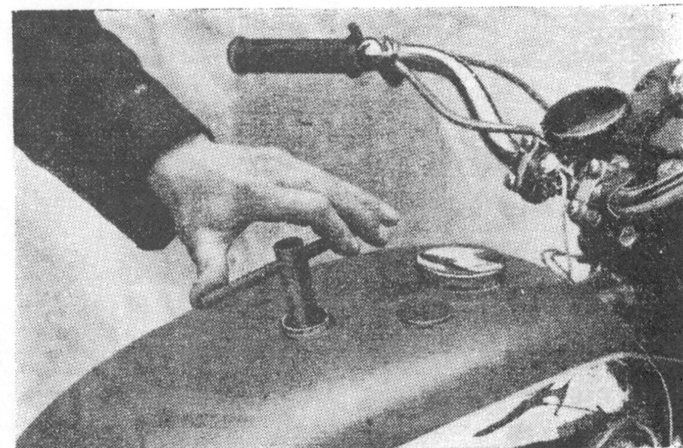

Left : Brake adjustment is effected by means of a self-locking fulcrum pin, not by the cable stop. Right : The single, fuel tank-retaining bolt is concealed by a rubber plug in the tank top. The bolt is reached by a tubular spanner

it was capable. Area of the friction linings is generous and no adjustment was called for during many hundreds of miles of hard riding. Both brakes are cable operated. The cable adjusters provided are intended only for initial setting, normal adjustment for wear being made at the fulcrums.

Originally the gear change was rather stiff though the stiffness eased considerably as the mileage totted up. A leisurely pedal movement was required to ensure noiseless upward changes, especially from second to third where the difference between the ratios is wide. The downward change from third to second was most cleanly effected if the throttle was blipped appreciably. Neutral could be selected without difficulty from bottom or second gears. A slight click of dogs accompanied the engagement of bottom gear from neutral when the engine was idling. Moderately light to operate, the clutch was smooth but firm in its take-up of the drive.

Though no automatic lubrication is provided for the enclosed rear chain, it benefited greatly from the protection. The messiness from oil which usually accumulates on and around the rear wheel was non-existent, while the chain retained its well-cared-for appearance and required no adjustment during a test which would certainly have necessitated resetting of an exposed chain. By contemporary standards the engine, gear box and primary chaincase retained their oil well but the same cannot be said of the oil tank. During a long, fast run seepage from the filler cap resulted in a film of oil forming on the inside of the rider's right leg.

It was necessary to remove the strip of rubber beading from the front edge of the headlamp cowl before the lamp could be swivelled upward far enough to obtain a beam setting suitable for out-of-town riding after dark. When correctly set, the beam permitted speeds of 60 to 70 m.p.h. to be maintained with safety on unlit main roads.

Front and centre stands are standard equipment on the A7; a prop stand is an optional extra and was fitted to the model tested. The prop was accessible to the foot and supported the machine safely on all normal road cambers. Though equally reliable in use, the centre stand required some knack and muscular effort to bring into operation. Incidentally, the foot of the prop stand did not foul the ground readily on left-hand corners provided the rear shock absorbers were correctly adjusted for the load carried.

Of average quality, the toolkit was adequate for routine adjustments. Several features of the design have a particular appeal to riders who conscientiously carry out their own maintenance. For instance, removal of the petrol tank for access to tappet adjustment is simple because the tank is retained by a single bolt (normally hidden by a rubber plug in the tank top); a strap bracing the two halves of the tank must also be removed before the tank can be lifted clear of the machine. Although the battery is concealed beneath the dual-seat, removal of the two seat-securing bolts gives access for topping-up. Rear wheel removal is not hindered by the chaincase: withdrawal of a rubber plug from the case reveals the heads of the four wheel-retaining nuts. The adjusters for the primary and rear chains are easy to reach, as are the contact-breaker points. Incorporated in the fork upper yoke is an anti-theft steering lock.

With its smart maroon and chromium-plated finish, its refined performance and ample speed, the B.S.A. A7 is one of the most attractive of touring five-hundred twins.

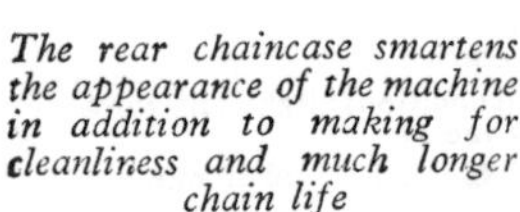

The rear chaincase smartens the appearance of the machine in addition to making for cleanliness and much longer chain life

The "GOLDEN FLASH"
40 CUBIC INCH VERTICAL TWIN

BSA
BIRMINGHAM SMALL ARMS CO. LTD.

BUILT TO HIGHEST QUALITY STANDARDS — FOR HIGH SPEED PERFORMANCE ON THE ROAD

Straddle the BSA "Golden Flash"—feel that soft spring suspension ease down under your weight—kick her over once—hear that powerful twin purr to life—shift into gear, let out that velvety BSA clutch — twist that throttle — and wham! You are off for the thrill of your life.

If you haven't yet ridden the latest BSA "Golden Flash"—you have a treat in store. Don't let another day go by—see your nearest BSA dealer and test ride the world's most modern twin!

40 CU. IN. O.H.V. TWIN, smooth as a kitten with acceleration like a jackrabbit. Down-draft Amal carburetor with air cleaner.

OIL TANK on right exposed to air stream for oil cooling. Tool box identical in shape on left, with battery mounted in between.

SWINGING ARM rear frame adjustable for the ride you want—either soft or firm.
LARGE COMFORTABLE DUAL-SEAT, rear foot-rests, jiffy stand, stop light, 120 m.p.h. speedometer and quick detachable rear wheel — ALL AT NO EXTRA COST. Precision built to highest quality standards and finished in luxurious colors offset by ample chrome plate.

Your BSA is a race-bred motorcycle! At the 1954 Daytona 200-mile National BSA came in 1st, 2nd, 3rd, 4th and 5th, THE FIRST TIME IN HISTORY that any motorcycle accomplished such a record-breaking victory!
BSA also won the 1954 Willow Springs 125-mile National Championship road race, and the 6-mile National at Richmond, Va. this year!

When you ride a BSA
You ride a Winner!

See your BSA Dealer today

Distributed in the East by
BSA INCORPORATED
639 Passaic Ave., Nutley 10, N. J.

Distributed in the West by
HAP ALZINA
3074 Broadway, Oakland, Calif.

October, 1954

BSA WINS
FIRST FIVE PLACES IN 1954 200 MILE DAYTONA NATIONAL

National Champion—Winner!
Bobby Hill on BSA "Shooting Star"
Time— 2 hours 7 minutes 22 seconds

Championship!

Second Place Winner!
Dick Klamfoth on BSA "Shooting Star"
Time— 2 hours 7 minutes 42 seconds

make your next motorcycle a BSA

MORE POWER
MORE SPEED
GREATER DEPENDABILITY
INCREASED SAFETY
BETTER APPEARANCE
PROVEN RELIABILITY

In The East   RICH CHILD CYCLE CO.,
639 Passaic Ave., Nutley 10, N. J.

In The West   HAP ALZINA,
3074 Broadway, Oakland, Calif.

Canadian distributors: Arlington Cycle & Sports Ltd., 1194, University St., Montreal, Que.   British Car Sales, Ltd., Cnr. North Park & Cornwallis Sts., Halifax, Nova Scotia.   Browns Sports & Cycle Co. Ltd., 343, Yonge St., Toronto, Ont.   Fred Deeley Ltd., 606, East Broadway, Vancouver, 10, B.C.   Edwin Murray Ltd., 256, Water Street, St. John's, Newfoundland.   Nicholson Bros., 245, 2nd Avenue North, Saskatoon, Sask.

August, 1954

BSA
Twins for 1954

BSA 650 c.c. O.H.V. "Road Rocket" with Alloy Head

An entirely new model for 1954, the "Road Rocket" embodies all of the proven features of the "Super Flash," but has the new type of swinging arm frame, new gas and oil tanks, separate engine and transmission as well as a polished motor, racing cams, racing carburetor, tachometer, and many more racing refinements.

BSA 500 c.c. O.H.V. "Shooting Star"

Another brand new model to "give you more for '54," The "Shooting Star" is a 500 c.c. vertical twin with light alloy cylinder head, new lightweight frame, and swinging arm rear suspension. With even greater performance than the popular "Star Twin" the "Shooting Star" is designed to go places fast with a minimum of effort.

BSA 650 c.c. O.H.V. "Golden Flash"

New design, new styling, new tanks, swinging arm frame and many other refinements plus the speed and reliability of the previous models go to make the new "Golden Flash" one of the most attractive dollar bargains on the market this year.

1954 B.S.A. vertical twins are all fitted with handsome and comfortable Dual-seats, assuring the greatest riding ease even when riding "two up." Instruments are neatly housed in a streamlined cowling built around the headlight. 1954 models are available in a variety of striking colors, offset with high quality, triple-plated chrome fittings.

"Trade Today for a BSA"

FRANCHISES AVAILABLE TO DEALERS.

In The East   RICH CHILD CYCLE CO.,
639 Passaic Ave., Nutley 10, N. J.

In The West   HAP ALZINA,
3074 Broadway, Oakland, Calif.

January, 1954

BSA Successes at Daytona Beach!

1ST Place Winner of the 50 Mile Race!
Nick Nicholson on BSA "Star Twin" averaged 93.99 mph to set new Daytona Beach speed record!

2ND PLACE WINNER—BOB WINTERS on BSA!

DAYTONA RELIABILITY RUN WINNER — Ralph Davis. Ralph beat a field of seasoned experts to win this annual event on his dependable BSA "Gold Star," losing only 15 points out of a possible 1000.

Visit your local BSA-SUNBEAM dealer today and place your order for the road version of the highly successful Daytona proven BSA

Star Twin

100 MILE RACE WINNERS
Bob Winters on BSA 2nd
Alex Pittson on BSA 3rd
Norm Lyon on BSA 4th
Wayne Adams on BSA 6th
Harold Ball on BSA 8th

200 MILE RACE WINNERS
Warren Sherwood on BSA 5th
Johnny Haskell on BSA 8th
Gene Theissen on BSA 9th
Trevor Deeley on BSA 15th
Pete Knight on BSA 19th

Nick Nicholson on Prize Winning 30.50 cu. in. BSA "Star Twin"

DEALERS
Get on the BSA Bandwagon for 1953 profits
Write your BSA-SUNBEAM Distributor for exclusive franchise particulars now!

East Coast BSA-SUNBEAM Distributor:
RICH CHILD CYCLE CO., INC., 639 Passaic Ave., Nutley, N. J.

West Coast BSA-SUNBEAM Distributor:
HAP ALZINA — 3074 Broadway, Oakland, Calif.

It's time you had a BSA

The 646 c.c. o.h.v. Vertical Twin
"ROAD ROCKET"
B.S.A.

Impressions of a Potent Small Heath Product just off the Export-only List

DESIGNED as a road-going solo with just that little extra in the way of speed and specification luxury likely to make it a dollar earner, the B.S.A. "Road Rocket" well fulfilled its original purpose in the export field and made a mid-season debut on the home market a few weeks ago. Almost at once B.S.A.s responded to a request that *Motor Cycling* should carry out a road test of this reputedly most powerful of the Small Heath twins and, therefore, this article becomes the first test report of the "Road Rocket" to appear in a British motorcycling journal.

Basically, the machine is a highly developed version of the 646 c.c. A10, featuring an aluminium-alloy cylinder head, "Nimonic 80" exhaust valves, a toughened, high-duty crankshaft and high-compression pistons giving a ratio of 8 : 1. For this power unit the makers record a conservative figure of 40 b.h.p. at 6,000 r.p.m. Listed with a 4.53 top gear as standard, the machine is said officially to have a maximum

speed in the region of 105 m.p.h., which, again, would appear to be a modest claim.

Tested under almost ideal weather conditions, the "Road Rocket" gave the initial impression that a slightly higher gear-ratio could have been used; indeed, the tester was pleasantly surprised that, at the quoted maximum rate of r.p.m., the speedometer needle was just passing the "ton" and that there was a degree of power still in hand. Actually, on several timed test runs, slightly more than 110 m.p.h. was speedo-recorded. It is true to say, however, that such speeds cannot necessarily be regarded as a day-to-day certainty. On the other hand, a more enduring feature is the fact that one can

---

TESTER'S ROAD REPORT

Maximum Speeds in :—

Time from Standing Start

Top Gear (Ratio **4·53** to 1) ..**109**.. m.p.h. = **6,200** r.p.m. **42⅕** secs.

Third Gear (Ratio **5·48** to 1) ..**88**.. m.p.h. = **6,300** r.p.m. **20** secs.

Second Gear (Ratio **7·9** to 1) ..**67**.. m.p.h. = **6,500** r.p.m. **12** secs.

Speeds over measured Quarter Mile :—

Flying Start ..**108·4**.. m.p.h.   Standing Start ..**58·06**.. m.p.h.

Braking Figures On DRY TARMACADAM **Surface, from 30 m.p.h. :—**

Both Brakes **28** ft.   Front Brake **33** ft.   Rear Brake **72** ft.

Fuel Consumption :—

30 m.p.h. **90** m.p.g.   40 m.p.h. **70** m.p.g.   50 m.p.h. **50** m.p.g.

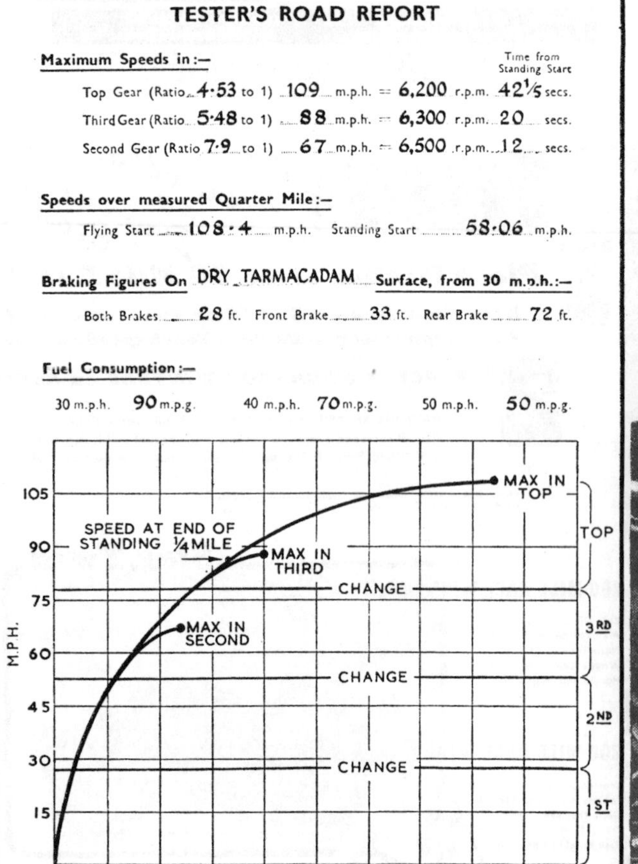

(Right) Essential with such a machine the rev.-counter, matching the speedometer, is carried just where the rider's eye can read it with the minimum deflection from the view ahead. Note also the steering lock keyhole.

(Below) A picture to delight the eye of any motorcycle enthusiast—the 650 c.c. o.h.v. twin engine of the A10RR.

Under suitable conditions, any private owner could simulate the riding positions with which the speeds recorded here were obtained.

rely on the "Road Rocket" for sustained high average speeds irrespective of the "ceiling." This B.S.A. model, designated the A10RR, could be cruised without signs of fatigue at speeds between 95-100 m.p.h. —given suitable road conditions, of course. But it is the kind of motorcycle which a foreign-touring enthusiast would find delightful to own. It would be invaluable as a means of rapid, yet rock-steady, transport on journeys over the straight and relatively traffic-free *routes nationales* or *autobahnen* of Europe. Nearer home, the chief appeal of the "Road Rocket" lies, not so much in its top-speed capabilities, which, alas, cannot always be fully used, but in acceleration qualities.

Off the mark like a shot in bottom gear, the model has an acceleration curve that rises steeply and consistently, there being no sign of "flat spots" in the carburation provided by the Amal 10TT9 instrument. The gears are well selected and the gearchange excellent. As might be expected, with an 8 : 1 c.r., tick-over and slow running were a little erratic but, by discreet use of

the manual ignition control, the tendency towards uneven firing at low r.p.m. could be minimized. When once on the move the control could be advanced fully and, unless pinking was provoked by intentional hamhandedness, the power build-up could be used efficiently right up to maximum speed.

Although listed as an extra, the Smiths rev.-counter fitted to the test machine was regarded as an almost essential complement to the speedometer, particularly in view of the engine's willingness to soar up above manufacturer's recommended maximum. At the top-speed second- and third-gear readings recorded on the graph, valve-float was *just* audible.

Generally Handling

Handling, by which is meant steering and the general ease of riding, earned full marks and there was nothing which could be "blacked" from a comfort point of view. The action of the suspension units, front and rear, was smooth but there was the sound of metallic impact somewhere in the front fork assembly on occasions when a

ridge or depression happened to be struck at speed and, apparently, at a certain angle. The sound occurred only two or three times in the course of several hundred miles and did not appear to be a symptom of any serious fault. Criticism could legitimately be levelled also at the efficiency of the rear brake. Both brakes applied together produced an excellent stopping figure and the forward brake, which was used for about 80% of the stopping work, proved to be completely reliable and fade-free. Operation of the back "stopper" produced a spongy reaction which did not improve as the test proceeded.

High-speed performance does not usually go hand-in-hand with economy in the amount of fuel consumed and the A10RR, with its T.T.-type carburetter carrying a 340 main jet, could hardly be an exception to this general rule. In fact, first experience, which comprised riding in city, suburban and high-speed main road environs—good, mixed going—a 175-mile journey served to empty completely the four-gallon tank that had been filled at the works before starting out. And that meant an average of about 43 m.p.g.! But like many high-performance models with a high compression ratio, the "Road Rocket" acquitted itself well in the fixed speed tests.

Fittings, generally, were of good quality and substantial; full marks went to the dual seat, correctly angled to give comfort in conditions produced by hard acceleration and braking. The seat blended well with the lines of the tank, the sides of which are flattened at knee level for the same reason. A centre stand was fitted but seldom used because of the existence of a much more easily operated prop-stand. This, wrongly in the opinion of the tester, came under the heading of an extra. The chromed hand-rail behind the seat added to appearance value and provided satisfactory handhold for the passenger or while manoeuvring the machine.

Pillion foot rests were well positioned for their purpose which was not that of providing a species of alternative racing rests to suit a racing poise. That scheme was not practicable, at least not to a rider of the stature of either of *Motor Cycling's* men in the Midlands, and for this reason (amongst others) all the graphed speeds were recorded with the tester normally seated, if crouching a little so as to present minimum frontal resistance.

A newcomer with good and not-far-distant ancestry, the "Road Rocket" assuredly will add to both home and overseas prestige of British-made motorcycles.

FULL ADVANTAGE can be taken of the sporting character of the 497 c.c. "Shooting Star" B.S.A. without serious detriment to a good all-round fuel-consumption figure. Over a period of several weeks, a current production "Shooting Star" was on loan to *Motor Cycling* for test purposes and the model was used for practically every conceivable type of work, the mileage covered exceeded 2,000 niles and the overall consumption was 64 m.p.g. Ownership of a high-performance model is often associated with heavy pecuniary demands for fuel but, bearing in mind the sparkling road performance of which this machine is capable, the fuel-consumption figure mentioned gives a clear indication of the machine's ability to combine speed with acceptable running economy.

In 1953, when B.S.A.s generally adopted rear swinging-fork suspension, a much-improved version of the popular "Star Twin" was introduced, one of the main attractions of which was, in fact, the new frame, but it was renamed the "Shooting Star" because of other specification changes which further increased the high-performance characteristics of the established 497 c.c. model A7. The present "Shooting Star" specification, after seasonal modifications,

The 497 c.c. Twin-cylinder o.h.v.
Model A7 "Shooting Star"
B.S.A.

A Versatile Sports Machine with Good Road-holding, Flexibility and Running Economy

Finished in two-tone green with chromium-panelled tank, the "Shooting Star" is a good-looking mount.

(Below) Nearside close-up of the "engine room." Oil stains were commendably absent.

TESTER'S ROAD REPORT

Maximum Speeds in:—

Top Gear (Ratio 5·28 to 1) 93 m.p.h. = 6,300 r.p.m. Time from Standing Start 33 secs.

Third Gear (Ratio 6·38 to 1) 84 m.p.h. = 6,800 r.p.m. 19 secs.

Second Gear (Ratio 9·28 to 1) 59 m.p.h. = 6,900 r.p.m. 7⅗ secs.

Speeds over measured Quarter Mile:—

Flying Start 92·75 m.p.h.   Standing Start 56·25 m.p.h.

Braking Figures On DRY TAR CHIPPINGS Surface, from 30 m.p.h.:—

Both Brakes 29 ft.   Front Brake 38 ft.   Rear Brake 69 ft.

Fuel Consumption:—

30 m.p.h. 98 m.p.g.   40 m.p.h. 84 m.p.g.   50 m.p.h. 74 m.p.g.

includes a light alloy cylinder head, high-compression pistons, high-lift cams and full-width alloy hubs.

A creditable feature of the test machine was the oil-retaining qualities of the power unit. At the close of the test period, slight smears were in evidence chiefly around the gearbox inspection plate, the oil-tank filler cap—this leaked when the machine was driven hard for any length of time—and on the underside of the primary chaincase. The upper half of the engine remained almost factory-fresh.

Quite tireless, the power unit would maintain high r.p.m. rates over prolonged periods. No symptons of overheating were perceived and mechanical noise—the operation of the valve gear could just be heard—and the exhaust note were at a low level. No bother was experienced in starting the engine, whether it was in a hot or a cold state.

The orthodox procedure of retarding the ignition by means of a long, slender lever on the left handlebar, closing the air supply and flooding the float chamber, always gave first-time starting results. When pulling away from a standstill, slight retardation of the ignition made for a smooth get-away (operation of the ignition lever could be accomplished simultaneously with the release of the clutch lever, for it was ideally positioned), but even if the spark were disregarded, only " fist-fulls " would induce incipient pinking.

Carburation is by the now-common Amal " Monobloc " instrument which, on the " Shooting Star " is set at a shallow down-draught angle. There is a drip-tray situated beneath the carburetter to deflect petrol drippings from the magneto but, in fact, this was a superfluous item for no leakages occurred whether the petrol taps were left open or not. An air cleaner is not fitted as standard to the " Shooting Star," but one is listed as an extra, price 19s. 10d. Carburation at all throttle openings was perfect; only the throttle-stop screw was reset to give a more reliable tick-over.

The four-speed positive-stop gearbox was in semi-unit with the engine and, apart from the change-down selection of first gear from second, which was stiff, engagements in either direction were quiet and certain. Clutch operation was light and the drive take-up progressively smooth. First thoughts about the overall gear ratio were that it was rather low; it seemed at times that the engine was racing unduly and this prompted early selection of top gear. However, the manufacturer's claimed maximum b.h.p. output of 32 occurs at 6,250 r.p.m. and, as the test graph shows, this figure was exceeded by

" Nothing was wrong with the model's handling at any speed or over any surface."

only 50 r.p.m. at the most favourable top gear speed.

The model was always good for a sustained 80 m.p.h. and, when conditions were good, near-90 m.p.h. readings were not difficult to achieve, particularly if third gear was held up to the late seventies. Weather and road conditions current when the machine was undergoing maximum speed-testing were ideal; the air was still and the road surface dry. As a matter of interest the recently released 100-octane-grade petrol was used for the speed tests.

With regard to suspension one criticism arose, for the adjustable rear Girling dampers could not be " pre-loaded " for pillion-passenger work by the C-spanner provided in the toolkit. The spanner twisted upon application without turning the 'cam arrangement.

Nothing was wrong with the model's handling at any speed or over any type of road surface. Well-balanced, the machine called for little physical effort when being ridden either in city traffic or at speed on the open road. Below 50 m.p.h., or thereabouts, the suspension was noticeably hard but the long, well-damped action of the telescopic front and pivot-fork rear assemblies made for superb machine control and a high comfort factor at higher speeds.

Slight vibration was felt through the handlebars and tank in the 65 m.p.h. region for a brief period. Perhaps this caused the lower near-side fixing point of the headlamp cowl to fracture about its bolt during the first few hundred miles of test riding.

B.S.A.s continue to list the prop-stand as an optional extra at 18s. 8d. The design and positioning of the stand ensured easy operation and a secure prop for the model although towards the end of the machine's test life the return spring lost a lot of its tension. The prop-stand was used much more frequently than the rather strenuous-to-operate centre-stand, and should be a standard, rather than an extra, fitment.

Both brakes were efficient and lining wear is readily taken up by means of the fulcrum adjusters; a suitable spanner for this purpose is included in the toolkit. Grab-free and reasonably fade-free, the purposeful-looking alloy brakes needed but light pressure to operate satisfactorily.

The rear chaincase with which the road-test " Shooting Star " was equipped undoubtedly kept the rear of the machine in a cleaner state than is to be expected when the chain is exposed.

Finished in two-tone green, the " Shooting Star " is a good-looking mount. Certainly in its specification nothing has been sacrificed which in any way contributes to comfort and economy plus performance.

BRIEF SPECIFICATION

Engine: 497 c.c. twin cylinder four-stroke: bore 66 mm. by stroke 72.6 mm.; cast-iron cylinder; alloy head; overhead valves; push-rod operated; C.R. 7.25 : 1. Claimed b.h.p. 32 at 6,250 r.p.m.: Amal carburetter, type Monobloc 376/15, 1 in. choke, 270 main jet.

Transmission: Four-speed gearbox; positive-stop footchange; ratios, 5.3, 6.4, 9.3 and 13.6 :1; primary drive by chain ½ in. by .305 in.; final drive by enclosed chain ⅝ in. by ⅜ in.

Frame: All-welded Duplex cradle type.

Wheels: WM2-19 rims, carrying Dunlop tyres; 3.25 by 19 in. ribbed front; 3.50 in. by 19 in. universal rear; hubs incorporate 7-in. full-width alloy brakes at front and rear with fulcrum adjusters.

Lubrication: Dry-sump lubrication with double gear type oil pump; oil tank 5½ pints capacity.

Electrical equipment: Lucas magneto with manual ignition control; 6v. 60w. dynamo with C.V.C. unit; 12 a.h. battery; 7-in. diameter prefocus head lamp unit; stop/tail light incorporating reflector; electric horn; dip-switch.

Suspension: Telescopic front forks of B.S.A. design, controlled by hydraulic damping; rear springing by swinging fork; movement controlled by Girling adjustable units with hydraulic damping; spindle adjustment by means of abutment screws.

Tank: Welded steel fuel tank, of 4 gall. capacity.

Dimensions: Wheelbase 56 in.; ground clearance 6 in.; unladen seat height, 30 in;. dry weight 416 lb.

Finish: Duo-green. Exhaust system, wheel rims, handlebars and other bright parts chrome plated. Fuel tank with chrome panels.

General equipment: Full kit of tools; tyre pump; 120 m.p.h. Smiths speedometer; pillion footrests; steering damper.

Price: £202 10s. plus £48 12s. P.T.= £251 2s.

Annual tax: £3 15s.; quarterly, £1 0s. 8d.

Makers: B.S.A. Motor Cycles, Ltd., Small Heath, Birmingham, 11.

Extras fitted: Prop-stand, 18s. 8d. (inc. P.T.); rear chaincase, £3 2s. (inc. P.T.).

Total: £255 2s. 8d.

ADAPTING SWINGING ARM UNITS TO A 1953 SPRING FRAME BSA

By Paul Cowles

CONVERSION: The BSA Gold Flash in the picture was converted from a spring frame to a swinging arm rear suspension setup. Note the elongated frame and the robust rear shock installation. Here's a neat "home-brew" springer of the type very prevalent before swinging arm became standard equipment on virtually every make of machine.

PERHAPS some of CYCLE's readers might be interested in the swing arm conversion we did last winter for John Stockwell of Burr Oak, Mich., on his 1953 BSA Golden Flash.

As you know, the Flash had a spring frame, but it still rode too hard to suit John, and he wanted a longer wheelbase so his passenger would have a better ride too. We discussed his ideas, and ended up with a plan for a swinging arm on a wheelbase 7½ inches longer than original.

To start with, I stripped the machine down, then took out the upper rear frame through-bolt under the seat and, after disassembling the rear spring unit, I unbrazed the spring frame brackets (be sure to remove the assembly dowels before this operation—they're ⅛" rod through the forging and frame section to hold alignment during brazing, and so nicely finished you have to really look for them), and, after heating above the brazing temperature, knocked them off. This operation brings to mind the old adage "Don't force them, just use a bigger hammer!"

At this stage, I was ready to start building back up. There is nothing sticking out behind the seat post but the lower frame tubing. This is carefully heated, and formed upward. Then form the upper frame sections so they're approximately parallel to the ground and each other, and formed around end lines in to the lower section. I reamed a piece of one inch pipe for each side, to join the upper and lower sections as shown. I then added the upper shock end supports. The half-inch pipe is bent and welded on to hold the muffler and foot rests, and the frame is ready.

The rear fork, or swinging arm units, were made from seamless tubing. The bearing section is bored from either end to receive a Timken bearing, the quarter-inch plate is shaped and brazed to the frame with care to keep them parallel to each other and square to the machine in general. To locate the swivel for the rear swinging arm, I set the machine on a steel plate and squared it up carefully. I marked the horizontal location from the plate with a surface gauge, squared up the front wheel and swung my vertical locations with a large divider from the front spindle bolt. I carefully drilled and checked until I was sure they were as near perfect as possible. The through-bolt is a ream fit on the right side and is tapped into the plate on the left side.

The swinging arm fork was carefully positioned and welded to the bearing tube, and the new rear axle supports were welded in. John made up the mount blocks, and turned a tapered shank on the forward end. These we pressed into the seamless tubing to fit, and shrunk them in before welding, so we have a very strong and rigid construction.

You'll notice we made the fender a part of the swinging arm so it doesn't need to have a lot of clearance for the rear wheel movement. We used Harley K shocks. We had to cut off a couple of coils to make the springs work to our satisfaction—probably due to the difference in weight distribution.

This machine has had considerable riding under all conditions, and the only "bug" we've had was the chain guard. It didn't have enough clearance, and the chain slapped it. With this one exception, the BSA has been a honey on all counts — riding, handling, and, we think, all around appearance.

I'd like to add, in closing, that I wish some of the manufacturers would build a machine with more room for passengers, without making them ride the rear wheel.

SPRING: Harley-Davidson K shock absorber units were the basis of the swinging arm conversion detailed in the accompanying article. Note welded-up frame extension.

I'm sure we're not the only ones that like the lighter machines with their zip, economy and ease of handling, but hate to give up the roominess of a machine *built* for two, and not just equipped with a dual seat as an afterthought. ●

NEW BSA WAREHOUSE

B.S.A., Incorporated have a newly-acquired property to be used as an additional warehouse for storage of motorcycles and parts.

646 c.c. B.S.A. Road Rocket

Extremely Attractive Vertical-twin Roadster Which Combines a Super-sports All-round Performance
With the Tractability of a Touring Mount

THE Road Rocket was evolved three years ago to satisfy the American demand for an ultra-high-performance roadster and an anglicized version (with flatter handlebar and more efficient silencers) was first released on the home market last June. Chief variations from the popular Golden Flash twin, of which it is a derivative, are high-compression pistons, a special camshaft, a racing carburettor and manual ignition control.

In the super-sports model the makers are to be congratulated on achieving a really high level of speed and acceleration without sacrificing any of the unobtrusiveness for which the Golden Flash is notable. At all speeds and throttle openings the exhaust note of the Road Rocket is pleasant and well subdued, while mechanical noise is also damped to a commendable degree. Mild piston slap could be heard during acceleration for the first three or four miles following a cold start but as soon as the engine had attained a normal working temperature the only audible mechanical noise was a rustle of well-lubricated machinery.

Maximum speed was more than 100 m.p.h. and only a super-sports 1,000 c.c. vee-twin has returned a better time on road test for the standing-start quarter-mile. Yet tractability is such that riding on congested roads presents no difficulties. True the engine repays use of the ignition control in traffic but so small is the demand (provided the highest grade fuels are used) that an automatic control might well be expected to be satisfactory. Indeed, if there is anything about the Road Rocket which proves slightly irksome when riding in heavy traffic it is not a need to tame the engine; rather is it the comparatively long reach to the clutch and front-brake levers, the slight heaviness of the clutch and gear change, and the high seat level (32in) coupled with the model's weight.

An unusually wide spread of high torque is another characteristic for which the Golden Flash engine is well known. The trait seems to have been enhanced rather than impaired on the tuned engine. Torque value on the Road Rocket is higher than on the Flash while its spread is equally wide. In practice this means that really

lusty acceleration and power reserve for gradients, head winds and passenger carrying are available over a broad engine-speed range. Silky transmission made it possible for the rider to exploit the engine's resources to the full without any feeling of guilt. Smoothness was good for a vertical twin of conventional layout; there was a feeling of solidity about the unit and though some vibration could be felt from 55 to 65 m.p.h. in top gear it was not severe enough to be noticeable so long as the handlebar and petrol tank were not gripped too tightly.

It is, of course, on the open road that the Rocket really comes into its own and there it furnishes a performance to gladden the heart of any sporting rider. To hold a speed of 70 m.p.h. requires

Deep finning characterizes the cylinder block and light-alloy head, thus ensuring rapid heat dissipation. Taper-cock petrol taps are used

Capable of an extremely high performance, the Road Rocket has first-class traffic manners. Mudguards and tank panels are chromium-plated. The kick-starter has a folding foot-piece

a throttle opening of no more than a quarter. Eighty-m.p.h. cruising is child's play. That is to say the speed is rapidly reached, needs less than half throttle under average conditions and can be maintained easily however adverse the wind or gradient.

A throttle setting of two-thirds is regarded by many experienced riders as affording the happiest compromise between zestful road performance and engine longevity. Use of that throttle opening on the Road Rocket resulted in an indicated speed of 85 to 90 m.p.h. with the rider normally seated—a rate which few riders maintain for long but which the B.S.A. proved willing to sustain indefinitely. When the twistgrip was rotated fully the speedometer needle lost little time in moving round the dial to the 96 m.p.h. calibration—still with the rider sitting upright. Indicative of the engine's outstanding pulling power is the fact that even at 80 m.p.h. in top gear a healthy forward surge was felt as soon as the throttle was snapped wide open.

The carrying of a pillion passenger did not substantially affect cruising speeds. Runs were made in opposite directions along a fast stretch of road with two adults on the dual-seat. Both were suitably clad for the very cold weather and their total weight was 23 to 24 stones. Yet with a fresh three-quarter tail wind the Road Rocket held an indicated 90 to 95 m.p.h. on two-thirds throttle while, in the opposite direction, 80 m.p.h. was sustained on the same setting. Incidentally, the passenger found the handrail behind the seat most useful during hard acceleration or braking and it obviated entirely the need to grasp the rider. The seat is a trifle thinly padded at the rear edge but the passenger's leg position is comfortable and insulation from bumps is first class.

When checked by stopwatch, speedometer readings proved to be about five per cent optimistic throughout the model's speed

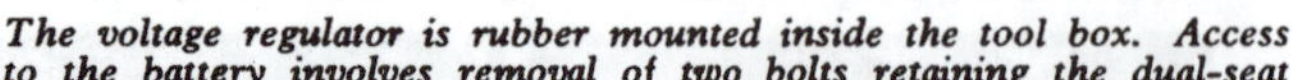

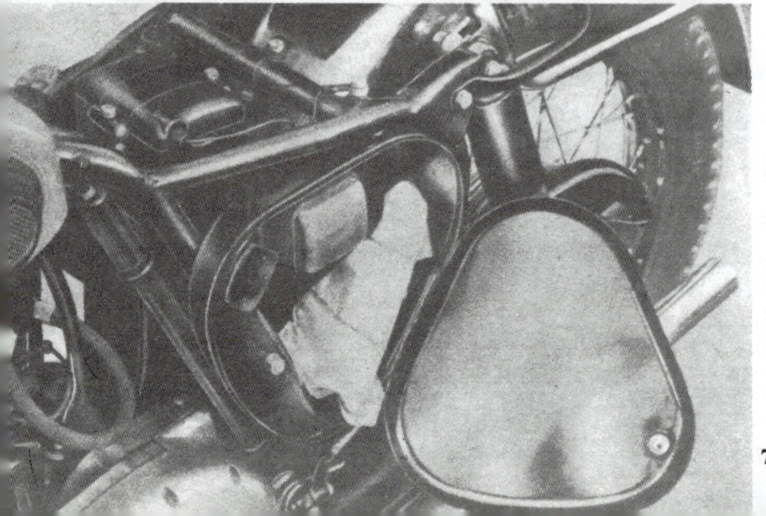

range. Listed as an optional extra for the Road Rocket, a rev-meter was fitted to the test model. (The two instruments are rubber mounted side by side on a bracket at the top of the front fork.) While engine speed is not critical for ordinary road work, the rev-meter can provide academic interest so long as the rider resists the temptation to divert attention from the road at high speeds. Knowing that peak power (claimed to be 40 b.h.p.) is produced at 6,000 r.p.m., that maximum torque occurs around 3,500 to 4,000 r.p.m. and that valve float sets in at 7,400 r.p.m., the rider can adjust his technique to suit any particular whim.

During the course of the test a considerable mileage was covered in London traffic and it was usual to retard the ignition only for starting and idling. For the latter purpose about half retard was used and the resultant tickover was as slow and reliable as that on any vertical twin. Naturally, the engine's response to throttle opening was comparatively sluggish on a retarded ignition setting; so, when moving away from a standstill, it was found best to return the ignition lever to the fully advanced position as soon as the clutch was home in bottom gear or even before the clutch was engaged. The latter technique is quite simple on the Road Rocket since the long ignition lever is extremely well placed and all that is required is to thumb it lightly forward after selecting bottom gear and while releasing the clutch lever. (The object of delaying full advance until after bottom gear is selected is, of course, to ensure almost noiseless engagement of the dogs.)

As implied earlier, the B.S.A. would burble along quite happily at 30 m.p.h. on full advance. Indeed the only time the ignition was retarded other than for starting or idling was when the model was ridden in a dense stream of nose-to-tail traffic which proceeded in fits and starts along London's Oxford Street. Under those conditions, use of about one-third retard blunted the engine's edge appropriately.

Carburation was a trifle lumpy just off the pilot jet and a very precise and small throttle opening below that spot was required for a slow tickover. There is no throttle stop on the Amal T.T. carburettor and it was found much more satisfactory to set the tickover by means of the throttle-cable adjuster than to try to achieve the delicate setting with the twistgrip. (The adjustment was carried out with the front wheel pointing straight ahead since turning the handlebar slightly raised or lowered the throttle slide.)

Uncramped and comfortable, the riding position was suitable alike for slow or fast riding and no distress was felt at the conclusion of a day's hard riding. The criticism that sustained speeds of between 80 and 90 m.p.h. necessitated a fair pull on the handlebar to counteract wind pressure is largely academic and an improvized backrest reduced the strain on the rider's arms under those conditions. Except that the headlamp switch is partially masked by the speedometer and rev-meter, all controls are well placed for convenience of operation.

At no time during the test was it necessary to put any restraint on the use of the Road Rocket's performance for reasons of handling. A steering damper is a standard fitment but there was never the least temptation to bring it into use. Steering was equally positive and responsive at high or low speeds and whether the model was following a straight path or being heeled through bends or corners. The B.S.A. could be steeply banked with every confidence; although the prop stand touched the ground on extreme left bank, grounding was not serious enough to restrict cornering technique.

For solo riding the springing was a shade on the firm side but it was well suited to the Road Rocket's performance. There was never any serious pitching and the adjustment of the rear suspension units proved adequate for passenger carrying.

Initially the brakes seemed a little below par but they improved appreciably with adjustment and bedding during the test. Smooth and controllable at all speeds, they were powerful enough for all normal occasions. But, though it may seem frivolous to criticize brakes capable of stopping a model in 34ft from 30 m.p.h., a trifle more bite in the front brake would have been appreciated in view of the Rocket's speed capabilities and weight.

The most important requirement for cold starting was a lusty thrust on the kick-starter pedal to spin the engine briskly; because of the high seat level, riders of small or medium stature found it helpful to position the model alongside a left-hand kerb. Provided the carburettor was flooded moderately and the air lever closed, a second-kick start was usual from cold. Full advance could be used for starting without a kick-back provided the throttle was opened only the merest trace but a small degree of retard made throttle setting less critical. After a cold start partial closure of the air lever was desirable for the first mile or so. The air lever could be left open for warm starting though a brief dab on the carburettor tickler was sometimes advantageous.

The clutch freed completely, took up the drive sweetly and was quite unaffected by a quick succession of six standing-start, quarter-mile sprints. For clean upward gear changes a rather deliberate pedal movement was required; the downward change from third to second gear needed an appreciable increase in engine speed if it was to be noiseless. Neutral was easy to find from first or second gear when the model was on the move but was sometimes a trifle elusive from second gear at a standstill.

The headlamp beam was up to the best contemporary British standard and permitted the safe use of fairly high speeds on unlit main roads after dark. Of average quality, the tool kit was used for all normal routine maintenance except valve-clearance adjustment for which there was no suitable spanner.

With its chromium-plated mudguards and red petrol tank with chrome side panels, the Road Rocket has a slightly flamboyant appearance to conservative British eyes but is nothing if not distinctive. In exhilarating measure it achieves its purpose in providing a super-sports road performance. That it does so with such exemplary manners adds greatly to its appeal.

The picture above shows the speedometer and rev-meter mounting and the convenient ignition-lever position inboard of the clutch lever. Below may be seen the racing carburettor and rev-meter drive

Information Panel – 646 c.c. B.S.A. Road Rocket

SPECIFICATION

ENGINE: B.S.A. 646 c.c. (70 x 84mm) overhead-valve vertical twin. Valve gear operated from a single camshaft. Light-alloy connecting rods; plain big-end bearings. Crankshaft supported in roller bearing on drive side and plain bearing on timing side. Compression ratio, 8 to 1. Dry-sump lubrication; oil-tank capacity, 5¼ pints.

CARBURETTOR: Amal T10TT9; air slide operated by handlebar lever.

IGNITION and LIGHTING: Lucas magneto with manual control. Separate Lucas 60-watt dynamo. Lucas 6-volt, 12-ampere-hour battery. Lucas 7in-diameter headlamp with pre-focus light unit.

TRANSMISSION: B.S.A. four-speed gear box with positive-stop foot control. Gear ratios: bottom, 11.68 to 1; second, 7.96 to 1; third, 5.48 to 1; top, 4.53 to 1. Multi-plate clutch with fabric inserts. Primary chain, ⅜ x 0.305in in oil-bath case. Rear chain, ⅝ x ⅜in with guard over top run. Engine r.p.m. at 30 m.p.h. in top gear, 1,750.

FUEL CAPACITY: 4 gallons.

TYRES: Dunlop: front, 3.25 x 19in ribbed; rear, 3.50 x 19in Universal.

BRAKES: Both 7in diameter x 1⅛in wide; fulcrum adjusters.

SUSPENSION: B.S.A. telescopic front fork with hydraulic damping. Pivoted-fork rear springing employing coil springs and hydraulic damping; three-position adjustment for load.

WHEELBASE: 56½in unladen. Ground clearance, 5¼in unladen.

SEAT: B.S.A. dual-seat; unladen height, 32in.

WEIGHT: 450 lb fully equipped, with full oil tank and approximately half a gallon of petrol.

PRICE: £217 10s. With purchase tax (in Great Britain only), £269 14s. Extras: prop stand, 15s (p.t., 3s 8d); rev meter, £6 12s 6d (p.t., £1 11s 10d).

ROAD TAX: £3 15s a year; £1 0s 8d a quarter.

MAKERS: B.S.A. Motor Cycles, Ltd., Small Heath, Birmingham, 11.

DESCRIPTION: *The Motor Cycle, 20 September 1956.*

PERFORMANCE DATA

MEAN MAXIMUM SPEED: Bottom: *49 m.p.h.
Second: *73 m.p.h.
Third: 95 m.p.h.
Top: 102 m.p.h.
* Valve float occurring.

HIGHEST ONE-WAY SPEED: 105 m.p.h. (conditions: strong cross wind; rider wearing bulky two-piece plastic suit and overboats).

MEAN ACCELERATION:

	10-30 m.p.h.	20-40 m.p.h.	30-50 m.p.h.
Bottom	2.5 sec	2.5 sec	—
Second	3 sec	3 sec	2.6 sec
Third	5.5 sec	4.4 sec	4.2 sec
Top		5.4 sec	5.5 sec

Mean speed at end of quarter-mile from rest: 85 m.p.h.
Mean time to cover standing quarter-mile: 15 sec.

PETROL CONSUMPTION: At 30 m.p.h., 100 m.p.g.; at 40 m.p.h., 92 m.p.g.; at 50 m.p.h., 74 m.p.g.; at 60 m.p.h., 54 m.p.g.

BRAKING: From 30 m.p.h. to rest, 34ft (surface, dry tarmac).

TURNING CIRCLE: 14ft.

MINIMUM NON-SNATCH SPEED: 13 m.p.h. in top gear on full retard.

WEIGHT PER C.C.: 0.7 lb.

497 c.c. B.S.A.
Shooting Star

A Super-sports Model with Punch and Charm

High Performance Combined with Docility,

Quietness and Economy

The deep finning on the light-alloy cylinder head and cast-iron block not only ensures freedom from overheating during the hardest use, it also gives the engine a robust appearance

A 90 M.P.H.-PLUS roadster five-hundred is nothing new; such performance was offered by a few super-sports models even before the war. But if the B.S.A. Shooting Star is taken as an example, then what distinguishes the modern road-burner from its pre-war counterpart is the docility, unobtrusiveness and economy which are blended with the high performance. Commendable though it is, the B.S.A's mean timed maximum speed of 94 m.p.h. is more of academic than practical significance under present-day road conditions. None will deny the thrill of crouching over the tank with the speedometer needle flickering around the 100 m.p.h. calibration; but such speeds are of more value as a subject for clubroom boasts than in everyday riding. For most practical purposes the ability to sustain 80 to 85 m.p.h. tirelessly and with the rider normally seated is adequate. Indeed, the number of riders who habitually use that level of performance is comparatively small.

The Shooting Star is among the models which satisfy that requirement. Moreover, both exhaust and mechanical noise are inoffensive. Throughout the normal range of cruising speeds petrol consumption is unusually economical. Finally, top-gear performance is flexible and, though a manual ignition control is featured, no special skill is required to obtain the best results. These characteristics have distinguished the Shooting Star during its four years on the market and it is significant that few specification changes have been made during that period. Full-width hubs and fulcrum-adjuster brakes were adopted for 1956; at the same time came integral formation of cylinder head and inlet manifold. Rear-chain enclosure has been an optional extra for the past two years and is such an obvious boon that its popularity is understandable.

Contributing much to top-gear tractability is the well chosen gear ratio. At 5.28 to 1 this is lower than average for a 500 c.c. vertical twin but it is theoretically correct in so far as it permits the engine to reach peak r.p.m. at maximum road speed. In practice the lowish ratio ensures that the engine is spinning freely at 30 m.p.h. in top gear so that town riding does not involve repeated gear changing. This lack of fuss at 30 m.p.h. is an endearing feature which distinguishes the Shooting Star among super-sports five-hundred twins and which is enhanced by clean carburation and a relative insensitivity to ignition setting.

No longer is skilful manipulation of the ignition control a necessary art for the rider of a sporting roadster. Provided the gears were used to prevent the engine from labouring at ultra-low r.p.m., the ignition lever could be left at full advance for all conditions except starting (half retard) and tick-tocking along at about 5 m.p.h. in dense city traffic without slipping the clutch (up to full retard). That does not mean that the indirect gears had to be used excessively to avoid pinking. In built-up areas it was commonplace to come down below 30 m.p.h. in top gear on full advance. And when accelerating away the throttle could be banged wide open without changing from top gear or retarding the ignition; smooth, gentlemanly acceleration resulted and there was no trace of pinking or harshness. Because it was rarely necessary to retard the ignition the impression was formed that equally good results could be obtained with auto-advance. Of course, premium grade petrol was used throughout the test.

Obviously, however, the model's sporting characteristics were best revealed at comparatively high engine speeds. With upward gear changes made at about 30, 50 and 75 m.p.h., acceleration through the gears was very satisfying yet always marked by a delightful impression of gentlemanliness. Half throttle furnished a give-and-take cruising speed of about 75 m.p.h. one- or two-up, and 80 to 85 m.p.h. was sustained on approximately two-thirds throttle under average conditions. Speedometer flattery was roughly five per cent throughout the model's speed range.

No parallel-twin four-stroke is entirely free from perceptible engine vibration; whether or not it can be regarded as a serious fault depends on its magnitude. To all intents and purposes the Shooting Star was smooth in operation up to 70 m.p.h. in top gear but vibration was apparent, chiefly through the tank, from that speed upward or at corresponding speeds in the indirect gears. So long as the rider refrained from gripping the tank between his knees, however, the tremor did not prove troublesome.

Engine starting was a first-kick affair, whatever the temperature of the unit. The only precautions required for a cold start were the usual closure of the air lever and momentary depression of the float tickler. Half-retard was normally employed as a safeguard against backfiring but full advance could be used

INFORMATION PANEL

SPECIFICATION

ENGINE: B.S.A. 497 c.c. (66 x 72.6mm) overhead-valve vertical twin. Valve gear operated from a single camshaft. Light-alloy connecting rods; plain big-end bearings. Crankshaft supported in roller bearing on drive side and plain bearing on timing side. Aluminium-alloy cylinder head. Compression ratio, 7.25 to 1. Dry-sump lubrication; oil-tank capacity, 5½ pints.

CARBURETTOR: Amal Monobloc; air slide operated by handlebar lever.

IGNITION and LIGHTING: Lucas magneto with manual control. Separate Lucas 60-watt dynamo. Lucas 6-volt, 12-ampere-hour battery. Lucas 7in-diameter headlamp with pre-focus light unit.

TRANSMISSION: B.S.A. four-speed gear box with positive-stop foot control. Gear ratios: bottom, 13.62 to 1; second, 9.28 to 1; third, 6.38 to 1; top, 5.28 to 1. Multi-plate clutch with fabric inserts. Primary chain, ½ x 0.305in. in oil-bath case. Rear chain, ⅝ x ⅜in. in pressed-steel case. Engine r.p.m. at 30 m.p.h. in top gear, 2,040.

FUEL CAPACITY: 4 gallons.

TYRES: Dunlop: front, 3.25 x 19in ribbed; rear, 3.50 x 19in Universal.

BRAKES: Both 7in diameter x 1⅛in wide; fulcrum adjusters.

SUSPENSION: B.S.A. telescopic front fork with hydraulic damping. Pivoted-fork rear suspension employing Girling units with coil springs and hydraulic damping; three-position adjustment for load.

WHEELBASE: 56½in unladen. Ground clearance, 5½in unladen.

SEAT: B.S.A. dual-seat; unladen height, 32in.

WEIGHT: 448 lb fully equipped, with full oil tank and approximately one gallon of petrol.

PRICE: £213. With purchase tax (in Great Britain only), £264 2s 5d. Extras: rear chaincase, £2 11s 3d (p.t., 12s 4d); prop stand, 16s 6d (p.t., 4s).

ROAD TAX: £3 15s a year; £1 0s 8d a quarter.

MAKERS: B.S.A. Motor Cycles, Ltd., Small Heath, Birmingham, 11.

DESCRIPTION: *The Motor Cycle,* 20 September 1956.

PERFORMANCE DATA

MEAN MAXIMUM SPEED: Bottom:* 42 m.p.h.
Second:* 62 m.p.h.
Third:* 90 m.p.h.
Top: 94 m.p.h.
*Valve float occurring.

HIGHEST ONE-WAY SPEED: 98 m.p.h. (conditions: moderate tail wind; rider wearing two-piece plastic suit and overboots).

MEAN ACCELERATION:

	10-30 m.p.h.	20-40 m.p.h.	30-50 m.p.h.
Bottom	2.7 sec	2.6 sec	—
Second	4 sec	3.6 sec	3.5 sec
Third	—	6 sec	5.5 sec
Top	—	7.6 sec	7.8 sec

Mean speed at end of quarter-mile from rest: 75 m.p.h.
Mean time to cover standing quarter-mile: 16.9 sec.

PETROL CONSUMPTION: At 30 m.p.h., 115 m.p.g.; at 40 m.p.h., 90 m.p.g.; at 50 m.p.h., 77 m.p.g.; at 60 m.p.h., 65 m.p.g.

BRAKING: From 30 m.p.h. to rest, 29ft 6in (surface, dry tarmac).

TURNING CIRCLE: 14ft.

MINIMUM NON-SNATCH SPEED: 13 m.p.h. in top gear on full retard.

WEIGHT PER C.C.: 0.9 lb.

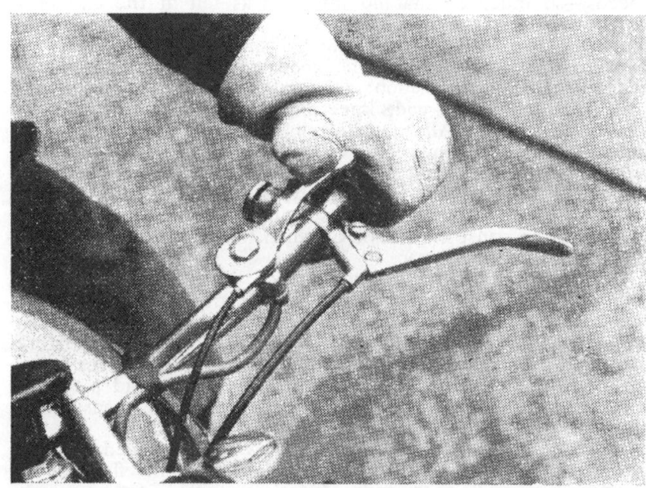

Above: Operation of the ignition control could scarcely be easier; the lever is long and easily reached with the left thumb. Below: Since 1956 the Shooting Star cylinder head has had an integral inlet manifold

in safety provided throttle opening was only minute. As would be expected, idling was lumpy on full advance and improved progressively as the ignition lever was moved backward. A midway setting gave satisfactory results; on full retard, tickover was as slow as the beat of a clock. Fairly hard sparking plugs are standardized (Champion NA10) and it was necessary to clean them once during the 800-mile test.

Provided the engine was idling slowly, only a slight click accompanied bottom-gear engagement. Both upward and downward changes were of average lightness and speed. In both directions it was the middle change which required the greatest care if clean engagement was to result; a leisurely pedal movement was called for on the upward change while the downward change was best made at not too high a speed and with an appreciable increase in engine r.p.m. Though the clutch freed and gripped perfectly, its take-up of the drive was not so smooth as is usual on a B.S.A.: on normal getaways engagement was jerky though full-power starts concealed the roughness. Transmission was commendably smooth on drive or overrun.

For sustained high speeds, a riding position giving a slight forward crouch is desirable to minimize stress in the arms arising from wind pressure, but at moderate speeds an excessive crouch places too much weight on the rider's wrists. The Shooting Star riding position affords a fine compromise for low and high speeds—so much so that no fatigue was felt at the end of a day awheel embracing both town riding and fast open-road touring. The handlebar is wide by contemporary standards—unnecessarily so in view of the good steering—but it provided a comfortable arm position; relationship of seat and footrests gave a commendably wide knee angle thus precluding all possibility of cramp. All controls fell readily to hand or foot as the case may be. However, two minor criticisms may be made of riding comfort. First the dual-seat felt a trifle hard towards the end of a day's riding. Secondly, the combination of a high seat and a heavy machine occasionally proved awkward for a small rider in dense city traffic or when manœuvring at very low speeds in a confined space.

Cornering and curve-swerving were delightful for steering was steady and reasonably light at all speeds. The only exception occurred on fast bends having bumps or undulations which were severe enough to reveal a slight inadequacy of front-fork damping. With the exception of occasional pitching at the front, springing was well suited to the Shooting Star's road performance. Bump absorption by both front and rear suspensions at high speeds was first class.

Provided a fairly close adjustment was maintained braking power was ample and there was no falling-off in efficiency in heavy rain or on flooded roads. Gentle operation of the controls was desirable at low speeds, however, if the initial action of the brakes was not to be rather sudden. Night riding called for no more than average restriction on speed for the headlamp main beam was well up to par. The beam could not be elevated to the correct level, however, without first removing the rubber beading from the front edge of the headlamp cowl.

On a model with such nice manners for its class it is a pity that no positive remedy has yet been found for oil leakage from the tank filler. No trouble was experienced at moderate speeds but whenever the model was ridden hard oil seeped past the filler cap washer and fouled the back of the rider's right leg. On the model tested, minor seepage also occurred from the exhaust rocker compartment, primary chaincase filler and gear box. When using the prop stand for parking care was required to position the model so that it could not roll forward. The centre stand provided firm support for the machine but required an appreciable effort to bring into use.

Routine maintenance presented no problems. Enclosure of the rear chain greatly reduces the need for resetting and renders the job far less messy; adjusters for both chains are readily accessible. Removal of the rear wheel is not hampered by the chaincase and both wheels are quickly detachable. Tank removal is, of course, necessary before valve clearances can be checked or adjusted, but the well known single-bolt fixing greatly simplifies the job. Contact-breaker adjustment is easy to effect but withdrawal and replacement of the pick-up brush holders for cleaning requires some manual dexterity.

In brief, the Shooting Star provides all the performance required of a sporting five-hundred without the noise, intractability and extravagance once accepted as the inevitable price. It is this blend of punch and charm which is the especial appeal of the model.

Above: Rear-chain enclosure and quick detachability of the wheel are not incompatible; removal of a rubber grommet from the chaincase gives access to the wheel nuts. Below: Finish of the Shooting Star is two-tone green

Missile with Muscle

ROAD TEST

ROAD TEST OF THE
BSA SUPER ROCKET

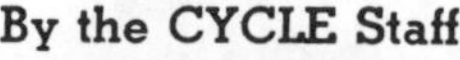

By the CYCLE Staff

The term "bomb" has been overused of late, but its application to the new Super Road Rocket by BSA fits like a fuse in a blockbuster.

The standard Road Rocket introduced to the American market in 1954 was a pretty potent pack of power that caused a good many boys with supposedly "hot" machines to hustle back to the speed shop for more modifications after being bested in a drag race or high-speed run against the Rocket. When these same speed-riders come up against the new Super Rocket their cries should be heard all the way to Birmingham as the improved BSA bomb once again hustles past their quick machinery.

In designing the original Road Rocket the BSA engineers were instructed to develop a motorcycle that would appeal to the tastes of the American rider. That their efforts met with approval on this side of the Atlantic is evident by the quick acceptance that the Rocket enjoyed in this country. What was probably more surprising to the Rocket's designers was the fact that a great many of the machines were also sold in the British Isles, proving that Americans are not the only people who appreciate power, comfort, and good-looking motorcycles.

The Super Road Rocket combines its amazing power with good manners and is equally at home in congested traffic and wide-open spaces. Too often low end performance must be sacrificed in order to gain power like the Rocket's, but unlike many factory hop-ups, the Super Rocket is easy to start and stays flexible throughout its entire speed range—which reaches well over the century-mark. But don't think for a moment that the Super Rocket is all go and no show. As a look at the pictures will prove, it is a handsome motorcycle with excellent detail finish, appealing lines, and enough chromium to outshine a searchlight. This lavish use of chrome is expected to appeal to the American market, and undoubtedly it will—but one item leaves us a little cold. It is that Detroitish Rocket emblem on the front mudguard. This doodad will probably appeal to the Christmas-tree school of motorcycle design, but those of us who feel that a motorcycle should look like a motorcycle will whip out a suitable wrench and transfer that particular feature to an Oldsmobile, where it belongs.

There is a type of motorcyclist who feels that his mount is well suited for short jaunts but a little too uncomfortable for cross-country trips. To those riders we say just rest your rear on that cushy dual-seat, bounce the swinging-arm over a couple of chuck-holes and see how slight an edge the old armchair holds over the Super Rocket. You'll find that the front forks are too soft for much cow-trailing—they bottomed rather easily during our test—but otherwise the suspension on this cycle is good. A great many

CYCLE tester Asher Lee reports the Super Rocket scaled hills like this easily.

things combine to place the Super Rocket above the average on the comfort scale: the seating positions for rider and passenger are good, the controls are right where they can be most easily operated, and except for some excessive effort required to operate the clutch—which is otherwise smooth in its action—and a gearshift lever that could stand a little lengthening, the handling of this machine is second to none. The gearbox turned out to be an enthusiast's delight and in spite of the stubby lever it could be shifted up or down at any speed with as little clash of cogs as a politician changing his mind.

Voltage regulator and tools repose in this spacious jockey box. Object on box cover is owner's handbook.

The huge T.T. carburetor fitted to this machine responded instantly to the quick-acting twistgrip and under its urging the 40 cu. in. vertical twin displayed more snap than a gross of rubber bands. This outstanding performance was not without its price, however. The two-gallon fuel tank fitted to our test machine tended to empty otself rather quickly, so if long trips are anticipated it would be advisable to fit the four-gallon tank which is standard equipment in the East and available as optional equipment on western models. This is the price that must be paid, since economy and high performance have never come in the same package. The less demanding rider may be able to lower his fuel consumption figures somewhat by reducing the power settings that were employed in the test.

One minor but embarrasing annoyance noticed during the test was that while the throttle action on the machine was smooth and the power response just as smooth, sharp right turns caused the throttle

A trim and businesslike engine. Note heavy cylinder base flange and T. T. carburetor.

cable to bind and speed up the engine. Rerouting or lengthening the cable should eliminate this problem.

It is obvious that the tremendous power of the Super Rocket engine demands exceptional brakes, and the stoppers on this machine are just that. Whether applied singly or in unison they bring the moving missile to a safe stop without a hint of grab or shudder. A welcome combination of speed and safety.

Now let's check the Birmingham beauty for technical details. During the test many of the break-in miles were put on at night and the lighting proved to be excellent, although a light for the tachometer should be provided. The rear chain is totally enclosed and this admirable optional feature kept the rear of the machine as clean as a parson's conscience. Unfortunately, enough oil seeped from the primary chaincase and gearbox to spot up the garage floor, but the rest of the mechanical components remained oil-tight.

Completely enclosed chainguard is optional. Full-width hub houses powerful rear brake.

Heavy chromium plating protects and enhances the tank, fenders, fenderstays, exhaust pipes and mufflers, and a bevy of small parts. This machine should be a joy to keep clean with its high-quality chrome and enamel.

Looking into the specifications, the "Super" engine features enlarged inlet ports, heavy-base cylinder block and an extra-heavy crankshaft to withstand the jolt of 650 booming ccs. displacement.

Gear ratios are well spaced for road work, with a close ratio between 3rd and 4th.

To eliminate any doubt about what is going on in the engine room, a tachometer is fitted in addition to the usual speedo. Handlebars are high and wide, a design that pleases Californians and distresses Britishers and some U. S. riders. The dualseat features a hand-hold for the passenger which can also be used for pulling the Rocket onto its center-stand. The impressive and desirable T.T. carburetor should cause the connoisseaur's mouth to water and the healthy exhaust note will delight his ear without offending any of the neighborhood gendarmes.

Forks are equal to dips like this, bottom on rougher stuff.

The BSA Super Road Rocket packs enough punch to hustle across the American continent and back in quick comfort yet it is pleasantly docile in going-to-work traffic. Its beauty spells pride of ownership and its performance will keep its owner happy for many years. The BSA firm's skillful wedding of utility with enjoyment is bound to please the most exacting motorcyclist.

With full equipment, top speed of the Super Rocket was 112.11 m.p.h.; and, without mufflers, when ridden by Neil Keen, top speed was 116.26 m.p.h. This test will be the last one CYCLE will conduct with mufflers removed from the test ma-

*chine. Some readers have criti-
cized the testing of road machines without mufflers, and/or
with the rider lying in a prone
position for top speed, which
has been discontinued.*

*Only on Scrambles models
will future tests be made without mufflers.*

*In each instance CYCLE will
request that one representative
of the manufacturer, dealer, or
importer be present when the
speed tests are made.—Clymer.*

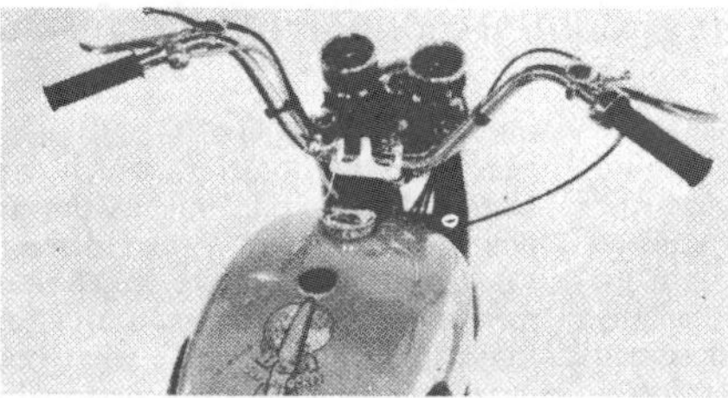

Standard equipment includes tachometer, steering head lock, steering dampner and manual spark advance.

Performance Summary

MAXIMUM SPEEDS:
3rd gear 103:96
4th gear 112:11
without mufflers...........................116:26
ACCELERATION:
1/10 mile drag.....................8.3 seconds
1/4 mile drag.....................14.1 seconds
BRAKING DISTANCE:
panic stop from 20 M.P.H.
front only ....24' 2"
rear only ....37' 5"
both ....13' 0"
SLOW RUNNING:
high gear without chain
snatch ....19.5 M.P.H.
GASOLINE MILEAGE:
average for test.....................50 M.P.G.

Specifications

ENGINE: 650 c.c. (40 cubic inch) overhead valve Twin; alloy cylinder head with valve seat inserts, racing valves and springs; Amal T.T. racing carburetor; super-sports camshaft, heavy base cylinder block, high compression pistons. Engine has Rocket type heavy duty crankshaft and is tuned at the Factory for maximum horsepower output. A Smith's precision 8000 r.p.m. tachometer is provided to protect the engine.
TRANSMISSION: Engine shaft cushion drive; B S A four speed gearbox with foot operated positive stop change lever, multi-plate clutch, primary chain in oil bath, full rear chain enclosure optional at extra cost.
IGNITION: Lucas magneto with manual advance and retard for maximum efficiency.
LIGHTING: Lucas gear driven generator, Lucas 7" diameter headlight incorporating parking light, tail and stop light with reflector.
FRAME: Welded double tube frame, spring up center stand, jiffy stand and front wheel stand, key operated steering head lock, new "Twin-Solo" dualseat with chrome handrail and passenger footrests. Telescopic front and swinging arm rear suspension are both hydraulically controlled. Rear springing is adjustable according to load. Full width alloy hubs with powerful centerline brakes.
FINISH: Sapphire Blue and Chrome tank with SUPER ROCKET insignia, heavy chrome plate on fenders, exhaust system, handlebars, wheel rims and many small parts. Polished alloy primary chain cover and gear box cover. Frame is lustrous black baked enamel. Note: Eastern models have 4 gallon tank and Twin Solo dualseat. Western models have 2 gallon tank and Sports type dualseat.
MANUFACTURERS: BSA Motorcycles Ltd., Birmingham, England.
U. S. DISTRIBUTORS: East—BSA Incorporated, Nutley, N. J. West—Hap Alzina, Oakland, Calif.

Continued from page 56

to the Birmingham M.C.C., the club under whose banner they were entered. After the trial, George Savage returned to England and Bert Perrigo took on the role of conductor, piloting the machines through Stuttgart, Frankfurt, Cologne, Hanover and Hamburg to the Nyborg Ferry, where the party was water-borne into Denmark at Korsor. Followed a route that led through Copenhagen into Sweden via Malmo and Gothenburg to Oslo, the terminal point, which was reached on September 30.

Scenes of great enthusiasm were witnessed as the trio rode into the city to a fine reception organized by the local B.S.A. distributors. The 4,900-mile objective had been magnificently achieved and Mr. McNulty put his signature to his report on the last day on which competition for the Maudes Trophy could be accepted for the 1951-1952 season. Since it is now not possible for further observed tests to be submitted for the current year to rank in competition for the Trophy, and because there has not been any other certified test in post-war years, it would seem fairly certain that this coveted award, which is given for the most meritorious motorcycling performance carried out in any one year under A.-C.U. observation, will pass to B.S.A.s, who will doubtless give it a deserving place of honour on their stand at the forthcoming London Show.

The Austrian B.S.A. distributor, Dr. H. Alt, welcomes George Savage and the three riders as they reach Vienna, the eastern-most extremity of their journey and well behind the Iron Curtain.

CHOICE of a sidecar for the stage-two test of B.S.A.'s A10 " Golden Flash "—the solo test report was published in *Motor Cycling* on January 2—fell upon the Watsonian " Avon," a single-seater of established design which has retained its popularity in this era of increasing demand for the larger " family " models.

The tester's first personal experience of the " Avon " was as a passenger, when he was helping to report the 1952 " Exeter." Memories of that run added to the interest of reassessing the sidecar—now a sprung-wheel model—in unit with the B.S.A. A10, the frame of which was extensively redesigned for 1958 with just this sort of usage in mind. At all except the swan-neck location, sidecar lugs and pick-up points are now an integral part of the machine's fabricated and welded frame. Riding the outfit with the " Avon " attached in this way, one is aware of its excellent rigidity; from the outset, there is a sense of handling a unified vehicle, rather than an assembled combination.

For normal touring purposes, the 12.9 : 1 bottom gear was suitable for pulling away under load, but to get off the mark really sharply it was necessary to permit a little clutch-slip, or the engine, which still had the standard 7.25 : 1 compression ratio, would pink slightly for a moment. Acceleration in the 8.8 : 1 second gear could be used to the

The 646 c.c. Vertical-twin o.h.v.

B.S.A. A10 " Golden Flash " and Watsonian " Avon "

A Combination Providing Comfort and High Performance

full, when the speedometer needle would move rapidly around the dial to near the " 60 " mark. In these working conditions the unit was turning over smoothly right up to peak r.p.m.; there was no vibration at any stage—a tribute, probably to the redesigned and considerably stiffened crankshaft introduced on the A10 series as a 1958 improvement.

Speed-test figures were determined on an airfield, in good weather but with a side wind. A nine-stone passenger was carried in the sidecar, and in these conditions second and third gears had really to be " wound on " to establish the graphed acceleration curve; " top," it was felt, might have produced more than the graphed 72 m.p.h. had there been room to " work up." In third

gear the speedometer, which was accurate, recorded 67 m.p.h. but, as the graph shows, changing to " top " then demanded a considerable dwell before much more than 70 m.p.h. could be obtained. and the maximum figure pin-pointed. Say what one will, however, 70 m.p.h.-plus is a reasonable top speed to claim for a sidecar outfit; and in this case it could be obtained without fear of fatiguing the engine or introducing any factor detrimental to the comfort of either driver or passenger.

Passenger impressions revealed little criticism. There was appreciation of general comfort at all the speeds quoted, despite the fact that this part of the test was carried out on a particularly cold March day. The Perspex screen with its large frontal area,

TESTER'S ROAD REPORT

Maximum Speeds in :—

				Time from Standing Start
Top Gear (Ratio 5·0 to 1)	72 m.p.h. =	4700 r.p.m.	42 secs.	
Third Gear (Ratio 6·0 to 1)	67 m.p.h. =	5200 r.p.m.	21 secs.	
Second Gear (Ratio 8·8 to 1)	58 m.p.h. =	6700 r.p.m.	14 secs.	

Speeds over measured Quarter Mile :—

Flying Start 69 m.p.h.   Standing Start 46 m.p.h.

Braking Figures On DRY CONCRETE **Surface, from 30 m.p.h. :—**

All Brakes 36 ft.   Front Brake 52 ft.   Rear Brake 63 ft.

Fuel Consumption :—

30 m.p.h. 72 m.p.g.   40 m.p.h. 60 m.p.g.   50 m.p.h. 50 m.p.g.

The well-established " Avon " combines with the " Golden Flash," now equipped with sidecar fittings, to make a taut and business-like outfit. The windscreen fairing is not standard.

NOTE: Figures in the test report sheet were obtained with a nine-stone passenger in the sidecar and the screen/fairing unit fitted to the machine.

served well to deflect side draught and engine noise, and the separate folding hood, allowing a 34-in. seat-to-roof dimension, gave adequate weather protection without inducing claustrophobia. Arm-rests would give an " Avon " passenger that extra comfort appreciated on long runs.

Watsonian's sprung wheel served further to improve the passenger's lot as compared with memories of that " Exeter " run; but, equally important, the sidecar brake, controlled by a pedal located alongside that for the rear brake of the machine, emphasized the point that in these times a three-wheeler without three brakes is an incomplete vehicle. Quite apart from the safety implicit in being able to pull up squarely to any obstacle, the special steering facility obtained from discreet toe pressure on the " chair " pedal at left-handers made the rider wonder how he had ever managed to get around such corners by any other means.

Allied to consideration of cruising speeds is the question of fuel economy. In solo form, the " Golden Flash " had shown a slightly weak cut-away setting which resulted in intermittent spit-back at this stage of carburation. Corresponding weakness was apparent during the sidecar test, particularly when the engine was in the warming-up stage, but, without doubt, this setting contributed materially to a satisfactory m.p.g. figure at low to medium cruising speeds. For town work at 30 m.p.h. about 70 m.p.g. was recorded, and on a fixed-speed airfield test that figure increased to an average, with and against the wind, of 72 m.p.g. The most

The generous area of the " Avon's " windscreen is well shown in this on-the-road picture.

Cockpit view of the " Avon " ; note the neat, covered hood stowage behind the seat.

significant figure, perhaps, was that of 50 m.p.g. at a fixed speed of 50 m.p.h. At speeds above " 50," a fairly high fuel-consumption rise was noted.

Facilities for sustained speeds above " 60 " are rare in this country, and therefore for all practical purposes it would be fair to consider the 54-58 m.p.g. recorded over the period of the entire test, some of which was carried out with the sidecar empty, as being a reasonable figure to expect from this high-compression, semi-sports roadster outfit.

Handling was assessed on performance in city streets, the open road and airfield conditions; in all circumstances, handling was excellent. The generous steering lock earned full marks and, from the rider's point of view, the suspension of the outfit, although harder than that of the solo version, gave no cause for complaint. Mileages of up to 120 at a stretch produced no abnormal fatigue.

The exhaust note, although pronounced, was not objectionable. It was accentuated to some extent by the presence of the sidecar, but during a long run, settled to a pleasant " woofle " objectionable to neither rider nor passenger. Particular attention was paid to this aspect because the " Golden Flash " carried a " Gazelle " windscreen and fairing unit, a Metal and Plastic Compacts product. Such equipment, while offering maximum frontal protection without detriment to performance, inevitably has a sounding-board effect and it is important that small mechanical sounds thus magnified, and the noise of wind impact, be carefully assessed.

With such factors weighed up, the value of a fairing as fitted to the A10 seemed to be high. It was the first time that equipment of this type had been used for a full road test and, on the findings, the innovation was judged to have been well worth while.

BRIEF SPECIFICATION

Engine: 646 c.c. vertical twin-cylinder four-stroke; bore 70 mm. by stroke 84 mm.; cast-iron cylinder and head; o.h. valves, push-rod operated; C.R., 7.25 : 1; claimed b.h.p., 34/5,750 r.p.m.; Amal " Monobloc " carburetter, type 376/80; 240 main jet; 25 pilot jet; 376/3½ throttle slide; 0.1065 needle jet with needle in No. 3 notch.

Transmission: Four-speed gearbox; positive-stop foot-change; ratios, 5.0, 6.0, 8.8 and 12.9 : 1; primary drive by ½-in. by .305-in. chain; final drive by ⅝-in. by ⅜-in. chain.

Frame: All-welded duplex tubular cradle with integral lugs for sidecar attachment; roll-on centre stand.

Wheels: WM 2-19 rims, carrying Dunlop tyres; 3.25-in. by 19-in. ribbed front; 3.50-in. by 19-in. " Universal " rear; full-width hubs with cast-iron drums and finning, accommodating 8-in. brake at front, 7 in. at rear, and incorporating straight spokes.

Lubrication: Dry sump with double-gear type oil pump; pressure feed through timing-side bush to big-end assembly, cylinder walls and rocker mechanism; return by gravity to timing wheels and sump; oil-tank capacity, 5½ pints.

Electrical Equipment: Lucas K2F magneto gear-driven from camshaft and incorporating A.T.D.; chain-driven Lucas 6-v. 60-W. dynamo, C.V.C.-governed; output to 6-v. 12-a.h. battery; Lucas 7½-in.

pre-focus light unit with cowl flush-fitting to upper fork structure; cowl carries illuminated speedometer, switch and ammeter, and houses 6-v. electric horn. Bulb ratings: headlamp 30/24 W.; tail and stop light, 6 v. 6/18 W.

Suspension: Telescopic front forks of B.S.A. design with heavy-duty springs and hydraulic damping; rear springing by swinging-fork assembly and sidecar-rated Girling suspension units with hydraulic damping and three-stage pre-loading adjustability; spindle adjustment by abutment bolts.

Tank: Welded steel fuel tank, of 4 gal. capacity.

Dimensions: Wheelbase, 56 in.; ground clearance, 6 in.; unladen seat height, 30 in.; dry weight, 425 lb.

Finish: Beige with chrome-panelled petrol tank and black frame.

General Equipment: Full kit of tools; tyre pump; 120 m.p.h. Smiths speedometer; pillion footrests.

Price: £210 plus £51 19s. 6d. P.T. = £261 19s. 6d.

Extras fitted to test machine: Rear chaincase, £3 4s. (inc. P.T.); M. and P. " Gazelle " screen fairing unit, £8 1s. 3d.

Annual Road Tax: £5; quarterly, £1 7s. 6d.

Makers: B.S.A. Motor Cycles, Ltd., Small Heath, Birmingham, 11.

THE SIDECAR

Body: Single-seater; timber frame construction panelled with 22-g. steel sheet sections; fully sprung seat and squab, finished in high-grade leathercloth; " Rexine " material trimming; fold-away hood; Perspex frontal screen; dash and door in one piece and double hinged; luggage boot with barrel-type lock. Finished beige to match B.S.A. colour scheme. Dimensions in inches (see diagram): A, 84; B, 52; D, 21; weight of body, 110 lb.

Chassis: VG21 with fully sprung wheel carrying 3.25-in. by 19-in. Dunlop tyre; hub incorporates sidecar brake operated by independent pedal and cable linkage.

Price: £62 18s. 6d. plus P.T. £15 11s. 6d.= £78 10s.

Extras fitted to test model: Sprung sidecar wheel, £5 10s.; sidecar brake, £5 10s. (inc. P.T.).

Makers: Watsonian Sidecars, Ltd., Albion Road, Greet, Birmingham, 11.

A "100 mph-plus" forty cu. in. road bike is certainly nothing new in 1959. In addition, such performance has been achieved by quite a few super sports mounts for several years. But if we consider the BSA Super Rocket as an example, then the excelling factors on this modern road burner are the silence, ease of handling and economy which are blended with its ultra high performance. Under present legal highway regulations its top speed (well in excess of 105 mph) is attractive to the owner's ego rather than being of substantial value. However, for most

The front forks' rubber dust covers, the fully enclosed rear chain and the roomy twin seat are some of the fine points of the new Super Rocket.

BSA SUPER ROCKET

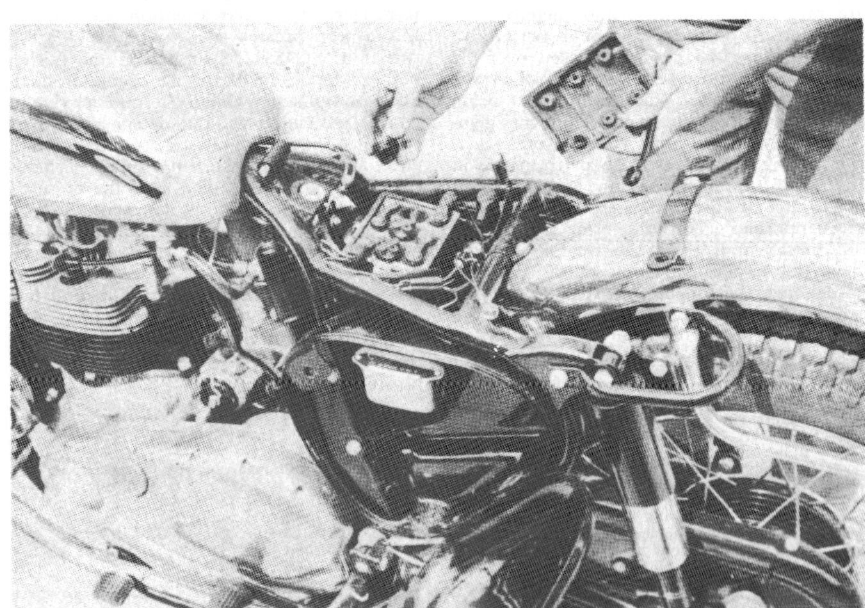

The battery is located right under the seat and is very well protected. Notice the rubber-mounted voltage regulator bolted inside the tool box.

power reserve for grades, headwinds and extra passenger are available over a wide range of engine speeds. Carrying a passenger did not substantially affect cruising speed. In a motor that can be wound up to top rpm's with extreme ease, the Smith tach is a most welcome feature to protect engine life. As might be expected with an 8.5:1 compression ratio, idling and slow running were a trifle erratic but, with proper use of the manual ignition con-

"The Super Rocket engine purrs like a kitten," said Asst. Editor Carol Anderson, here shown, not so coincidentally, with a small feline friend.

practical purposes the ability to sustain 80 to 85 mph tirelessly and "packing double" is adequate. Incidentally, the number of riders who indulge in such a high level of performance is comparatively small. The BSA Super Rocket is the mount that will satisfy that requirement even if a round trip coast-to-coast spin is being considered! This month's test bike was furnished to CYCLE staff by BSA Dealers Le Bard & Underwood, of Los Angeles, Calif.

From the very beginning of the test

and during the ten days that the machine was in our possession, its excellent ability to start at the first or second attempt—disregarding engine's temperature—was remarkable indeed. The tone of the engine was adequately controlled by a pair of Burgess type mufflers. Its torque and flexibility through gears was another highlight of this worthwhile high performance version of the successful and reliable Golden Flash. In practice this means that really superb acceleration and trol this minor problem could be easily solved. A big size Amal mono-bloc carb has been fitted replacing the TT type featured in 1958 models. This change accounts for a substantially higher gas mileage without impairing acceleration to a noticeable extent. The smooth transmission made it possible to take full advantage of the engine's resources without abusing it. Gear ratios are well selected and shifting is sheer pleasure in spite of the comparatively short lever.

Handling was well above average with the suspension a trifle on the stiff side. Incidentally, we consider this is a desirable feature in a high performance machine like the Super Rocket. The rear shocks can be adjusted to three different positions in order to meet different requirements of load and road conditions.

A two-wheeled 650 cc and a four-wheeled 600 cc side by side!

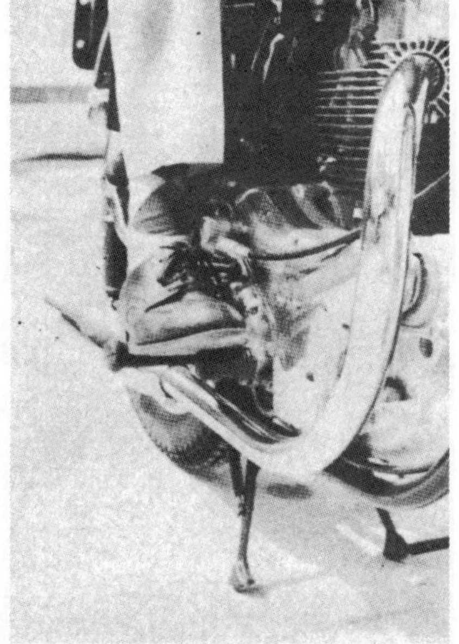
The protruding tach drive rubbed against the rider's right ankle and foot.

Full width and deeply finned front and rear brake drums are good features. However, on the test bike the rear binder operation was somewhat spongy, definitely requiring much more foot pressure than normally expected.

Clutch, front brake and twistgrip control cables are neatly concealed inside chromed guides along the handlebars. With the exception of the headlamp switch, which is partially covered by the speedo and tach clocks, all the other controls are very well placed and light to operate.

The magneto cutout is located right at the middle of the handlebar and close to the steering head damper knob. The air control lever has been relocated and is now on the right hand side of the machine between the seat and the gas tank.

Both fenders are chrome plated and match the tank panel, fork upper covers, exhaust systems, wheel rims and spokes.

The forks' legs feature rubber dust covers for extra protection and better looks. The gas tank is rubber mounted and can be removed, via a single bolt, in a matter of minutes. The rear chain is fully enclosed, assuring longer chain life and a minimum of noise at any speed. This valuable feature also precludes the necessity of removing the chain every month for cleaning purposes.

The battery is located under the roomy western-type twin seat and is very well protected from weather or eventual bumps. In order to reach the battery, the seat is removed by undoing a couple of bolts under it. The carb air filter has an extra large cleaning unit providing a maximum of efficiency and an almost negligible resistance to the carb air flow.

The voltage regulator unit is rubber mounted and bolted inside the tool box. Some minor criticism might arise

LEFT: The newly fitted Amal monobloc carb accounted for a minimum number of gas stops.

ABOVE: CYCLE tester Castro receives the keys of the BSA from Dealer Le Bard.

The relocated air control lever, folding kick starter pedal and chromed gas tank panels are features.

regarding the capacity of the latter. The tool kit is of average quality.

The 7½″ diameter head lamp with pre-focus light unit provides more than adequate illumination for safe and

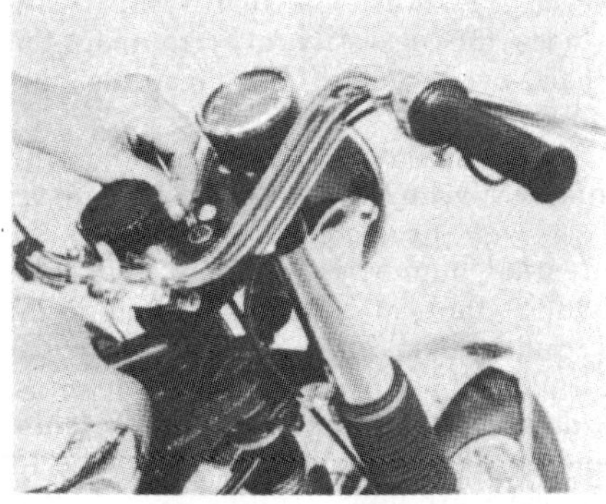

The anti-theft lock is a practical and useful addition.

consistently high speed cruising at night. By means of the convenient side lifting handle, the machine can easily be placed on its excellent center stand. The jiffy stand, although efficient, is a little hard to reach with the foot.

Another minor criticism was that the oil tank cap, with extremely fine thread, was a bit troublesome to remove or replace. At this point, and bearing in mind the beautiful and high quality craftsmanship of the Super Rocket, we would heartily welcome a quick-action type cap instead of the one furnished with the bike. At the conclusion of the test, the BSA was delivered back to the Dealer with real regret. It had shown itself to be a thoroughly attractive and powerful mount. It should appeal strongly to any type of rider—either beginner or

seasoned.

It possesses excellent maneuverability and speed coupled with a reasonable gas mileage and a second-to-none comfort for long distance rides. It is equally as attractive to those who ride their bike to and from work six times a week and have to fight the heavy traffic of the suburban areas.

BSA SUPER ROCKET

SPECIFICATIONS

ENGINE: 646 cc, OHV, four-stroke with fully enclosed valve gear and high performance camshaft; aluminum alloy cylinder head and 8.5:1 compression ratio. Bore and stroke: 70 x 84 mm. 46 HP @ 6200 RPM. Crankshaft drive-side supported by roller bearing, timing side by white metal bush. Light alloy rods. Single camshaft at rear with gear drive to magneto; dry sump lubrication with double gear type oil pump. Amal monobloc carburetor 389/31.

TRANSMISSION: BSA four-speed gear box with foot control. Gear ratios: 1st, :11,68; 2nd. :7.96; 3rd. :5.48 and 4th. :4.53. Five-plate fabric insert clutch and a fabric lined chain-wheel; primary chain ½ x .305″ with double cam cush drive on engine shaft; chain running in an oil bath case. Rear chain: ⅝″ x ⅜″.

IGNITION: Lucas magneto with manual control and separate chain driven 6-volt C.V.C. generator; Champion N-3 spark plugs. 7½″ diameter headlamp with pre-focus light unit and parking light; 12 amp. hr. battery.

TIRES: Front, 3.25 x 19
Rear, 3.50 x 19

BRAKES: Full width hubs with high grade cast iron drums; straight spokes. Front brake 8″ x ⅛″; rear brake 7″ x ⅛″, both with finger adjustment.

SUSPENSION: BSA hydraulically damped telescopic front fork with rubber dust covers on each leg. Swinging arm rear suspension with Girling shocks adjustable for weight in three positions.

FRAME: All welded duplex tubular cradle; easy-action roll-on central stand; key operated steering head lock; detachable rear wheel; western dual seat and passenger pegs.

CAPACITIES: Gas tank: 3 gal.
Oil tank: 5.5 pints
Gear Box: 14 fl. oz.
(400 cc)
Front fork legs: 7½ fl. oz.
(213 cc) in each leg
Primary chain case: 8 fl.
oz. (225 cc)

DIMENSIONS: Wheel base: 56″
Ground clearance: 6″
Overall length: 85″
Unladen seat height: 30″
Dry Weight: 413 lbs.

Minimum non-snatch speed: 15 mph in top gear on full retard.
Braking Distance for 30 mph: 27′
Gas mileage (overall avg.): 56.8 mpg

Ease of handling and rock-steady stability when cornering are two of the many fine features of the BSA Super Rocket, reported CYCLE staff tester A. Castro.

At the final control in the ACU Rally. The A7 finished in perfect condition with no oil leaks —and a first-class award as well

is little noise, and by rolling the grip back in the early hours of the morning I was able to burble through sleeping villages without even waking the dogs.

How about vibration, the curse of the vertical twin? On the A7 I would prefer to call it a slight tremble—strongest at 50, it almost disappears at 60.

The lights are very good indeed and enabled me to do 32 miles in 35 minutes on one not-so-straight stretch. Cats-eyes or no cats-eyes, you can't do that sort of motoring without a decent headlamp.

The petrol consumption varied very little whether the machine was ridden in traffic or fast on the open road. Owners who drive a little less enthusiastically will be able to improve on our overall figure of 74 m.p.g.

Nothing is perfect—not even the A7. This is a heavy bike, and the first-class prop stand listed as an optional extra should be fitted as standard. The headlamp switch is a good

600 NON-STOP ON A B.S.A.

THIS BSA is probably the friendliest bike I have ever ridden. I practically lived on it for a week—covering 1,264 miles. Drove it up and down the A5. Drove it two-up 60 miles a day in heavy traffic. Drove it all over London. And for good measure I did the ACU National Rally on it—600 miles virtually non-stop in 24 hours, then home again. And if a machine and rider can't get to know each other in that time they never will.

First I must make it quite clear that nobody is going to break any speed records on the A7, nor is it specifically designed for hauling a sidecar—BSA make other machines for that sort of thing. This is a sports twin equally suitable for fast touring or riding to work. It will meander along in built-up areas without fuss in top gear, yet can be cruised on the open road in the upper 70s. That is the great beauty of this bike—flexibility.

It handles extremely well—the steering was spot-on at all speeds. Yet the suspension was so soft and comfortable that it was difficult to detect a change of road surface.

This is a quiet bike. Even at speed there

arm's length away from the throttle, and the ammeter invisible at night. The brakes were good—very good. But would it cost a lot more to fit the fabulous 8-inch front stopper from the Gold Flash?

To sum up, then. Here is a sound, British-made machine—reliable and well built. It is as much at home on a run to the north of Scotland as it is on a shopping expedition down the High Street on a Saturday afternoon. A first class all-rounder.

Yes, it was a sad moment for me when I had to return this machine to the BSA factory.—DAVID FROST.

'M.M.' MACHINE TEST REPORT No. 5

Machine B.S.A. Model A.7. (GREY) c.c. 497

TEST Mileage 1264 Price new £249-1-10 Examiner D. Frost
(CHAINCASE EXTRA).

Supplied by B.S.A. MOTORCYCLES LTD.

Maximum Points 10 (compared with machines in same c.c. and price range)

Brakes (front)	8	Lights	9
Brakes (rear)	8	Engine accessibility	9
Brakes (both)	8	General performance	9
Steering at high speed	9	Overall finish	8
Steering at low speed	9	Electrical layout	8
Gearbox action	8	TOTAL	93

OVER WHOLE TEST
Fuel consumption 74 m.p.g.

Acceleration 0-50 7.25 secs.

Top speed 85 * m.p.h.

* Remarks MAX. SPEED OBTAINED ON STRAIGHT LEVEL ROAD, NO WIND, RIDER CROUCHED SLIGHTLY FORWARD

BRAKING GRAPH

M.P.H.

STOPPING DISTANCE IN FEET

---

646 c.c. B.S.A. AIO Golden Flash

AN OUTSTANDING TWIN WITH THE SPRIGHTLY

BUT UNOBTRUSIVE ALL-ROUND PERFORMANCE

THAT APPEALS TO THE CONNOISSEUR

by **HARRY LOUIS**

NO model produced in Great Britain has retained its identity, prestige and following better than has the B.S.A. Golden Flash. When introduced almost ten years ago it was heralded as a powerful luxury mount to provide that balanced combination of effortless high-speed performance and docility sought by discriminating riders who use their machine for all-round road work. It was an immediate success and has remained in the forefront ever since. To say that its charms are usually appreciated more by experienced riders than by comparative newcomers is to offer the highest praise. The latter group, for example, will probably be attracted by the more sporting six-fifties offered in the B.S.A. and other ranges but they may not know that on the give-and-take going of British roads the Flash is capable of averages that are unlikely to be bettered by the versions with slightly higher maximum speeds. Yet the machine has advantages of a lower level of mechanical and exhaust noise and better mudguarding.

It is difficult to imagine a more suitable mount for long-distance trips. The overall top-gear ratio of 4.53 to 1 means rather less

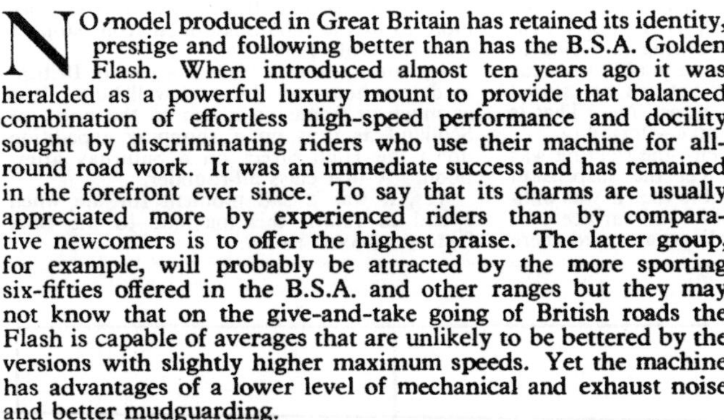

ENGINE: B.S.A. 646 c.c. (70 x 84mm) overhead-valve parallel twin; plain bearing big ends; crankshaft supported in roller and plain bearings. Compression ratio, 7.25 to 1.

CARBURETTOR: Amal Monobloc type 376 with air filter.

ELECTRICAL EQUIPMENT: Lucas magneto with automatic advance. Separate Lucas 60-watt dynamo. Lucas 7in-diameter pre-focus light unit with integral pilot light. Lucas 6-volt, 12-amp-hour battery.

TRANSMISSION: B.S.A. four-speed gear box driven by ⅜ x 0.305in chain through a multi-plate clutch with fabric inserts. Gear ratios: top, 4.53 to 1; third, 5.48 to 1; second, 7.96 to 1; bottom, 11.68 to 1. Final drive by ⅝ x ⅜in. chain.

SUSPENSION: Telescopic front fork with two-way hydraulic damping. Pivoted rear fork controlled by adjustable Girling spring units incorporating hydraulic damping.

WHEELS and TYRES: 19in-diameter wheels with full-width, cast-iron hubs. Dunlop tyres, Ribbed 3.25in front, Universal 3.50in rear.

BRAKES: 8in-diameter front, 7in-diameter rear.

FUEL CAPACITY: 4 gallons.

OIL CAPACITY: 5½ pints.

DIMENSIONS: Wheelbase, 56in; ground clearance, 5½in unladen; seat height, 30in; dry weight, 430 lb.

PRICE: £253 6s 3d (including £43 6s 3d British purchase tax). Extras: prop stand, 19s 11d (3s 5d); rear chaincase, £3 1s 10d (10s 7d).

MANUFACTURERS: B.S.A. Motor Cycles, Ltd., Small Heath, Birmingham, 11.

than 4,500 r.p.m. at 75 m.p.h. and there is 20 m.p.h. in hand at a twist of the grip. At speeds in the seventies the engine purrs like a contented cat, and the noise level is so low and the road-holding and steering so good that high averages without conscious effort become commonplace. When traffic enforces reduced speeds one can make the most of opportunities for overtaking since, as might be expected with an engine producing its maximum torque at 3,500 r.p.m. (60 m.p.h.), top-gear acceleration from about 45 to 65 m.p.h. is outstanding—and, because of the machine's unobtrusiveness, satisfying to use. Stop-watch tests showed a time of 12s for top-gear acceleration from 45 to 75 m.p.h.

The two-way mean maximum speed of the Flash is over 95 m.p.h. and 100 m.p.h. can be exceeded in slightly favourable circumstances. In fact, the three-figure mark could probably be achieved as a mean speed if the rider were clad in a one-piece racing suit and tucked in as much as possible to reduce windage. The important point is that 90 m.p.h. is easily obtained with the rider in ordinary weather gear and sitting up normally. Alternatively, 90 m.p.h. is on tap as the maximum in third gear. The engine is smooth up to about 63 m.p.h. (in top gear), when a vibration period sets in and can be felt at the tank and handlebar until nearly 70 m.p.h. Above that speed the period is completely lost. The level of vibration is by no means acute; it is what is normally experienced with all types of parallel twin.

As compared with the engine of a few years ago, the 1959 unit has a higher compression ratio (7.25 to 1) and the Super Rocket camshaft giving more valve overlap (although earlier closing of the inlet valve). The most noticeable effect is that fuel consumption is considerably lower than before. On long runs involving hard driving, 60 m.p.g. can be bettered and at fast touring speeds well over 70 m.p.g. is usual. Precise checks on measured quantities of fuel at exactly sustained speeds revealed the following: 70 m.p.h., 62 m.p.g.; 60 m.p.h., 69 m.p.g.; 30 m.p.h., 97 m.p.g. Premium fuel is desirable and in the middle throttle range slight pinking can be provoked by brutal grip twisting when the engine is hot after long periods of wide-throttle work. The chances are, however, that the average rider would cover thousands of miles without involuntarily causing pinking.

Although it is indisputably a heavy machine, the Golden Flash belies its weight immediately it is on the move. It has inherently good balance and can be ridden feet up at less than walking pace. At traffic crawls there is a complete absence of that steering heaviness sometimes felt with machines providing faultless high-speed steering. During the test period extending over 2,000 miles almost every conceivable type of road surface was encountered and on no occasion could the steering be awarded less than full marks. The suspension characteristics, too, are a happy compromise of the softness required for comfort and the firmness necessary for good handling at speed. The Girling hydraulically damped spring units at the rear have three-position adjustment for loading; the slackest position was used for solo work and the middle position when an adult passenger was carried.

Both brakes were spongy and the rear brake lacked bite. In contrast the front brake was extremely powerful and pleasureably light in operation; it could be made to squeal the tyre at all speeds by only light pressure and, used alone, gave a stopping distance of 44ft from 30 m.p.h. From the same speed both brakes brought the machine to rest in 34ft. Adjustment of the front-brake cable was required at approximately 500-mile intervals.

Hot- or cold-engine starting was easy and certain but the effect of really low temperature could not be ascertained since the weather throughout the test period was unusually summer-like. The engine idled with the slight unevenness common to parallel twins but the tickover was completely reliable. Carburation was clean throughout the range. Like almost all modern clutches, that on the Golden Flash would not free to give noiseless engagement of bottom gear on the first start of the day unless the plates were freed initially by operating the handlebar lever and depressing the kick-starter. Also a slight tendency to stickiness of the plates made it difficult to locate neutral when the machine was stationary while the engine was idling. But in the take up of the drive and in its lightness the clutch was faultless.

Gear changing was up to average standards—positive in all circumstances and very quick if need be. For completely clean changes a slowish movement of the pedal was desirable, particularly when engaging third from second. However, experience with B.S.A. gear boxes suggests that a lengthy mileage—up to 5,000—is often necessary before the gear box is free enough for the best results. Second and third gears were slightly noisy on both drive and overrun.

At times during the test the weather was abnormally hot, yet all the engine joints remained oil-tight and the gear box could be faulted only for a very minor leakage at the foot-change and kick-starter spindle bushes. In giving the machine a thorough clean down after 1,500 miles it was a far longer task to remove squashed bugs from the headlamp, front fork and tank than to obtain a pristine finish on the engine, chaincase and gear-box castings.

As is usual with all B.S.A.s, the riding position was suitable for a wide range of statures and proved absolutely comfortable for a rider of 5ft 9in. Although the rear-brake pedal is no longer fitted with an adjustable stop its position is excellently chosen and the short-travel gear pedal can be set on its splines to be equally well placed. The handlebar can be swivelled in its clips and the control levers are fully adjustable.

In spite of its weight the Flash can be rolled on its centre stand quite easily by depressing the rubber-covered pedal while a pull is exerted on the conveniently placed lifting handle. An excellent beam with a sharp cut-off on dip was provided by the headlamp. The range of adjustment of the light unit within the nacelle was adequate.

For 1959 the familiar all-beige finish was relieved by black enamel for the frame, engine plates, fork, shock-absorber covers, hubs and (if fitted) rear chaincase. The result is, unquestionably, a more attractive ensemble which reduces the apparent bulk of the machine and is probably more durable. An all-black finish is offered as an alternative. Wheel rims, exhaust system, tank panels, handlebar and controls, the headlamp rim and other detail parts are chromium plated and the aluminium primary chaincase cover, timing cover and gear-box cover are highly polished.

Two extras were fitted to the test model—a prop stand and a rear chaincase. The stand is commendably sturdy and easy to operate but could with advantage retract farther since it is likely to be grounded during cornering to the left, especially when a passenger is carried. The chaincase is a boon and well worth its price of just over £3; it keeps the chain completely free from grit and water and ensures that the rear drive is as good as noiseless.

No machine can aspire to match everyone's ideal. Each has its points of appeal, and the Golden Flash offers most of those sought by real enthusiasts and earns its place in the affections of knowledgeable, hard riders by genuine merit.

The black, beige and chromium finish is attractive without being garish

Left below: The power unit is outstanding for its quietness in operation and oil-tightness. The middle picture shows the dual-seat removed—by undoing two nuts—to give access to the battery. The tank is retained by a single bolt. Right: Chain tension can be checked quickly after removing a rubber grommet. Although not an oil-bath, the case keeps the chain in good condition and muffles chain swish

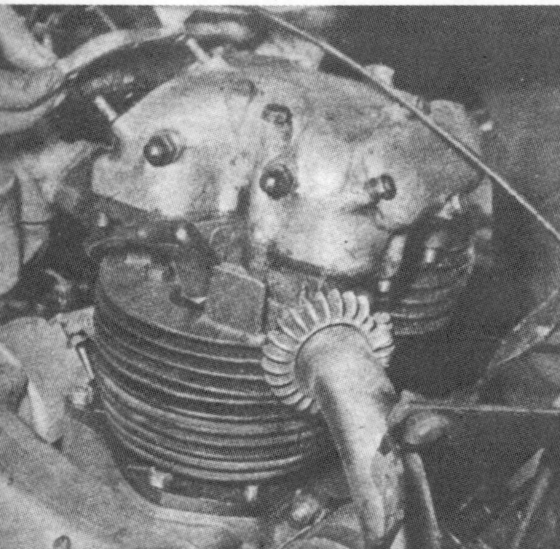

After removing the saddle and petrol tank take off the tappet covers to reveal the rocker box securing nuts

The carburetter being removed from the manifold. The exhaust pipes are also taken off the head at this stage

The rocker box being lifted from the cylinder head. Take care to slacken the tappets first to prevent damage

The first job on any overhaul—removing the petrol tank

OVERHAULING A BSA TWIN

JOHN CLARK describes how he

overhauled a badly neglected BSA Twin

IN our last issue we mentioned the reader who had been unfortunate enough to purchase a 500 c.c. BSA A7 in need of considerable overhaul. This has now been done and we have noted step by step the work that was done. It will be of great use as a guide to all A7 owners.

Dismantling this model was not a difficult job. After draining the tank and removing the petrol pipes, the two tank retaining bolts were undone. The dual seat was then taken off the machine—allowing removal of the petrol tank.

The tappet covers were next removed, this being necessary to give access to the rocket box securing nuts that were inside. The rocker box oil feed pipe was loosened and tied back against the machine's frame with a piece of string.

Before removing the rocker box the tappets were slackened—the reason for this was the prevention of possible distortion of the box during removal.

It was found that the only work necessary to remove the exhaust pipe was the slackening of the connections of the silencers and the removal of the finned collars next to the cylinder heads. The pipes could then be pulled away leaving the silencers *in situ*.

The knurled ring on the carburetter was then undone and the throttle and air slides removed from the body of the carburetter. They were then taped to the frame out of harm's way. The carburetter body could now be removed from the manifold.

The studs holding the head to the cylinder barrel were then released and, with the sparking plug in place, the kick starter was given a sharp prod. The resulting compression forced the head from the pots.

An examination of the head valves of this machine showed that the guides were so badly worn that oil was being induced into the combustion chambers from the rocker box via the valve guides, resulting in heavy oil carbon deposits on the chambers and valve heads.

Weak springs allowed the valves to wobble in the guides and this in turn caused incorrect seating in the head—

With the cylinder head nuts undone and the plugs still in place a swing on the kickstart will free the head

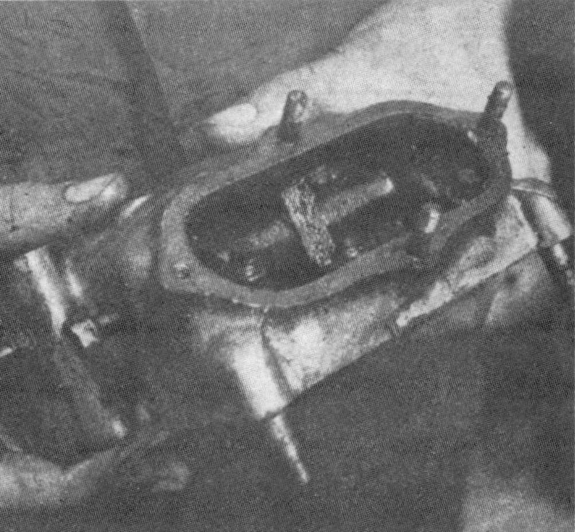

The filthy state of the rocker box with burnt oil and sludge shows how seriously this machine was neglected

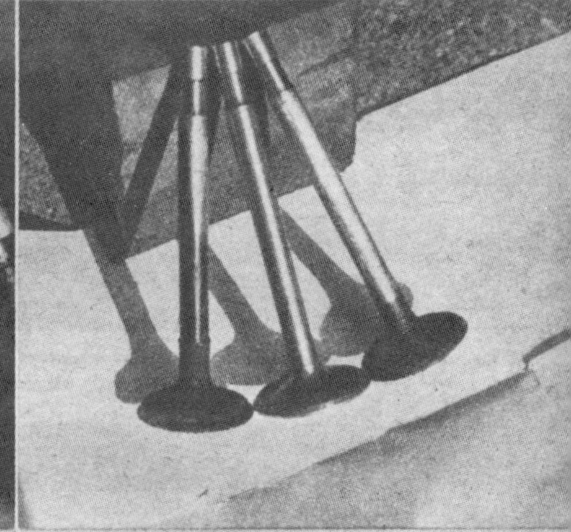

The valves were badly worn and had to be scrapped. Compare worn stems on old valves with the new one in middle

also wear on the circumference of the heads of the valves.

Wear on the barrel was not excessive and we decided that new oil control rings would save cash and would be suitable. The nuts securing the barrel were then removed and the pots lifted clear of the crankcase.

The small and big end wear was negligible but there was considerable shake in the crankshaft assembly. The primary chaincase was removed and it was found that the primary chain and the clutch sprocket bearings were in bad shape.

The hardened steel chain tensioner was slackened. The split pin holding the engine shaft nut was withdrawn and the shock absorber assembly removed.

The clutch cover was held in place by 2BA nuts. These were undone and the cover was eased away from the studs. The clutch springs and cups were released by undoing the slotted nuts.

Withdrawing Clutch Plates

The clutch plates were then withdrawn from the clutch housing giving access to the centre nut, the clutch thrust rod was left in place through the centre of the main shaft. The gearbox crankshaft was prevented from rotating while the clutch centre nut was being undone by putting the box into gear and holding the rear brake on hard.

As the primary chain is of the endless variety it was necessary to remove the engine and clutch sprocket at the same time.

We found that there were two rollers missing and this no doubt accounted for the wobble on the clutch sprocket. When the back plate was removed the collar fell away in two pieces. This is, however, quite normal and allows easy fitting to the shaft.

We began to dismantle the offside of the motor and when the timing chest cover was removed discovered a large amount of old grease, filth, carbon, etc., instead.

Wear on the dynamo drive chain was considerable and a new one was obviously the solution. Removal of the drive sprocket from the idler shaft allowed the removal of the dynamo drive chain—it was not necesary to remove the sprocket from the end of the armature.

We encountered further troubles after removing the centre section of the timing chest. The cork disc connecting the camshaft drive gear to the rotary breather was broken and a new one required. The cork seal on the idler shaft was also damaged.

By slackening off the dynamo securing band it was possible to slip the dynamo from the cradle to the nearside of the machine.

The lock-nut on the end of the main shaft and the oil pump were next removed. Both of these have left-handed threads. The oil pump retaining nuts were undone and the pump was then drawn from the studs.

The drive gear on the mainshaft was coaxed off with the aid of a tyre lever. The curved end was placed under the edge of the gear and only a little gentle pressure was required to ease the gear off the end of the shaft. We were then able to examine the main bearing.

It was obvious that the caged roller drive side bearing and the plain timing side bearing had seen better days and were in fact so sloppy that they allowed the shake previously mentioned.

We decided to remove the remainder of the engine from the frame (and record here that this is the easiest engine removal we have ever experienced). Previously four front plate bolts had been removed and the removal of a further four allowed the engine and gearbox to be lifted from the frame—the secondary chain, clutch cable and oil and crankcase having first been disconnected.

We released the magneto drive gear. As this incorporated the automatic advance and retard mechanism little difficulty was experienced in releasing the gear from the taper on the shaft. We did this by undoing the shaft nut and removing the split washer and back plate. We then slackened off the three nuts holding the magneto to the timing chest and gave the nut on the end of the magneto shaft a sharp tap with a hide-faced hammer—this was quite successful.

One of our reasons for removing the magneto was to have reasonable access to the gearbox securing bolts. As these hold the gearbox in the motor they must be removed before it is possible to split the crankcase.

The sump plate and filter on the crankcase were next to be removed.

Splitting the crankcase was not difficult and we gave it a few gentle taps round the edges—this did the trick.

The complete list of replacements were written down as they were needed while the motor was being stripped.

The new main bearings were fitted in the same manner as suggested in our August issue. The crankcase halves were heated in a kitchen oven, the old bearings being tapped out and the new ones pushed into place. During this time the complete c r a n k assembly was thoroughly cleaned.

It was noticed that the end float on the main shaft had permitted the drive end bobweight to scuff against the casing —no doubt this accounted for some of the noise we heard from the engine whilst it was running.

The camshaft drive gear was left in position while the crankcase was in two halves but we saw that any future removal would certainly require the splitting of the crankcase with the engine out of the frame.

Flushing the Gearbox

We flushed out the gearbox and re-tensioned the kick-start return spring which had been incorrectly fitted by a previous owner. All that was needed was the removal of the end cover with the gear change lever and kick-start in place. We then wound up the spring with two turns of the kick-start lever— then having cleaned up the face joint we replaced the end cover.

We rejointed the two crankcase halves making sure the two halves were square— being certain that the camshaft underwent this performance carefully. The gearbox was then refitted to the crank case.

We decided it was easier to refit the magneto on the bench so we stripped and cleaned it. During this operation, we found that the carbon brush on the

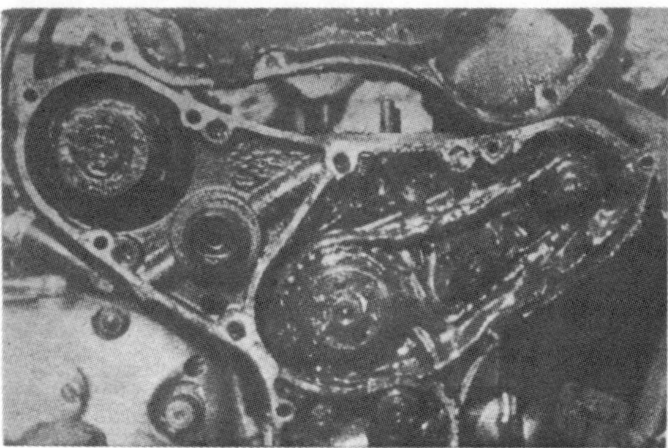

Removal of timing case cover showed a mass of old grease, sludge and oil

The mainshaft pinion being eased off its taper with the aid of tyre lever

Refitting cylinder barrel. Note how pistons are held in place with blocks

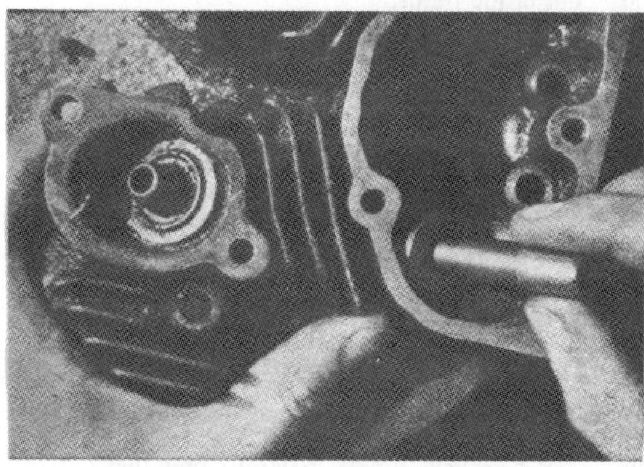

Replacing a worn valve guide into the cylinder head, which had been warmed

BSA TWIN—STEP-BY-STEP GUIDE

drive side of the magneto was completely adrift and that there were small broken pieces of the brush in the bottom of the magneto case. There was no sign of the spring and we found that it had been chewed up. This brush was replaced and the magneto refitted to the engine with the new chain gasket.

The reversal of the removal procedure was all that was necessary when refitting the motor back in the frame. The main point to be remembered being the fitting of the front plates before finally securing all the bolts.

We then checked the dynamo and found that the commutator end plate was loose. The dynamo was then slipped into the cradle on the front of the engine.

All engine parts which had been removed during dismantling were cleaned in a cleansing solution—fifty/fifty diesel oil and paraffin. They were scrubbed with an old paint brush to remove all the filth.

The engine and clutch sprockets were fitted together with the primary chain in place. (This applies equally to the type of chain with a connecting link. As it is a duplex chain it is impossible to replace the long connecting link—there being insufficient room behind the chain and the back of the primary chain case.)

We first fitted the splined sleeve to the engine mainshaft ready to receive the sprocket split collar and the clutch back plate. No trouble was experienced when reassembling the clutch centre rollers as plenty of grease kept these in place.

By slipping the chain round both sprockets and holding one in each hand, they were offered up to their respective shaft. A little careful manipulation and they were held in place. We then replaced the face cam shock absorber, spring and end plate. Screwing in the end plate as far as possible, we fitted a new split pin.

The clutch centre nut was tightened with a box spanner while holding the shaft still by the same method as used for slackening. Incidentally, the adjustment of the clutch spring should be done to your own tastes and needs, remember that more spring pressure is advisable if a sidecar is to be used. *Be certain that the clutch clears squarely.* This is done by viewing across the face of the clutch and gently pressing the kick start.

We then fitted the clutch plate cover ensuring that the oil seal was in good condition. Next the outer cover and foot rest. This is fitted with a nut with a left-handed thread and care was taken to see that it fitted correctly.

With care we replaced the drive to the main shaft and made sure it keyed correctly in place—the small key must fit properly in the key-way before the drive gear is slipped into position.

The oil pump was put into place using the new gasket and then the oil pump drive gear was screwed on to the shaft—this too has a left-handed thread. After inserting the locker washer and fitting the locknut we secured the nut and gear together. The next step was to refit the idler gear and to time the camshaft. On the drive gear there is a small spot punched on a tooth—this we engaged with a similarly marked place on the idler gear. On the camshaft gear there is a small line marking a tooth—this must correspond with a mark on the idler gear. This done the timing is correct.

Before fitting the centre screw on to the timing chest it was found necessary to get a new cork drive for the end of the camshaft gear driving the rotary crankcase breather. We also fitted a new joint gasket here before fitting the centre section in place.

No trouble was experienced in refitting the magneto drive gear and after fitting a new cork seal it was pushed into place against the timing chest. A new cork washer was fitted into the end of the idler shaft.

The dynamo chain tension was adjusted by rotating the dynamo in its cradle until there was about a quarter of an inch up and down movement at the centre of the chain.

Before fitting the cylinder barrels they were given a coat of cylinder black and whilst this was drying the pistons were fitted to the con rods. This was facilitated by heating the pistons in the oven. When they were really hot they were then slipped over the con rods and the gudgeon pins were pushed into place. New circlips were fitted and the new block/crankcase gasket was put into place ready for the fitting of the barrels.

This was made easier by the fitting of two pieces of wood across the crankcase supporting the pistons in a level position. The barrels were gently lowered over the piston and the rings were compressed by hand as it was lowered into place. The two pieces of wood were then slipped out and the block allowed to drop over the studs.

Ignition Timing

Ignition timing was done with the head off — this ensures absolutely correct measurement of five sixteenths of an inch before top dead centre. Next we fixed the auto advance in the fully advanced position with a chip of wood. The drive gear was loosely fitted over the magneto shaft.

Next we turned the contact breaker assembly until it just opened (we used a thin cigarette paper to check this).

We gave the drive gear a sharp tap to fix it on to taper of magneto shaft.

We then turned the engine over several times and rechecked the timing. The setting was correct and the magneto drive shaft nut was tightened and the timing checked *again* to see that it had not moved while tightening. When we were satisfied that all was well, the dynamo chain compartment was filled with clean grease and the timing chest cover refitted.

We then started on the cylinder head. After removal of the valves and springs we cleaned the head thoroughly and removed the valves guides with a bronze drift. It was then completely decoked.

The head was heated in the oven to the same temperature as the crank case had been. It was removed and the new valve guides were carefully tapped into place with a soft square headed drift. After the head had cooled the new valves were ground to form a perfect seat in the head. The new valve springs were then

—continued page 138

THE B.S.A. GOLDEN FLASH 650 c.c. O.H.V. TWIN
MODEL A10

George Wilson, Assistant Editor of "The Motor Cycle" says "I consider this B.S.A. model to be just about the best value for money available today." Extract from "What I Rode in 1952" in "The Motor Cycle," January 1st, 1953.

B.S.A. CYCLES LTD., 47, ARMOURY ROAD, BIRMINGHAM 11

Highlights from a brilliant range

This year prove for yourself what thousands upon thousands of satisfied owners already know. This, B.S.A. is today's very best motorcycling value. Look at it *every* way. Initial cost. Fuel economy. Minimum maintenance. You get MORE for LESS with a B.S.A. Yet this all-round economy is coupled with sparkling performance, superb roadholding and comfort—plus the widest range in the world. Bantam to Golden Flash, you're better off on a B.S.A.

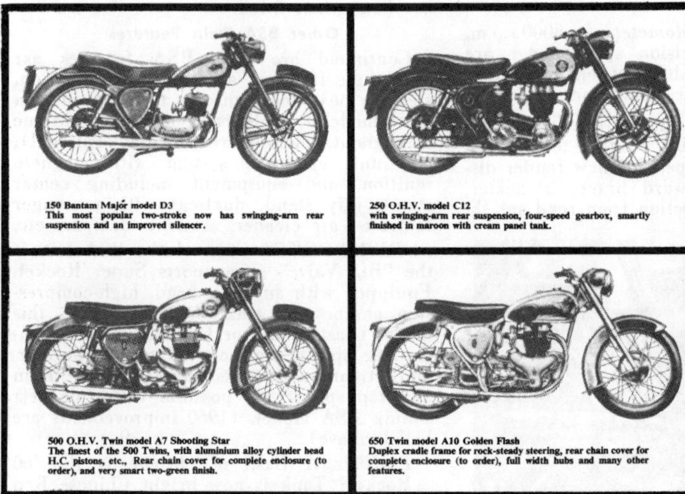

150 Bantam Major model D3
This most popular two-stroke now has swinging-arm rear suspension and an improved silencer.

250 O.H.V. model C12
with swinging-arm rear suspension, four-speed gearbox, smartly finished in maroon with cream panel tank.

500 O.H.V. Twin model A7 Shooting Star
The finest of the 500 Twins, with aluminium alloy cylinder head H.C. pistons, etc., Rear chain cover for complete enclosure (to order), and very smart two-green finish.

650 Twin model A10 Golden Flash
Duplex cradle frame for rock-steady steering, rear chain cover for complete enclosure (to order), full width hubs and many other features.

Please send catalogue showing complete B.S.A. range—BANTAM TO GOLDEN FLASH.

Name..

Address..

B.S.A. MOTOR CYCLES LTD., 47, ARMOURY ROAD, BIRMINGHAM, 11.

The Reference in this advertisement to an A.C.U. Official Test has been approved by the A.C.U.

ESSO PETROLEUM COMPANY, LIMITED, 36 QUEEN ANNE'S GATE, LONDON, S.W.1.

B.S.A. MOTORCYCLES FOR 1960

BSA goes into 1960 with a 17 model motorcycle range incorporating many refinements and improvements. Both mechanically, and from the appearance standpoint, 1960 BSA motorcycles are among the finest ever offered by the Birmingham, England factory, and the range is broad enough to completely cover the motorcycle market. In addition to motorcycles, BSA offers also the improved Sunbeam twin-cylinder scooter.

THE BSA RANGE

In the popular 40 cubic inch twin class, BSA offers the popular "Big Valve Super Rocket Sports Twin," and the newly renamed Royal Tourist (formerly Golden Flash). The Spitfire Scrambler, a competition model, is also a 40 incher. 500 cc twins are represented by the 500 Flash and the Shooting Star.

Big Singles, for which BSA is well known, are represented by the Gold Star Road

Racer (in road trim) and the Catalina Scrambler. Both models are 500 cc capacity and are also available to special order in 350 cc engine size. The popular Sportsman 500 road single is also continued.

In the increasingly popular 250 cc class, BSA offers the improved 250 Star and the recently introduced 250 Starfire Scrambler.

BSA two-stroke models are comprised of the sturdy 125 cc Bantam and the 175 cc Bantam Super. The 175 is also available in an under-5-horsepower model for states with special licensing regulations for younger riders.

The BSA "Sunbeam Scooter" in improved form is now offered in attractive metallic zircon (light green) color.

That is the range, now for details of 1960 improvements.

1960 IMPROVEMENTS

Better Braking: An improved rear brake is now fitted to all twins and the Sportsman Single. A repositioned brake operating lever, and improved brake cam action give powerful braking with less pedal effort. BSA twins all have the rigid full width type hubs with polished alloy brake plates and chrome end covers. Cable adjusters are now fitted at the handlebar end of both brake and clutch cables.

New Clutch Adjustment Access Opening: A large diameter plug is now fitted in the primary drive of all BSA twins, making clutch spring adjustment quick and easy.

New Oil Level Check and Drain Plug: All twins now have a new oil level check and drain plug fitted to the bottom of the primary drive case. Oil level in primary drive may be accurately checked or completely drained without disturbing other parts.

New Tachometer Drive: A neat, new tachometer drive is now fitted to the Super Rocket and Gold Star Road Racer. Drive is now taken from the front of the timing chest, entirely eliminating the former right angle drive.

Tachometer and Speedometer: An 8000 r.p.m. tachometer and precision speedometer are mounted on a twin bracket on the Super Rocket and Gold Star Road Racer.

New Style Fenders: An entirely new, self-supporting front fender is fitted to all road twins. Of valanced type, this new fender dispenses with the forward brace, is neater, and offers more protection from road splash.

On the Rocket, a new semi-bobbed fender of valanced type is fitted. Fenders on the Rocket are heavily chromed, other road models are enameled. A neater rear fender brace is also fitted to 1960 twins.

Larger Carburetors: On the Super Rocket with its large diameter valves introduced in 1959, a larger carburetor adds even more performance. The Royal Tourist also has a larger carburetor.

New Dip Switch & Horn Button Fitting: A neat new ring-type fitting on the left handlebar now incorporates horn button, dip switch ·and magneto cut-out, eliminating much external wiring.

New Tank Badges: On most larger models, the four gallon tank is now fitted with new streamlined tank badges of handsome appearance. (3-gallon sports tanks have round badges.) All BSA badges are of three-dimensional design in gleaming lucite plastic material. Tanks are also fitted with new design knee grips.

Longer Fork Top Nuts: A longer threaded portion on fork top nuts now allows for space taken up by windshield mounting brackets when fitted.

Other BSA Twin Features

Continued are such BSA features as: Twin tube frame of all welded construction, steering head lock, chrome tank panels (on most models), and generous use of chrome throughout, enclosed rear chain (optional), two unit electrical system with magneto ignition, and equipment including center stand, jiffy stand, dualseat with passenger footrests, air cleaner, steering damper, etc.

SUPER ROCKET: Top of the BSA line is the "Big Valve" super-sports Super Rocket. Equipped with an alloy head, high-compression engine and maxium sized valves, this model boasts many performance features including sports camshaft, bigger carburetor, and streamlined ports. Lively acceleration and top speeds are possible with this best selling BSA model. (1960 improvements are listed above).

Finish: A flash of chrome is the '60 Rocket! Tank is now bright Chinese Red with large chrome panels and new style tank badges, fenders are completely chrome plated. Many other chrome plated parts

BSA. New rear brake drum and cable

B.S.A. MOTORCYCLES FOR 1960

include fork top tubes, wheel rims, entire exhaust system, handlebars, levers, and brake end plates. Frame is black.

ROYAL TOURIST: The re-named Golden Flash with many improvements as outlined above, continues to be a favorite touring model. More power through a larger carburetor in the 1960 model should make this BSA twin a top choice of the highway and byway wanderer. Finish specifications make the Royal Tourist especially attractive with the BSA Accessory Group available through BSA dealers.

FINISH: Jet black with gold striping and large chrome tank panels. Many parts in chrome or polished alloy.

SHOOTING STAR: 500 FLASH: Two fine-performing 500 cc twins of similar basic specifications and with many 1960 improvements as outlined above. The Shooting Star

B.S.A. Sunbeam Scooter

parts in gleaming chrome plate.

250 STARFIRE SCRAMBLER: A high performing, extremely attractive competition model, the new BSA Starfire Scrambler has already made a fine reputation in motorcycle sport circles. Featuring a special high-output scrambles engine, this model has scrambles gear ratios, engine undershield, sports tires and other competition items plus complete lighting equipment.

Finish: Sapphire blue tank with chrome panels, chrome fenders, black frame and many parts finished in chrome.

BANTAM 125: Reliable, highly economical, and dependable, the BSA Bantam is continued without change for 1960. A highly developed 125 cc two-stroke engine furnishes ample power for quick cross-town jaunts or byway pleasure riding.

Finish: Bright red tank with cream panels, red fenders with white striping, black frame and many parts in gleaming chrome.

BANTAM SUPER 175: Good power output,

has an alloy head engine with high compression pistons for more performance. The 500 Flash offers more than adequate power for many riders and is the lowest priced BSA twin.

Finish: Shooting Star, jet black with gold striping and 500 Flash, sapphire blue with gold striping. Both models have generous areas of bright chrome.

SPITFIRE SCRAMBLER: The BSA 40 cubic inch Scrambles model, the high performance Spitfire is supplied in complete scrambles trim. Specifications include a high-performance engine with racing camshaft, high compression pistons, maximum diameter valves, and larger carburetor. Scrambles gear ratios, sports tires, sports fenders, racing dualseat are also supplied. Generator and regulator are standard equipment (no other electrical equipment or wiring supplied).

Finish: Sapphire blue tank with chrome panels, chrome sports fenders, rubber fork gaiters, and many other parts in chrome.

GOLD STAR ROAD RACER: The well-known Gold Star in road trim. Continued in 1960 are such high-speed specification items as dynamometer-tested and tuned 500 cc o.h.v. engine, racing cams, racing valves and springs, racing carburetor, and road racing brakes. This is a model for the rider who is interested in competition or in a fast road single.

Finish: Deep blue tank with chrome panels, chrome sports fenders, chrome upper fork covers with rubber gaiters, many other parts in chrome or polished alloy. Frame is black.

CATALINA SCRAMBLER: The Gold Star in full scrambles trim with engine specially tuned and set up for scrambles type compe-

tition. Specifications include scrambles gearbox, engine under-shield, racing oil tank, quick-fill gas tank, and many other equipment items designed for scrambles competition.

Finish: Sapphire blue tank with chrome panels, chrome sports fenders and black frame.

250 STAR: Popular new addition to the BSA line in 1959, the lively 250 cc o.h.v.

reliability, and fine appearance in a lively two-stroke. Featuring a unique lubrication system with direct oil feed to main bearings, the Bantam Super also has such refinements as hydraulically controlled front fork, swinging arm rear suspension, dualseat with passenger footrests, and many other equipment items for motorcycling enjoyment.

Finish: Bright red tank with cream panels, red fenders with white striping and black

B.S.A. Tachometer & Speedo—On Super Rocket and Gold Star Road Model

"250 Star" has a brand new finish, and detail improvements resulting in even better performance in the 1960 model. Light and peppy, this is the BSA entry in the fast growing lightweight market.

Finish: Two-tone tank in Sapphire Blue and Ivory with gold striping and new streamlined badges in gleaming red lucite. Fenders blue, frame black, with many

frame. Many parts in bright chrome plate.

Thus, for 1960, BSA has lined up a fine array of top quality motorcycles with more performance, more chrome, and more value for the purchaser's dollar, plus BSA dependability. Every motorcyclist will find a model of special appeal in this comprehensive range.

4,500 miles in a fortnight! That's the plan, says BOB WEBB, as he points to the turn-round oasis in the Sahara Desert

Monty, the racing rider and builder of many successful racing machines. Ron will be recording the trip on film and Geoff is driving one of the outfits and is organising the technical side of the venture. Ron will also act as spare rider.

The machines will be examined at the RAC offices at the start of our journey and will again be examined when we-return. We hope to do the complete trip without touching either machines or side-cars with a spanner.

The organisation has been lengthy but, I hope, thorough. We have made several visits to the French Consulate and between us filled in 24 different forms for the Sahara crossing alone.

John Clark, one of our staff, is in charge of the route marking, working on maps supplied by Michelin. The RAC supplied the basic route and have assisted with all the documentation.

We propose to leave from the RAC, Pall Mall, London, early in January, and will then drive to Lydd Airport. We will

Sahara Safari

WE have devised the toughest road test for machines and equipment that has ever been attempted by a motorcycling magazine. Over 4,500 miles of the roughest roads in the world—sand, grit, gravel and rocks. The machines will be driven as hard and as fast as is possible in temperatures ranging from freezing to over 100 degrees. We are driving from London out into the Sahara Desert and back—in 14 days.

What special machines and equipment have been specially designed to withstand this sort of treatment? The answer is NONE—everything is " straight from the assembly line." No special mods.

We have chosen two 1960 BSA 650 c.c. Golden Flashes, and they have each been fitted with a Watsonian sidecar—one a passenger-carrying Avon and the other a commercial box to carry our spare petrol and water (27 gallons of liquid—at the order of the French authorities).

The Plastics Division of ICI stepped into the breach and have given us 15 one-gallon Alkathene water containers. No rattles, squeaks or thumpings in the side-car, and the plastic jerrycans pack into quite a small space. ICI are also responsible for the Perspex screens that are fitted on our streamlinings.

With me on the trip are Ron Spillman, writer and photographer, and Geoff

fly by Silver City Airlines to Le Touquet, and will then drive direct to Marseilles. This is one of the very long stretches on the trip, but to save time we will do it in one run with only a brief rest midway.

At Marseilles we board a steamer for Algiers, and this part of the trip will be spent checking the machines and resting. The passage takes 20 hours, and we lose almost two days' running time from our 14 days.

At Algiers we drive due south on a well-shod road for some 200 miles through the Atlas Mountains. Then the road finishes and the desert begins. Although popularly believed to consist mainly of sand, the desert is in fact

Watsonian Director Mr. G. C. Bennett shows us a frame

Ron Spillman tries this "Avon" for riding comfort

This Benjamin Edgington tent is our portable home

Sleeping is important and so we decided on this Lilo

largely rock, and we drive through one continuous mountain range broken only by strips of sand till we arrive at Hoggar, 1,485 miles from Algiers.

Just what sort of treatment the machines will get we will leave to your imagination—but we will report on their progress on our return.

Fuel and Oil

Fuel for the trip was an important consideration, and we decided to ask Mobilgas for their help and advice. They have arranged petrol for us at various stages throughout the trip, as well as a complete oil change twice at Algiers.

The machines are shod with Dunlop tyres—Trials on the rear and Universals on the front—our only breakaway from standard equipment. I think that this is quite justifiable in view of the nature of the tracks to be covered. All tyres are fitted with security bolts to allow running at low tube pressures.

Clothing for this sort of trip is all-important, and we have to equip ourselves for two different climates—cold in Europe and hot in Africa. We plumped for Barbour suits with fleecy inner linings in the jackets. S. Lewis have supplied us with a new line in riding boots. These are really something quite special, with a tough shoe and with the full knee-length upper made from the same leather as their racing horsehides. They are soft

and comfortable to walk in and wonderful for riding—whether it be on the race track or road.

Our scarves and body belts came from Aviakit—the scarf is made from towelling and slips through the loops at the neck of the suits. The body belt helps to hold us connected inside over the rough roads—it makes a lot of difference to the comfort of long-distance riding.

Goggles were a problem—we all had different ideas. Stadium Ltd. came to the rescue with Mk. 9 goggles for myself, a pair made to fit over spectacles for Ron, and a panoramic type for Geoff.

We are using two types of glove by Slazengers. A light racing gauntlet for the hot riding and heavy fleecy-lined mittens for the cold weather.

Benjamin Edgington, who have equipped many expeditions—including Sir John Hunt's Everest party—suggested and supplied what camping equipment we will require. It is all light and cut to bare essentials. The tent (a Monarch) weighs only just over seven pounds, but will hold the three of us with Lilo beds as well. The Lilos weigh only two pounds apiece and pack small. Lilo also make a two-gallon rubberised canvas water carrier with a tap at the bottom, and we are carrying two of these for emergencies.

Reg Cross, of Louth, has made us three Italian styled racing overalls to wear for driving in the heat. These serve a double

use—they are extra clothing in the cold but ideal for summer riding.

Naturally enough, we are taking tools —we'd be foolish not to, although we don't think that they'll be needed. Gordon Tools have supplied a very complete kit.

Some special equipment is being carried. A Timex watch is being strapped to the steering head of my machine—I don't know how many times it will be shaken up and down, but it will be a very severe test.

Streamlining

For our own comfort, both machines are being fitted with "Avonaire" Dolphin streamlinings. These will give us protection in snow or rain, and also in sand. For further protection we are also wearing helmets—we all decided on the American types, and Ron and Geoff are using the new Everoak Racemaster and I am remaining faithful to the one I have been using for the past six months—the Aviakit Super Jet. These types of helmet are comfortable and very protective.

The past few weeks seem to have been filled with " string " vests, inoculations, snake-bite kits, tyre and petrol companies and reams of documents. It's my firm belief that the hardest part of the trip has been the planning. I shall be quite glad to get into the middle of the desert 2,250 miles away—just for a rest !

BOB WEBB

Special new racing boots made for us by S. Lewis Ltd.

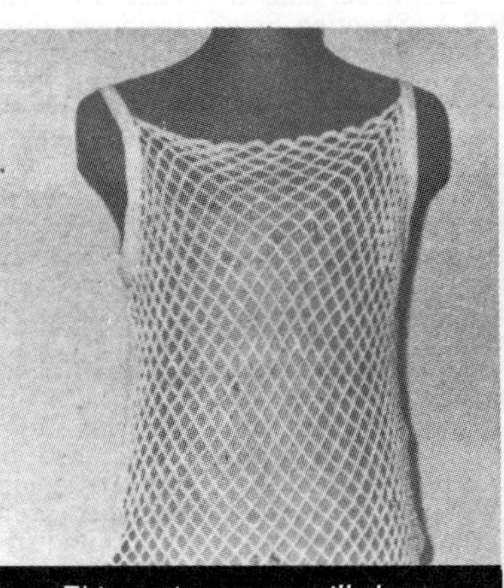

This string vest will keep the cold out and the heat in

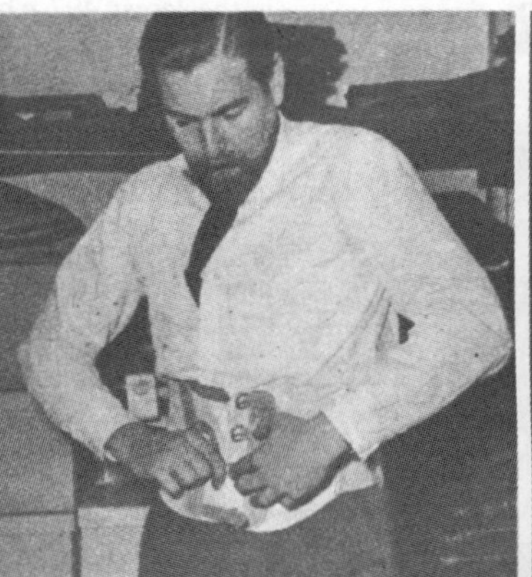

For long rough riding a body belt helps to keep body and soul together. D. Lewis (Aviakit) recommended this and towel scarves

497 c.c. B.S.A. Shooting Star

ONE OF THE WORLD'S MOST REMARKABLE TWINS : FLASHING ACCELERATION, HIGH AVERAGES, ROCK STEADY AT SPEED, DOCILE IN TRAFFIC

PERFORMANCE over the years has always been something of a compromise: underline one particular aspect of it and, in general, somewhere along the line another has suffered in

A deep section and absence of forward stays give the front mudguard a neat appearance

some degree. In terms of refinement, what does one expect to pay for a top speed of close on 100 m.p.h. in a roadster five-hundred twin? And for the ability to reach 80 m.p.h. at the end of a standing quarter-mile and to cruise indefinitely at 80 to 85 m.p.h. on little more than half throttle?

These are outstanding abilities in a medium-capacity twin. To what extent need they involve noisy running, vibration, heavy petrol consumption, tricky starting, poor tractability at low speeds or, at least, a knack in juggling the controls? Time was when those short-comings were an inevitable part of the price cheerfully paid for such vivid performance. But that time has passed if the model chosen is the latest 497 c.c. B.S.A. Shooting Star twin.

Its top speed and, more important, its acceleration and effortless fast cruising would do credit to a good six-fifty. Yet the Shooting Star is among the smoother vertical twins and can hold its own with the best for fuel consumption. The level of exhaust and mechanical noise is no higher than one would expect from a model of much more moderate performance, so the rider has no fear of giving offence to any reasonable bystander. And although a healthy sucking sound comes from the carburettor intake when the throttle is snapped open, the noise is by no means obtrusive and soon escapes notice.

Starting required little effort and was dependable whether the engine was cold or hot. As for low-speed tractability, it

was good enough to take all the irritation out of traffic crawling. True, it was usual to retard the manual ignition control for starting, idling and tick-tocking along at 5 or 6 m.p.h. in bottom gear with the clutch fully home; but even manual retarding might well be avoided by a change to auto-advance, for the usual centrifugal control would do all that the engine requires.

The basic layout of the Shooting Star is by no means new. The model was derived five years ago from the Star Twin, a high-performance variant of the A7 introduced immediately after the war. But unobtrusive changes year by year serve to keep it right up to date in looks and convenience as well as in performance. For instance, there is a deeper-section front mudguard this year that dispenses with the need for front stays. A slight alteration in the shape of the dual-seat makes for greater comfort on long runs. And the latest primary chaincase has not only an ingenious level-cum-drain plug but also an extra inspection hole through which the clutch springs may be adjusted in a trice; since stiffnuts replace the earlier lock nuts, the job needs only a box spanner.

Performance-wise the most significant recent alteration is the raising of the compression ratio to 8 to 1. This has pepped up acceleration appreciably, yet the engine remains completely free from pinking on ordinary premium petrol and no benefit was found in using the dearer 100-octane grade.

Of course, the engine needs to be turn-

Left: The rear-brake adjuster is knurled for finger setting and has a nut for locking purposes.   On the right can be seen the plug giving access to the clutch-spring adjustment.   The voltage regulator is in a compartment of the tool box.   Below are details of the primary chaincase drain-cum-level plug

ing over briskly to give its best power; but that does not imply harshness at low r.p.m.—merely a more moderate response to throttle opening. Indeed, not only was the Shooting Star quite happy at 25 to 30 m.p.h. in top gear (and on full advance at that) but it would accelerate smoothly from that speed merely at a twist of the grip. To a considerable degree this commendable top-gear flexibility stems from the makers' good sense in avoiding the pitfall of overgearing: at 5.28 to 1 the Shooting Star's top-gear ratio is lower than that of all other five-hundreds, even allowing for some of them using smaller wheels.

But to the sporting rider one of the prime joys on the Shooting Star is to push the speed swiftly up to 55 m.p.h. in second gear and 80 m.p.h. in third before settling down to sustained high speeds. For riders of sufficient experience and ability that sort of technique was enough to put a

mile into every minute on long main-road journeys without using the motorway. At high speeds a slight tremor could be felt through the handlebar but certainly not enough to cause discomfort. Incidentally, the speedometer was more accurate than most: maximum error was 2 m.p.h. (fast) from 90 m.p.h. upward.

On a machine of the Shooting Star's versatility, riding position is particularly important. If the footrests are well forward, there may be ample comfort at low speeds but the rider will have to pull continuously on the handlebar at high speeds to counteract wind pressure; if the rests are too far back, the improvement at high speeds may be at the cost of too much weight on the wrists at low speeds.

The B.S.A. footrests are set far enough forward for comfort in town but the need to pull on the handlebar is reduced to a minimum by the chocking effect of the slightly raised rear half of the dual-seat.

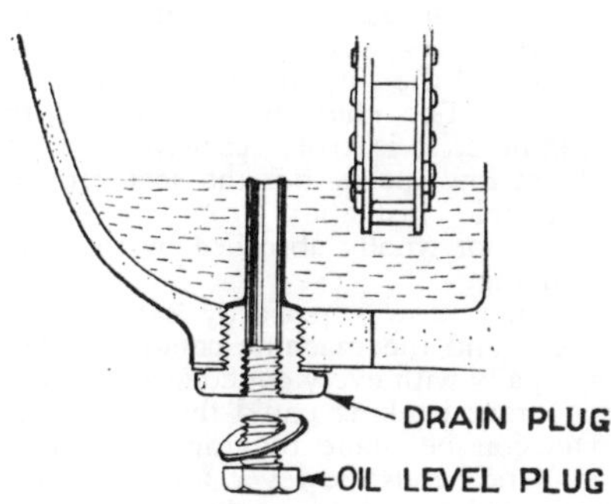

Relative positioning of seat, footrests and handlebar is widely spaced enough to ensure uncramped angles at the rider's knees, hips and arms.

Controls are very conveniently placed. Some tidying of the handlebar has resulted from positioning the air lever

Specification

ENGINE: B.S.A. 497 c.c. (66 x 72.6mm) overhead-valve vertical twin. Valve gear operated from a single camshaft. Light-alloy connecting rods with lead-bronze big-end bearings. Crankshaft supported in roller bearing on drive side and lead-bronze bush on timing side. Aluminium-alloy cylinder head. Compression ratio, 8 to 1. Dry-sump lubrication; oil-tank capacity, 5½ pints.

CARBURETTOR: Amal Monobloc; aid slide operated by lever under dual-seat nose.

IGNITION and LIGHTING: Lucas magneto with manual control. Separate Lucas 60-watt dynamo. Lucas 6-volt, 12-amp-hour battery. Lucas 7in-diameter headlamp with pre-focus light unit and 30/24-watt main bulb.

TRANSMISSION: B.S.A. four-speed gear box with positive-stop foot control. Gear ratios: bottom, 13.62 to 1; second, 9.28 to 1; third, 6.38 to 1; top, 5.28 to 1. Multi-plate clutch with fabric inserts. Primary chain, ½ x 0.305in in cast-aluminium oil-bath case. Rear chain, ⅝ x ¾in, in pressed-steel case. Engine r.p.m. at 30 m.p.h. in top gear, 2,040.

FUEL CAPACITY: 4 gallons.

TYRES: Dunlop: front, 3.25 x 19in ribbed; rear, 3.50 x 19in Universal.

BRAKES: Front, 8 x 1⅛in with finger adjuster; rear, 7 x 1⅛in.

SUSPENSION: B.S.A. telescopic front fork with hydraulic damping. Pivoted rear fork controlled by Girling spring-and-hydraulic units with three-position adjustment for load.

WHEELBASE: 56½in unladen. Ground clearance, 6½in unladen.

SEAT: B.S.A. dual-seat; unladen height, 32in.

WEIGHT: 440 lb fully equipped, with full oil tank and approximately one gallon of petrol.

PRICE: £213; with purchase tax (in Great Britain only), £256 18s 8d. Rear chaincase, £3 1s 10d extra.

ROAD TAX: £3 15s a year; £1 0s 8d a quarter.

MAKERS: B.S.A. Motor Cycles, Ltd., Small Heath, Birmingham, 11.

PERFORMANCE DATA

(Obtained at the Motor Industry Research Association's proving ground at Lindley.)

MEAN MAXIMUM SPEED: Bottom*: 43 m.p.h.
Second*: 63 m.p.h.
Third*: 92 m.p.h.
Top: 95 m.p.h.
*Valve float occurring.

HIGHEST ONE-WAY SPEED: 98 m.p.h. (conditions: moderate tail wind; rider wearing two-piece plastic suit and overboots).

MEAN ACCELERATION:

	10-30 m.p.h.	20-40 m.p.h.	30-50 m.p.h.
Bottom:	2.6 sec	2.6 sec	—
Second:	3.8 sec	3.4 sec	3.4 sec
Third:	—	5.5 sec	4.8 sec
Top:	—	7.3 sec	7 sec

Mean speed at end of quarter-mile from rest: 80 m.p.h.
Mean time to cover standing quarter-mile: 16 sec.

PETROL CONSUMPTON: At 30 m.p.h., 100 m.p.g.; at 40 m.p.h., 83 m.p.g.; at 50 m.p.h., 75 m.p.g.; at 60 m.p.h., 65 m.p.g.

BRAKING: From 30 m.p.h. to rest, 29ft (surface, dry tarmac).

TURNING CIRCLE: 14ft.

MINIMUM NON-SNATCH SPEED: 14 m.p.h. in top gear on full retard.

WEIGHT PER C.C.: 0.9 lb.

under the right-hand side of the seat nose. During the warm weather of the test period, when the lever was fully opened immediately the engine fired, the new location had no drawbacks; but it might prove less convenient than the old position on the bar in wintry weather when the lever might need to be used for the first mile or two following a cold start.

The clutch was very light to withdraw, free from drag and smooth yet firm in taking up the drive. A restart on a 1 in 3 slope proved to be child's play. With the engine idling slowly—which it did very well with the ignition at half retard—bottom gear could be engaged at a standstill with only a minor clonk. When coming to a halt, neutral could be selected with ease and certainty from bottom or second gear, regardless of whether the machine was rolling or stationary. To achieve really clean changes between bottom, second and third gears it was necessary to use a slowish pedal movement going up, and to blip the throttle briskly and make the change at a fairly low road speed when coming down. No such precautions were required for the change from third to top and *vice versa*.

At high speeds the Shooting Star held the road very well without the slightest pitching of the suspension under any conditions. The characteristics giving this steadiness, it is true, resulted in a firm ride at low speeds but the seat provided reasonable insulation from those road shocks not wholly absorbed by the wheel springing.

Cornering was perfectly steady at all speeds and the machine could be heeled over gaily with every confidence. Only by exuberant banking could the centre-stand extension be made to ground lightly on left-hand bends; however, for convenience many riders might prefer to specify a prop stand (available as an extra) and that is normally slightly easier to ground.

The generous steering lock was appreciated when manœuvring in confined spaces, though for short riders the advantage was largely offset by the seat height (unladen) of 32in. At no time was it found even remotely desirable to use the steering damper. There is no doubt that the makers' precaution of balancing the wheels has a lot to do with the machine's general steadiness at high speeds.

Front-brake diameter is increased this year from 7 to 8in while reversal of the rear-brake cam lever results in greater effort going to the leading shoe. Both brakes were smooth, progressive and amply powerful to pin the machine down really firmly whatever the speed.

Lighting was up to par and the headlamp beams are controlled from a combined dip switch, horn button and magneto cut-out just inboard of the left handlebar grip. The possibility of an unpleasant black-out when changing from one beam to the other is obviated by overlapping of the contacts in the mid-position of the dip switch. During the test a short circuit developed in the unit, cutting the engine and main beam; removing the lead from the contact breaker cover enabled the engine to be restarted.

The oil tank was changed when a welded seam began to leak, and the

Steadily improved over a number of years, the B.S.A. Shooting Star engine gives the model a fine blend of pep and good manners

speedometer-drive cable also had to be renewed. Rather more austere than those of earlier models, the tool kit lacked spanners for removing the petrol tank and valve covers and for holding the valve-clearance adjusters. Though the instruction book is in the main excellent, there are shortcomings that might puzzle the newcomer if not the experienced owner.

These are minor criticisms of a remarkable machine that must make an enormous appeal to the rider seeking a tip-top five-hundred. In spite of the Shooting Star's zestful performance being used without stint for many hundreds of miles, the machine remained commendably clean externally and the rear chaincase (an optional extra) proved a very worth-while fitment.

The 1960 B.S.A. Shooting Star has an 8in-diameter front brake and a comfortably shaped dual-seat

Sahara Safari

The roughest, toughest road test of all time — 4,500 miles driven in ice, snow, rain, mud, sand and sun.

BRITISH motorcycle products, machines and accessories are the best in the world. They can withstand the most arduous and trying conditions that can be found anywhere. We know—they took us across the Sahara Desert and back.

Our machines were two 1960 BSA A10's, 650 c.c. twins coupled to Watsonian sidecars. The only non-standard fittings were manually operated advance and retard mechanisms on the mags, large section trials tyres and gaitered front forks. Both machines wore Avonaires and carried Stowaway panniers.

One of the sidecars was a commercial box and carried spare petrol, water, tools and tinned food—plus sleeping bags, camping equipment and various odds and ends. A total load of OVER 500 lb. excluding the extra weight of two spare wheels carried between the box and machine in a special rack. The amount of gear was so great that special racks were made by Terry Fry of Hampton.

The other sidecar, a normal touring model, carried a passenger, and various photographic equipment. It also had a spare wheel, five gallons of extra petrol and two gallons of water loaded on to various parts of the chassis.

All refuelling at points throughout the trip was done by the Mobil Oil Company, they provided petrol, oil and grease. We fully endorse their products and the efficiency, courtesy and help given to us by their stations in England, France and Africa.

Climatic conditions were varied. Below freezing in France and over 98 degrees in the desert. We had rain, snow and ice in Europe; sand and blazing sun in Africa.

The roads and tracks were as varied as the weather. Some Algerian roads as good, if not better, than the M1. Others rutted and stony tracks, deep in sand and corrugations that shake the fillings out of your teeth.

This is the day by day diary of the trip. . . .

DAY 1 Left RAC club, Pall Mall, London, after examination of machines by RAC Chief Engineer. Arrived Lydd Airport and crossed to Le Touquet by Silver City freighter. Total time of crossing, including all formalities with French Customs, less than $\frac{1}{4}$ of an hour. Weather rainy as we drove south to Paris. City very crowded with evening traffic. Found Mobil Station and refuelled then rode on to Evry-Petit-Bourg where we had an evening meal and a couple of hours rest at the home of two French motorcycle enthusiasts Alain and Francis Gannon. Total mileage 223.

DAY 2 Left at 3 a.m. and continued south towards Marseilles. Decided to alter alignment of sidecars to suit camber of French roads. North of Valence Geoff Monty noticed that his ammeter showed no charge—hasty check indicated fault in cut-out. At Mobil Station in Valence we stripped out the regulator and found two wires loose—no doubt due to vibration of *pavé* roads. Repaired these but still no charge. Found armature burnt out. Impossible to find dealer at this late hour so continued on to Marseilles. As Geoff's battery became flat we changed it with the one from my machine, then changed again. Reached Marseilles at 2.30 a.m. spent rest of night in café. Mileage 516.

Both the pictures on this page show typical desert tracks—the deep sand frequently stopped the bikes

Above left : a quick stop for a glucose drink. Above right : this track was a corrugated bone shaker

DAY 3 Found Lucas dealer in Marseilles and waited at doorstep until he arrived. Very cooperative man who supplied us with new armature. Rushed to dockside and spent next hour trying to get on to boat. Very confusing performance both to Frenchmen and foreigners like ourselves.

Machines lifted on to ship by cranes and then packed into hold. We retired to cabin to catch up on sleep. Crossing rough but we appreciated French food and enjoyed company of French soldiers returning to Algeria after leave.

DAY 4 Entered Algiers harbour at dawn. Passed through customs with no trouble. Representatives of the Mobil Oil Company waiting on dockside with Rene Goetz the Algerian Moto-Cross champion. They led us to petrol station and Rene organised a replacement for the cut-out. He and his brother worked with us while we changed the armature.

Mr. Alfred Fox of the British Embassy gave us information on the road conditions and we left Algiers at mid-day. Wonderful drive in sunny weather up over the coastal mountains and then through the fabulous gorges of the Atlas mountains. Geoff's dynamo was now charging.

French military road blocks every few miles reminded us that this country was at war. We turned a corner of the road and found ourselves in the middle of a company of French artillery mortaring the hillsides—we left rapidly.

Past the mountains the country began to get browner—the road rougher—and we stayed the first night at Boughari. Local Gendarmerie were very friendly. We had first Arab meal of cous-cous in native café.

Camping here was forbidden because of terrorists and we spent night in an ancient " hotel."

DAY 5 Ancient hotel had modern fleas —this encouraged early rising and we were on the road before dawn. With machines coated in ice we drove south through a light mist. Glad of Barbour suits with thick woolly linings. Sun rose as we approached first road block and military waved us through after examining papers. Road only one vehicle wide but southbound traffic has the right of way—this is because of the blinding glare of the sun. We changed the lenses in our goggles to a dark green.

At noon the sun was hot and as the long fast ride heated the engines Geoff recommended that we changed oil at every refuelling station. The first was at Djelfa and our machines caused quite a stir in the small Arab town.

The road now had deviations at various points and was quite rough. This cut down our speeds. Dangerous bends were navigated with care as the road was not wide enough to carry two vehicles side by side. Both machines running well.

Towards Ghardaia the road became first class. Very wide and very smooth we were able to drive at 60 m.p.h. plus. We arrived at Ghardaia just as the French Military closed the road for the night. After reporting to Gendarmerie and having documents stamped we left machines under guard in the barracks and found small hotel for the night. The Hotel Rocher was clean and comfortable and we enjoyed a good night's rest.

DAY 6 We again began before dawn and noticed along the route that hundreds of telephone poles had been cut down by terrorists. Sight of armed convoys brought back unpleasant memories. We wondered if the sub-machine guns carried by French sentries at the road blocks were loaded—later found that they were loaded *and cocked*.

Road surface was good but there were drifts of deep sand across it. These are invariably round fast corners and we had a few exciting moments navigating them. The road was incomplete here and we had several long stretches which gave us a good indication of what we were going to meet ahead. The tarmac ended and we found nothing but a rutted track ahead, sand and dust are over a foot deep in places and we were soon smothered in a layer of red. There were pot-holes and rocks and it became difficult to do more than 10 miles an hour. The country was now barren, just large sand hills hundreds of feet high and occasionally the tents and camel herds of wandering Arab tribes.

At lunchtime we arrived at El Golea, the town where the Duke of Edinburgh rested on his way to Ghana. We had ridden well into the desert. After refuelling and changing the oil we drove out of the town. There was no road whatsoever. Just tracks, deep rutted through soft sand. Large hidden rocks became a constant menace.

We had to strip and clean both carburetters. Sand and dust jammed open the slides. I lost the large nipple that fits into the twistgrip but we made up one out of a short length of wire wrapped round the cable. The track became corrugated and this shook the machines and sidecars badly at any speed over fifteen miles an hour. We saw a lorry and stopped to ask the driver of the road conditions ahead. He told us that they would be the same all the way south.

We decided that in order to complete the mileage we must ride fast regardless of the possibility of damage to equipment.

We climbed on to the Tadamait Plateau through deep sand. A few miles farther on we found that Geoff was no longer with us. On returning we saw him examining his sidecar wheel. The suspension spring unit had been smashed off by a rock. We jacked up, the sidecar and changed the unit. We had two spares for the sidecars and two for the machines (the latter two units were Geoff's personal property).

Within 20 miles the second unit broke and we replaced it again. We dug the machines out of the sand every few minutes.

It was dark when we arrived at Fort Mirabel, once built for the Foreign Legion this is now used by the infantry. We were invited to dine with the French officers and spent the night in one of the " cells."

DAY 7 The Plateau consisted mainly of small rocks over a black sandy crust. There were no hills to break the monotony and the horizon was perfectly circular. Nothing living could be seen. Only the tracks of previous vehicles indicated the route. The suspensions took a terrific hammering. Geoff's machine broke a third unit and the wheel began to lean in dangerously. The heavy weight it carried strained everything over the rocky track. We had now only one unit left.

Cleaning the carburetters became an hourly job. Mirages made driving uncomfortable as we became more and more tired. The others were now envious of the peak on my helmet.

We lost our way in the afternoon and after driving for a couple of hours decided to retrace our steps. It had become dark and I slid the outfit into a heap of rocks. At first we thought that the machine was a write-off but the fairing took most of the impact and the damage was restricted to the mudguard, front wheel rim, forks and exhaust pipes. Ron was thrown through the sidecar windscreen and cut his nose.

After finding the original track we carried on to Ain Salah. Leaving the dreadful plateau was a great relief although in the dark everything still looked the same. We had a strange illusion that we were driving through forests—this must have been because we were now very tired.

After again reporting to the police we spent the night in the only hotel in the town. Mileage for the day was 315.

DAY 8 Awake early we found that this was indeed a beautiful town. No trace of Western modern civilisation. Just mud huts and a majestic ancient fort captured by the Foreign Legion. All the inhabitants wore native dress and camels and donkeys seemed to be the only means of transport. The French soldiers in Saharien dress, baggy pantaloons and long white cloaks with red bandoliers of bullets looked very picturesque.

After a couple of hours work on the machines—just regular maintenance, checking cables, adjusting brakes and clutches, resetting tyre pressures to cope with almost red hot sand, we again drove south.

The road was deep in sand and we had to dig out the machines time after time. This frayed tempers but any anger was directed against the track rather than each other. At three in the afternoon we turned about at Tiguelguemine and headed north again for the return trip. This was very hard to do for not far south of us were better tracks and Nigeria, swimming pools and English speaking company.

We passed Ain Salah in early evening and made the run up to the Plateau again. The evening became night and we were sore and almost exhausted with the hardest day's run of the trip when we reached Fort Mirabel again at 2 a.m. after 405 miles of rough going.

Ron's work was harder than Geoff's or my own. He was recording the trip both on tape and film. His gear suffered badly with dust and constant vibration and he was a mass of bruises. We made rope handles for him to hold on to on the sidecar. Over the very rough ground he sat on the back of the seat—trials fashion.

The guard at Fort Mirabel lent us three straw mattresses and we just had enough strength to crawl into our sleeping bags—fully dressed.

DAY 9 In the morning, by the light of a torch, we found that the last suspension unit had broken on Geoff's box sidecar. The shock of the road without this fractured a joint of the suspension lug and the wheel was now leaning even further towards the machine.

Geoff found a discarded lorry inner tube on the desert, it was the biggest we had ever seen and Geoff strapped it on to the sidecar. This tube saved the day, for cut into bands. we were able to make a rough but efficient suspension by looping the rubber around the swinging arm and pulling it back to the sidecar mudguard's rear stay.

Geoff coupled two spare chains together and made one end fast to the inner side of the sidecar chassis, the other side he fastened to the wheel suspension. This prevented the wheel from leaning in any further.

This work took most of the morning and we seemed to be miles away from anywhere. With the engines stopped on the

Wherever we stopped in the towns large crowds gathered around the machines. They were all extremely helpful and friendly, sometimes riding on the sidecars to show us the Mobil Stations

The gorges through the Atlas Mountains were extremely beautiful but they hide also the camps of many of the Algerian terrorists and we were warned not to stop for more than a few moments

Fort Hassi El Fahl was built by the Foreign Legion and we were entertained in traditional style. The young French soldiers are stationed here for months many miles away from the towns

First essential on any long trip is a comfortable camp and we were than more satisfied with the Benjamin Edgington equipment, the tent was warm and insect proof and quite simple to erect

Sahara Safari

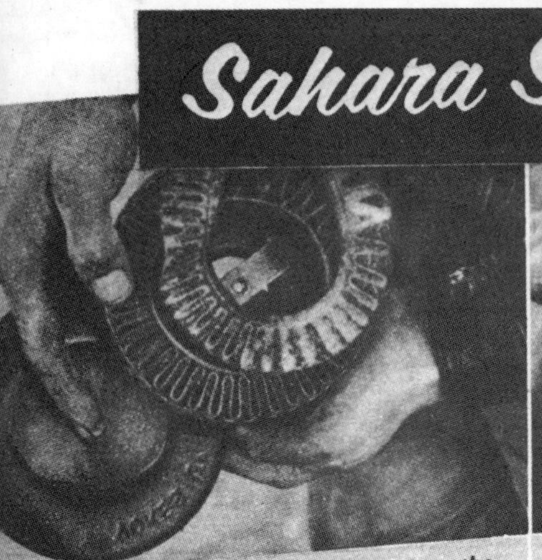

The sand and dust was so fine that the filters needed cleaning every few miles, we tied oily rags around the air intake

Once the dust had penetrated the filter it jammed open the slides of the carb, this meant frequent stops to clean them

Greatest danger was from large rocks and here I am examining the damage caused by hitting one hidden in the soft sand

This was the result of the crash but Geoff was confident that all the gear would return home with us

This "spanish windlass" of chains held the suspension until we found a garage to straighten the tubes

Ever seen anything like this ? It gives some idea of the road surfaces that were encountered on the trip

The fully loaded box sidecar—it carried as much weight as could be carried in a light truck or car

plateau there was absolutely no sound at all. The only living thing we saw in the desolation was a huge red locust.

We were now all very saddle sore and Geoff was sitting on a sheepskin waistcoat. Our knees were skinned where they had been touching the tank rubbers and it was easier to ride standing up.

Late in the afternoon we reached El Golea again and managed to find a garage with brazing equipment. After unloading the box we repaired the damage done by the rocks of the plateau. Geoff also managed to repair one of the suspension units and so back in our original condition we reached Fort Hassi El Fahl, as the road was closed for the night.

Here again, as on many occasions during the trip, we were all very grateful for the guidance of Benjamin Edgington, the camping equipment people. The camping gear they supplied us with was ideal. The sleeping bags were warm and comfortable and the tent easy to erect, draughtproof and light.

DAY 10 The going was better again and we were making good time although there had been sandstorms in the previous few days and the roads were covered in some places. The machines kept running well and we wrapped oily rags around the filters to help keep out the dust—this meant that we could go for as long as four or five hours without cleaning them.

There were the wrecks of abandoned cars along this section of the road and obviously some of them have been here for many years. A grim reminder of previous unsuccessful attempts to cross the desert.

A French officer asked me if we would be in Algiers on schedule, I replied that with luck we would be. His answer was that of the hardened Saharien, "You'll find no *good* luck in the Sahara Desert."

At about six p.m. we reached Fort Tilrempt and shortly after we had been stopped and informed that this was as far as we were allowed to travel that night, we found that the pilot jet cap screw had dropped off my carburetter. Geoff's ingenuity came to the rescue again and he astounded the garrison mechanics by effecting a repair with a short length of plastic tube, a small bolt and a length of wire.

He pushed the tube up over the bottom end of the pilot jet securing it in place with the wire. He blocked the other end of the tube by screwing in the bolt and then tied the tube up against the carburetter—result, no leaks and the machine was running.

The French were most hospitable and we answered hundreds of questions about the machines and equipment.

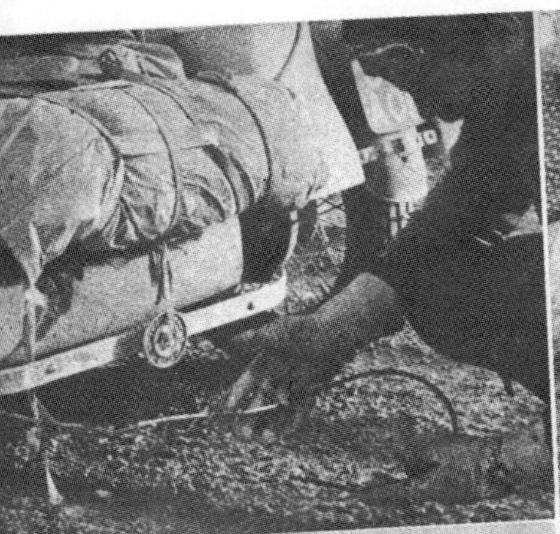

We had to keep up high speeds although his guaranteed damage to our gear and his sidecar brake was torn clean away

The suspension springs were smashed by stones and the great weight of the gear we carried—nothing could have survived

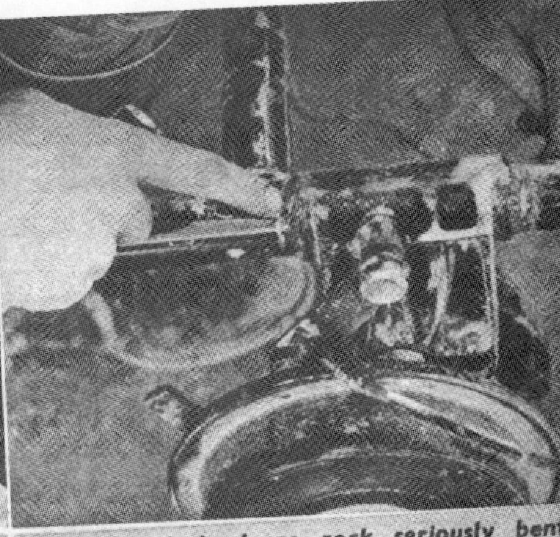

A particularly large rock seriously bent the suspension unit where it sleeved on the heavy tube chassis of the box sidecar

DAY 11 Some 20 kilometres after leaving the Fort we saw the tops of oil derricks in the distance some miles off the track. It was just dawn and we decided to take time off to investigate these. They belonged to a German company searching for Butane gas. They had built a portable town in the middle of nowhere. They had drilled their own well and their cabins were air-conditioned. We were given an English breakfast washed down with very French Cognac and coffee.

We became rather angry later that day as we were stopped on the road at four-thirty p.m. The French N.C.O., refused to let us go through to Boughari although we would have been there within half an hour.

This put us behind schedule. Later when the Commandant arrived we learnt that there had been two terrorist attacks on vehicles on this road within the previous three days—the day before one of the Foreign Legion platoons fought a battle with some terrorists in a nearby village.

DAY 12 Up before light and we were ready to go as soon as permission was granted. We got away at first light and some hundred yards down the road found a whole company of horse-mounted Foreign Legionaires. Their officer clapped his hands as we rode by and the men waved their kepis and shouted to us. They were a wonderful sight with red and blue cloaks and white belts.

As we drove up into the mountains the machines seemed to run easier in the cooler air. After the heat of the desert this was comfortable riding. No more trouble with the filters and although the roads were bumpy by English standards we found them easy going.

We stopped at Boughari to say goodbye to the Gendarmes who had helped us on our way south. They told us that on the day we had left the town it had been attacked by terrorists who were firing down from the hills. More telephone wires were cut and the road signs along the route we saw were riddled with bullet holes.

At last we entered the gorges again and rode down through the fields of orange trees. We stopped and Ron and I picked some to take home to our families.

Ron's chest was giving him a lot of trouble and we thought that he had torn a ligament. We all showed signs of wear and Geoff's nose would be worth a story all of its own.

We reached Algiers and the friends we made in the British Consulate and the Mobil Oil Company. We were entertained at the Consulate in the evening and began to feel civilised again. The machines spent the night in the workshop of Rene Goetz.

DAY 13 When we collected the outfits from Rene in the morning, in order to load them on to the boat, we found that he had already repaired another suspension unit, this time for my own sidecar. It had been missing completely but I had not noticed. This oversight must have been due to tiredness as I had remarked that the machine was pulling to the left but thought this was due to the heavy camber of the narrow road.

We loaded the machines at 9 a.m., and then treated ourselves to the pleasures of a haircut and shave at a local barber's.

At last we were on board the ship bound for home. Although we had only left Algiers a little way behind it was already getting colder. We ate heavy meals to prepare for the last part of the trip and went off to bed early.

DAY 14 France — almost home again It was minus seven degrees centigrade a n d really freezing hard. We had more trouble leaving the port—a very complicated procedure made worse by the fact that our French was a little rough. We eventually got away at 10.15 a.m.

After driving for a while we were freezing and no matter what we did we had to stop every half an hour and thaw out by violent roadside exercise.

Geoff had very bad cramp in his shoulders and my right hand began to give me some trouble. We found that by wrapping the sleeping bags round our legs we made better time. We did not stop during the night.

LAST LAP It was dawn as we passed through Paris and refuelled in the city centre. We were feeling the trip now far more than the machines. They just seemed to keep on running. It had begun to snow and the roads had a coating of ice.

At last Le Touquet and an understanding Silver City official found us room on the first available plane, within half an hour we were back in England.

We left the airport and were pleased to find the roads clear of ice although it was still cold. This last leg became a major physical effort and we were grateful when we met Alec Smith, a personal friend and contributor to this magazine. He led us back to our final destination at the RAC club. We had driven non-stop from Marseilles, 739 miles in 37 hours.—BOB WEBB. ●

EQUIPMENT USED AND CARRIED

2 BSA A.10's. 650 c.c. Twin cylinder machines.
2 Watsonian Sidecars.
Mobil Oil Company fuel and lubricants.
Dunlop tyres.
Lucas Electrics.
Renolds Chain.
Avonaire Fairings. Fitted with ICI Perspex Screens.
Stowaway Panniers.
Champion Sparking Plugs.
Wipac filter links and Dip Switches.
15 one gallon ICI Alkathene water containers.
3 4½ gallon petrol cans.
2 Special Tubular carriers by Terry Fry Products, Station Road, Hampton, Middlesex.
3 Alkathene drinking cups.
3 Barbour Suits.
3 Aviakit 'Super Jet' Helmets.
S. Lewis racing boots.
3 Lilo air beds.
2 Lilo water bags.
1 Remington razor.
3 Timex Watches.

6 Stadium Goggles.
Boots Chemists medical equipment.
Maconochies tinned food.
Dictaphone 'Dictet' recording equipment.
Jenolite rust neutraliser.
Complete Tool kit (personal).
3 prs. Slazenger racing gloves.
3 prs. Slazenger Touring gauntlets with waterproof covers.
3 D. Lewis body belts.
3 prs. D. Lewis sea boot stockings.
3 prs. D. Lewis Tuffler scarves.
3 prs. Reg Cross racing overalls.
Michelin Road Maps.
Benjamin Edgington supplied the following equipment :
3 sleeping bags.
3 sets eating irons.
One petrol Primus stove.
3 plastic plates.
Tent with flysheet and built-in groundsheet.
6 string vests.
Each rider was allowed one pannier for personal clothing.
Total weight of gear—over 700 lb.

The 646 c.c. B.S.A. Model A10SR 1960 ROAD TESTS

'SUPER ROCKET'

Motorway performance

combined with

docility and economy

Specification

ENGINE

Type	Parallel-twin four-stroke
Bore	70 mm.
Stroke	84 mm.
Cubic capacity ..	646 c.c.
Valves	Overhead (push-rod)
Compression ratio	8.3 : 1
Carburetter	Amal " Monobloc," $1^{5}/_{32}$-in. choke
Ignition	Lucas K2F magneto, manual control
Maker's claimed output	42 b.h.p./6,000 r.p.m.
Lubrication	Dry sump with double gear pump
Starting ..	Kickstarter (folding pedal)

TRANSMISSION

Separate gearbox with footchange

Ratios	4.5, 5.5, 8.0, 11.7 : 1
Speed at 1,000 r.p.m. in top gear ..	17 m.p.h.

Speed equivalent to revs. at maximum power rating :

Second gear	60 m.p.h.
Third gear	87 m.p.h.
Top gear	106 m.p.h.

Primary drive	$\frac{1}{2} \times .305$ in. chain
Final drive	$\frac{5}{8} \times \frac{3}{8}$ in. chain enclosed
Clutch	Multi-plate in oil bath
Shock-absorber	Cam type on engine shaft

CYCLE PARTS

Frame	Full duplex cradle, all-welded
Front suspension	Telescopic front forks with coil springs and two-way hydraulic damping
Rear suspension	Swinging fork with two adjustable Girling hydraulically damped spring units
Tyres ..	Dunlop. Ribbed 3.25×19 in. front, " Universal " 3.50×19 in. rear
Brakes	8-in. front, 7-in. rear. Total lining area 34 sq. in.
Fuel tank	4 gal.
Oil tank	$5\frac{1}{2}$ pints
Generator ..	Lucas D.C.-output dynamo with compensated voltage control
Lamps ..	30/24-w. head; 3-w. pilot; 6/18-w. tail/stop; 1.8-w. speedometer
Battery	Lucas 6v., 12 a.h.

Speedometer ..	Smiths 120 m.p.h. with trip
Seating.. ..	Two-level, styled dual seat
Stands	Centre roll-on type
Tool kit	Spanners: 1 combined plug spanner/screwdriver; 4 tubular; 2 open-ended; 1 double-ended ring; 1 combined ring and " C "; 1 special Girling. Tyre lever. Push-rod assembling guide.
Toolbox	Partitioned to enclose Lucas c.v.c.
Finish ..	Royal red; black frame, forks, head-lamp and seat; chromium-panelled tank

OTHER EQUIPMENT

Tyre pump

PRICES

Machine	£273 16s. 5d. (inc. £46 16s. 5d. P.T.)
Extras ..	Rear chaincase, £3 3s. 8d. (no P.T.)
Total as tested	£277 0s. 1d. (inc. £46 16s. 5d. P.T.)
Tax	£3 15s. 0d. p.a. (£1 0s. 8d. quarterly)
Makers	B.S.A. Motor Cycles, Ltd., Armoury Road, Birmingham, 11.

'Motor Cycling' Test Data

Conditions. *Weather: Fair, with showers (Barometer 29.30 in. Hg. Thermometer 66°F. Wind W.N.W. 0–6 m.p.h.). Surface (braking and acceleration): Dry asphalt. Rider: 11 stone 8 lb., 5 ft. 8 in., wearing one-piece suit and safety helmet; normally seated (except for " Best certified M.I.R.A. maximum "). Fuel: Premium grade (96 research method octane rating).*

Venue: *Motor Industry Research Assoc. Station, Lindley.*

Speed at end of standing 1,000 yd.:

East	100.20 m.p.h.
West	86.25 m.p.h.

Best certified M.I.R.A. maximum (rider prone) .. .. 108.5 m.p.h.

Braking from 30 m.p.h. (all brakes): $11\frac{1}{2}$ yd.

Fuel consumption:

At constant 30 m.p.h. ..	101 m.p.g.
50 m.p.h. ..	76 m.p.g.
500-mile overall figure ..	62 m.p.g.

Speedometer

30 m.p.h. indicated =	29.12 m.p.h. true
40 m.p.h. indicated =	39.95 m.p.h. true
50 m.p.h. indicated =	49.52 m.p.h. true
60 m.p.h. indicated =	58.54 m.p.h. true
70 m.p.h. indicated =	69.53 m.p.h. true

Mileage Recorder .. Accurate

Electrical Equipment

Top gear speed at which generator output balances:

Minimum obligatory lights	20 m.p.h.
Full lights	28 m.p.h.

Weights and Capacities

Certified kerbside weight (with oil and 1 gal. fuel) ..	439 lb.

Weight distribution, rider normally seated:

Front wheel	38%
Rear wheel	62%

Tank capacity (metered):

Total	4 gal.
Reserve	$3\frac{1}{2}$ pints

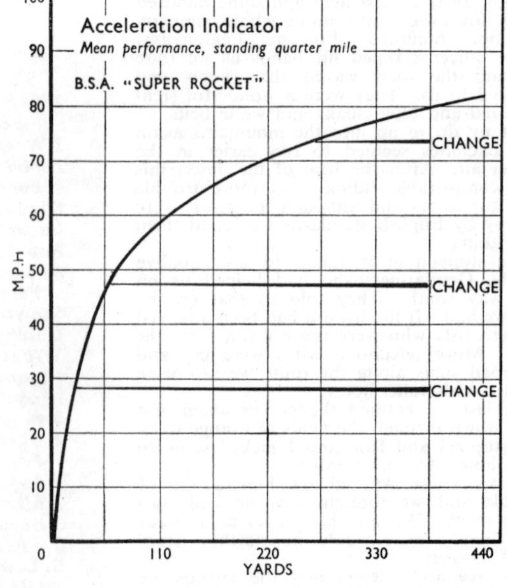

GENERAL efficiency throughout a very considerable speed range has been the objective of the development work devoted to the 646 c.c. B.S.A. "Super Rocket" during the past three years. The result is a full-blooded sports machine with a docility and economy which make it entirely suitable for every-day use.

The "Super Rocket" has a near-three-figure cruising speed—a performance to meet the *autobahn* ambitions of foreign-touring enthusiasts, or those who buy motor-cycles with an optimistic eye to the extension of motorway travel at home in the not-too-distant future.

On the other hand, the current model can be throttled back to accept happily the inevitable limitations of built-up-area riding. In these less spectacular circumstances, one's patience in jogging along at 30 m.p.h. or so is rewarded by a remarkable—for a lusty 650 c.c. twin—fuel consumption also in the three-figure class.

In their obvious desire to provide the "Super Rocket" owner with the best of two worlds, it seems that the Small Heath designers have wisely evaded the lure of spectacular speed claims. The maximum

speed of the 1960 A10SR is about on a par with that of the comparable model tested by *Motor Cycling* in 1956. But improvements to the cam gear, the greater rigidity of the crankshaft assembly and the raising of the compression ratio have all played their part in making an already adequate performance more pleasant—and more economical—to use.

For example, throughout the test no more than one sharp dig at the kickstarter crank was needed to bring the engine to life. One is accustomed to recording that generally this or that engine started well. But with the "Super Rocket" this behaviour was *invariable*—a point frequently noted by knowledgeable onlookers during the past three weeks.

For starting, the ignition was retarded by means of the long lever on the left handle-bar. The air lever, mounted below the saddle nose, could be returned to its normal running position as soon as the engine had settled to a tick-over.

Ignition had to be advanced more gradu-ally, for the 8.3 : 1 compression ratio is the highest of any current standard tourer equipped with a single Amal " Monobloc " carburetter. In other words, while the A10SR is not a specialized machine with twin or racing-type carburetters, it has the advan-tage of a high c.r. which, if handled properly, results in a good performance build-up, plus the boon of economical fuel-consumption.

Indiscreet acceleration with the ignition control thoughtlessly advanced would pro-duce pinking. Consequently, while working through the gears in a hurry, it was always wise to co-ordinate throttle and ignition-lever movement. Whilst 100-octane fuel did obviate pinking, its use was not essential; indeed, the test was conducted on the cheaper, premium grade.

The A10SR gearchange mechanism had a soft action, permitting slick engagements in keeping with the acceleration of which the motor was capable. The clutch was a little heavy—at any rate, to a hand of fairly small span—but the plates parted to permit, clean

Engine of the 1960 B.S.A. "A" series of o.h.v. twins. The "Super Rocket" version has high-compression pistons and the automatic advance-retard unit shown here is replaced by manual control.

Splined countershaft of the cable-operated rear brake, air control lever beneath the seat nose and carburetter drip-shield are details visible in this close-up.

this stage, the " normally seated " road-test rule.

Possibly the most outstanding point about this jaunt was the subsequent check on petrol used. It worked out at about 57 m.p.g. There were no hills to obstruct and no gear changes to waste fuel; none the less, the figure is still a very creditable one.

The standard of comfort was excellent. Normal touring handlebar bends discourage any form of racing crouch for ordinary riding, when quite high averages can be maintained without fatigue. There was evidence of slight vibration in the 50-60 m.p.h. speed-band; it was noticeable also during deceleration in top and in the intermediate gears at equivalent revolution rates.

During the fixed-speed tests, both brakes pulled up the machine reasonably well, but at speeds above 60 m.p.h. one wished for slightly stronger and more progressive stopping. There were no panic sessions; but complete assurance of one's own safety, and that of others, is essential when dealing with the cruising speeds of which this machine is capable.

The same limitation applied to the lighting, which is standard equipment fitted to a number of current machines, irrespective of top-end performance.

Credit points went to ease of maintenance. Tappet adjustment calls for tank removal, but this involves no more than disconnecting the fuel lines, a frontal brace and a centre fixing bolt—a minute or two's job. Clutch adjustment, facilitated by the 1960-modified chaincase, which has a handy aperture, calls for no dismantling work at all. The rear chaincase—an extra, and well worth the money—cuts maintenance to a minimum because of reduced wear and tear. The q.d. rear wheel can, of course, be taken out leaving the transmission undisturbed. Sparking plugs and contact-breaker points are accessible and by modern standards the tool-kit is beyond reproach.

Altogether, this popular " 650 " has been considerably improved by patient development without the sacrifice of a single good feature.

changes at all speeds. More important, perhaps, was the rider's ability to tread swiftly and easily into neutral with the machine stationary at traffic lights.

Normal gearchange points are indicated on the quarter-mile acceleration chart, but to get the best possible performance it was practicable to use the rev. range to the full and hang on to second gear right up to 65-70 m.p.h. Absolute maximum in third gear was in the early 90s; it was obtainable in good conditions over a quarter-mile distance in about 15 sec. Wringing the utmost performance from the engine in this manner produced no symptoms of flagging or mechanical distress.

A steering damper is a standard, but apparently decorative, fitment. It was kept only finger-tight throughout the test which, as a matter of interest, included a trip along the *pavé* at the M.I.R.A. track. No steering upsets were apparent.

One nostalgically recalled rapid trips in the past along Belgium's *autoweg* and the *autobahnen* of Germany; so, in simulation, the speed test was concluded by a 50-mile cruise with the needle of the Smiths speedometer—a remarkably accurate instrument, incidentally—clawing around the 85-90 m.p.h. mark. For comfort rather than performance, a concession was made to wind resistance by temporarily relinquishing at

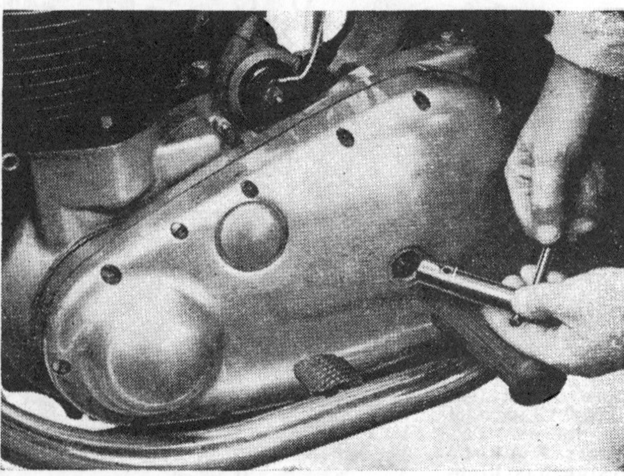

(Left) Adjusting the contact-breaker points. Clutch adjustment (above) is carried out after removing only the access plug in the primary chaincase.

EASIWAY TUNE-UP

B.S.A. "TWINS"

Keeping the Popular Small Heath "Multis"
up to Performance Par

THIS information applies in essence to 497 c.c. A7 and 646 c.c. A10 twins, with swinging-fork rear suspension, produced in either touring or sports roadster form. Primary transmission details illustrated have application to all "A" models excluding pre-swinging-fork version, which had a built-on gearbox and duplex chain with a tensioner. Recent change to roadster A10 and "Super Rocket" ignition setting recommends 13/32 in. before t.d.c.; previously the dimension for the "Golden Flash" was 11/32 in. and for the A10 sports—listed initially as the "Road Rocket" and now the "Super Rocket"—$\frac{3}{8}$ in. These changes, current from early 1960, do not apply to the A7 or "Shooting Star," for which an ignition advance of 5/16 in. and $\frac{3}{8}$ in. respectively is still recommended. Details of modified tappet settings, also a mid-1960 season alteration, are dealt with in Operation 10 describing this simple routine work.

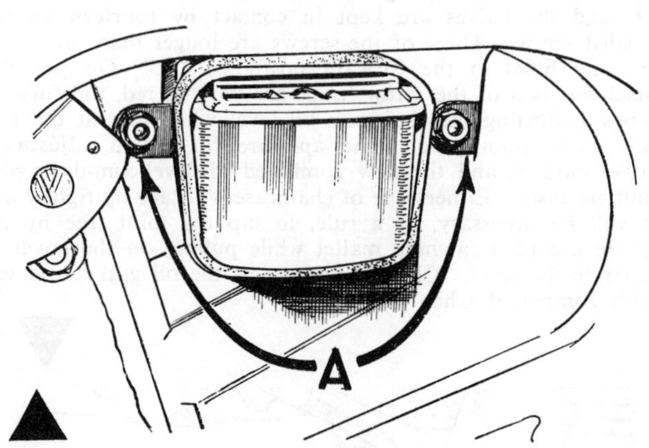

1. ELECTRICS

EQUIPPED with separate magneto and dynamo equipment, the "A" range "electrics" incorporate a Lucas compensated voltage control unit to determine the rate of charge to the battery. This unit is non-adjustable and is given maximum enclosure and protection from damage so that attention to it is seldom necessary. The mounting provides for a degree of flexibility and a thick rubber band stretched around the C.V.C. cover acts as a shock-absorber. But this degree of permitted movement becomes excessive if the two securing bolts and nuts, "A," are permitted to slacken. In this condition the C.V.C. suffers vibration with resulting derangement of the fine settings which control the charging rate and cut-out contacts. Periodically take out the unit and check that the wiring connections with the remainder of the loom are sound.

2. MAGNETO CHECK-UP

THE Lucas K2F contact-breaker is protected by a screw-on cap in the centre of which is an earthing contact with a yellow cable connection to a push-button "Earth" on the handlebar. The object of this is to stop the engine but if the assembly is neglected ignition may cut out of its own accord. A chaffed cable may cause this trouble. Pre-1958 models have a button in the magneto end-cap. Unscrewing the cap gives access to the points for adjustment but it is as equally important to check the condition of the pick-up brushes (one of the two is shown inset) which should be a free and springy fit in the holders. Renew if worn down to the spring retainers. A length of thick pencil lead makes an emergency get-you-home brush. The H.T. leads must be kept in good condition.

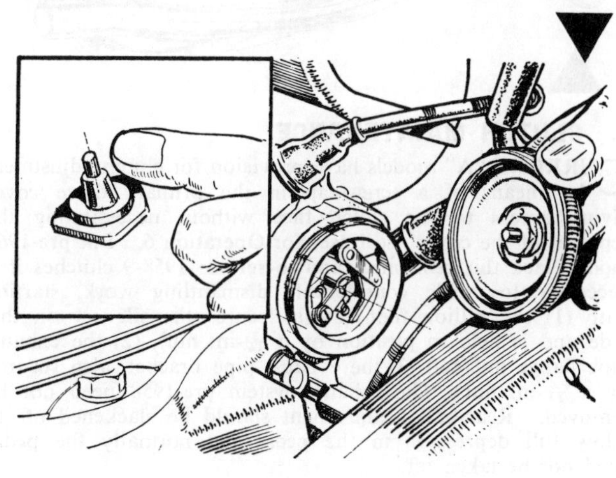

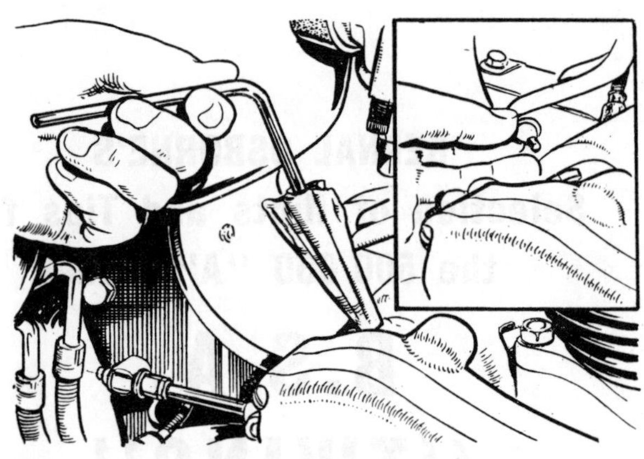

3. IMPORTANT CONTACT POINTS

PICK-UP brushes kept in good condition justify corresponding care in seeing that the slip-ring segments are clean and that the earthing brush is doing its job properly. A pick-up ring is cleaned by pushing a scroll of fine sand-paper into the pick-up aperture and holding it in contact with the ring, while the engine is spun over several times. Finish off with a petrol-damp cloth to clear the ring of sand-paper fragments. Do not let any metal part of the cleaning device, or your fingers, touch the slip-ring as it rotates or an electric shock will be felt! The earthing device is a spring-loaded carbon pencil (inset) located at the end of the magneto and its contact with the armature also must be free of grease or dirt.

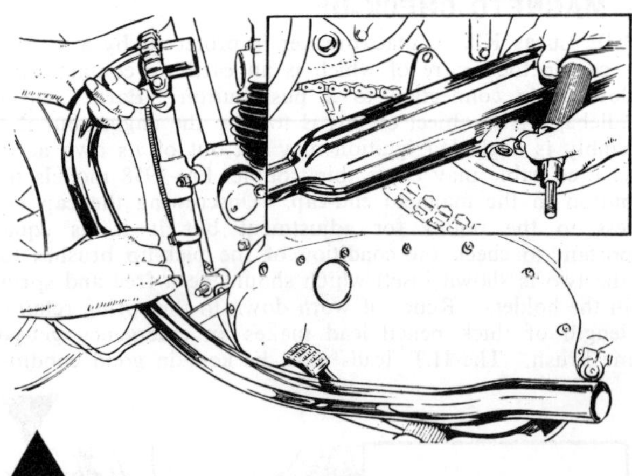

4. CLUTCH MAINTENANCE

CURRENT "A" models have provision for clutch adjustment by means of a screw-cap in the primary drive cover giving access to the clutch face without necessitating the removal of the cover—see inset for Operation 6. But pre-1960 models lack this refinement and to service 1958-9 clutches it is necessary to tackle considerable dismantling work, starting with (1) the pillion foot-rest (it secures the silencer on this side and is held in position by a $\frac{3}{16}$-in. nut), (2) the exhaust pipe flange nut and (3) the exhaust pipe bracket, also secured by a $\frac{5}{16}$-in. nut. The exhaust system pre-1958 need not be removed. Rear-brake adjustment should be slackened off to allow full depression to the pedal but normally the pedal need not be taken off.

5. OFF WITH THE FOOT-REST

THE foot-rest hanger is splined to a shaft to permit fine adjustment and first assessment of the job may give the impression that the hanger can be left in position while the chaincase cover is drawn away. In fact, usual practice is to pull off the hanger (inset) so that the rest of the work is unimpeded. So take off the securing nut and, while pulling steadily on the hanger, tap around the boss with a mallet to free the splined fit. The machine dealt with for the purpose of this feature had a tight hanger assembly and the work took considerable time. Avoid temptation to use the chaincase as a leverage point. A little paraffin, or penetrating oil, sprayed on the parts and left to soak in overnight is a useful freeing agent.

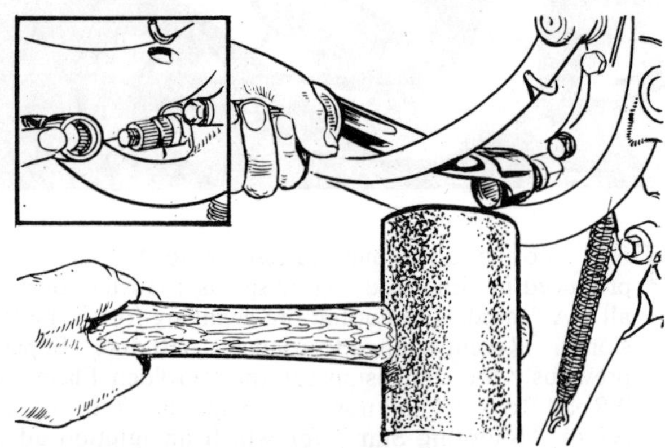

6. MORE MALLET WORK

THE cover faces up tightly in order to contain chaincase oil and the halves are kept in contact by fourteen cheese-headed screws. Three of the screws are longer than the others and are fitted in the forward positions, "A." On pre-1960 machines two of the screw heads are painted red, the forward screw indicating the chaincase oil level while that at the rear acts as a drain plug. The aperture for clutch adjustment (1960 models) and the new combined oil-level-cum-drain-plug unit are inset. Either type of chaincase will face up tightly and it will be necessary, as a rule, to tap the joint free by the gentle use of a rawhide mallet while pulling on the cover to separate the joint. Clean it and renew the oil gasket and seal with compound when assembling.

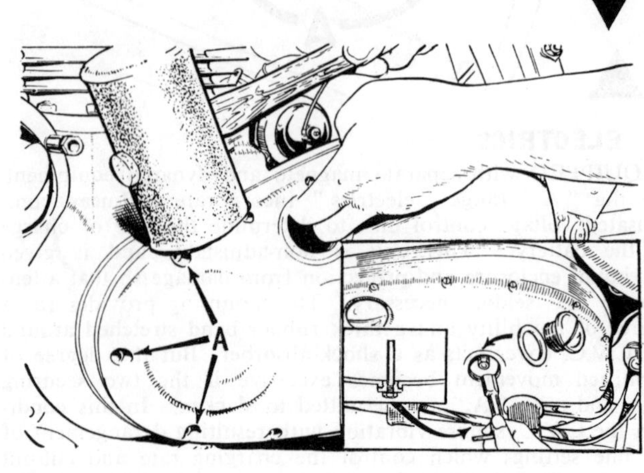

7. THE PRIMARY TRANSMISSION

ALTHOUGH current "A" models have the convenient chaincase aperture for adjustment of the six nutted clutch-spring retaining assemblies, a thorough check of clutch condition is best carried out with the cover removed. Then uneven spring pressure, betrayed by the tilting of the outer plate when the clutch lever is drawn in, becomes a visible fault easily corrected by the screwing in, or out, of the appropriate adjuster nut (toolkit spanners do the job) and tightening the locknuts to retain this condition. Suddenly noisy transmission and rough running at tick-over engine speeds may be due to the shock-absorber nut "A" having worked loose on the engine shaft.

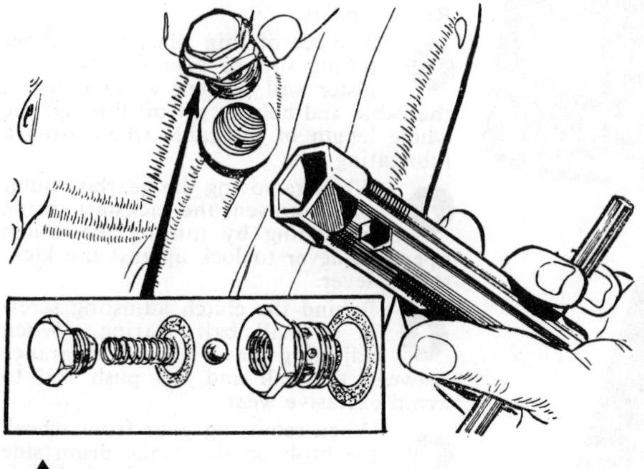

8. LUBRICATION

PERIODIC flushing out of the lubricating system and the washing in paraffin of the main filter (attached to the hexagon at the base of the tank) is an obvious chore carried out when a new machine has completed 500 miles and thereafter at much greater mileage intervals. Less obvious, because it is located in the crankcase and partially screened by the timing cover, is the pressure-release valve. Attention to this unit should be part of a 10,000-mile check: there is no spanner in the kit to fit the A/F 1⅛-in. dimension of the major hexagon which must be slackened first. Then secure the assembly in a vice and unscrew the smaller hexagon to release the spring and ball (inset). Thoroughly clean the parts, and the housing, and refit, placing the shims in the positions previously occupied.

9. TAKING OFF THE TANK

TAPPET adjustment and work generally on the cylinder head are facilitated if the fuel tank is first removed. The task is a simple one, involving on current models the dismantling of fuel feed and the removal of the transverse strap which acts as a steady at the front of the tank. Toolkit spanners fit the ¼-in. nuts. The main anchorage is a centre bolt screwing down into a lug on the top frame rail. A rubber cover blanks off the well but with this cover removed, application of a box spanner with a $\frac{5}{16}$-in. Whit. hexagon completes the job in a few moments. Rubber sleeves interpose between the frame and tank centre to prevent drumming: take care that these are neither lost nor moved.

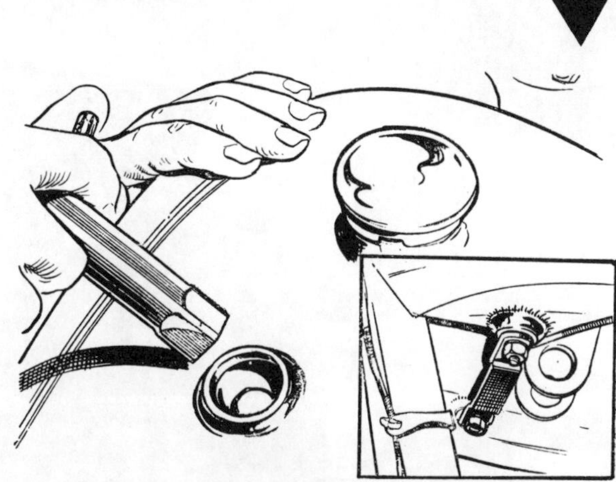

10. TAPPET ADJUSTMENT

IRRESPECTIVE of engine capacity or type, all current "A" model units are subject to a service amendment (December 1959) which provides now for .008-in. inlet and .010-in. exhaust valve clearances. This, it is claimed, results in quieter running but the previously recommended .010-in. and .016-in. settings are still applicable and can be used by owners in search of maximum performance at the expense of mechanical noise. Access to the locknuts and adjusting pins is gained by removing the two rocker covers, each being secured by studs and pillar nuts. Appropriate spanners are supplied in the kit but a good feeler gauge to check the adjustment (inset) is an essential extra.

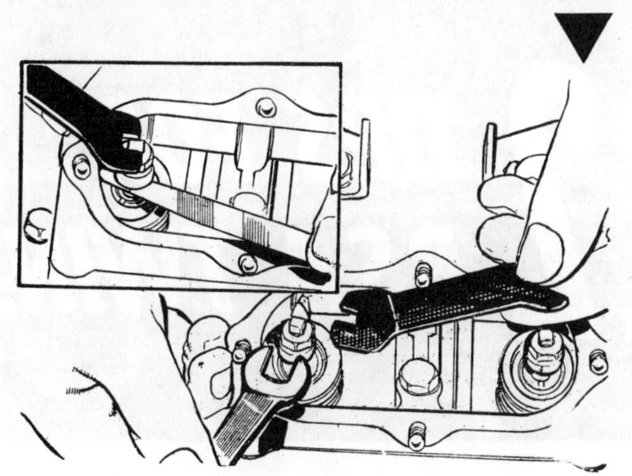

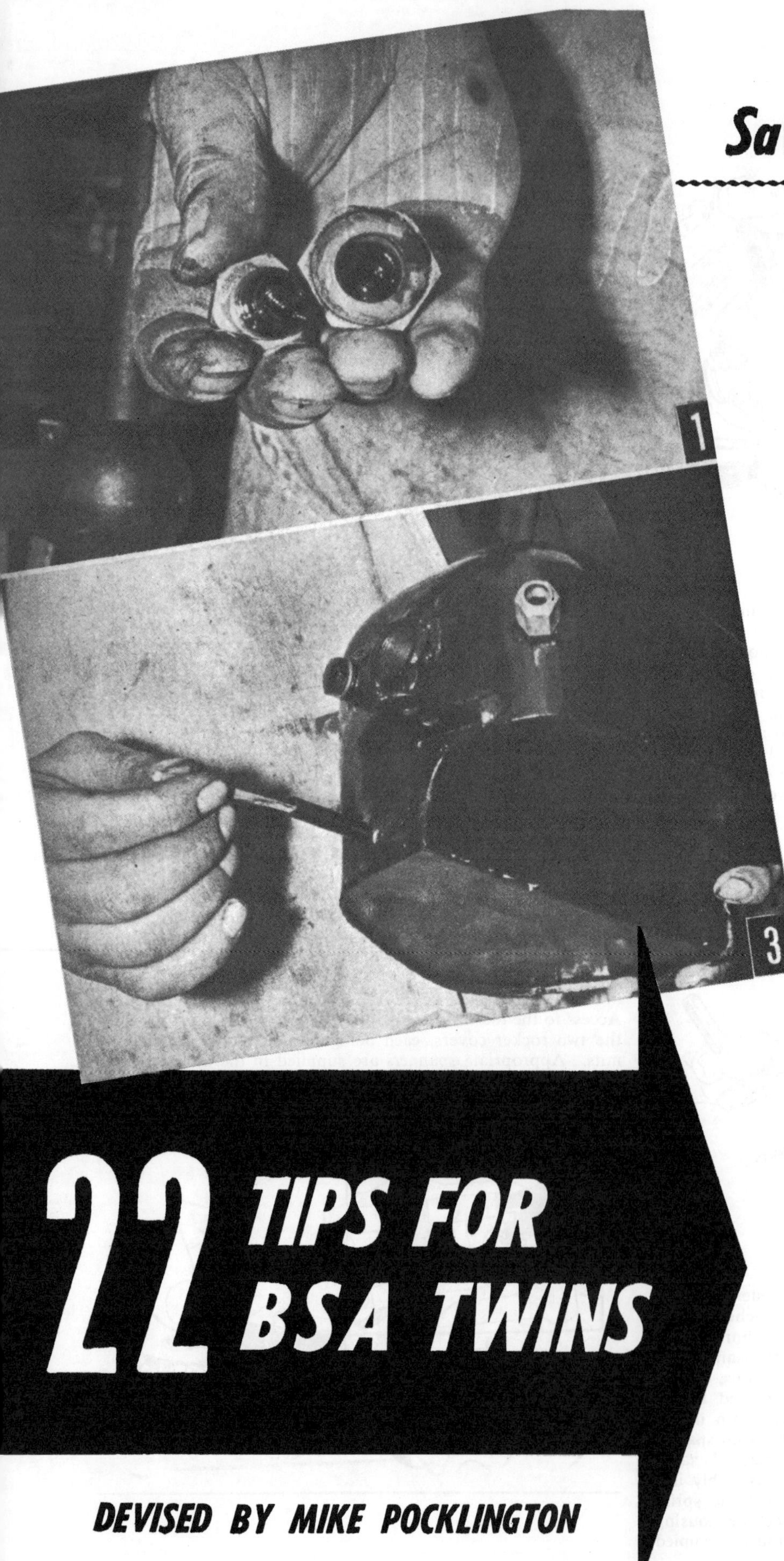

1 When carrying out an oil change **always** remove the pressure release valve. Wash it in petrol and replace when completely clean and dry —screw it home tight. Failure to seat correctly can cause oil starvation to the crankshaft and big end bearings. Oi' will also drain from the tank to the crankcase.

2 Check that the oil is returning to the tank. If not, then the anti-syphon valve in the crankcase may be stuck to its seating.

3 If oil persists in leaking at the oil tank filler cap, the oil tank breather pipe may be blocked, clean out with a piece of wire or remove tank and flush with petrol.

4 Excessive oil consumption can often be traced to worn or sticky piston rings, blocked return pipe, clogged oil filters or an air leak in the sump. Any restriction in the oil system will cause high crankcase pressure.

5 To clean sticky piston rings give them a Redex treatment. Remove the plugs and pour Redex through the plug hole. Leave to soak overnight and then kick over the engine to get rid of surplus Redex. Replace the plugs and run the engine for a few minutes to clear the oil. The correct amount of Redex for your machine can be obtained from Redex dealers.

6 A piece of thin plastic or rubber tubing slipped over the cable adjuster will prevent water entering the cable and help to get oil through the whole length of the cable when using a lubricating gun.

7 When removing the gearbox outer cover, prevent the kickstart spring unwinding by turning the clutch operating lever to lock against the kickstarter lever.

8 Behind the clutch adjusting screw is a small ball bearing. When adjusting leave a small clearance between the ball and the push rod to avoid excessive wear.

9 When removing your front wheel, the bush on the brake drum side is often drawn into the hub. It can easily be replaced with the aid of the wheel spindle.

10 When removing the steering column see that the ball bearings do not fall out. It's a good idea to pump plenty of heavy grease into the steering head before starting to dismantle this part. When reassembling again use heavy grease to hold them in position.

11 On A.10 models ignition timing is automatic. The automatic timing unit is to be found in the timing case, and is fitted to the magneto pinion. This unit should be removed when resetting the timing. Wash thoroughly in petrol and inspect carefully to see if it is functioning correctly. When dry squirt oil on the working parts. It is most important that the timing is accurate. Follow the handbook instructions to the letter.

22 TIPS FOR BSA TWINS

DEVISED BY MIKE POCKLINGTON

with these ideas

12 When on the rare occasions a horn needs adjusting it is a good policy to correct the horn in series with an ammeter. Turn the adjusting screw very carefully until you have a good tone and as low a reading as possible. Never let a horn take more than 4 amperes of current even if it has a good tone. This will help your battery to hold its charge better.

13 **Never** leave a battery in a discharged state. It will eventually be ruined.

14 When servicing your dynamo make sure the bushes work freely in their holders and the commutator is clean and not unduly worn. Clean the segments with a clean cloth dipped in petrol. If this fails very fine glass-paper may be used. Cut the mica to a depth of 1/32 in. The segments should be squared edged with the mica.

15 When grinding in valves insert a light spring behind the valve head. This will help to get an " all round " and even seating. Replace valve springs at every decoke. Weak springs cause loss of power.

16 When removing pistons from the " con " rods, mark the pistons on the inside to ensure they are replaced in the correct place.

17 On dismantling tappets remove the inlet tappets first and then the exhaust ones. Reverse the procedure when replacing them. They are **not** interchangeable.

18 It is worthwhile obtaining the correct B.S.A. service tool for locating the pushrods (Part No. 67-9114). It makes the job twice as easy and removes the risk of damage. It is a flat piece of metal with six wide recesses cut into one side. The outer pair are fitted behind the two rear bolts on the rocker box. The inner four locate the push-rods.

19 Be very careful when replacing the rocker box as it is easy to foul the valve collars and bend the stems.

20 When stripping any part of the engine carefully note the position of all shims and washers. If you find any "play" anywhere don't shim it up until you find out if the play is intentional as is the play on the crankshaft end in the A.10 engine. Here the play should be .005 inch.

21 On recent models, with totally enclosed chaincases, it is important to check regularly the tightness of the four rear wheel holding nuts hidden in the chaincase. If these work loose they may jam against the casing.

22 If your machine has a sidecar attached it is unlikely that the lifting handle on the rear mudguard stay is ever used. If this is removed with the bolt lugs and turned in the same place it will make a good hand grip for a pillion passenger when bolted or screwed into a suitable position on the sidecar body.

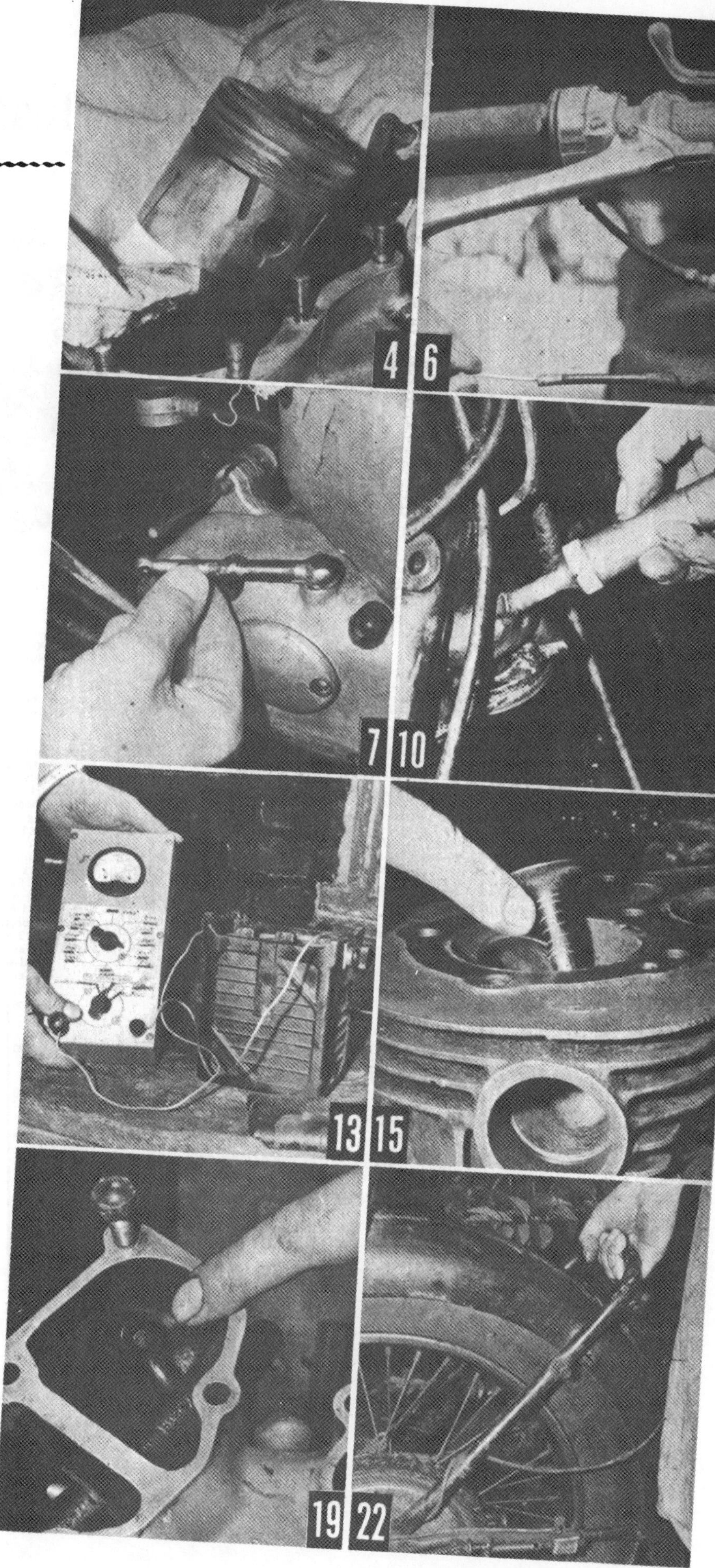

646 c.c. B.S.A. A10 'Golden Flash'

and Canterbury 'Arrow'

Sidecar

A flexible 'work horse'

in harness with a sports tourer

Specification

ENGINE
Type	Twin-cylinder four-stroke
Bore	70 mm.
Stroke	84 mm.
Cubic capacity	646 c.c.
Valves	Overhead (push-rod)
Compression ratio	6.5 : 1
Carburetter	Amal " Monobloc," 1 $\frac{1}{16}$-in. choke
Ignition	Lucas magneto, automatic control
Generator ..	Lucas 6-v. 60-w. dynamo with automatic voltage control
Makers' claimed output	37 b.h.p. at 6,000 r.p.m.
Lubrication ..	Dry sump, double gear pumps
Starting	Kickstarter

TRANSMISSION
Separate gearbox with footchange
Ratios	5.3, 6.4, 9.3, 13.5 : 1
Speed at 1,000 r.p.m. in top gear ..	15 m.p.h.

Speed equivalent to revs at maximum power rating:
Second gear	51 m.p.h.
Third gear	74 m.p.h.
Top gear	90 m.p.h.
Primary drive.. ..	Single-row chain
Final drive	Single-row chain
Clutch	Multiplate in oilbath
Shock-absorber	Spring-and-cam type on engine shaft

CYCLE PARTS
Frame	Duplex cradle type
Front suspension	Telescopic forks with coil springs, hydraulically damped
Rear suspension	Swinging fork, with hydraulically damped three-position Girling units
Tyres ..	Dunlop " Universals," 3.25×19 in. front, 3.50×19 in. rear
Brakes ..	Front, 8 in. dia.; rear, 7 in. dia. Total lining area 34 sq. in.
Fuel tank	Single-bolt fixing
Oil tank	5½ pints
Lamps ..	30/24-w. head, 3-w. pilot, 1.8-w. speedometer, 18/6-w. stop/tail
Battery	Lucas 13 a.h.
Horn	Electric
Seating..	Dual-seat
Stand	Centre

Tool kit	Spanners: 4 box, 1 double-ended, 1 Magdyno, 2 combined, 1 rear spindle, 1 rockerbox cover, 1 suspension-unit; 1 tommy bar, 1 tyre lever, 2 feeler gauges, 1 push-rod assembly tool
Toolbox	Semi-pannier position on left side, hinged lid, Dzus fastener
Standard finish	Sapphire blue tank and guards, black frame and forks

OTHER EQUIPMENT
Tyre pump, finger adjusters to clutch and front-brake levers, air cleaner, carburetter drip tray

PRICES
Machine	£259 6s. 11d. (inc. £44 6s. 11d. P.T.)
Arrow sidecar on GMC/10A chassis (inc. brake)	£93 15s. 3d. (inc. £14 17s. P.T.)
Total as tested	£353 2s. 2d.
Tax ..	£5 p.a., £1 17s. for four months
Makers	B.S.A. Motor Cycles, Ltd., Small Heath, Birmingham 11

'Motor Cycling' Test Data

Conditions. *Weather: cold, drying after recent rain (Barometer 29.60 in. Hg. Thermometer 38°F.). Wind: South, 2 m.p.h. Surface (braking and acceleration): Dry asphalt. Rider: 11½ stone, wearing two-piece suit, wellington boots and safety helmet, normally seated (except for " Best certified M.I.R.A. maximum "). Fuel: Premium grade (96 research method octane rating).*

Venue: *Motor Industry Research Assoc. Station, Lindley.*

Speed at end of standing 1,000 yd.:
East	65½ m.p.h.
West	58½ m.p.h.

Best certified M.I.R.A. maximum (rider prone) : 71.0 m.p.h.

Braking from 30 m.p.h. (all brakes): 15 yd.

Fuel consumption:
At constant 30 m.p.h. ..	66 m.p.g.
50 m.p.h. ..	46.8 m.p.g.
500-mile overall figure ..	44.8 m.p.g.

Speedometer
30 m.p.h. indicated	= 29.9 m.p.h. true
40 m.p.h. indicated	= 39.4 m.p.h. true
50 m.p.h. indicated	= 48.5 m.p.h. true
60 m.p.h. indicated	= 58.2 m.p.h. true
70 m.p.h. indicated	= 68.0 m.p.h. true
Mileage Recorder ..	1% optimistic

Electrical Equipment
Top gear speed at which generator output balances:
Minimum obligatory lights	20 m.p.h.
Full lights	25 m.p.h.

Weights and Capacities
Certified kerbside weight (with oil and 1 gal. fuel) .. .. 686 lb.

Weight distribution, rider normally seated, sidecar ballasted with 9 st.:
Front wheel..	37%
Rear wheel	43%
Sidecar wheel	20%

Tank capacity (metered):
Total	3.65 gal.
Reserve	3½ pints

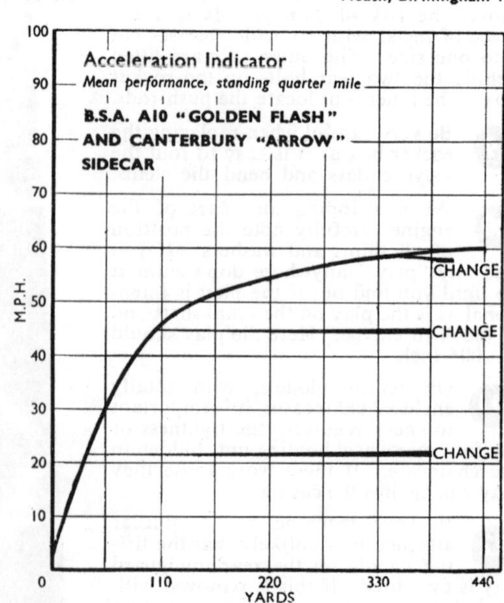

FIRST 'LEG' OF A TWO-PART TEST

SIDECAR enthusiasts are apt to complain that their choice of prime mover has been sadly restricted since the demise of the slogging side-valver and the V-twin. And it is true enough that the modern machine, for all its generally higher performance, often lacks the extreme flexibility and sheer low-speed punch that many three-wheeler owners would like to have.

Often, but not always. Proof that the traditional qualities of the sidecar haulier *can* be combined with the reigning parallel-twin formula is the 650 c.c. B.S.A. A10 " Golden Flash "—a machine which, with its beefy power output almost irrespective of revs and its general docility, comes nearer to the old " big twin " ideal than any other of its type that we have tested.

Experience of the " Flash " extended to 4,500 miles because it was used for an experiment—a two-part test designed to give a direct comparison between the performances of the same machine with sidecars of widely different types. First the B.S.A. was hitched to the single-seater Canterbury " Arrow " sports tourer, then the full drill was repeated with the same manufacturer's three-seater " Carmobile " (both on the GMC/10A springer chassis). The second " leg " of the test will be reported next week.

The sidecar was laden throughout the test (except for " light-handling " trials). When no passenger was carried, the seat was slipped out and 9 stone of ballast put in its place.

The B.S.A.'s qualities as everyday transport became apparent during its first spell

of duty in London traffic. A tick-over, car-like in its smoothness and utter reliability, a totally fuss-free pull-away at low revs and a smooth clutch took much of the fatigue out of queue-crawling.

At the other end of the scale the proving-ground record shows, graphically enough, how powerful and useful is the *type* of performance available. The maximum speed of 71 m.p.h., rider crouched right down, is in accordance with " 650 " standards, but more significant is the exceptionally good " sitting-up " speed, only 3 m.p.h. slower.

The engine shone at staunch pulling at low revs, exhilarating and rapid pick-up through the range, very satisfying acceleration when using the gearbox to get away from rest, and the most useful ability to maintain high speeds under adverse conditions. So far as the three upper ratios were concerned, the standard sidecar sprocket converted the internal reductions to something very near the ideal, although top was theoretically a little high.

Thanks to the untiring engine and freedom from rider-fatiguing vibration, main-road cruising was practicable at anything up to 65 m.p.h.

" Top-gear-only " power characteristics reduced strain on the pilot by cutting down the number of gearchanges and the need to think about keeping the motor in a restricted rev band.

1-in-3 Restart

Only on one occasion was there any protest from the engine department. An anvil chorus set in when doing the arduous stop-and-restart test on M.I.R.A.'s 1-in-3 test hill —and this is a gradient, as steep as any metalled road in the U.K., on which the majority of *cars* fail. It is to the B.S.A.'s credit that a restart was possible, albeit with generous use of the clutch and throttle.

A 1-in-4 test was straightforward, requiring no dextrous contrapuntal variations between the bass and treble hands, and producing no pinking on the 96-octane fuel used throughout. The standard sidecar sprocket gives a highish bottom gear for " chair " work.

Under normal road conditions, the tester never gave a second thought to the transmission. The clutch was sweet and there was not the slightest difficulty with gear selection, despite some initial stiffness in pedal movement. Downward changes were exceptionally pleasant. When slowing right down, one merely slipped the cogs in without throttle-blipping; no grating resulted.

Neutral was found with ease, in motion

Cutaway sides, ample height above the passenger's knees and high, comfortably raked backrest are practical features of Canterbury's latest, the smartly styled "Arrow" sidecar.

Design of the "Golden Flash," sidecar haulier of the B.S.A. range, is essentially sturdy and straightforward, with "iron" head and barrel, separate four-speed gearbox and magneto ignition.

or at rest, whilst the engine was running. Paradoxically, it was not easy to locate when the motor was dead; one tended to slip through it.

The first gear engagement of the day was quiet; no "pre-freeing drill" was required. Second gear whined slightly, but this did not increase with mileage. Pedal movement was short and general action taut. The kickstarter was well placed.

Starting was truly exceptional. Given choking *or* "tickling" and one priming kick from dead cold, the engine infallibly fired on the next thrust of the foot. Indeed, on occasions the priming kick did the deed if one used a little vigour. Hot starting was just too easy. Magneto ignition removed any cause for worrying about battery state.

Full marks were awarded to the "old-fashioned" dynamo, which gave more than enough current to balance lighting loads in all gears at all speeds above non-snatch levels and kept the battery fully up, thanks to regulation of output by an orthodox a.v.c. unit.

The headlamp threw a brilliant beam. Its cowl, which incorporates a joggle rim for beam alignment, holds the ammeter on the left and the switch on the right. We would have preferred them the other way about, so that the switch would fall naturally to the left hand instead of being a long arm's stretch across one's front. On the other hand, the cut-out/horn/dipswitch cluster by the left grip was the last word in accessibility.

Suspension

A good level of comfort was imparted by the suspension systems of machine and sidecar, which harmonized in the laden state (unladen, that of the sidecar was, naturally, the "harder"). Sway was undetectable on right-handers; on turns to the left, some depression of the machine's rear occurred, but this became of account only when a pillion passenger was carried. (The remedy would have been to "jack up" the adjustable rear spring units, but an attempt to do so merely bent the toolkit C-spanner.)

However, for general usage, the standard springing was quite o.k. Handling was actually improved with the chair loaded;

Wheel of the Canterbury GMC/10A chassis is mounted on a short trailing arm.

the plot could be taken up to tyre-scream point both to the left and the right.

By sports standards, the handling would have been rated heavyish; but this is primarily a serviceable workaday outfit. Use of the steering damper cut down low-speed handlebar flutter to an acceptable minimum.

For a laden outfit which spent most of its time either stopping-and-starting in London or being driven hard on the open road, the overall fuel consumption of 44.8 m.p.g. was in step with general results.

Braking provided the only substantial point of criticism. Not only is 15 yd. from 30 m.p.h. among the higher figures returned by modern outfits, but considerable pressure on all three anchors was required for a reasonably smart stop. The eight-inch front brake alone, applied really hard, would deal with more normal situations.

The linkage between the pedals of the machine's rear brake and the sidecar brake was not the happiest of marriages.

The sidecar itself is Canterbury's latest—and very nice it is, too. It has notably clean lines, is well finished, is mounted on a sturdy sprung chassis and is available with or without the braked disc wheel.

Designated a "sports tourer," it does in fact combine low head resistance with accommodation far more comfortable than that of the average "sports" job. The occupant has plenty of leg, arm and shoulder room and sufficient headroom, if of average stature, when the hood is erected. Really luxurious was the tall and well upholstered seat back, which had just the right rake.

A capacious external boot, guarded by a lockable lid, is located behind the passenger's seat. It would swallow two week-end cases—and leave room for oddments—this in addition to providing stowage for the hood and tonneau cover. Its internal finish was markedly better than one has (regrettably) learned to expect of the average boot.

We were particularly pleased with the colour match that Canterbury had managed to achieve, the sidecar being finished in the exact shade of sapphire blue used on the machine. The two components blended harmoniously into an outfit which was undeniably handsome, as well as possessing the more solid qualities which gave us many miles of pleasant, reliable riding in a completely fuss-free manner.

NEXT WEEK: Same mount, same chassis—and Canterbury's "Carmobile" body. Object—comparison.

THE SIDECAR

Chassis

Model GMC/10A; welded steel tubes with integral suspension-unit abutment

Machine connection: Four-point attachment by means of clamped-on tubular fittings

Wheel suspension: Trailing link controlled by Armstrong or Girling unit with alternative spring poundages to suit load

Tyre: Dunlop "Universal" 3.25 × 16 in. on q.d. disc wheel mounted on taper-roller bearings and incorporating 7 in. dia. brake

Assembly details: Lean-out at head, 2 in.; track, 44 in.; toe-in, 1½ in.; wheel lead, 6 in.

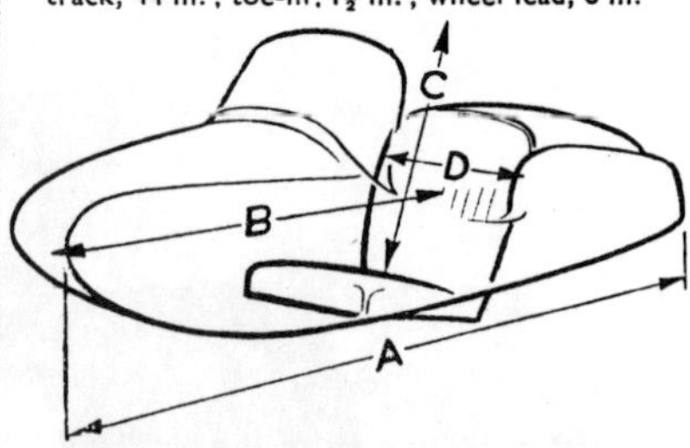

Dimensions : A = 86 in. ; B = 47 in. ; C = 35 in. ; D = 21 in.

Body

Single-seat tourer of sporting aspect

Construction : Hardwood frame ; plywood panels covered with aluminium sheet ; luggage compartment at rear ; panoramic screen ; side panel cutaway for easy access (no door); detachable hood or tonneau cover

Standard finish : Two-tone in popular machine colours

Body mounting : Direct to chassis rails (i.e. no body springs)

Equipment : Detachable key to boot lid; separate sidecar brake pedal with full cable control

Price : £86 17s. (inc. £14 17s. P.T.) ; braked disc wheel £6 18s. 3d. (inc. £1 3s. 8d. P.T.)

Makers : Canterbury Sidecars Ltd., Arisdale Avenue, South Ockendon, Romford, Essex

646 c.c. B.S.A. A10 'Golden Flash'

and Canterbury

'Carmobile'

Second instalment of a two-part

test: switch-over to a family outfit

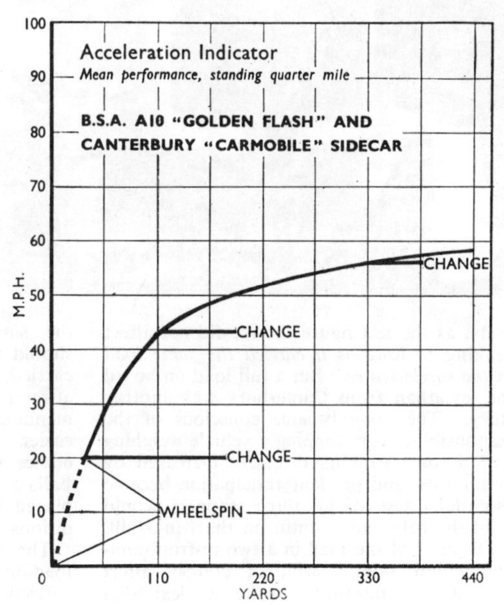

FIT a really large family sidecar to your machine instead of a single-seater—and what happens to performance? To answer that question, *Motor Cycling* undertook a novel two-part road test, of which this is the second instalment.

The prime mover used throughout was a B.S.A. A10 "Golden Flash." Last week we reported fully on its behaviour with a Canterbury "Arrow" *monoposto* sports tourer. Now we give directly comparable data on its performance with the same manufacturer's three-seater "Carmobile."

And the result? It's a surprise. Both on the road and through the electronic timing trap, the difference made by fitting one of the largest sidecars in the world was far less than would have been expected!

Maximum speed with the rider prone fell by only 2 m.p.h. to 69 m.p.h.; with the rider normally seated, the 68 m.p.h. maximum of the smaller outfit was cut by 4 m.p.h.

There was no significant change in fuel consumption, the cost being 3 m.p.g., bringing the "Carmobile" figure down to 42. The closest assessment of braking revealed no difference (with identical loads). Handling was, of course, heavier.

With the "Carmobile" carrying the same 9-st. ballast as the single-seater, the standard sidecar gearing, giving a 5.3 top and 13.6 bottom, proved too high (as B.S.A. agreed), so the normal 19t. gearbox sprocket was replaced by a 17t. component. This had the effect of lowering top and bottom to 5.9 and 15.2, respectively, giving higher maximum speed, better throttle response in top and less gearchanging, and making standing starts possible on *both* of M.I.R.A.'s test hills, the 1-in-4 and the 1-in-3.

On the open road and in traffic, the outfit was far more pleasant on the lower ratios and dealt with adverse conditions even better than previously. The lower gearing, with its associated SC3305-06 speedometer head, can be specified by a customer at no extra cost.

The effect of using the standard speedometer head with the revised gearing is shown in the test data panel. It will be seen that the error, although considerable, remains within the legal limit.

That the two fuel-consumption figures should have tallied so closely was both pleasing and surprising. It is assumed that consumption, like general performance, benefited from the fact that the "Carmobile" gearing was even more "right" than that used with the "Arrow."

Due, possibly, to more uniform weight distribution over the three wheels, the larger

---

Specification

646 c.c. B.S.A. A10 " Golden Flash "
Specification as for first part of test (Feb. 16 issue) except :—

TRANSMISSION

Ratios (17t. gearbox sprocket)
  5.9, 7.1, 10.4, 15.2
Speed at 1,000 r.p.m. in top gear 13 m.p.h.
Speed equivalent to revs at maximum power rating :

Second gear	.. ..	46 m.p.h.
Third gear ..	.. ..	67 m.p.h.
Top gear ..	.. ..	81 m.p.h.

'Motor Cycling' Test Data

Conditions. *Weather:* Cold, dry (Barometer 29.55 in. Hg. Thermometer 36°F.). *Wind:* light and variable. *Surface (braking and acceleration):* Dry asphalt. *Rider:* 11½ stone, wearing, two-piece suit, wellington boots and safety helmet, normally seated (except for "Best certified M.I.R.A. maximum"). *Fuel:* Premium grade (96 Research Method Octane Rating).

Venue: *Motor Industry Research Association Station, Lindley.*

Speed at end of standing 1,000 yd.:

East	63 m.p.h.
West .. .. ♦ ..	61½ m.p.h.
Best certified M.I.R.A. maximum (rider prone)	68.9 m.p.h.
Braking from 30 m.p.h. (all brakes):	15 yd.

Fuel consumption:

At constant 30 m.p.h. ..	64 m.p.g.
50 m.p.h. ..	43 m.p.g.
500-mile overall figure ..	42 m.p.g.

Speedometer (with SC3305–04 head)

30 m.p.h. indicated =	27.5 m.p.h. true
40 m.p.h. indicated =	35.0 m.p.h. true
50 m.p.h. indicated =	42.3 m.p.h. true
60 m.p.h. indicated =	51.4 m.p.h. true
70 m.p.h. indicated =	60.0 m.p.h. true

Mileage Recorder   Overreading 15%

Weights and Capacities

Certified kerbside weight (with oil and 1 gal. fuel)		767 lb.
Weight distribution, rider normally seated, sidecar ballasted with 9 st. in place of front seat:		
Front wheel		37%
Rear wheel		33%
Sidecar wheel		30%

Acceleration Indicator
Mean performance, standing quarter mile

B.S.A. A10 "GOLDEN FLASH" AND CANTERBURY "CARMOBILE" SIDECAR

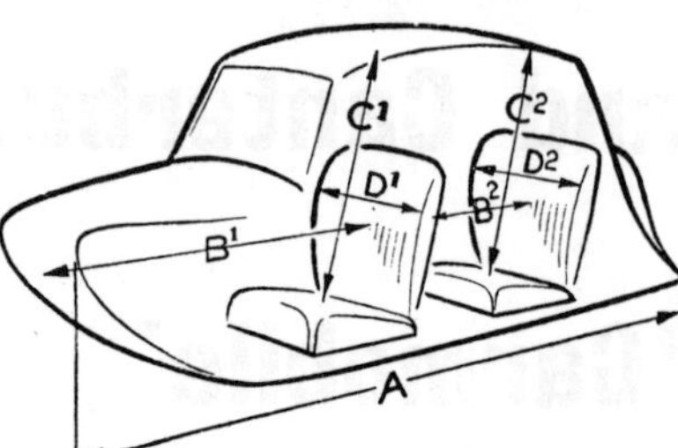

The following is a specification box:

THE SIDECAR

Chassis
Model GMC/10A.
Specification as for first part of test (Feb. 16 issue) except:
Assembly details: Lean-out at head, 2 in.; track, 44 in.; toe-in, 2 in.; wheel lead, 6 in.

Dimensions: A=92 in.; B¹=43 in.; B²= 25 in.; C¹=33 in.; C²=31 in.; D¹=31 in.; D²=21 in.

Body
"Carmobile" Mk. III three-seater family saloon; single seat at rear, double-adult bench seat at front.
Construction: Hardwood frame; plywood panels covered with aluminium sheet; single door at front; lift-up front seat with hinge-forward backrest for access to rear seat; luggage compartment at rear; roll-forward sunshine roof; opening front and side windows; ventilation louvres; light-alloy rear bumper
Standard finish: Two-tone in popular machine colours
Body mounting: Direct to chassis rails (i.e. no body springs)

Equipment: Detachable key to boot lid; separate sidecar brake pedal with cable connections

Prices: £129 4s. 10d. (inc. £22 2s. P.T.); braked disc wheel, £6 18s. 3d. (inc. £1 3s. 8d. P.T.); total as tested, £136 3s. 1d.

Tax: £5 p.a., £1 17s. for four months

Makers: Canterbury Sidecars, Ltd., Arisdale Avenue, South Ockendon, Romford, Essex.

This family was a light load for the "Carmobile," which can carry three adults. The roll-forward sunshine roof is standard equipment, the braked disc wheel an optional extra.

With the front seat swung out of the way, the rear passenger goes aboard. Adults found the sill height more convenient.

body, as the test figure shows, did not affect braking *so long as it carried the same load as the single-seater.* But a full load on board the leviathan from Canterbury was another story. Then one became conscious of the responsibility for stopping a vehicle weighing half a ton. Braking distances increased by about 15% and prudent anticipation became essential. Use of all three stoppers would hold the fully laden outfit on the 1-in-3 hill.

Disposal of the load in a two-in-front-and-one-behind sidecar will, of course, affect handling. Canterburys make it clear that the heaviest passenger should be carried in the single rear seat—and so, it follows, should the one passenger, when only one is carried. But for the average user the obvious attractions of the front seat, with its tremendous elbow-room, better visibility and easier access, would probably outweigh advice from absent manufacturers. So the ballast for our standard-payload tests was placed in front. Handling under these conditions was quite satisfactory.

The soundness of Canterbury's advice on loading was apparent when one child was carried in the rear and another, with its mother, in the front. The rear wheel of the machine was then light enough to demand respect on hard right-handers. This arrangement was adopted, incidentally, because it would have been unwise to carry a child in the seat adjoining an unlockable door—and one which, on the test model, did not always latch securely.

Space inside the "Carmobile" is lavish. Here is a sidecar that is, in the current phrase, "the mostest." There is really room for a 6-ft. man at the rear and for two other adults, side by side, on the bench-type front seat. All have adequate head-room and elbow-room. Anyone at the front has an abundance of leg-room, but there is only just enough for an adult at the rear. Similarly, while access to the front is car-like, that to the rear is less convenient.

The "chair" is well appointed. The front window of safety glass gives true vision and can be opened at the bottom for ventilation. On the right is a hinged window panel for communicating with the driver. Internally there is a space for small articles over the wheel arch. The lockable boot can carry quite a large suitcase, or can be hinged down for tray-like support of a bulkier load. There is a roll-forward sunshine roof; it proved to be weathertight.

Final verdicts. On the "Carmobile": a practical three-seater which imposes surprisingly little penalty for its bulk and weight. On the "Golden Flash": an excellent sidecar machine. On the outfit as a whole: a worthwhile proposition for the family man at £395 10s. all told.

ALABAMA BOUND

by Patrick Heffron

When I first considered the possibility of making a 2,000 mile trip from Pasadena, California, to Tuscaloosa, Alabama aboard my year-old BSA my relatives and friends were all very dubious about my chances, to put it mildly. But all their protests availed little when the idea of riding free and unfettered for such a distance really began to take hold. Aside from the initial thrill every cyclist experiences at the anticipation of such a trip, there were many practical reasons for my pilgrimmage to Alabama.

For the last year and a half, though actively engaged as a social case worker for Los Angeles County, I had eagerly looked forward to the day when I might again resume my career as a free-lance writer, putting into tangible form some of the ideas acquired over the years. Tuscaloosa, Alabama, offered itself as a likely spot in which to allow the fermentation and expression of these ideas to take place.

My trusty two-wheeler and companion of a year, which I had surreptitiously named "Nicole", was a brilliant blue, black and chrome BSA of 500 cubic centimeters. Purchased new in October of 1961, it had been given the ultimate in care and maintenance, and certainly was a worthy vehicle on which to make the trip.

After a week of careful preparations, following an elaborate tune-up by the Pasadena BSA dealer, sorting and organizing my gear and systematically planning the placement of it on the cycle, the fateful day arrived.

Late on a warm Sunday afternoon my relatives and friends were gathered

Alabama Student Union Building located on campus of the University of Alabama. It is one of the most important in the country and many thousands of students enjoy its benefits.

around Nicole and myself watching as I performed last minute adjustments. The air had become slightly cooler after sun-

The historical Vicksburg battlefield. Note the sign denoting Vicksburg Siege. Highways around this area are excellent.

set and I was glad that our parting had been delayed till evening, thereby avoiding the worst of the desert heat and dryness. After much last minute enthusiasm

and advice, waving arms and ringing farewells, I pulled Nicole away in a wide semi-circular swing through the driveway and out into the clear October night.

From Pasadena I rode steadily along Rosemead Boulevard toward Temple City and U.S. 99. I had already begun to have difficulty with the dirt track goggles and mask I had specifically bought for the trip. The interchangeable amber lens, supposedly designed to reduce headlight glare, was badly distorted, and I was forced to change back to the clear lens. Wind had also begun to seep in under the nose opening of the goggles and I knew my eyes would not take this for very long. The mask and goggles were, of course, very useful in protecting against large bugs and other flying insects. For additional hiway safety during periods of night driving I wore a white ski parka over my jacket which

Holiday Beach, an Alabama recreational park and lake. Miniature "Natchez Queen" is seen in foreground. It is a perfect replica and attracts lots of favorable comments and admiration.

"Nicole", as the author named his mount, stands in foreground near Tuscaloosa bridge spanning Black Warrior River. This photo was taken at the end of the long trip.

Just before departure in Pasadena. Note mask to protect against wind, rain and bugs on the open road. Twin rear view mirrors are mounted for extra safety.

Denny Chimes and Tower, prominent landmark of the University of Alabama. There is a beautiful and well-kept park around these buildings.

isolated dips or canyons. The engine droned along with the evenness of a fine watch, but the increasing heat and dryness seemed to cause it to run hotter. It was nearly 3:00 in the morning when I approached the inspection station on the Arizona side of the state line, and, either out of courtesy or from weariness, the guard passed me through with a wave of his hand. Suddenly I was in Yuma, Arizona. A brief search for an inexpensive motel followed and the first night's journey, somewhat reluctantly, was at an end.

After leaving Yuma the next lap followed U.S. 80 almost due east, traversing bleak desert country under broad skies which grew warmer and more intense as the day passed. Here and there, the flat, colorless terrain would be relieved by cactus, an occasional roughly shaped hill, or an isolated rest stop which would loom up beside the road with the most delightful frequency and under the most incongruous conditions.

The rest stops, incidentally, were one of the real pleasures of this extended trip. Just at a time when my back would be straining for the last ounce of endurance, while following what seemed to be

served the obvious purpose of spurring the attention of less alert drivers, and had the additional advantage of keeping

a table and bench under a hastily constructed canopy, while others were elaborate little canopied villages, complete

This powerful and old steam locomotive provided a real contrasting background for the motorcycle. This location is almost a must for all tourists and their cameras.

Memorial at Vicksburg to Union soldiers from Iowa who died there. This place is a center of attraction for all tourists from every part of the country.

my leather jacket free of bug stains.

Following U.S. 99 to Indio, California, a small desert oasis of 7,000 souls, I pulled into a service station for fuel. As I had many times in the past, I casually reached over to press the ignition cut-off button and thereby stop the engine. This time, however, as I pressed the button, nothing happened! I pressed again. Still the engine continued to run. It was beginning to remind me of a scene in a very funny Charlie Chaplin movie. Finally, in desperation, I pulled the sparkplug cables with a simultaneous jerk and the engine stopped. Nicole's eagerness to keep going amazed me!

Leaving Indio the night became warm with occasional patches of cooler air in

an endless road, a rest stop would pop up out of nowhere to provide a moment of still, vibrationless comfort and relaxation. Some of the rest stops were merely

This highway rest spot with protective roof was a real treat in itself for the tired traveler, either on two wheels or four! The one shown here is located east of Yuma, Arizona.

with fireplaces, trash cans, parking areas, camping facilities, water taps, and a score of other little refinements. For the person driving an auto across the country these rest stops may be considered merely as handy places to have an impromptu picnic; for the cyclist they are real havens of comfort.

Nicole was performing exceptionally well under the tortuous regimen of the road and I considered myself very fortunate that, at this point, I had not encountered any major difficulties. Still, the only infuriating problem was the ignition cut-off and the failure of the engine to stop when I wanted it to. Near Casa Grande, on close inspection of the engine, I discovered that the wire connect-

The author's faithful BSA parked on shoulder of highway in Arizona. The desolate mountains in background provide excellent theme for any lover of Nature.

ing the cut-off button with the ignition had broken apart from its soldered metal fastening. I determined to make the repair the following morning under better light.

After darkness and many hours on the road, Tucson seemed a thriving metropolis with its brightly illuminated city streets and bustling sidewalks. I stopped here briefly to pick up a pocket knife for repair of the ignition wire, replacing one I had misplaced earlier. Later, under a crisp, starlit sky, I pushed on to Benson, Arizona, final destination for the day.

The next morning, after leaving Benson, I continued east via State Route 86 thru the fascinating Texas Canyon with its unusual rock formations, and very soon afterwards came to the Texas Canyon Summit rising to an elevation of 4,975 feet, the highest point of the entire trip. My eyes had become very bloodshot with the constant flow of wind thru the nose opening of the goggles and so at Wilcox I stopped to buy some adhesive tape with which to seal up this gap. The expedient of the tape worked very well and I was not bothered by the wind after this.

At Lordsburg, New Mexico, U.S. 80-70 becomes an impressive four-lane divided section of Interstate Hiway 10, sometimes stretching for several miles of completed roadway. This frequency of good hiway continually pleased and amazed me. At least 40% of the journey so far had been traversed upon fine completed sections of the Interstate hiway system, which, in the distant future, is expected to connect entirely the west and east coasts of our country.

At Deming, New Mexico, cattle grazing and farming center of the Mimbres Valley, the influence of Mexican and Indian culture is keenly evident. Many of the citizens of Deming, a town which gives the impression of having grown up spontaneously along one main thoroughfare, still converse in Spanish amid a setting which hearkens back to visions of Custer, Geronimo and Buffalo Bill. At the outskirts of Deming, near a remnant of a bygone steam locomotive era, Nicole stopped long enough to have her picture taken in an attempt to contrast one powerful engine with another.

Beyond Deming, the road becomes two-lane again but was not heavily traveled so I was able to make very good time, arriving at the Rio Grande River

just at sunset. From the Rio Grande crossing, which is quiet high, the road wends downward steadily to Las Cruces, a breathtaking spectacle in the twilight hours. Ahead, the faintly flickering lights of the city could be seen burning brighter and more intense as the sky darkened.

After a brief stop in Las Cruces for a pecan pancake dinner, in deference to a fine suggestion of my friends. I proceeded on to El Paso, Texas, a distance of forty-eight miles. Running free through the blamy, windless night, under a full moon that shone at intervals between puffy cumulus clouds, I was exuberant with the natural splendor of the evening and was hardly aware of the miles I had so rapidly put behind me. Finally, settled in El Paso, the mood of the evening was further enhanced by the nearness of my room to the border. Looking out my window, beyond the

This "post-card background" belongs to a roadside park located east of Texas. It was commendably neat and well provided with tables and benches.

Rio Grande riverbed which fell away sharply from the hiway at the western edge of town, I could see the feeble glimmer of street lights and the softly illuminated glow of lanterns. Over there, I though to myself, over there was Mexico.

Outside of El Paso U.S. 80 runs southeast and parallel with the Rio Grande for many miles, through the small villages of Ysleta, Tornillo, and McNary, before turning away from the river in a more easterly direction. At Ysleta, home of the last surviving members of the Pueblo Indians in Texas, the buildings fairly reeked with western flavor, while at Tornillo cotton is everywhere and in great abundance.

Leaving the Rio Grande the hiway begins to climb across barren country

Mississippi farmhouse and barn under broad clear skies. In spite of their age, most buildings of this type still remain in excellent shape and are a proof of their builder's craftsmanship.

with fewer and fewer tokens of civilization until it culminates, nearly a thousand feet higher, at the windswept crest of Sierra Blanca, a small mountain village at 4,500 feet elevation. Although Sierra Blanca was not the highest point of the trip, it was undoubtedly the steadiest, most prolonged endurance trial over rugged terrain that I had come to and would have broken the spirit of lesser bikes.

Descending for the next thirty miles to Van Horn, I stopped to check for general delivery mail, and then pushed on to Pecos, Monahans and Odessa, a progressive oil-rich town, where I stayed the night.

Early the next day, while passing through Midland, twenty miles east of Odessa, I noticed that a police officer had pulled up beside me on a large Harley-Davidson. He motioned with his hand to the side of the road, and I began to wonder what law I had broken now. As I edged up beside him, he turned to me with a fraternal smile and launched into a discourse about·the virtues of his husky Harley-Davidson. He was, above all things, a cycle enthusiast! With trepidation I ventured a few favorable comments on Nicole and BSA's generally, wondering what the size of my ticket would be if I happened to say the wrong thing. But he was a good sport and admitted that there were, after all, a few other motorcycles in the world.

Later, at Big Spring, I pulled into a service station for fuel. The manager of the station and his son had only recently come to this country from England and were quite taken with the BSA. Before leaving England they had both owned cycles and commented that cycling there was very widespread. They were "friendliness" personified in their eager efforts to offer tools and helpful advice to me, and, I thought, if these two were examples of the people currently emigrating to this country, then let's have more like them!

It had just gotten dark when I arrived

The beautiful and wild Texas countryside was a permanent temptation for repeated stops to enjoy its colorful tones and amazing variety of shades at different times of the day.

at Eastland, Texas. As I cruised somewhat wearily into town I could hear the

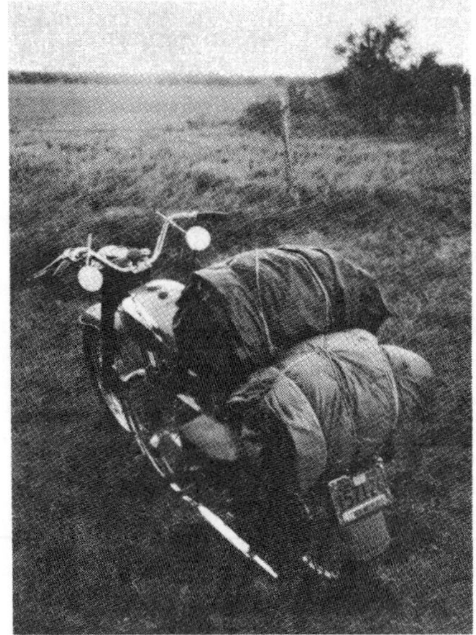

Texas rest stop at sunset, some three miles east of Marshall. The motorcycle seems dwarfed by the huge gear loaded on her back!

violent cheers and massed singing of an assembled group of teenagers who were standing before the county courthouse in

This Louisiana road was one of the most fascinating encountered by the author along his 2,000 mile trip. It provided hours and hours of sheer motorcycle pleasure since traffic was not heavy.

the center of the small town. Now and then the high school band would break into a brassy accompaniment as the football fight song predicted the downfall of tomorrow's rival. Overhead the sky was leaden with the look of rain.

Driving from Eastland to Weatherford the next morning I encountered heavy rain, sometimes turning to hail. Ahead of me, over the lush green fields, hilly and scattered with clumps of trees, the violence of the storm could be seen as it was punctuated at irregular intervals by sudden flashes of lightning and reverberating rolls of thunder. My boots were waterlogged from the cosntant splash of the front wheel and the rain, finally, came down so heavily that it became very difficult to see the road. At a crucial moment I saw a small general store by the side of the road and pulled off hurriedly beneath its corrugated metal canopy until the worst of the storm had passed. The proprietor and his wife, a middle-aged couple, were astonished to see a motorcyclist in this weather. They were very friendly, though, offering me a much appreciated cup of coffee and talking to me about twenty minutes or until the rain subsided. By the time I arrived in Fort Worth my clothing had dried out under a blistering sunlit sky and my spirits had risen accordingly.

At high noon, after a short but rapid run on the Dallas-Ft. Worth Turnpike, I landed in the center of an impossible downtown traffic tangle. Dallas, or "Big D" as the citizens affectionately call it, was playing host to the supporters of Oklahoma University prior to the football game with Texas the following day, and this partly accounted for the very heavy traffic. After another thirty minutes of navigating the congested streets, I found the BSA dealer garage near the edge of town. Wheeling Nicole in the entrance door I was surprised to discover that the garage was equipped with three to four hydralic lifts which could easily raise the cycle to the height of a mechanic and make repairs easier, quicker and with less physical strain.

At first, because of the loss of power in low gears, I had assumed the trouble was in the clutch, but toward the end of the tuning operation the mechanic recognized the symptoms of a badly seared right exhaust valve and pointed out that at low speeds I had actualy been running on only one cylinder. He felt, however, that I would be able to make Alabama in good shape.

From Dallas, Nicole and I, with a momentary mechanical reprieve, hobbled further into the Deep South via Interstate Hiway 20 and U.S. 80. Mineola, Texas, where I stayed the night, represented a clear transition from the rugged western plains and cattle country to the charming old tradition of the agricultural south. The people here seemed to follow a more leisurely pattern of living, a gentler understanding of serene human values. During my late dinner at a nearby cafe several elderly women and an elderly man were lingering over the last of their evening meal, laughing almost childishly with the sudden spontaneity of life-long friends, creating a delicate unhurried mood which, with its soft accents, echoed an era that was nearly forgotten.

Continuing on my journey I stopped at Gladewater, Texas, the following day for a late breakfast of *beef* bacon and eggs, and, of course, now, wherever I went, I was offered the usual additional items of hominy grits and coffee with chicory.

Shreveport, near the Red River, struck me with its oldness and typical antebellum architecture, although many areas of the city were run-down and neglected.

At Tallulah, ninety-two miles beyond Ruston, Louisiana, I was struck by the brilliant lights and gaiety of this small southern town. It was Saturday evening, a balmy night, and all the Negro men and women were massed in the streets, walking and talking, laughing riotously and parading proudly up and down the sidewalks in their weekend finery.

Beyond Tallulah the land became really flat, the road straight as an arrow, and I sensed that I would soon be approaching the banks of the mighty Mississippi. Near the river the gradient of the road began to rise, becoming more of an aqueduct, then, suddenly bursting out of the trees lining the water, I was awed and thrilled by the moonlit mystery of the Old Man. And across the river —*Vicksburg!* What historical impact that name carried!

After a comfortable night's rest, I proceeded eagerly toward the Vicksburg Military Park, an immense shrine of 1,323 acres dedicated to the memory of the men, both North and South, who lost their lives in a memorable 47 day seige of the city. The year had been 1863; the place, where I was standing!

Straining an inner ear I could almost hear the thunder of artillery pieces, the wild shouting of Yankee infantrymen assaulting a Southern position, and the equally determined crack of Rebel rifle fire. The monuments to the dead heroes moved me, and for a moment, standing there on the battlefield, I could not believe that they were forever dead, or that their spirit could ever really die.

Near Forest, Mississippi, I stopped at a roadside park to give the cycle a breather. The eighty mile stretch from Vicksburg had been a prolonged test of endurance for both of us.

As I drove the last few miles in Mississippi, passing through Hickory, Meridian, Toomsuba, and Kewanee, I thought how valuable the trip had been to my understanding of people, how close I had come to the natural glory and splendor of this country, and, not least, how much freer, sincere and wholeheartedly had people along the way responded to questions and comments, partly perhaps, because I was riding a cycle.

True, the trip had not been a profitable venture in money saved. The gas and oil for the eight day journey amounted to over $16.00, lodging was $33.00, food a little over $16.00, and, of course, the service and mechanical work in Dallas came to nearly $13.00. Total cost of the entire trip ran to about $78.00. Even this did not include the eventual labor and parts that went into the replacement of the exhaust valves, undertaken several days later. But, still, I felt that I had profited immensely.

With a mixed feeling of reluctance for the journey's end and thrilling anticipation of my next several months in Alabama, I turned left at Cuba, just inside the state border, passed through York and Livingston shrouded yet in the amber glow of twilight and droned steadily toward my final destination, Tuscaloosa.

FORMER MOTORCYCLIST, JOHNNY MANTZ, AWARDED $300,000 JUDGMENT FOR CAR CRASH

A $300,000 judgment was recently returned by Circuit Court in St. Louis, Missouri and is reported to be the largest ever awarded in St. Louis. The award was in favor of Johnny Mantz, of Duarte, Calif. who sued the Southwest Freight Lines of St. Louis for a very serious car collision accident in which Mantz was badly injured on Jan. 11, 1962 near Rolla, Missouri. Mantz was driving a camper truck and was hit in the rear by a tractor trailer. The collision resulted in long time hospitalization for Mantz and the removal of his left arm, thus resulting in his inability to earn a livelihood, in the testing and racing of automobiles.

Few people know it but Johnny Mantz is a former motorcyclist. In the early thirties, during the depression years, Johnny Mantz, Perry Grimm and Walt Faulkner were customers of Floyd Clymer's and rode Indian "74" Chief motorcycles in their work of delivering jewelry for the Columbia Optical Company and the Butler Service Company in Los Angeles. All three started racing in midget cars at Atlantic Stadium, and raced later at Loyola Stadium and Gilmore Stadium, all in Los Angeles. All three men raced for many years and became nationally known as excellent drivers of midgets, big cars and Indianapolis cars; and Johnny Mantz and Walt Faulkner were competitors in the Mexican Road Race.

Faulkner was killed in a racing car accident. Now Johnny Mantz is through with car racing; and what Perry Grimm is doing now we do not know. The last time we saw him he was in good health and good spirits.

The many friends of Johnny Mantz will at least be happy to know that he survived the crash and, even though he can not compete again, we hope he will be with us for many years to come.

The 497 c.c. B.S.A. A7 'SHOOTING STAR'

A smooth and docile

twin with a

near-100 m.p.h. maximum

Specification

ENGINE

Type .. .. Parallel-twin four-stroke
Bore .. .. 66 mm.
Stroke .. .. 72.6 mm.
Cubic capacity .. .. .. 497 c.c.
Valves .. .. Overhead (push-rod)
Compression ratio .. .. .. 8 : 1
Carburetter Amal " Monobloc," 1-in. bore
Ignition .. Lucas K2F magneto with manual control
Generator Lucas E3L 6-v. 60-w., D.C. output, with A.V.C.
Makers' claimed output 33 b.h.p. at 6,250 r.p.m.
Lubrication Dry sump, double gear pumps
Starting .. .. Kickstarter

TRANSMISSION

Separate gearbox with footchange.
Ratios .. .. .. 5.3, 6.4, 9.3, 13.6 : 1
Speed at 1,000 r.p.m. in top gear 14½ m.p.h.

Speed equivalent to revs. at maximum power rating :
Second gear .. .. .. 53 m.p.h.
Third gear .. .. .. 77 m.p.h.
Top gear .. .. .. 93 m.p.h.
Primary drive .. .. Single-row chain
Final drive Single-row chain, fully enclosed
Clutch .. .. Multi-plate in oilbath
Shock-absorber Spring-and-cam type on engine shaft

CYCLE PARTS

Frame .. .. All-welded duplex cradle
Front suspension Telescopic forks with coil springs and hydraulic damping on both strokes
Rear suspension Swinging fork, with two Girling three-position hydraulically damped spring units
Wheelbase .. .. 57 in.
Tyres .. Dunlop 3.25×19 in. ribbed front, 3.50×19 in. "Universal" rear
Brakes .. 8-in. dia. front, 7-in. dia. rear, both in full-width hubs. Total lining area, 34½ sq. in.
Fuel tank.. Welded steel; single-point fixing, rubber mounted
Oil tank .. .. 5½ pints

Lamps .. 30/24-w. head, 3-w. pilot, 18/6-w. stop/tail, 1.8-w. speedometer.
Battery .. .. .. Lucas 13 a.h.
Horn .. .. Lucas
Speedometer .. Smiths 125 m.p.h., trip
Seating .. .. Dual seat
Stands .. .. .. Centre, prop
Toolkit Spanners: 4 box, 1 double-ended, 1 plug, 1 magdyno, 1 combination. 1 tyre lever. 2 feeler gauges
Toolbox .. On left, below saddle nose; hinged lid, Dzus fastener
Standard finish .. Polychromatic green guards and tanks, black frame

OTHER EQUIPMENT

Tyre pump; q.d. rear wheel; pillion rests; finger adjusters to handlebar levers; steering-head lock; front wheel stand.

PRICES

Machine £255 2s. 6d. (inc. £43 12s. 6d. P.T.)
Extras .. Rear chain enclosure, £3 3s. 8d.; prop-stand, £1 4s. 2d.
Total as tested .. .. .. £259 10s. 4d.
Tax £4 10s. p.a.; £1 13s. per four months
Makers B.S.A. Motor Cycles, Ltd., Birmingham, 11.

'Motor Cycling' Test Data

Conditions. *Weather: Cold, wet (Barometer 29.15 in. Hg. Temperature 46°F.). Wind: East, steady at 5 m.p.h. Surface (braking and acceleration): Damp asphalt. Rider: 11½ stone, wearing one-piece racing leathers, boots and safety helmet, normally seated except for " Best certified M.I.R.A. maximum." Fuel: Super grade (101 research method octane rating).*

Venue: *Motor Industry Research Association Station, Lindley.*

Speed at end of standing 1,000 yd.:
East .. .. .. 74.7 m.p.h.
West .. .. .. 77.4 m.p.h.
Best certified M.I.R.A. maximum .. .. .. 98.8 m.p.h.
Flying lap speed .. .. 95 m.p.h.
Braking from 30 m.p.h. (all brakes) 10 yd.
Fuel consumption:
At constant 30 m.p.h. .. .. 88 m.p.g.
50 m.p.h. .. .. .. 73 m.p.g.
70 m.p.h. .. .. .. 48 m.p.g.
500-mile overall figure .. 66 m.p.g.

Speedometer
30 m.p.h. indicated = 30.0 m.p.h. true

40 m.p.h. indicated = 38.7 m.p.h. true
50 m.p.h. indicated = 47.7 m.p.h. true
60 m.p.h. indicated = 56.7 m.p.h. true
70 m.p.h. indicated = 66.6 m.p.h. true
80 m.p.h. indicated = 76.1 m.p.h. true
90 m.p.h. indicated = 85.0 m.p.h. true
100 m.p.h. indicated = 93.8 m.p.h. true

Mileage Recorder .. .. Accurate

Electrical Equipment
Top gear speed at which generator output balances:
Minimum obligatory lights 18 m.p.h.
Full lights .. .. .. 24 m.p.h.

Weights and Capacities
Certified kerbside weight (with oil and 1 gal. fuel): 430 lb.
Weight distribution, rider normally seated:
Front wheel 38%
Rear wheel 62%
Tank capacity (metered):
Total .. 3.55 gal.
Reserve (left side) .. .. 4 pints
(right side) .. .. ¾ pint

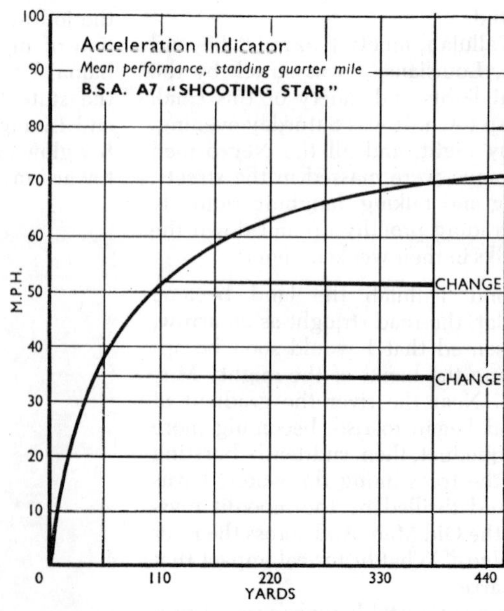

ONCE in every few years there swims into a tester's ken a mount that manages, in some vague and quite indefinable way, to be a " happy " motorcycle. It is impossible to pin down its appeal to the sum of certain good features, nor is it due merely to an absence of aggravating faults. Perhaps all one can say is that the machine is " right " and that the rider immediately feels at home with it. Such a product is the 1961 B.S.A. A7 " Shooting Star."

This sporting 500 c.c. twin was a delight for both driver and passenger. It was comfortable, handled nicely, had a normal two-up maximum in the eighties, possessed excellent brakes and, at 66 m.p.g. overall, was economical for this class and size of mount.

Unlike its " Gold Star " stablemate, it is not super-tuned. The 8 : 1 c.r. engine delivered good results all through the range. It ticked over slowly with utter reliability, manual ignition lever fully advanced; there was not a single occasion during the long test when the motor fluffed. Opening-up was clean carburation-wise and free from the temperament often associated with large-overlap big-ported sportsters.

It was the marvellous spread of power without concentration in any one part of the rev band that made the A7 such a delight to ride two-up in top gear. It was not necessary to " flog it up through the cogs " to overtake faster traffic—nor, indeed, was the box used very much at all on long main-road runs.

Thanks also to a correctly chosen gear, top-only acceleration was quite practicable from 28 m.p.h. onwards, again with the ignition lever fully advanced. In fact, it was never necessary to retard this lever *at all* —even for starting. It is a measure of the " Shooting Star's " flexibility that it could

run so excellently on what amounted to fixed ignition timing.

From very low engine speeds the power flowed in smoothly, the intake chuffing in a clearly audible way. At larger throttle openings, exhaust noise increased to a degree that called for restraint in residential areas at night. But the silencers did at least cut out crackle and the sharp, penetrating overtones that make all too many sports machines so unpopular with the public.

The engine's smoothness was remarkable.

A slight tremor came in above 70 m.p.h. in top, and then it was transmitted chiefly through the tank (which is rubber-mounted— a seeming paradox). Only at absolute revs in the intermediates was there anything that could strictly be termed vibration, and even then it was not enough to deter the rider from using these revs as often as he wished. Pillion passengers commented upon the complete freedom from " the tingles " through either their footrests or the seat.

One of the " Shooting Star's " most attractive features was its capacity for effortless motorway cruising at a continuous 75 to 80 m.p.h. The motor remained on tune and, after such a run, could be shut down immediately to a slow idle. Never, at any time, was there a tendency for the tickover to speed-up as a result of hard driving and its attendant extra heat.

During one period of 40 hours, towards the end of the test, the machine covered almost 900 miles, many of them at speeds up to 85 m.p.h. It behaved perfectly and the only adjustments necessary afterwards were to primary and final drive chains.

Another endearing characteristic was the ease of starting. Priming kicks are usually " not counted "—and with the " Shooting Star " were not necessary, anyway. It nearly always burbled on the first depression of the kickstarter—and on the other occasions it was in business on the second. It was undoubtedly one of the easiest starters in its class that we have tested.

Starting still remained first class after a night in the open. In March and April the choke was never needed (its control lever is tucked away under the seat).

A " kill " button for the magneto ignition is included in the neat dipswitch-horn fitting on the left bar. Here also is the timing control lever, sensibly placed for

Where 33 b.h.p. comes from. Above the separate gearbox can be seen the particularly accessible adjuster. Bottom left is the rear brake countershaft's operating lever.

TWO-PAGE DRAWING OVERLEAF

The 497 c.c. B.S.A. A7 'Shooting S

B.S.A. parallel-twin design is essentially sturdy, straightforward, without " frills."
A distinguishing feature of the engine is the operation of all o..h. valves from a single
camshaft, mounted to the rear of the cylinder block.   The sporting A7 has a light-
alloy head and single down-draught carburetter.   The rear swinging fork pivot
occupies all the available width between the members of the duplex cradle frame.
Full-width brake drums are fitted at front and rear.

FULL ROAD TEST REPORT ON

For tappet adjustment (left), removal of the tank, with its single-bolt fixing, is a five-minute job. To detach the tail of the chaincase (above) two bolts and two minutes.

B.S.A. 'SHOOTING STAR' Road Test

There is plenty of room to get at the brushes and contact-breaker cover of the magneto, which is shielded from fuel drip by a "tray" below the carburetter.

thumbing. The dipswitch has an action that permits the penetrating and intense main beam to be flashed while the dipped one continues in use (i.e., both filaments are " on " at once). The horn note was loud and clear.

The clutch was extremely light to lift, easy to feed in, and freed readily for the first gear engagement of the day. No slip was experienced, despite the light spring pressure. This fabric-lined component seemed insensitive to oil level in the primary chaincase.

Convenient finger adjusters are incorporated in the pivot lugs of the well-placed handlebar levers. That of the front brake was taken up from time to time. This full-width stopper was given a lot of work to do by the speedy passage of the " Shooting Star " and it was always up to its job.

When it was applied really hard—up to tyre squeal point, in fact—some fork judder became apparent. In wet weather the lever assumed a lazy action, despite oiling of the cable and greasing of the cam spindle; perhaps a stronger pull-off spring is indicated. The rear brake was quite adequate. The waterproofing of both was effective in rainy weather.

The gearbox was most pleasant to use for any kind of change, or for the selection of neutral, either from bottom or second, when coasting to a standstill or even when at rest. Given no more than normal throttle synchronization, all operations were smooth and quiet. Pedal travel was short and light.

No gear whine was audible, either in the intermediates or in top. The sole transmission sound amounted to a rustle from the chains, most apparent on the over-run. The rear chain was fully enclosed and required no adjustment after the post-running-in check of the machine; it did not clang on its case.

" Shooting Star " handling was good without approaching the superlative. Lack of ground clearance was the snag. The propstand persisted in offering itself for abrasion by the road surface as soon as hard left bank was applied. (The offending stand, incidentally, also holds the machine too near the vertical for security when it is in use; a single " mod " could remedy both faults.)

This sole black mark in the handling section (but a serious one) was notched much more readily when a pillion passenger was carried. To the right, however, really enthusiastic cranking-over was possible under all conditions.

There were some situations in which the wide handlebars had to be used to " boss " the steering—when hammering through undulating bends two-up, for example, or when cresting sharp rises with the suspension fully extended and the wheels all but off the ground.

Straight-ahead navigation at maximum velocity was absolutely stable, no matter how atrocious the surface. Generally, the handling gave lots of confidence on roads wet or dry. For pillion work with an 8-stone passenger, the rear units could be left in the " soft " position. With an 11-stone passenger they were jacked up, mainly to reduce front-end lightness at walking pace in traffic.

For comfort, the suspension earned top marks. It was supremely capable of absorbing punishment from rough roads. On smoother roads, the rear springing worked unobtrusively, but the front forks seemed to require somewhat greater impacts to get under way. With this, rather oddly, they combined a tendency to curtsey when the front brake was applied hard.

Another of the B.S.A.'s assets was the positioning of components. Everything, from the riding position to the location of the petrol taps, was just as it should have been. It was a pleasure to be mounted on a " 500 " without feeling like a monkey on a stick, perched miles up in the air. Feet could easily touch the ground and the entire mount felt compact.

For those who are running-in a " Shooting Star," it is useful to mention that we experienced a marked increase in power and " revability " during the course of a mere 200 miles, around the 800-mile mark. In fact, yet another endearing characteristic of this " hot " A7 is the apparently endless store of revs without fear of valve float, bounce or any other undesirable mechanical effects.

And that completes the picture of an exceptionally pleasant 500 c.c. twin which gave a hard-bitten tester, not easily raised to a crescendo of enthusiasm, some of his most enjoyable rides of 1961.

TUNE YOUR BEEZA

JOHN GLEED, OF EDDIE DOW'S, SHOWS HOW TO GET MORE POWER FROM THE A10 BSA

For just over 12 years, the B S A A10 parallel twin was one of the most popular bikes on the road. It appeared in 1950 as one of the first 650s, and powered the Golden Flash, the Super Rocket, the Road Rocket, and, in a more refined and tuned version, the Rocket Gold Star. It was replaced three years ago by the unit-construction engines.

Tuning can boost the top speed of Flash and the Super Rocket to over the magic "ton" by around at least 10 mph—and for the gen on how to do it we went to Eddie Dow, of Banbury.

Eddie Dow, of Southam Road, Banbury, Oxfordshire, is the complete B S A specialist, for either customising, tuning, or just straight repairing. The tune-up parts and service we show on the following pages will cost you just over £20—a modest fee for ton-plus performance.

Before you even touch a nut on your A10, you must establish whether it is possible to tune, or not. The first 650s appeared in 1950, with the sporting version—the Super Rocket—appearing later.

The early models will only take a moderate degree of tune because of their thinner crankshaft construction and weaker cylinder base make up.

Step up in the strength of construction, plus the switch to one-piece crank construction, took place around 1959. Have a careful look at your motor to see which type you have.

The early Flashes can take a step up in compression to around 8.5:1 only. Fitting the Spitfire cam (part number 67–357) is not possible, either, and you will have to settle for the slightly milder 67–356 camshaft.

Once you have settled that you have the stronger A10 engine, however, you can really start.

The first job after stripping the motor —and you will have to do this to fit the new camshaft—is a thorough check of all the bearings. An obvious point, you might think, but too many motorcyclists put new parts in old worn-out engines and are then surprised at getting little increase in performance. Main check point is the timing side main bearing which takes extra load with the high compression and bigger valve opening effort.

Most motorcycles have roller or ball-race bearings at this point, but B S A have always stuck to a plain bearing. It is copper-lead and you should look at it closely for corrosion, especially if you haven't changed the oil regularly.

Another point to watch if you are going to hot the motor is the bottom-end bolts. These stretch during use and should be replaced. A set costs £1 5s. 0d. Tighten with a torque wrench to 22 ft./lb.

Watch the washer

Assembly of the bottom half is quite straightforward, and the only point to watch is the cork washer on the end of the breather sleeve. These washers come in various thicknesses and should just be nipped by the outer cover.

The ignition timings recommended by Dow's are 13/32 in. before top dead centre, for compression ratios up to 9:1, and a slight increase to 11/32 in. btdc when the higher ratios of 10:1 and over are used.

An important point with the ignition timing is to check the spark timing on both cylinders.

If the timing is out on one cylinder the only real cure is to use an emery stone on the cam ring to alter the opening of the points. Failure to check on this balance of timing leads to burnt out pistons, and is surprisingly frequent.

The A10 inlet tract is difficult to modify, although it can be cleaned up carefully by hand. The oversize inlet valve— measuring $1\frac{1}{2}$ in. dia.—can usually be fitted, while the carb size can be stepped up. The maximum Monobloc throat diameter obtainable is the $1\frac{3}{16}$ in. size, but Dow's recommend stepping up only to $1\frac{5}{32}$ in. which will then allow standard carb settings to be used. The slightly smaller Monoblocs—which are only 1/32 in. under maximum in any case— are also easier to obtain.

Final piece of advice is to drop the size of the engine sprocket from 21 teeth to 20. The motor tends to be overgeared when new, and will rev comfortably to 6,500 or 6,700 without damage.

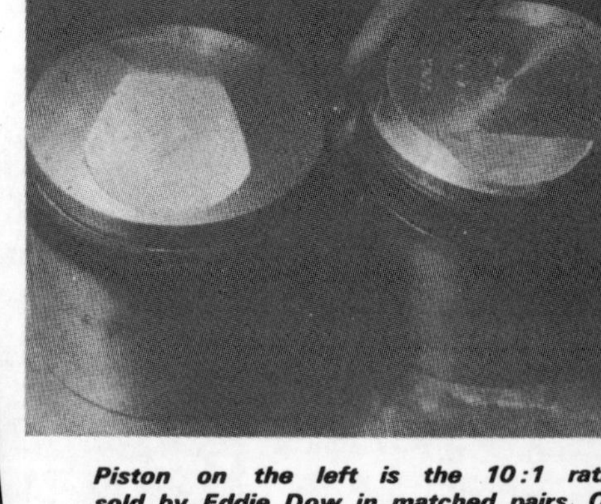
Piston on the left is the 10:1 ratio sold by Eddie Dow in matched pairs. On the right is the standard piston which gives the normal Rocket 8·75:1 compression

Expensive—but good. On the right are the American W & S valve springs, complete with their specially lightened Dural collars and big valve. Standard on left

First step is to find out if you have the later engine to take the tune. Earlier crank assembly shown has bolt-up centre section and thinner webs and end journals

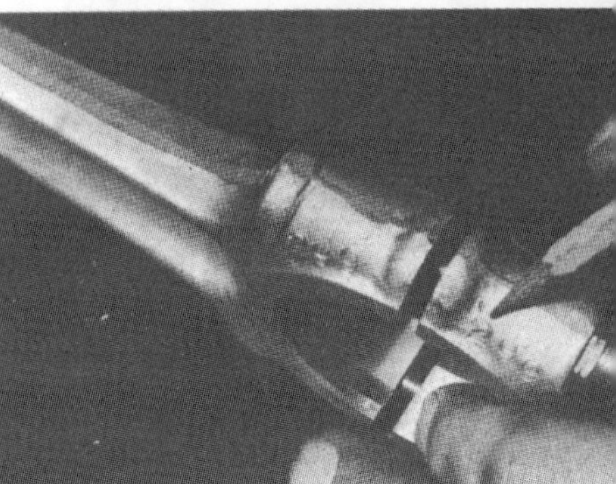
A certain amount of polishing can be done on the internals like flywheel and con-rod, but don't remove reference numbers which show how the lower half should be bolted

BEEZA TUNE: WHAT IT COSTS

Spitfire Camshaft	£4 1s. 0d.	Timing side bearing bush	£1	3s. 0d.
9:1 pistons with rings	£4 12s. 6d.	Set big end bolts	£1	5s. 0d.
10:1 pistons with rings	£5 8s. 0d.	Engine sprockets (19–23t)		19s. 6d.
American v/springs (set)	£9 10s. 0d.	O/size inlet valve	£1	0s. 0d.
Alloy v/collars (set)	£2	Terry sports v/springs	£1	13s. 0d.
Copper head gasket (approx)	15s. 0d.	Approximate cost of enlarging inlet valve seats	£8	9s. 0d.
Set engine gaskets	9s. 0d.			
Cork breather washers	0s. 2d.			

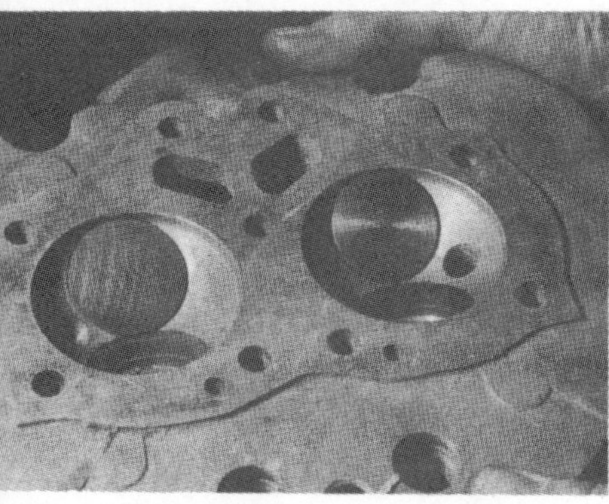

A bigger inlet valve is made and can be fitted after the head is machined. The standard size valve is $1\frac{7}{16}$ in., while the oversize—shown on left—is $1\frac{1}{2}$ in.

Fitting the Spitfire cam (part numbered 67–357) is straightforward. Only work which may be needed is removal of metal from trough edge for better clearance

Another small but important new part you will need is the cork breather seal. It comes in different thicknesses for better fit and should be oiled over when fitted

Some work can be done on the inlet tract with polishing and easing, but overboring is tricky. Carburettor bore can be increased from $1\frac{1}{16}$ in. to either $1\frac{5}{32}$ or $1\frac{3}{16}$ in.

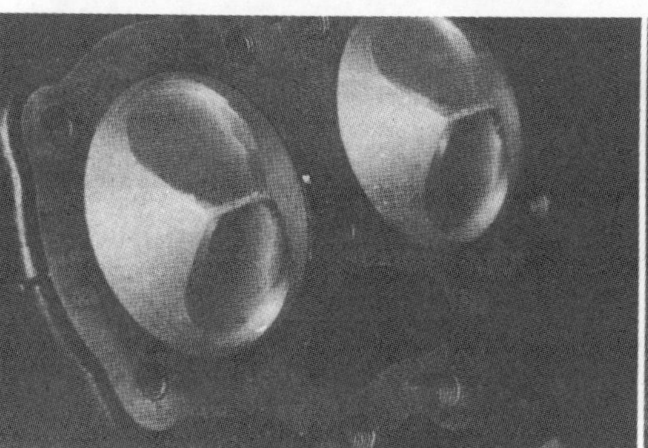

If you use these high compression pistons they have a solid skirt instead of being split as on standard. This means that they must be a good fit in bore or oil gets past

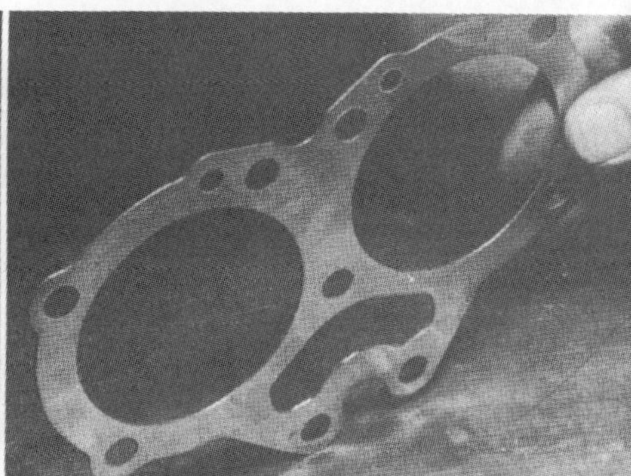

A specially thick cylinder head gasket is sold by Dow's. Extra thick at ·030 in., it helps quicker heat transfer from the head and cuts down the chance of the head warping

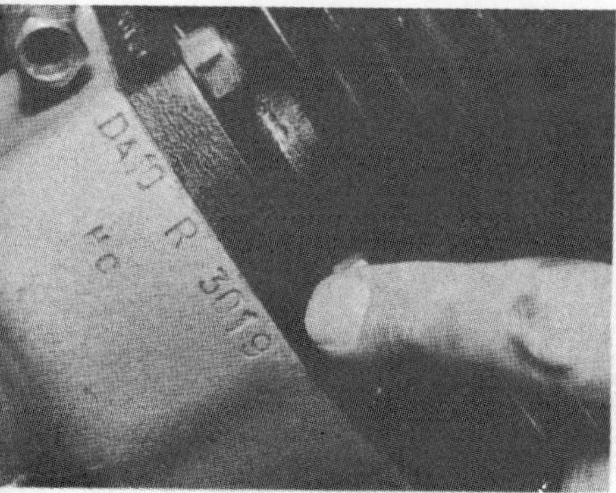

The next checkpoint is the base of the cylinder flange. Earlier models were thin here and cracked with too high compression ratios. New type is $\frac{1}{2}$ in. instead of $\frac{3}{8}$ in.

Rather rare for most bike engines, the A10 has copper-lead plain bearing on timing side—and it tends to wear. Check and replace before tuning increases loading

An obvious point but often overlooked is the cleaning out of the centrifugal sludge trap mounted in the bottom end web. Locking bolt in flywheel must be taken right out

It's no use fitting a new camshaft and then forgetting the followers. Some earlier followers wore rapidly, and in any case cam is worn, it's best to replace them

Three tiny set screws are used to lock the followers in their guides cast into the cylinder base. Undo carefully or you will have to drill them out and retap the hole

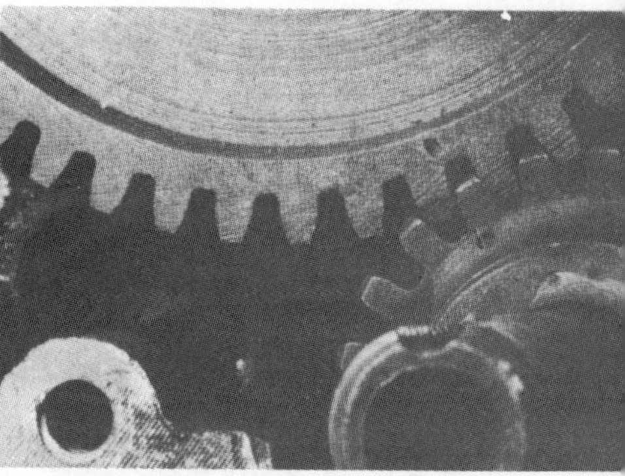

The same timing marks can be used with the new camshaft, as the timing remains just the same. Check the tooth condition for wear and replace if there is any sloppiness

1 Place selector plate in shell and locate selector plate in neutral position with the selector plunger shown. Ensure plunger is dirt free

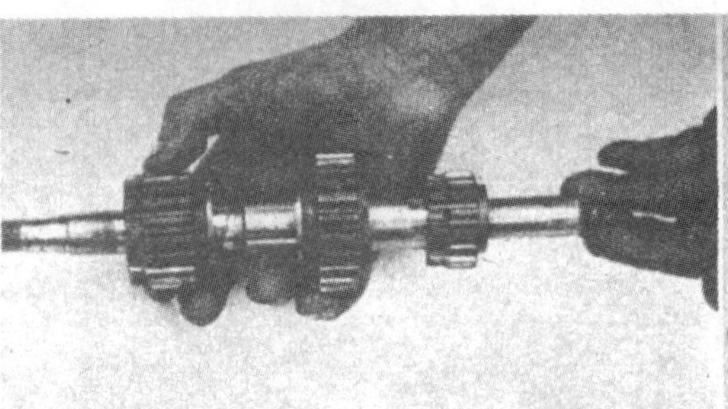

2 Assemble the mainshaft cluster of gears first. One fixed gear and two sliders. Note that the shoulders on the sliders face inwards as shown

3 Next assemble the layshaft cluster as shown, remembering it is most important to locate the thrust washer between first and end pinion

4 With both clusters assembled locate the selector forks. The forks are interchangeable and therefore they cannot be fitted wrongly positioned

5 The whole gear cluster, complete with selector forks, is now slotted into the main gearbox shell. It is a smooth slide fit into the shell

6 Position selector fork spindle in casing through selector forks. Note length of guide rod (rear of shell) to help in location of the spindle

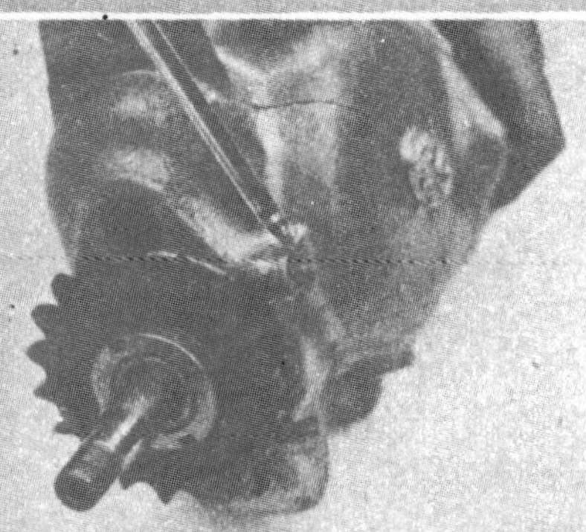

7 The selector fork spindle is held in position by grub screw. Note drive sprocket is not removed when stripping box. Mainshaft is in the centre

8 Fit inner cover plate ensuring the selector quadrant is correctly set in cam-plate. There are two dots as shown to help meshing of quadrant

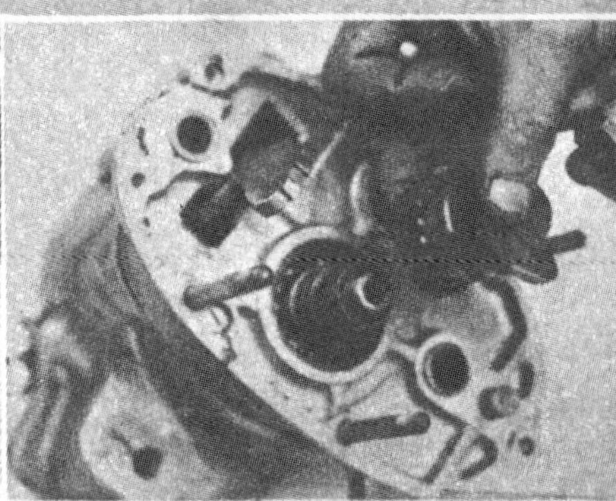

9 Now place thrust washer over mainshaft followed by bush, spring and kickstart ratchet as shown. A lock washer and nut secure this unit

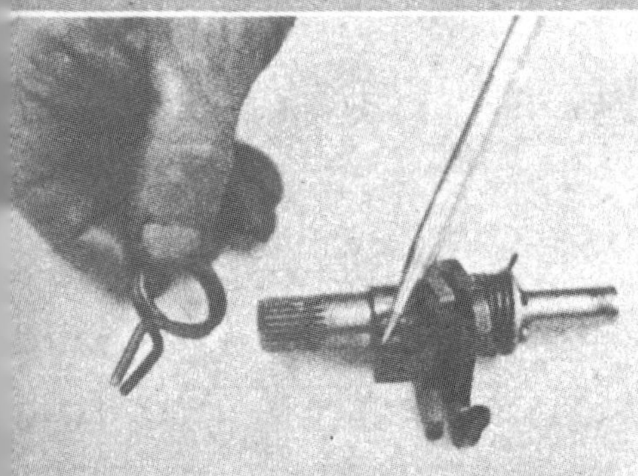

10 Here the gearchange return spring is being positioned on the selector claw. The spring fork must fit over the peg indicated by tip of pencil

11 Locate footchange mechanism into the outer cover as shown, locating the gearchange return spring on to boss cast into the outer box cover

12 After inserting kickstart quadrant into cover as shown, ensure that clutch operating arm is set correctly and offer up cover to gearbox

BEEZA BOX

GEARBOX design always seems to outlast engine design and although engines are modified, gearboxes seem to go on forever, with one type serving faithfully in many different capacity models.

This applies to the BSA gearbox as fitted to the 'A' and 'B' models. The swinging-arm B31, B33, A7 and A10 Beezas all have basically the same gearbox fitted and therefore, this build-up can apply to any of these machines. Even the Gold Star layout is identical except that it is fitted with a reverse cam-plate and plunger.

One advantage of having the same gearbox fitted to so many machines is that spares are interchangeable and all replacements are readily obtainable and very reasonably priced.

Fortunately, the BSA gearbox is very easy to dismantle and no special tools are required. Here, Lou Monnier, foreman fitter of BSA specialists, Owen Bros., of Battersea Rise, London, S.W.11, shows how to reassemble the Beeza Box. Naturally, Owen Bros., carry a full stock of spares . . .

KEY TO PARTS

1, Gearbox Outer Cover. 2, Gearbox Case. 3, Gearchange Lever Spindle. 4, Gear Pinions. 5, Gear Shifter Forks. 6, Gearchange Return Spring. 7, Layshaft. 8, Layshaft Thrust Washer. 9, Kickstart Return Spring. 10, Selector Fork Shaft. 11, Retaining Nuts and Bolts. 12 Kickstart Ratchet. 13, Cam-plate Plunger Unit. 14, Gear Selector Plate Spring and Washer. 15, Gear Control Cam-plate. 16, Mainshaft. 17, Gear Pinions. 18, Gearbox Inner Cover. ●

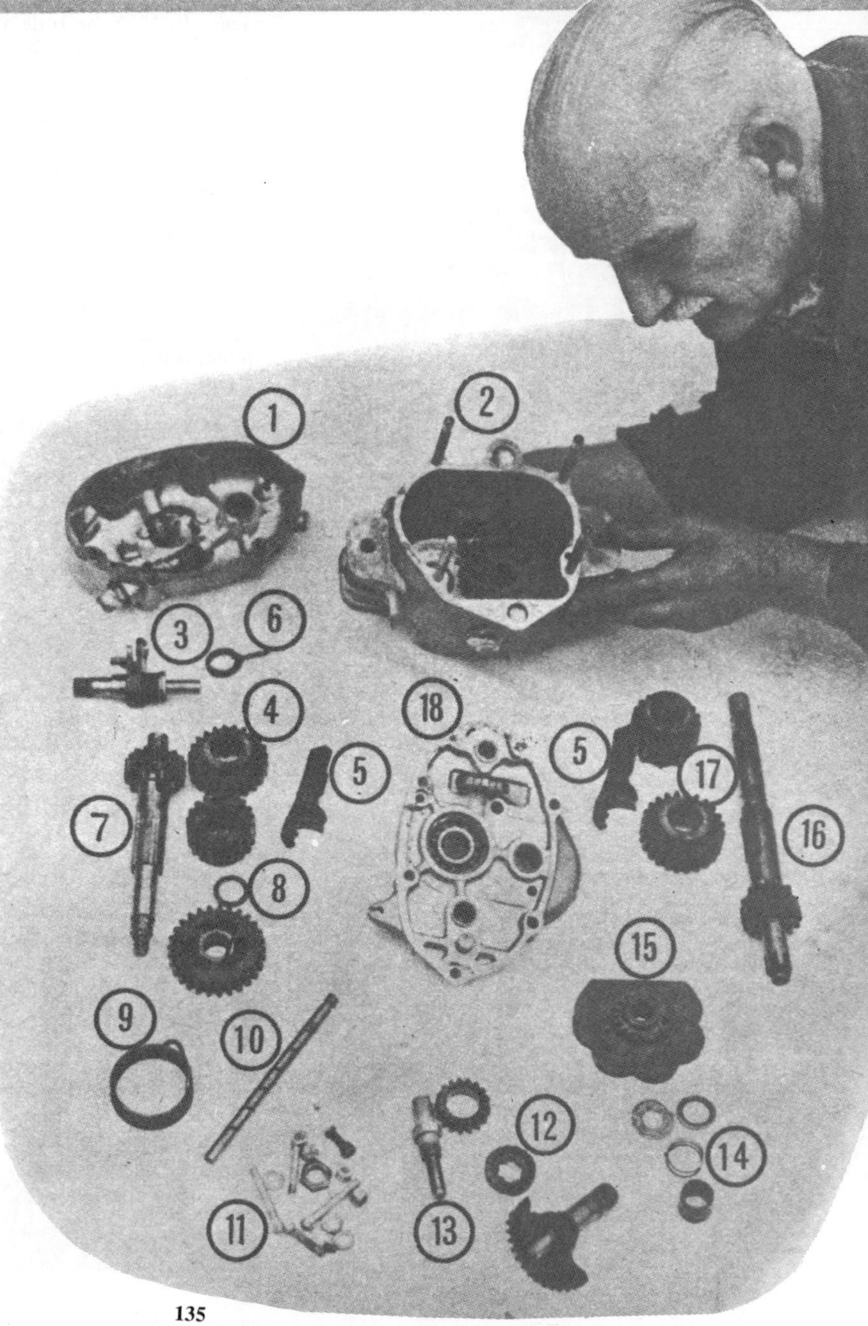

Rear end of the Rocket Gold Star. Note the Taylor Dow racing seat, track silencer

A very large B.S.A. alloy fuel tank holds five gallons. Sponge pad for rider comfort

Front wheel has steel rim (alloy ones optional) and the B.S.A. racing 190 mm. brake

Frame is normal B.S.A. tw duplex tube model. Siamese exhaust pipes give more pow

FOR many years now Eddie Dow, managing director of Taylor Dow Ltd., Southam Road, Banbury, has been specialising in sporting B.S.A. machines and entering them in the major production machine races. In 1955, he rode a 500 c.c. Gold Star himself and on this model he won the Clubmans' T.T. in the Isle of Man and the Thruxton Nine Hour race. Since then he has never lost interest in this type of racing and the Taylor Dow Gold Stars were a familiar sight to enthusiasts. When the Gold Star's popularity began to wane it was only natural that he should turn to B.S.A.'s latest sportster, the Rocket Gold Star —especially as it was due in no small way to his incessant pestering of B.S.A.s that they brought the new model out !

This year the Taylor Dow Rocket Gold Star was ridden at Thruxton b Dave Williams and Ron Langston an finished eighth overall after a stop t repair a broken oil pipe had dropped from the leading position. We took th bike over exactly as it finished the rac so readers should remember that suc things as braking figures may be eve better on a new model. The speed is ur likely to be as high, however, as the Do motor had naturally been prepared wit racing in mind.

Another point which should be mad is that—as in the case of the Thruxto Triumph which we tested recently—ou chart does not really apply to this typ of machine as certain instruments hav been taken off.

Special Engine

The engine fitted to the Rocket Gol Star is basically that which powers th Super Rocket—the A10 650 c.c. twin. has certain differences such as siamese

Over 120 m.p.h. from the Taylor Dow

BSA ROCKET GOLD STAR

Rearset footrests fold up so that the bike can be started on the kickstarter

Steel toolbox has plenty of room for toolkit and also houses the voltage regulator

Another rear-end view but from opposite side. Shows the sporting half-chainguard

The bike's roadholding was aided by this superb tyre. Dunlop "triangular" pattern

exhaust pipes with a "Gold Star" type silencer and what used to be called the "Spitfire" camshaft. The motor on our test model had also got 10.5:1 pistons and special valve springs which gave it an estimated power output of 51 b.h.p. at 7,200 r.p.m.

Taylor Dow are now marketing 10.5:1 pistons for those A10 riders who want extra power from their motor.

The gearbox is the RRT2 B.S.A. extra close ratio type and we faulted it because it persistently jumped out of third gear. This, however, was probably due to the fact that during the race Ron Langston had clouted a straw bale and had bent the gear lever, thus upsetting the selector mechanism.

Except for this the gearbox was perfect and thanks to the reasonably flexible motor the RGS was quite manageable even in London traffic once we had fitted soft plugs instead of the RL49 racing type.

The clutch—same as that fitted to the big Triumphs—was perfect under normal riding conditions but began to slip during our acceleration tests. Not surprising really because we were doing sprint-type starts and 51 b.h.p. is a whole lot of power for a standard clutch to cope with under those conditions. A private owner is unlikely to suffer any clutch trouble at all.

Handling the RGS at speed was fabulous. One could feel a slight wiggle but it was nothing to worry about and the fact that our tester was able to ground the bottom frame tube is testimony to the bike's roadholding !

Something which helped greatly in this respect was the Dunlop triangular tyre. Riding round bends at speed was child's play with this tyre fitted—the difficulty came when riding slowly ! On London's roundabouts in the wet—which one is forced to trickle slowly through thanks to the traffic and the greasy surface—

they felt rather dodgy.

Triangular tyres, however, are not meant for trickling through roundabouts! Fitted with the B.S.A. five-gallon alloy tank and the Taylor Dow Clubman seat, plus clip-on bars and rearset footrests, the bike looked like a thinly disguised racer. Despite this it was quite comfortable, though anyone not used to a racing style riding position might find their wrists aching on a long run.

Starting Problems

The rearset footrest folded up to allow the bike to be kickstarted but as this had been bent in the straw bale incident it still got in the way a little. This—combined with the extra high compression pistons—made the bike a real beast to start and quite often we did it by bumping it in racing style.

The mods. carried out by Taylor Dow's had made the RGS appreciably faster

continued on page 138

MOTORCYCLE MECHANICS ROAD TEST No. 68

Vehicle BSA Rocket Gold Star **Price new** £323 - 8s

Engine 650cc twin cylinder 51 bhp @ 7,200 rpm

Gearbox Four speed - Extra close ratio

Final drive Chain

GENERAL INFORMATION

Weight	405 lbs
Saddle height	29 ins
Turning circle	17 ft
Is toolbox lockable	No
Is steering lockable	No
Fuel tank capacity	5 Galls
Reserve capacity	approx 1 gall
Oil tank capacity	5½ pints
Gearbox capacity	3/8 pint
Fuel specified	100 octane
Overall consumption	41 mpg.
Braking from 30 mph	20 ft
Acceleration 0-60 mph	6·8 secs

SPEEDS IN GEARS (123 mph top)

EQUIPMENT SUPPLIED

STANDARD FITTINGS Clip-on bars. rev-counter 5 gallon alloy tank

OPTIONAL EXTRAS Taylor-Dow Clubman seat 190mm racing front brake (all extras)

SPARES PRICES

Engine gasket set	5s 6d
Set valves & guides	126s 0d
Piston with rings	45s 0d
Set of clutch plates	95s 0d
Silencer	108s 0d
Pr Exchange brake shoes	22s 6d

RATING CHART (points out of 10)

Control positioning and adjustment	6
EXTRA Instruments and equipment	0
Fuel reserve and tap operation	8
Ease of starting	5
Engine smoothness	6
Quietness of engine & transmission	6
Gearbox and clutch operation	6
Road holding	8
Braking efficiency	8
Comfort and ease of handling	8
Lighting efficiency	8
Stand operation	0
Tool kit	3
Overall finish	8
General performance & reliability	10
TOTAL (maximum points 150)	**90**

BSA Golden Flash

HERE'S A MODEL WITH UNIVERSAL APPEAL!

The BSA Golden Flash is the *right* motorcycle for more motorcyclists! Here is real *universe* appeal.

FEATURES *INCLUDED* IN THE PRICE!
Full width alloy hubs
Chrome plated tank panels
Centrally positioned brakes
Dual seat with chrome handrail and pillion footrests
Quickly detachable rear wheel
Enclosed rear chain
Extra strong double tube frame
Steering head lock
Adjustable rear suspension

The big husky "Flash" successfully combines smooth, flexible traffic docility with unusually potent acceleration, high cruising speeds, and, to quote a "Cycle" Magazine road test, "top speed in excess of 100 m.p.h.".

With finish in gleaming black baken enamel, rocket-fire red tank with chrome panels and lots of chrome and polished alloy, the Golden Flash is one of the best looking motorcycles on the market today.

Performance—Appearance—and above all, DEPENDABILITY ar yurs with a Golden Flash!

Visit your BSA Dealer — Make your own "Flash Test!"

BSA Road Rocket

FAST—
CYCLE magazine in road test report (Sept. 1954) gives electrically timed speed of 110.76 mph with full road equipment!

The BSA Road Rocket gives you more for your money than any other motorcycle on the American market!

- **Do you want chrome fenders?**
  —*You get them on a Road Rocket!*
- **Do you want a chrome panelled tank?**
  —*You get it on a Road Rocket!*

- **Do you want tachometer equipment— racing carburetor?**
  —*You get them on a Road Rocket!*

PLUS—Many DeLuxe features included in the standard retail price.

Double tube frame, ultra performance engine with alloy cylinder head, quick detachable rear wheel, dual seat with chrome handrail—everything you want in a fine high powered motorcycle. See your BSA dealer.

Write nearest Distributor for Dealership information ● (Rider-Dealer opportunities in certain open territories)

ROCKET/GOLD STAR
— continued from page 137—

than a standard one so we were not unduly surprised when we obtained a maximum speed figure of 123 m.p.h., the fastest ever attained by a machine on test by this magazine.

Speeds in the lower two gears were just as impressive—almost 90 m.p.h. in second and well over the ton in third.

Considering the extremely high first gear — which necessitated prolonged clutch slipping—the acceleration time of 6.8 sec. was quite fantastic.

It was obvious that the brakes had done a lot of hard work but even so a stopping distance of 20 feet from 30 m.p.h. was the result of our brake test! The bike had the B.S.A. racing 190 mm. front brake and racing linings both front and rear. Of the two, the rear brake was by far the best.

Taken all round the Rocket Gold Star proved to be a really thrilling bike and it is quite safe to say that such a machine could be bought and raced almost as standard by a private owner and still keep him up with the pack in short circuit races. Proving this is the fact that the RGS we tested could have been geared up even more by the fitting of an engine sprocket one tooth larger.

This would have given a top speed approaching 130 m.p.h.—as we said, quite a thrilling bike ! ●

OVERHAULING BSA TWIN *from page 94*

fitted and after a new cylinder head gasket had been given a coat of graphite grease the assembly was placed in position. After replacing the push rods the rocker box was then screwed down evenly to prevent distortion.

The tappets were adjusted to 10 thou inlet valve and 16 thou exhaust valve clearance—with the motor cold. After the tappets had been adjusted the oil feed pipe to the rocker spindles was put into place with a new fibre washer.

The torque stays were then fitted into position between the motor and the frame and exhaust pipes fitted between the ports and silencers.

When replacing the carburetter we took great care to see that the rubber air filter connector was correctly in place over the carburetter intake. Extra care was also necessary when making up the joint between the carburetter and the manifold.

It is important to see that it is absolutely airtight to avoid considerable carburetter troubles.

The rest of the assembly was straight-forward and we refilled the machine with new oil.

The kick starter was then given twelve quick sharp prods to get the oil circulating through the oil ways and pipes. We started the engine and checked the oil return pipe with the engine running fairly fast to make sure that the oil was returning to the tank.

Having fitted so many new parts we decided the machine should be run in as if new and so driving for the first five hundred miles was steady. ●

BEEZA TWIN TUNE-UP

Gold Star specialist, Eddie Dow, peps up performance on the BSA big twins . . .

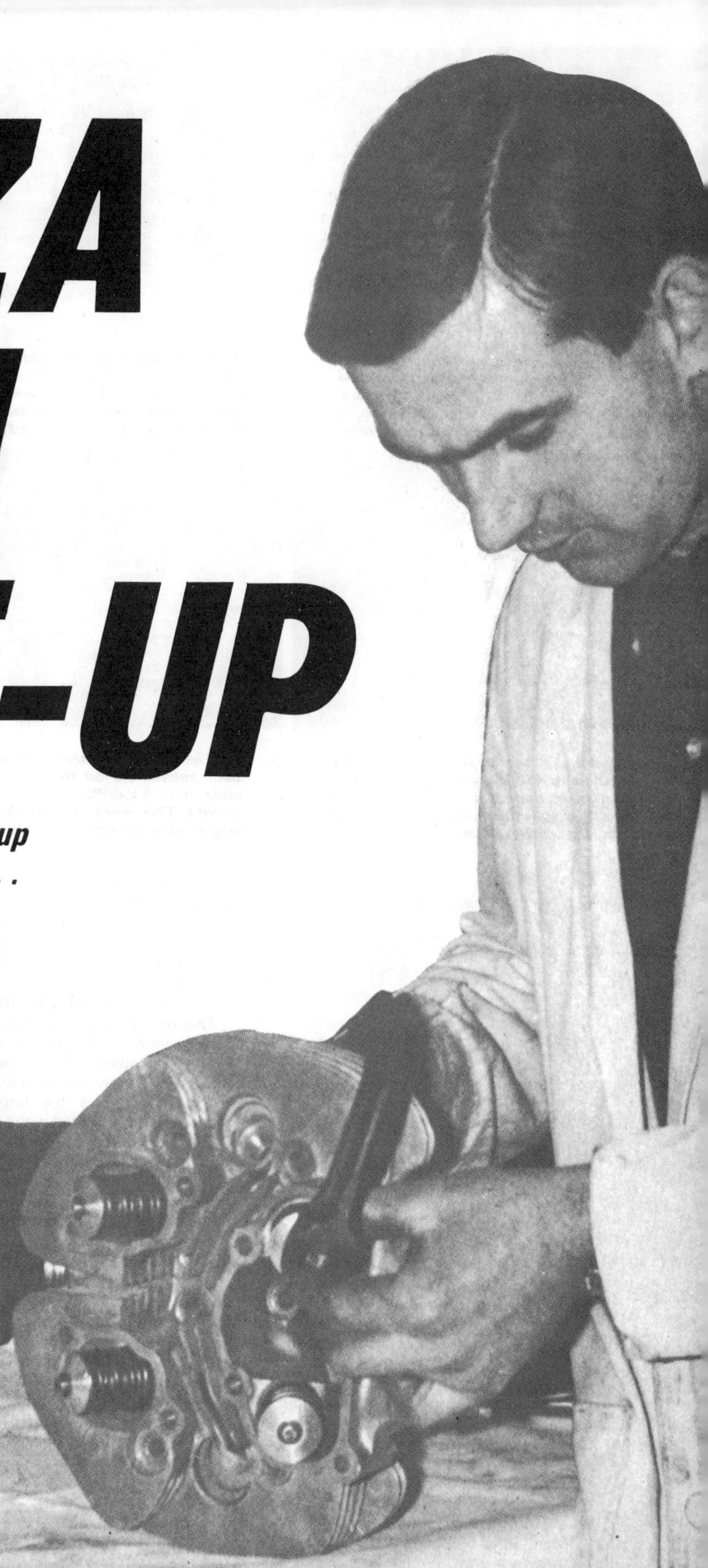

▶ WITH a following wind and the tarmac sloping in the right direction, the long-lived BSA A10 and A7 twins would comfortably top 90 and creep slowly towards the magic "ton".

But not all of the Beeza big twins were sluggards. The series which began with the introduction of the Golden Flash in 1950 culminated with the rip-snorting Rocket Gold Star of 1962, having a top speed approaching 115 mph.

Eddie Dow, famed for his work on the Goldie, also turned his hand to the RGS, producing a range of goodies to pep up the performance of all A7 and A10 models to RGS standards.

By fitting high-lift camshaft, racing valve springs and high-compression pistons, plus a measure of balancing, polishing and port enlarging, any of the big BSA twins can be whipped up to three-figure speeds.

Scrambler star Bill Gwynne, workshop foreman for Eddie Dow, shows the necessary engine mods that bring a big power bonus to the "A" series motors . . .

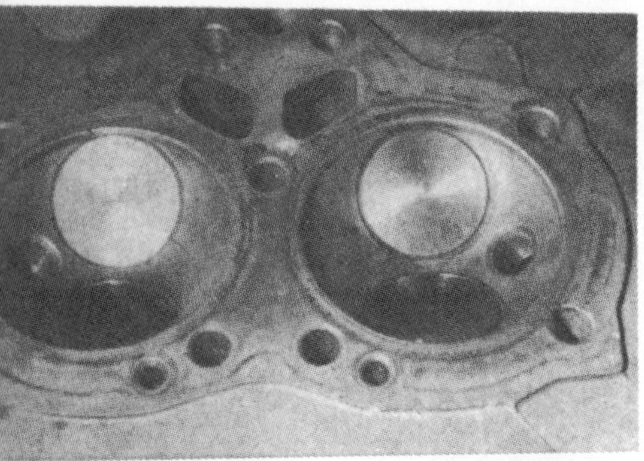

The inlet valve size may be increased to 1·455 in. These are the largest possible and larger seats have to be cut in head, plus port throat enlargement. Work costs between £3 and £5, including valves/guides

Used in conjunction with the Spitfire camshaft, W & S racing valve springs stop valve bounce and allow increased engine revs. Complete set with collars £11 0s. 0d. Gold Star springs may be used at £3 15s. 0d.

High compression 9·0 or 10·5 pistons for the "A" group twins cost £5 7s. 0d. a pair. They are necessary if advantage of other tuning is to be obtained. Con-rods buffed and polished to avoid cracks developing

The tappets can also be reduced in weight by lengthening the longitudinal slots with a carborundum-tipped drill. When finished all should weigh the same and have no burrs on the sliding faces of the tappets

The idler and camshaft pinions are more than substantial on the "A" twins. These units may be drilled and lightened to cut weight. This work is best done by a light engineering company or tuning specialist

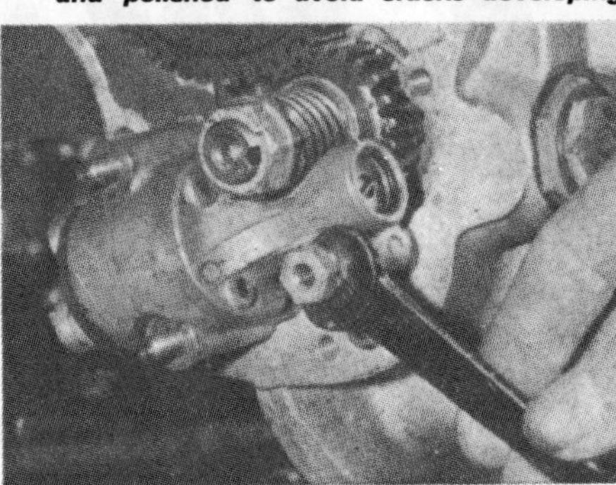

The oil pump does not need to be changed on the tuned engine, but it must certainly be in first-class working order. Dismantle and replace any component that is showing signs of wear. Only good lubrication will do

BEEZA TWIN TUNE-UP

▶ **Any cooking-type motorcycle engine can be tuned, witness the racing Bantams or the incredible Chris Vincent racing outfits. But what is it that makes these machines buzz like the proverbial cat with its tail on fire?**

A finger cannot be pointed at any one item to say that it alone has produced road-burning acceleration or a fantastic maximum speed.

Performance tuning is a combination of things from high compression pistons to polished ports, plus hours of painstaking labour in workshop preparation.

Eddie Dow of Banbury is renowned for his prowess with the legendary Gold Star singles and in latter years, the Rocket Gold Star. Consequently, to find out how we could get the best from a Beeza big twin, we visited his workshops to see what was involved in producing a Beeza twin with performance plus.

The answer is simply that the engine to be tuned is dismantled into sections, each of which receives individual tuning attention.

Cylinder head

The first modification made to improve performance is to obtain better filling of the cylinders. To achieve this, the inlet valves may be increased in size to 1.455 in. This is the largest size that may be accommodated in the head.

The port throat must also be enlarged to suit the bigger valves, with a diameter of 1.355 in. Templates showing the actual shape of the port are given in the Eddie Dow catalogue, together with a complete list of goodies available for tuning.

After enlarging the ports and valves, the inlet ducts are polished to a mirror finish to improve gas flow, and the inlet valve guides may be shortened by 0.187 in. where they protrude into the port. They can also be filed to an oval section, to offer less obstruction to gas flow.

On iron cylinder heads, a "Tufnol" packing piece, $\frac{1}{8}$ in. thick, should be set between the carburettor and cylinder head to act as a heat barrier.

On reassembly, stronger valve springs should be used in conjunction with a high-lift camshaft to increase revs and stop valve bounce.

The W & S road racing valve springs are available, but somewhat expensive. A Gold Star valve spring and alloy collar conversion may be used and is much cheaper.

The part number for the racing spring (outer) is 67-883 and (inner) 67-884. The outer spring has a closed-end coil, which must be located against the cylinder head.

The rockers can be lightened by reducing them slightly in size at the outer end and by removing all sharp corners.

Many enthusiasts are under the impression that to obtain real performance a twin-carburettor cylinder head is needed. But the cost of converting a B S A head to twin carbs is far too expensive for the benefit that would be obtained. Also, the cylinder head casting does not have sufficient material thickness to safely adapt the inlet tract.

Pistons and con-rods

At high rpm, it is obvious that reciprocating parts such as pistons should be equalised in weight to minimise engine vibration.

They can easily be checked on precision scales and the heavier piston lightened by removal of material from inside the casting.

The compression ratio of 9:1 on the Rocket Gold Star requires the use of a premium grade fuel and is considered to be high enough for road use. However, 10.5:1 pistons are available for competition use and should be used with 100 octane fuel.

As with the pistons, both connecting rods should be of equal weight. Also, the small-ends and big-ends should weigh the same.

These may be checked by first resting the bearings on the precision scales and suspending the rest of the rod horizontally. The heavier rod must then be filed on the

great deal is talked about balancing the
crankshaft, but for normal road use this
is not really necessary. The cranks are
all balanced sufficiently during production
at B S A. Rarely are they out of balance

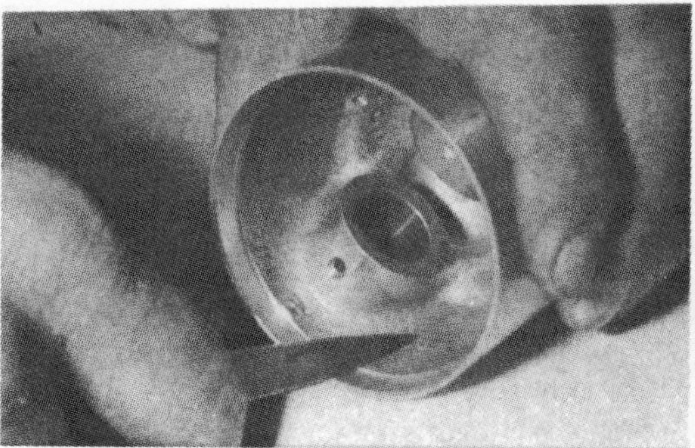

However, it is possible for the pistons to
vary slightly in weight and on a twin it
is necessary for them to weigh the same. A
slight scraping of metal from inside the
heavier unit should equalise the weights

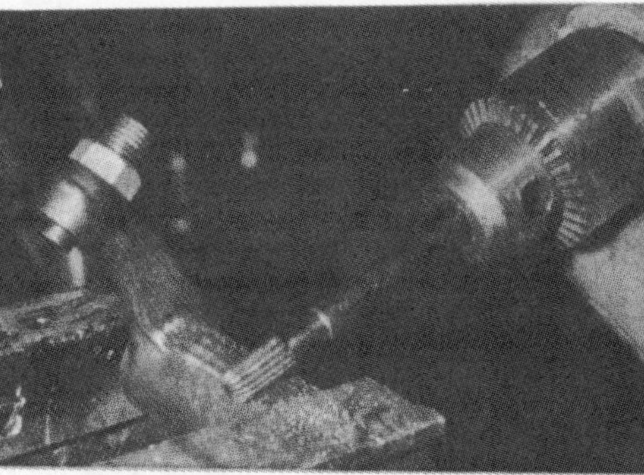

The rocker arms can be reduced slightly in
size at the outer end and all sharp corners
removed as shown. But don't overdo it as
they can easily be weakened to breaking
point. Finish off by polishing rockers

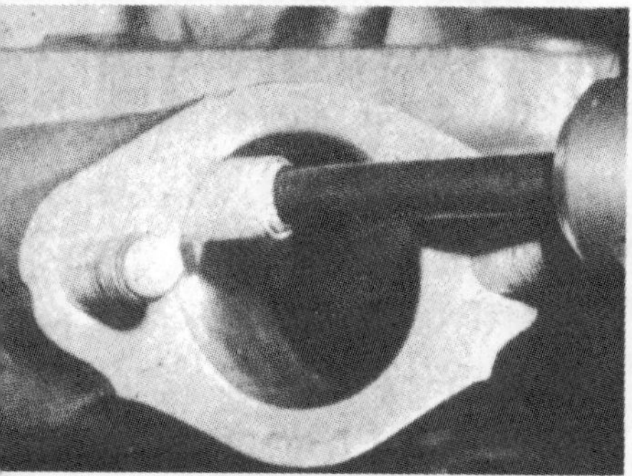

Polishing all exhaust and inlet ports will
improve gas flow. Begin with a rat-tail
file or drill-powered grinding tool to
remove rough cast. Next use fine emery to
smooth contours and finally, metal polish

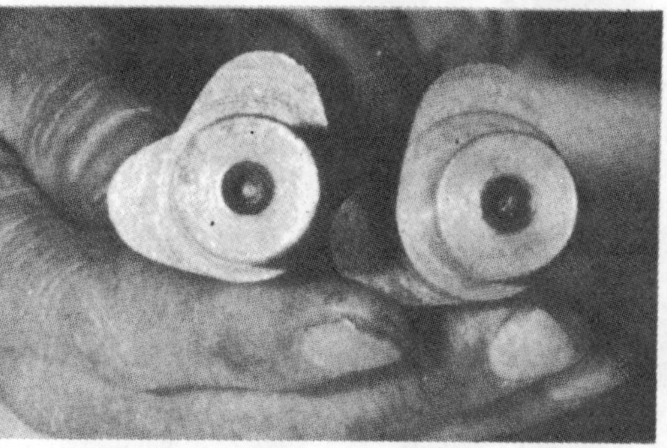

A B S A Spitfire camshaft used in conjunction
with tappet clearances of 10 thou (inlet)
and 12 thou (exhaust) will provide a marked
improvement in power. The camshaft costs
£4 11s. 0d. Standard cam followers are used

Finally, for maximum power at peak revs, a
siamese system with megaphone Gold Star
pattern silencer gives best results. Pipes
cost £5 0s. 0d. and Gold Star type silencer
costs £2 17s. 6d. from Eddie Dow Ltd.

gudgeon pin boss, until the same weight
reading is obtained for both rods.

Repeat the process for the big-ends.
Finally, file off all sharp edges on the rods
and mirror polish, giving a final weight
check afterwards.

The connecting rod big-end bolts are
highly stressed and it is advisable to renew
these on reassembly. They should be tightened with a torque wrench to 22lb./ft.

Camshaft

For improved engine performance, it is
essential to fit a high-lift camshaft as
included in the B S A Spitfire specification.

These are available over the counter,
although it is necessary to check that there
is sufficient clearance between the lobes
of the cams and the crankcase when fitting.

Sometimes the castings of the crankcases have a little too much material and
the cams will touch. Therefore, it may be
necessary to file away slightly part of the
casings on the inside.

Tappet clearances will also have to be
altered from standard to 0.010 (inlet) and
0.012 (exhaust).

Standard cam-followers are retained,
although they may be lightened by lengthening the slots. However, when this work
is done, it is necessary to ensure that they
weigh the same and also that there are no
burred edges.

For competition use, it is possible to
obtain "Stellite" faced cam-followers,
while ordinary cam-followers, if worn, can
be refaced with this extra-hard metal.

When tuning the big B S As, the later
crankshaft assembly is probably more
satisfactory for high rpm as it has larger
diameter crankpins, which are not so likely
to disintegrate with the increase in engine
power output.

Therefore, although earlier twins can be
tuned, it is wiser to obtain the later model
crank. This will also, of course, involve
buying connecting rods with the larger
diameter big-ends, as well as new main
bearings.

The assemblies are interchangeable as
the larger main bearings will fit the earlier
crankcases.

According to Eddie Dow, balancing of
the crankshafts is not necessary, as when
they are produced by B S A the cranks are
automatically checked and balanced on the
machining line.

Vibration

Only if there is an extraordinary amount
of vibration which shatters number-plate
brackets, headlamp mountings and such-
like, will the crankshaft be suspect.

In this case, it is easier to have a specialist such as Eddie Dow carry out the balancing act, than attempt the work yourself.

The flywheel may be lightened if
required, by skimming $\frac{1}{8}$ in. from each of
the side faces of the flywheel, without
machining any part of the bobweight. If
this is accidentally trimmed, it will affect
the balance factor of the crankshaft.

If the flywheel has been dismantled,
then the bolts should be treated with
"Loctite" on reassembly, to prevent any
possibility of their coming loose.

Finally, the crankshaft and flywheel may
be polished, but the utmost care should
be taken to avoid damaging the bearing
surfaces.

Both early and late model crankshafts
are fitted with sludge traps, which should
be cleaned on dismantling the engine. On
early models, this means removing the end
plugs on the crankpins and scraping out
the deposits.

On the later models, the end plug is removed and a sludge tube is withdrawn for
cleaning.

Plugs and exhausts

With a higher compression ratio and
tuned engine, it is necessary to fit hot
plugs. These should be Lodge 2HN or
2HLN or their equivalent in other types,
according to whether the head is iron or
aluminium.

While for really high-speed, long distance
motorcycling, Lodge RL49 or their equivalent racing plug may be used.

Finally, for maximum power at peak
rpm, siamese pipes in conjunction with
megaphone type Gold Star silencers will
give best results, although at medium
rpm, there is slight power loss compared
with twin pipes.

The pepped-up big twins should obtain
peak horsepower at approximately 6800
rpm, with a safe maximum of 7000 rpm
for sustained running.

With a tuned motor giving that extra
performance, it should always be remembered that all cycle parts, which means
brakes, tyres, steering, suspension and
controls, must also be in top trim.

It's no good being able to go if you can't
stop!

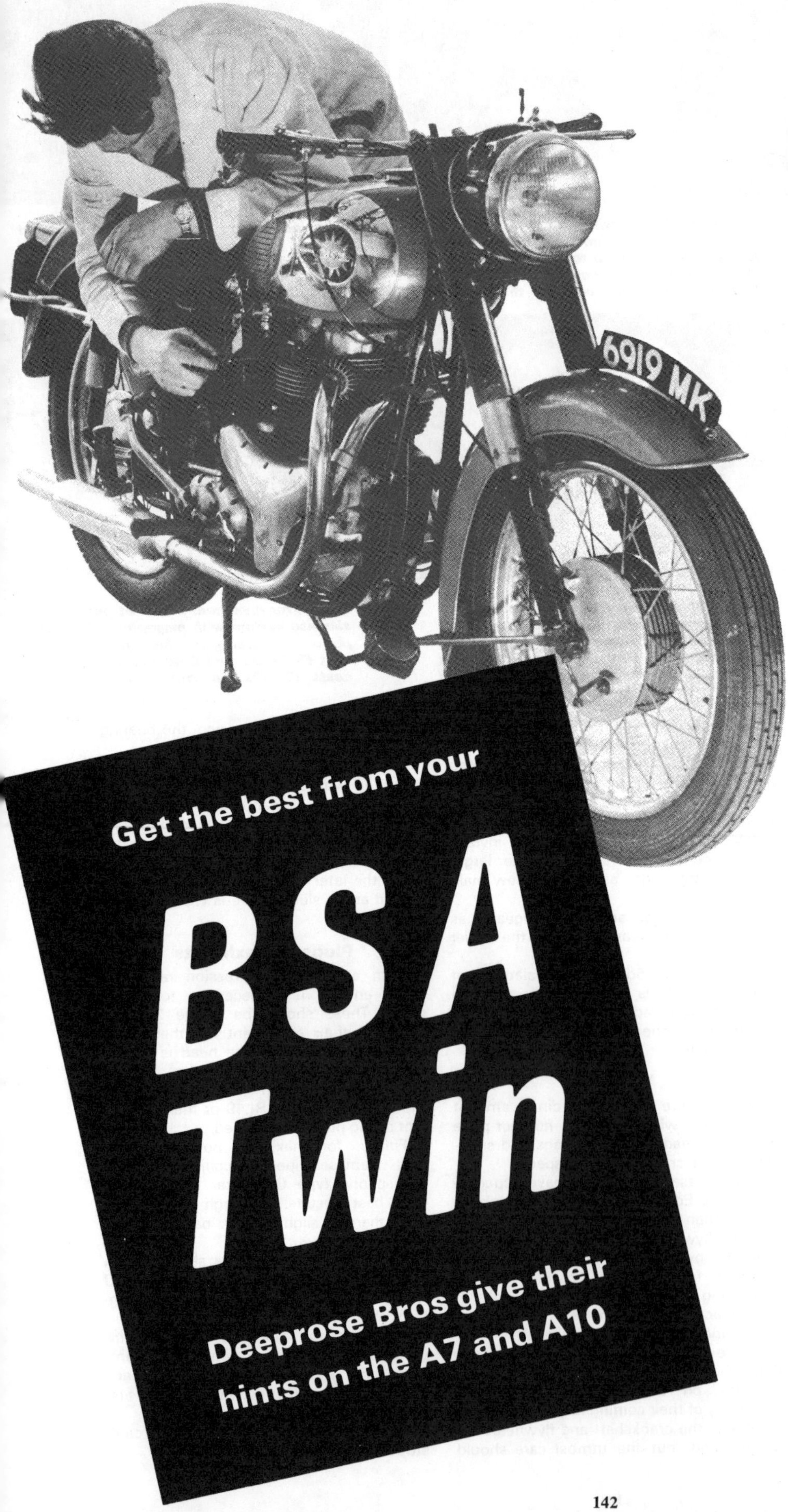

Lubrication is of vital importance on any machine. The gearbox holds approximately ¾ pint of oil (SAE 5Q). A level plug is situated at the rear of the box as shown and should be removed when filling unit

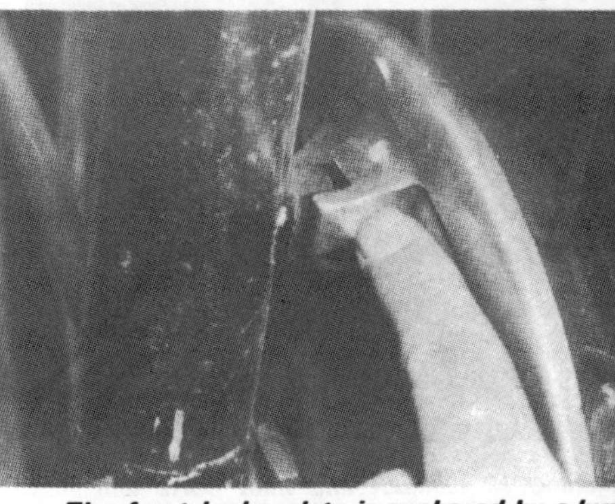

The front brake plate is anchored by a lug on the fork leg. When replacing the front wheel make sure the lug is pushed fully home in the brake plate notch before tightening clamp on wheel spindle

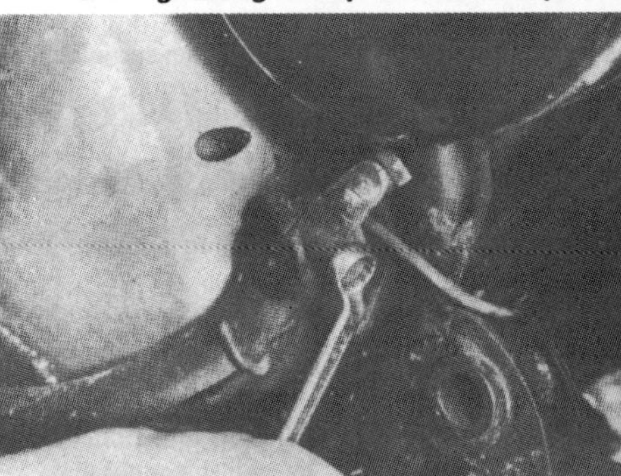

The rear brake is cable-operated on the right of machine. To avoid damage to the splines on brake spindle across the frame, make sure that the pinch bolts on both ends of the spindle are really tight

Get the best from your

BSA Twin

Deeprose Bros give their hints on the A7 and A10

● Although the heavyweight 500 cc A7 and 650 cc A10 B S A s are out of production and have been superseded by the A50 and A65 unit-construction machines, there are still a large number of these popular models on the road.

Like the A50 and A65, the A7 and A10 are almost identical; only minor differences such as front-brake size, colour schemes and bore sizes are variants. Therefore, although these photographs feature the popular A10 Road Rocket, the points apply to all 500 and 650 B S A twins.

With the large capacity models in the range, B S A retained magneto ignition

The rear brake torque-arm bolts on to the frame on the swinging arm. The bolt should have a castellated nut and a split pin. If this is not fitted, the nut can come off and the rear brake will lock on

Oil feed to rockers is through these two points. The retaining bolts are hollow and should not be overtightened as they easily break. Also, copper washers behind unions should be replaced on reassembling

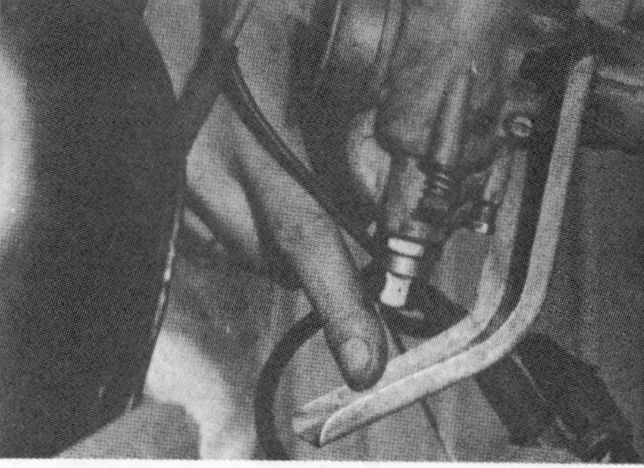

Remove this petrol-waste tray at your own risk. The purpose is to deflect any waste away from the magneto. If petrol is allowed to drip into magneto—one spark and you have the best bonfire on the road

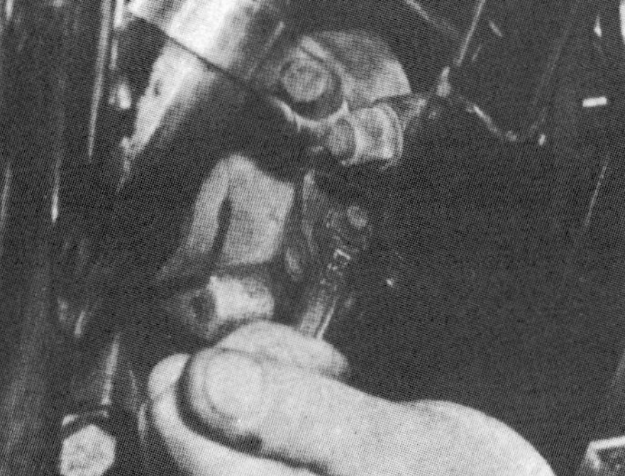

The BSA dynamo is chain driven and is retained only by a single clamp. If this clamp loosens, the dynamo can shift. Make sure the bolt is tight or the cork seal may fail and the chain drive be thrown!

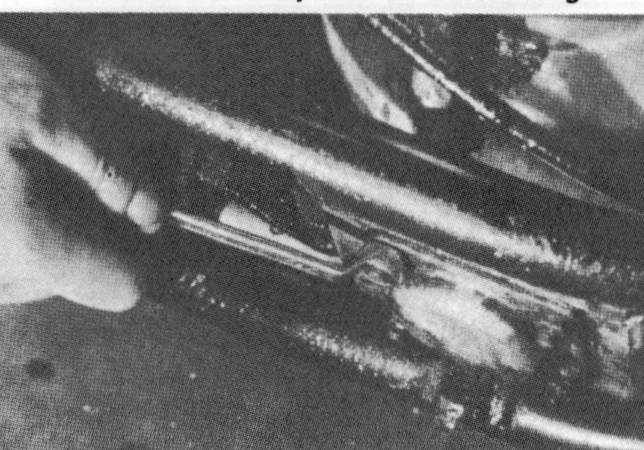

Beneath this sump plate is the first oil filter in the lubrication system. If you are making an oil change, don't forget to clean it. Also, take care when replacing nuts as these small $\frac{3}{16}$ in. studs are soft

Primary chain adjustment is carried out by shifting gearbox forwards or backwards with adjuster shown. However, don't forget that after adjusting primary chain, the rear chain will also need attention

The swinging arm sub-frame is held by the large nut indicated. This must be tight or swinging arm section will hammer the pivot hole in main frame out of shape. A check should be made weekly for security

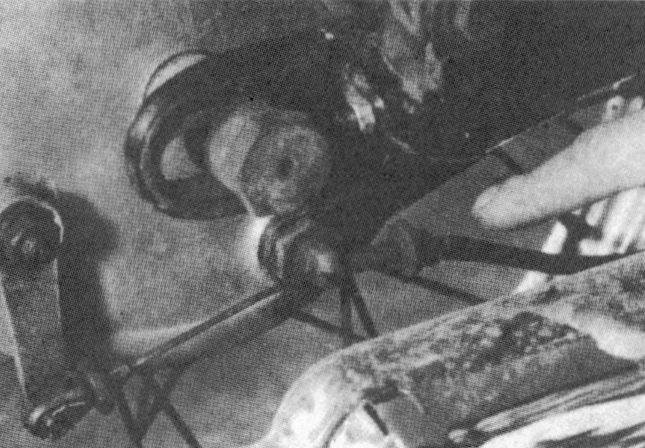

Brake adjustment here is at its limit, and although it could be due to lining wear, a stretched cable could be a cause of trouble. In this case, simply adjust by moving operating lever on its spline

Four bolts hold the sprocket to the hub, and should they become loose the sprocket will be hammered back and forth when accelerating and decelerating, until the holes become oval and the bolts all shear

and dynamo electrics until the change to unit-construction. Therefore, with all of the magneto ignition units, the contact breaker points should be set between 10 and 12 thou. Also, the ignition should be set $\frac{3}{8}$ in. btdc with the ignition fully advanced.

Battery check

Unlike coil ignition motorcycles, the A7 and A10 are completely independent of batteries except for lighting purposes. Therefore it is quite common to find a battery has "died" of neglect. A weekly check should be made to ensure that the battery is topped-up and also that the terminals are clean and firmly attached.

BSA forks have a one-way damping action, although it is possible to buy a conversion. However, the standard forks are rather unusual in that they need a surprising amount of damping fluid. Each leg should contain $7\frac{1}{2}$ fluid ounces of SAE 20 oil. The forks are drained from a small plug hole at the base of the leg and re-filled by removing the large cap-nut on top of the fork.

Tappet adjustment

The engines of the 500 and 650 models are also virtually identical except for the larger bore of the 650. Tappet adjustments are 8 thou for inlet and 10 thou for exhaust valves. Make sure these adjust-ments are perfect, as the motor can be very noisy with an alloy head. An oil pressure relief valve is set at the base and to the front of the timing case, and should excess smoke come from the engine, it could be due to grit or dirt sticking the valve.

Clutch adjustment is set through a hole beneath a cover next to the kickstart on the gearbox. The clutch arm is set at right angles to the casing seam with the aid of the pushrod adjuster nut. When the operating arm is at the correct angle, the cable is slackened off at the handlebar lever to give $\frac{1}{8}$ in. free play at the lever. If not, the clutch pushrod will bind and possibly become damaged.

Offside view of the meaty 650 motor shows the still immaculate chrome pipes and the clean and perfectly oiltight motor. Only flaw on bike was dented oil tank cover

Cowhorn bars had been added, with rubber shrouds over the levers. Another owner mod was the elegant—and useful—eye-level mirror. Rev-meter had been added, too

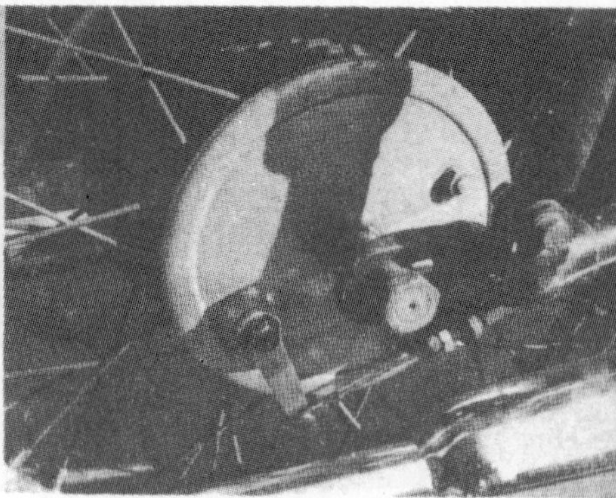

Full width rear brake is cable operated —and even when new was accused of spongy feel. Note angle of lever which undeniably betrays worn brake linings

ROAD TEST

● **With a shattering crackle, the motor burst into life at the second prod; smoothly the clutch fed in, and wallop, the acceleration whisked you up to 50 with the slightest twitch of the wrist.**

The A10 SR BSA was a secondhand model picked at random from the gleaming stock of bikes in the showrooms of Elite Motors, dealers of Garratt Lane, Tooting, London, S.W.17 —but two years and 20,000 on the clock had done nothing to cool off what is still one of the hottest production motors.

Top speed was still a comfortably reached 100 mph, which compares with the 108–110 mph claimed for the Super Rocket when new. The 8·3:1 compression ratio motor revved without effort up to a maximum of over 6,000, and not the slightest edge appeared to have been knocked off the tune by previous owners.

Maximum speeds of 30, 52, and 85 were screwed out of the intermediate gears without any feeling of "thrashing" the big-hearted 650 motor, while the acceleration was completely breath-removing, especially lower down the rev range.

Vibration was present to a certain extent, but it was no more than one finds in nearly all parallel twins, and it could never be called unpleasant. The first-class dual seat and well-positioned footrests transmitted none of the tingle, and what little was felt came mainly through the tank and "cowhorn" handlebars which had been added by an earlier owner.

Ageing gearbox

In the transmission department, the A10 SR is one of the last of the BSA big twins with separate gearboxes; unit construction was introduced the following year.

It was in this unit, however, in which time was beginning to tell. The change itself was positive but inclined to be

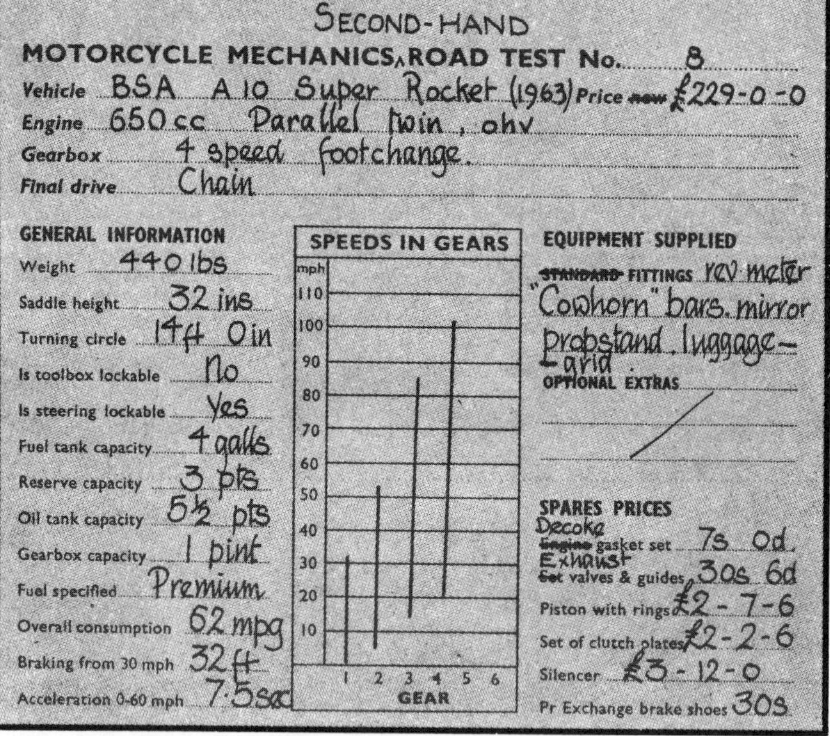

SECOND-HAND
MOTORCYCLE MECHANICS ROAD TEST No. 8
Vehicle BSA A10 Super Rocket (1963) Price ~~now~~ £229-0-0
Engine 650 cc Parallel twin, ohv
Gearbox 4 speed footchange.
Final drive Chain

GENERAL INFORMATION

Weight	440 lbs
Saddle height	32 ins
Turning circle	14ft 0in
Is toolbox lockable	No
Is steering lockable	Yes
Fuel tank capacity	4 galls
Reserve capacity	3 pts
Oil tank capacity	5½ pts
Gearbox capacity	1 pint
Fuel specified	Premium
Overall consumption	62 mpg
Braking from 30 mph	32 ft
Acceleration 0-60 mph	7·5 sec

SPEEDS IN GEARS

(bar chart, vertical axis mph 10–110, horizontal axis GEAR 1 2 3 4 5 6: gear 1 ≈ 32, gear 2 ≈ 52, gear 3 ≈ 85, gear 4 ≈ 100)

EQUIPMENT SUPPLIED

~~STANDARD~~ FITTINGS rev meter "Cowhorn" bars. mirror propstand. luggage-grid.

OPTIONAL EXTRAS

SPARES PRICES
Decoke
~~Engine~~ gasket set 7s 0d.
Exhaust
~~Set~~ valves & guides 30s 6d
Piston with rings £2-7-6
Set of clutch plates £2-2-6
Silencer £3-12-0
Pr Exchange brake shoes 30s

"clunky" with a rather harsh feel, while there was noticeable whine especially in third gear, indicating developing backlash on some of the teeth.

The clutch, however, gained top marks from all MM staffmen who rode the Rocket. Light and silky, it could be used all day without tiring the weakest wrist, or developing the slightest sign of slip—an all-too-common fault with many second-hand power mounts.

The rest of the transmission had stood up to the miles quite well, and the sprockets and chains were in very good order.

Biggest single criticism of the Rocket concerned the brakes. Any machine with as much "go" as this 650 needs plenty of "stop" if the performance is as difficult to resist as it was with the test mount. But both front and rear units were far from

satisfactory, with worn linings apparently the main cause.

The rear brake linkage follows a tortuous track from the nearside, through a transfer spindle and then out along the offside to the drum via a final cable, and this collection leads, in any case, to a nasty feeling of sponginess. Coupled with worn linings, it was at times a most frightening combination.

Biting brake

The front brake had its own peculiarities, and at first touch really bit, which gave rise to false confidence soon betrayed when pronounced fade set in almost immediately.

The test stopping figure of 32 ft. from 30 mph was obtained by leaping on everything; as speeds went up, braking effect

Handsome set of instruments include the optional extra rev-meter. Spring tongue locks the steering damper wheel to stop unscrewing. Steering lock shows on right

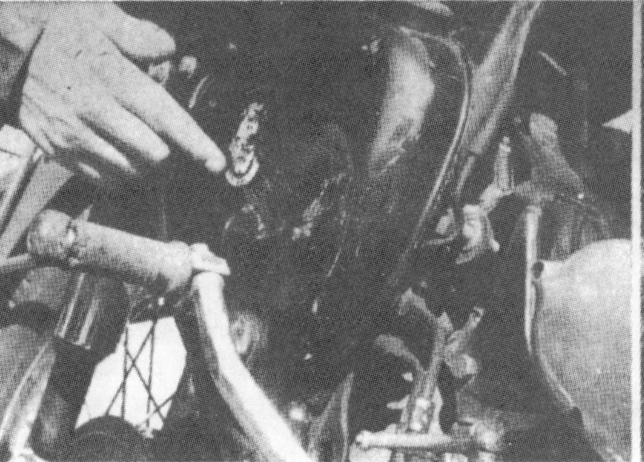

Dent in oil tank looked like result of a minor prang. The damage was a smooth push-in, and could probably be easily filled out with glass fibre material

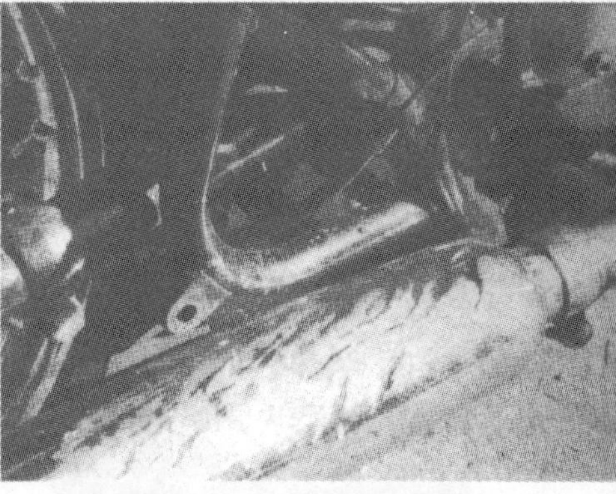

Chrome on silencer was damaged by acid from the battery which had run out from a cracked cell. Although only surface was affected the result was unsightly

ROAD-BURNING ROCKET

MM tests this secondhand hot-lot which hasn't cooled off in two years

dropped with alarming suddenness.

After some initial trouble with a dud battery, the electrical equipment worked without bother, although the horn seemed to be on its last legs. All the lights including the speedo pilot light and the rear stop lamp worked, and the dip, worked from a neat combined horn and "kill" button complex on the left bar was most effective.

Suspension was still of the well-known BSA comfort variety, although the front forks seemed more bouncy than usual. Roadholding was first rate.

Perhaps the nicest thing about the test bike was that it was perfectly oiltight and clean. Not a drop of oil was left wherever it was parked. Such cleanliness is a hall-mark of most Elite models—although their prices may be regarded by some as being slightly above average.

CONTROLLED POWER
B.S.A. SUPER ROCKET
£273.16.5
(including £46.16.5d. purchase tax)
and there's still more to BSA
To B.S.A. MOTOR CYCLES LTD.
465, ARMOURY ROAD · BIRMINGHAM 11
Please send me your latest catalogue
APRIL, 1960
NAME
ADDRESS
RAPID ACCELERATION
PERFECT BALANCE
EYE APPEAL
MORE M.P.G.
STOPPING POWER
EXTRA COMFORT
HAIRLINE STEERING

Everybody wants one!
BSA goes Everywhere
Send for YOUR copy of this NEW catalogue to:—
B S A MOTOR CYCLES LTD., 47 ARMOURY RD., BIRMINGHAM, 11.
Name
Address

rapid acceleration
BSA 650 O H V TWIN SUPER ROCKET
Price £273-16s-5d
(including £46-16s-5d purchase tax)
Emmwood
and there's still more to BSA
CONTROLLED POWER
STOPPING POWER
FLEXIBILITY
PERFECT BALANCE
HAIRLINE STEERING
EYE APPEAL
EXTRA COMFORT
ECONOMICAL RUNNING
To BSA MOTOR CYCLES LTD.
465, ARMOURY RD., BIRMINGHAM 11
Please send me your latest catalogue
NAME
ADDRESS
JUNE, 1960

ideal transport for the family
BSA
For reliable and economical travel the BSA 650 and
500 twins with sidecar make the ideal combination.
The lusty performance of these popular twins with any
sidecar is making them increasingly popular every day.
Remember you get the benefit of 50% insurance
reduction with a sidecar outfit.
650 TWIN GOLDEN FLASH
500 TWIN A7 or A7 SHOOTING STAR } with Sidecar
Please send colour catalogue.
B.S.A. Motor Cycles Ltd., 465 Armoury Road, Birmingham, 11.
NAME
ADDRESS

▶ *The pre-unit BSAs were among the most popular machines to come from Birmingham and although superseded by the unit-construction models, they still have a very large following.*

We went along to Stratford Motorcycles, of 38 Romford Road, London, E.15, where we watched BSA specialist Robert Flemwell strip an A10 engine.

The A10, Road Rocket, Super Rocket, etc, are all basically the same to work on, so the following article can be used on nearly all of the pre-unit Beeza big-twins.

BSAs have large spares stockists all over the country and prices compare favourably with other makes, but it is as well to check up on the availability of certain items, such as cam followers, if you think they might need renewing during the strip.

Apart from isolated items, however, BSA spares should present no problems.

ROBERT FLEMWELL DISMANTLES THE PRE-UNIT TWIN

BSA STRIP

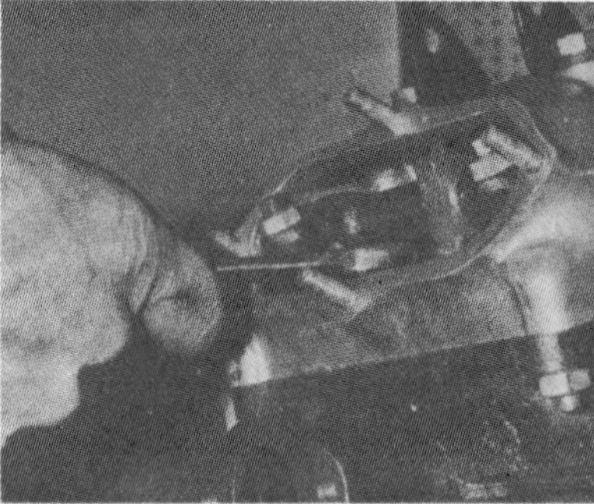

With engine on bench, remove the tappet covers and then rocker box which is held by four bolts on top and one more bolt inside

Lift off rocker box and take push-rods. A strong box span will be necessary to undo the head-holding bolts (all arrow

Remove dynamo complete with engine plate. On reassembly, renew the cork washer and push the dynamo hard against it

The best way to remove the d amo drive sprocket is to giv a tap with a soft-faced hamm to jar it from its taper s

Important: when rebuilding the engine, all oilways should be either blown clear with an air line, or with an oil gun as shown here

Lock the engine once again undo the mainshaft nut, which a left-hand thread. Use a g socket spanner to avoid dam

Lift off the timing-side case. The plain bearing is good for many thousands of miles. Heat is needed to remove and replace it

Lift the rest of the engine f its hole in the box to en the drive-side case to be tap from the mainshaft with a m

▶ **Start by removing the sump plate and draining off the oil. The sump plate has to be removed before the crankcases will part anyway.**

When the head is lifted off and the push-rods are taken out, you will see that the exhaust rods are longer than the inlets. The exhaust rods fit into the centre cam followers.

The only special tool you will require during the overhaul is an extractor with three sets of legs. This will extract both camshaft and mainshaft pinions and can be bought or hired from most large BSA agents.

OIL PUMP

The oil pump is in mesh with the worm drive and it is necessary to remove the pump first.

Unscrew the two bottom studs which hold the pump in place. By slipping a thin locknut over the existing nut, you'll find that the studs can be withdrawn easily. Swing the pump to one side. It can then be removed.

After undoing all the external crankcase nuts, don't forget the internal nut—many people do! The crankcase should part without trouble, but you may find it necessary to give them a tap with a hide or lead mallet. Don't hit thin parts of the case, like the magneto flange—it will surely break off.

Heat is needed to remove and replace main bearings. The plain bearing on the timing side does not require reaming, but camshaft bushes must be line-reamed—a job for the dealer.

The flywheel, provided it is not damaged at the ends, or in some other way which will render it unserviceable, can be exchanged over the counter for about £8 10s. Never face the big-end caps to take up play.

REASSEMBLY

Absolute cleanliness of parts is essential when rebuilding the motor. Clean off all parts in petrol and liberally oil bearings before replacing shaft, cams, etc.

By getting exchange con-rods at the same time as the shaft, you will not have the chore of small-end fitting. The big-end bolts are torqued to 28 lb. ft. and that is pretty tight. You will need a slim socket spanner for this but, of course, if you get exchange rods this will already be done for you.

Use new gaskets when assembling. It is particularly important to fit a new cork washer under the timed engine breather. This gets squashed flat in use and causes severe oil loss through the breather.

The other point to watch is where the dynamo joins the engine. Push the dynamo up hard against the cork washer before tightening clamp.

...light tap with a soft mallet ...ll release cylinder head. Undo ...the cylinder base nuts and ...efully lift barrels from case

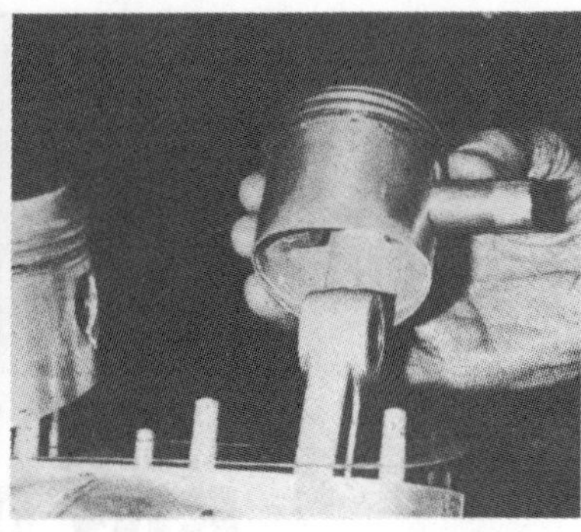

Prise out the gudgeon pin circlips with a screwdriver, warm pistons with a hot, wet cloth. The gudgeon pins should then push out

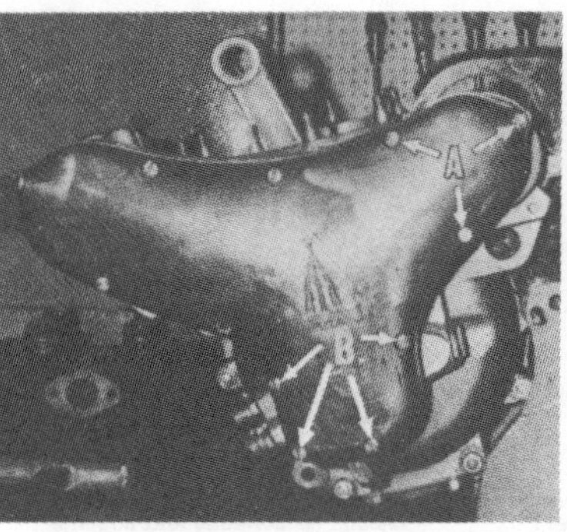

The timing cover screws are of differing lengths. Note where they come from. Those at A are short, B are long, the rest are medium

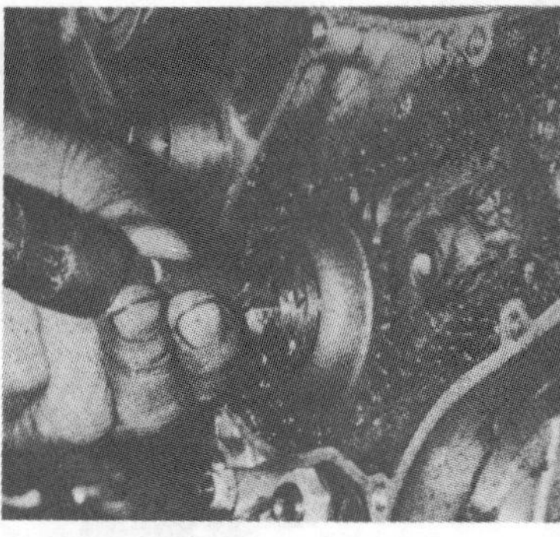

Knock back the tab washer on the dynamo drive sprocket. Lock the engine with a rod through small-end eye then undo nut

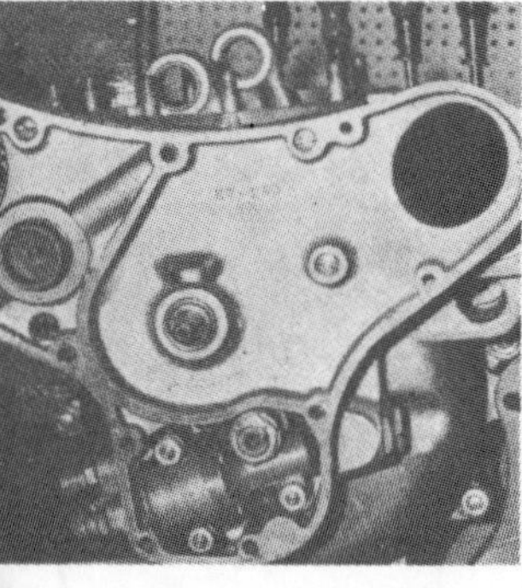

...ur recessed screws are used to ...d the inner timing cover. Take ...se out, tap cover and pull it ...to reveal timing pinions

Pull off the timed engine breather. Behind it you will see a large cork washer. This washer must be renewed at every overhaul

To remove the automatic advance and retard unit the engine must be locked. The nut will then extract timing pinion from taper

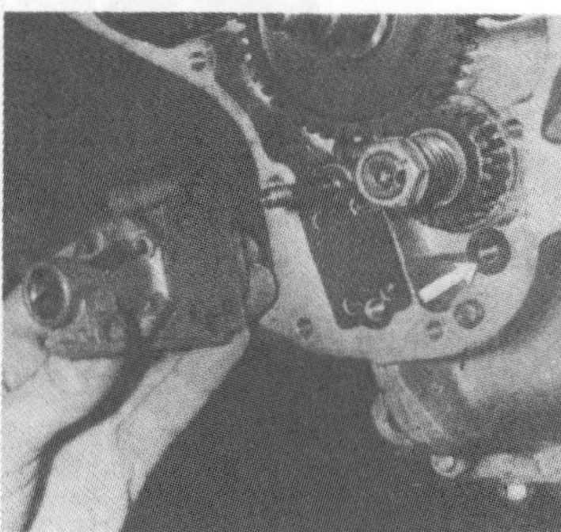

Remove the top nut and two studs to withdraw the oil pump. Renew all washers. Note the fibre compensating washer

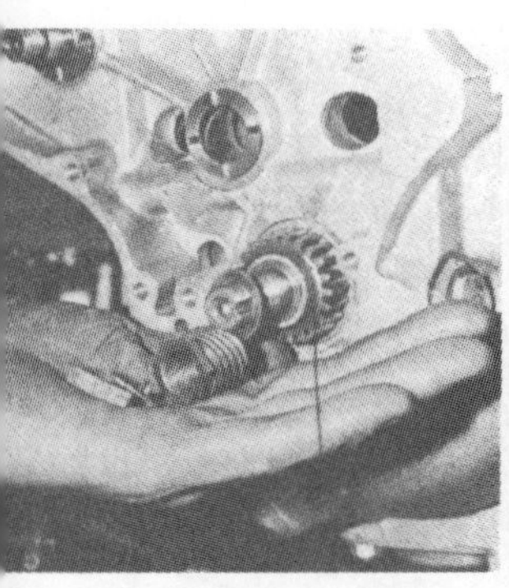

...pump drive assembly comes next. Note the sequence for ...uilding—steel washer, worm, ...washer and finally lock nut

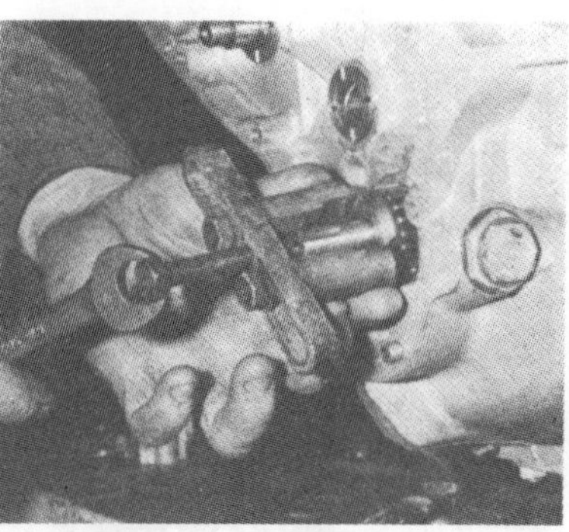

A special extractor is needed to withdraw the mainshaft pinion. It can be hired from a BSA dealer. No need to disturb Woodruff key

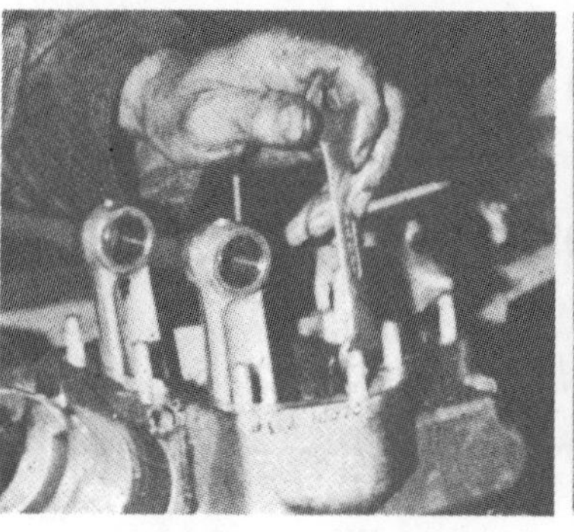

Remove all the external crank-case bolts, but do not forget the internal bolt shown. Don't forget to take the sump plate off

To part cases, place them on a box with a hole in it to take driveside mainshaft. Tap timing case side with a mallet

...w you remove the roller main ...ring is up to you. A pair of ...ewdrivers is as good as any. ...e note of shims behind bearing

You'll need a slim, tough socket spanner to undo the big-end nuts to take the con-rods off. Inspect shells and shaft for ovality

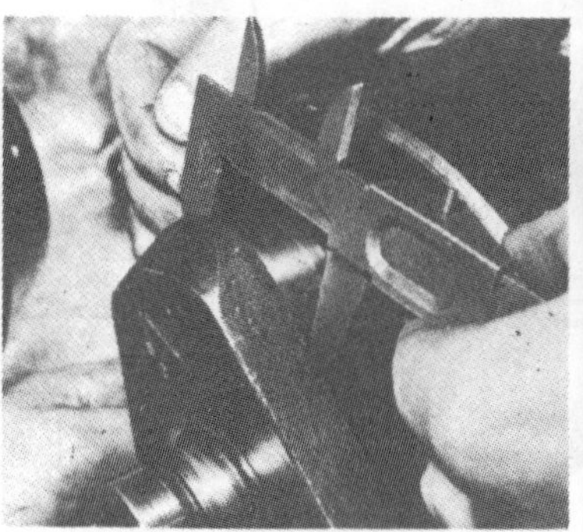

Maximum permitted ovality on the shaft is 2 thou. Get it checked by an engineer with a Vernier if you don't possess one yourself

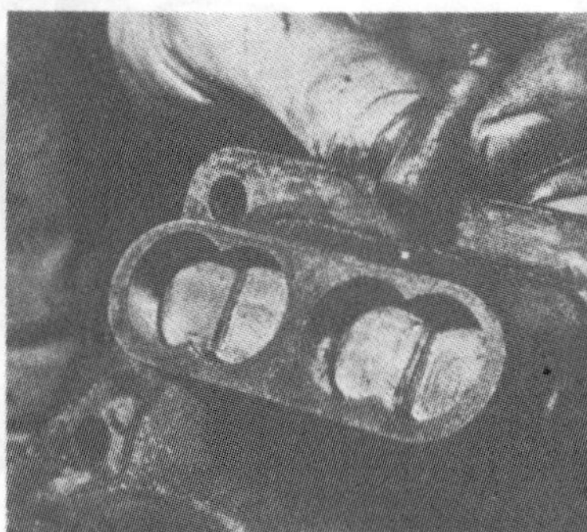

Don't forget the cam followers. These ones have really had it. Lesser wear can sometimes be remedied with a grindstone

MCM shows how to assemble a BSA pre-unit twin . . .

■ Outdated, old-fashioned, underpowered? Maybe it is all of these but the BSA pre-unit twin still soldiers on providing dependable transport for many motorcyclists. Development in motorcycle design may have outdated the old, twin-cylinder design, but for sheer guts and pulling power, especially with a sidecar attached, few modern multis get anywhere near them. We have taken a trip back in time to show you how to work on one these famous A7 or A10 engines.

REBUILD A FLASH

● *Basically, the BSA 500 and 650 twins are the same design with only a few differences between the two engines. It is essential to have a workshop manual at hand when working on one of these engines so that settings and clearances are correct.*

The pre-unit twin is noted for having a weak bottom-end and leaking oil at every joint, but neither of these two troubles are a design problem.

The oil leaks are due to lack of care during assembly. Mating surfaces on the twin are narrow by modern standards, and if these mating surfaces are not perfectly clean then oil will leak. A good jointing compound to use would be Locktite Plastic Gasket. Take care when bolting components up not to over-strain any of the bolts. The alloy cylinder head used on some of the models can be distorted especially if the bolts are not tightened in the correct sequence and at the right torque. All seals must be in perfect condition, especially the cork washer that seals the dynamo to the crankcases.

Bottom end

Troubles with the bottom end of the pre-unit engine are usually due to the way the engine has been treated. The BSA engine is noted more for torque than revs and if the engine is over-revved, main bearing and big-end failure comes very quickly.

Failure to change the engine oil at regular intervals will also lead to premature bottom-end failure. The BSA filter system is very wide mesh and small lumps of grit can soon get into the oil. For this reason the oil must be changed at the correct intervals or if the engine is used for short trips even sooner.

The only essential special tool is a push rod comb. This flat shaped piece of tin holds the push rods in the correct position while the rocker box is lowered into place.

Spares for the twins are becoming scarce but some of the leading dealers are still able to supply off the shelf.

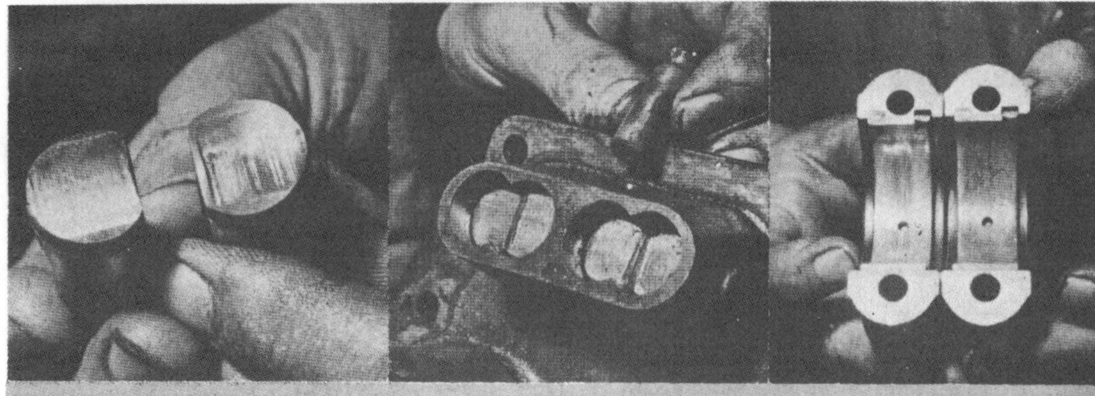

Excess wear causes excess noise. Items like worn cam followers must be replaced or reground flat again

Followers are held in place with this peg. After building make sure they are well-lubricated with engine oil

Don't take chances, alway fit new big-end shells. Us Loctite to secure the con rod cap bolts in plac

If the main bearings have to come off the shaft, gently lever away with a wedge as shown in the picture here

Cases are gently worked into place over the crank using a copper/hide mallet. Do not use too much force or . . .

. . . the cases will leak Don't overtighten the crankcase bolts as thi can also cause oil leak.

. . . it is fitted into the crankcases. Make sure the pump securing bolts are fully tightened up after

Cam timing is arranged as shown in the pic. Make sure the timing wheels are oiled to prevent wear on start-up

Crankcase breathing is fixe by this bush. Make sure th cork washer behind bush is i good condition when fittin

Timing cover securing screws are different lengths. Make sure you put them back in the same place they came . . .

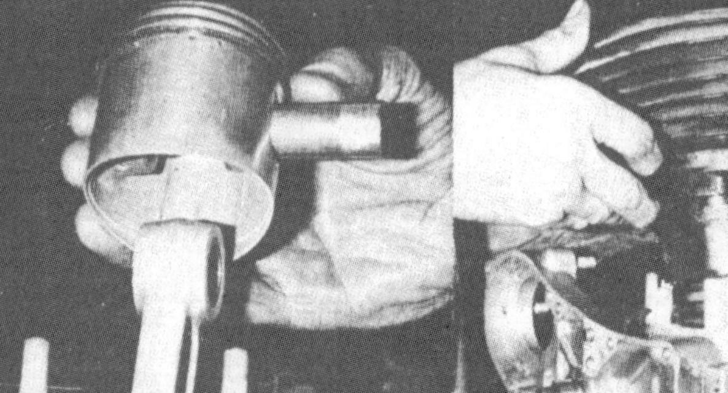

. . . out from. Pistons must be fitted the right way round. Oil the small-end bearings during assembly

Use piston ring compressor when fitting the barre Take care not to break th piston rings when fittin

Make sure shells are well-
oiled during assembly. A
mixture of Wynns and engine
oil helps with the assembly

New cams are expensive, but
a new cam will put new life
into the oldest engine. If
in doubt, fit a new camshaft

Whether fitting or removing
the engine crankcases don't
use too much force. Gently
tapping with a hide mallet ...

... is enough. Make sure
the oil return pipe inside
the case is clear before
starting to rebuild engine

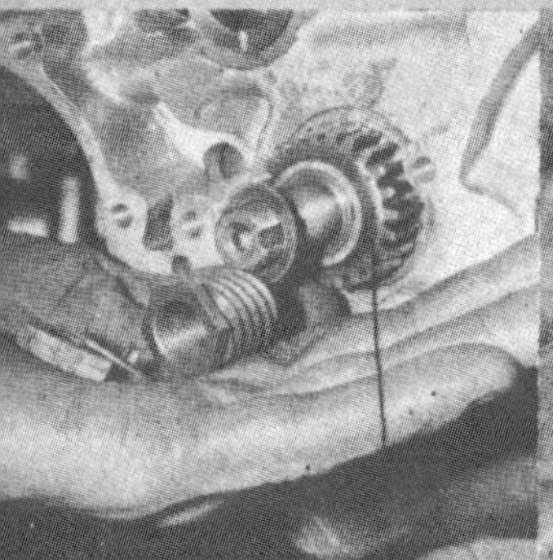

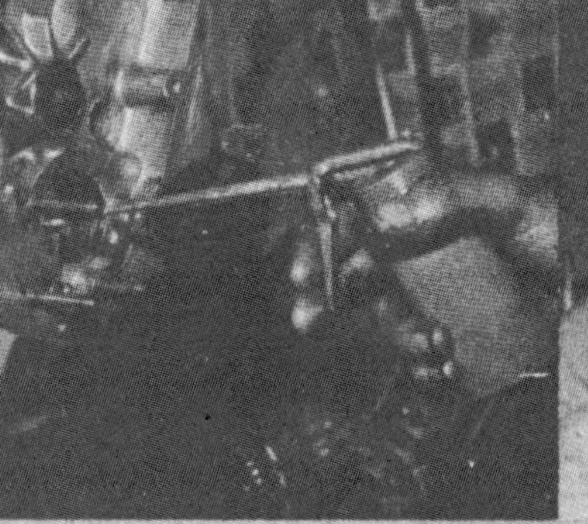

Oil pump drive is assembled
as shown in pic. Don't miss
out the washer behind drive
lock washer over the nut

Make sure the lock washer is
fully closed up or the pump
drive will fail. Loctite will
help hold pinion in place

During every stage of build
make sure that every moving
part is well soaked in oil.
Most wear occurs in the ...

... first seconds of a new
engine's life. Oil pump must
be cleaned out and fitted
with a new gasket before ...

Dyno drive cog can be tight
to fit or remove, but a light
tap with a hammer will make
the pinion fit every time

Dynamo to crankcase seal is
via this cork washer. Make
sure washer is fully home
before fitting the dynamo

Most mags are auto-advance,
but some models use a fixed
pinion with a hand advance
lever fitted to handlebars

Make sure the dyno pinion
is securely locked to the
shaft. If it comes undone
it will wreck the engine

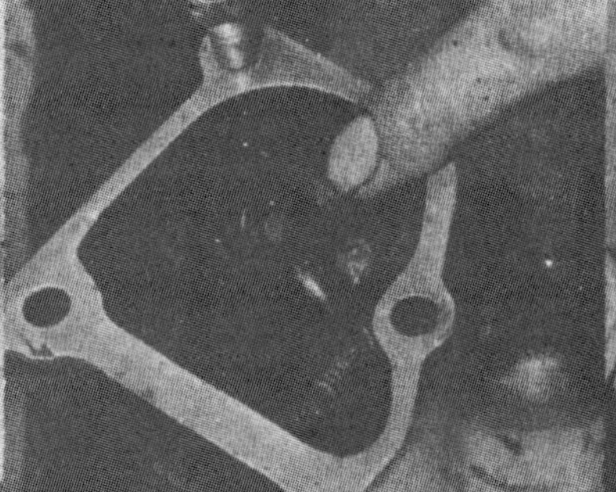

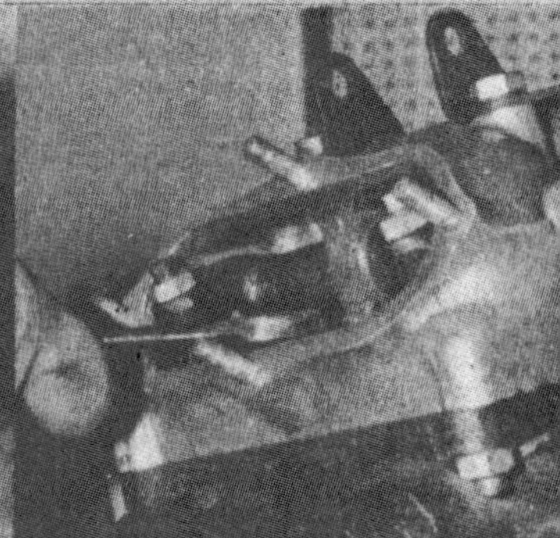

Copper/asbestos head gasket
must be renewed every time
cylinder head is removed
from the engine. Gasket ...

... can fail if the head is
not tightened up in the
right sequence. Don't forget
those hidden head bolts

Worn valve gear causes
noise and low performance
so replace if in doubt.
Make sure the rocker ...

... box is fully tightened
and check the tappets after
five hundred miles have
been travelled with the motor

Right: The handling on this example was peculiar, but the bike could still be flung round bends.

Above: Distinctive drive side cover conceals a beautiful clutch. 'Box is sweet too.

The golden mean

A factory shot of a slightly earlier model than that tested.

BERT Hopwood's inestimable contribution to the British motorcycle industry is documented elsewhere in this issue, but one of the most enduring of his designs must be the BSA A10 650cc powerplant. Started within four weeks of his joining the Armoury Road factory, the plans for the engine were completed by the end of June 1949. Announced in October 1950, the A10 was first produced in 1951 and given a name now redolent of an era — Golden Flash.

In the days when motorcycles were, for the most part, any colour you liked as long as it was black, the golden beige of the new BSA really shone out. In standard trim, the bike had a plunger frame, with a large capacity petrol tank. A home market version in black, with a rigid frame and smaller tank was available until 1951, when all twins were given the sprung frame.

The new model became a favourite with the road testers of the day, *Motor Cycling* achieving 104mph in top gear (with 89 in third and 66 in second), and a 15 second standing start quarter mile. The brakes were singled out for praise, being capable of stopping the bike in 25.5 feet from 30mph. This is a good figure even now, but from 30mph brake fade from heat build-up is not an important factor, and the BSA's brakes are not as good as that result implies.

The engine was a workman-like job, initially having an iron head and barrel, which was held onto the crankcase with nine studs. The inlet manifold was cast into the head, and permitted only a single carburettor — none of the A10 variants had twin carbs. Silicon alloy pistons were carried on alloy conrods, with split big-ends bearing on a forged crankshaft. A flywheel was bolted to the centre web of the crank, which ran in a roller bearing on the drive side, and a plain bush, through which oil was delivered to the big-ends, on the timing side. With hindsight, this arrangement could have been a lot better, as the bush is the weakest point of the bottom end, and when it wears, oil-flow is impeded. However, Hopwood and his team chose to follow the basic pattern laid down by the first BSA twin, a design widely attributed to Val Page.

As designed, the engine pushed out 35bhp at 5,500rpm, with 39ft/lb of torque at 3,900rpm. The figures really say it all — this was a touring motor, and in that guise the bottom end was perfectly satisfactory. As long as the oil was changed regularly a long and reliable life could be expected of it. When tuning pushed up the output, durability began to suffer, though the Achilles heel was not truly

revealed until the engine had been converted to unit construction, as the A65, but that does not concern us here.

The first major development of the popular bike came in 1953, when the Super Flash was developed for export to the USA. With high compression pistons, a special camshaft and an Amal TT carburettor, the motor pushed out 42bhp, giving the bike a top speed of 110mph. In turn, this extra performance highlighted the shortcomings of the plunger frame, and a swinging arm, duplex cradle frame was produced. At first this was available only on export machines, but in 1955 it was adopted on all the twins, and became well known for its good handling.

The new frame allowed BSA to alter the gearbox. Previously this had been in semi-unit with the engine, but on the new frame the heavyweight 'box (as used on the singles) was adopted, with its normal clutch. This had the drawback of making primary chain adjustment a matter of tensioning a drawbolt that pivoted the gearbox casing, but did allow a wide choice of ratios.

The America-only Super Flash was metamorphosed into the home market Road Rocket in 1954, and it was given an alloy cylinder head. The brakes were also uprated, but the following season all models got the benefit of a full width, seven inch front stopper, with the rear following suit in 1956.

In 1958 the Road Rocket became the Super Rocket, and the compression ratio on both this sports model and the touring Gold Flash was increased. The crankshaft was stiffened, the brakes were given another inch in diameter, and new silencers and a redesigned headlamp cowling changed both the noise and the appearance of the bike.

The basic machine continued virtually unchanged until it was replaced by the A65 in the summer of 1962. The sports version, however, had something of an Indian summer, with the Super Rocket surviving until mid-'63, and being joined by what to many is the apogee of A10 engineering, the Rocket Gold Star. Essentially this was a highly tuned motor in a Gold Star style frame, with suitably racey looking ancillary parts. It was an impressive way to bow out.

The model that forms the subject of this test, however, is the humble cooking version, the Gold Flash. Well regarded as both a solo and sidecar machine, the Flash had a quiet sort of life, was exported in great numbers and was sorely missed when it ceased production.

The test bike is owned by Maurice Belcher, who admits to being something of an A10 aficionado (he has two Rockets to prove it), and was one of the last to leave Small Heath, being produced in March 1962. Maurice bought it in 1979, more or less original and complete, and spent over two years bringing it back to peak condition. Starting with the frame, he rubbed it down by hand and sprayed it with black cellulose. He describes it as a cheap job, but it looks good to me. The golden beige paintwork was applied by his partner in a car-repair business, Ian Buckle, who just happens to have an A10 himself. The paint came from Bri-Tie Motorcycles, 1 Armstrong St., Swindon (31518), who can supply almost any BSA colour.

The front wheel was rebuilt with a new rim by E. Booth, rear of 3 Copperfield Rd, Coventry; while the rear came from an autojumble, complete and in pristine condition. Maurice has a lot of BSA stock in his garage, and many of the parts he needed were available off his own shelves. However, he did have to have the cylinders rebored and the crank ground, so this work was entrusted to F J Payne, Osney Mill, Oxford, who also supplied pistons and shells. New cam followers, timing side-bush, main roller bearing and fork seals and holders came from C and D Autos, 1193 Warwick Rd, Acocks Green, Birmingham.

The gearbox was dismantled, but showed no signs of wear, and the clutch plates were all serviceable. With new chains and cables that more or less completed the overhaul, except for the seat. This was retrimmed, in the correct colour material by Spencer Brownhill, a friend of Maurice's, and a professional upholsterer.

'The handling's a bit funny', I had been warned before starting off on the test, and yes, it was very funny. For a bike that was supposed to handle well, this A10 certainly showed little sign of it. The main problem was 'falling into' corners. Maurice has not experienced this on his other A10s, neither have other owners I've spoken to, and the early A65, which had very similar running gear did not display this trait. Talking it over with Maurice afterwards, we decided that this bike could have been fitted with the sidecar fork yokes BSA offered as an option. These rake out the stanchions slightly more than standard to increase the trail, making the steering geometry better suited to the strange demands an extra wheel makes. It is believed a chair was attached at some point in the bike's history, so the theory is quite plausible.

I am prepared to accept on trust the A10's handling capabilities, but the suspension is awful. Harsh and ungiving, it had me jumping around on even mildly bumpy roads, and conspired with the arms-akimbo riding position to give me a peculiar ache across the ribs. If this example is representative, and I think it is, the Gold Flash is one bike I would not like to ride on a long tour, without substantial

Above and right: The Flash retained iron barrel and head throughout its life — alloy versions being restricted to the sporting models. Primary chain is adjusted by gearbox drawbolt.

tailoring of the handlebars, footrests and suspension.

The engine, too, takes a little getting used to. Royce Creasey once attributed a quality of tenseness to parallel twins, and the A10 unit is a good example of what he means. At first, it feels unwilling to rev out, and would seem to be happiest cruising at around 50mph in top gear. Then, when boredom or increasing familiarity encourages further experimentation, the engine comes out of that period and into a more exciting one. It can be driven hard, but all the time feels as though it really would prefer not to. It is not, for example, as willing as the Triumph unit, though it would be most interesting to try one of the more highly tuned versions to get a more rounded view.

Below the initial tense period, the engine feels very sweet, and smooth (though it shakes vigorously at high revs). Easy to start with a serious lunge on the kickstart lever, it picks up quickly and pulls off from standstill in a most civilised manner. In 1949, Bert Hopwood designed an excellent unit, but events largely overtook it — improved roads, higher cruising speeds and the other demands made by modern traffic soon dated the basic motor. I cannot help but feel that

when BSA dropped the pre-unit 650 in 1962, they should have replaced it with something a little more adventurous than more of the same in a new shape — the expertise was there.

Be that as it may, parts of the A10 are very good indeed. A lighter clutch I have yet to find, with a nice spread of engagement to prevent kangaroo starts. The gearbox too is good, though it cannot be hurried, especially when changing down. With the choice of gear sets offered, the rider would have been able to cope with anything from mudplugging trials to high speed racing, and this inevitably imparted a flexibility to the bike that encouraged competition riders to use it, as well as the road rider.

Anyone using the bike for high speed work would, however, have had to do something about the brakes. The front brake is yet another of those units which feels as though it is going to be superb on first pressure, but rapidly fades away, increasing pressure at the lever merely

Maurice Belcher with one of his Rockets.

Standard rear suspension could use a little customising for comfort; rear brake is spongey and not very powerful.

Above and top: Handlebars are quite wide, tiring for long distance trips. Yoke cover and nacelle are totally styleless.

restoring the initial braking effort. The rear is, in a way, better in that it offers no pretence of being powerful. When he rebuilt the machine, Maurice was able to lock the rear wheel, but with use the effectiveness has dropped off. Some of the blame he puts on the cable operation, which must soak up a fair bit of effort. The stoppers on this bike were hardly up to the job of halting a Gold Flash in its mild trim, so how Rocket riders fared, I would be interested to learn. Photographer John Sandall remembered his A10 to be similar in this respect, so it can't be an isolated example.

Overall, the A10 is a handsome bike, but whoever thought-up that dreadful headlamp cowling-cum-top yoke cover deserves to be locked in a room full of biscuit tins. Not even lozenge-shaped chrome flashes, save it — and they prob-

ably shine brighter than the headlamp. 'It's bloody useless', said Maurice, 'How we ever did it years ago I don't know.' In its day it would have been standard issue lighting kit, but that standard has, thank goodness, improved immeasurably, and in my opinion restorer/riders who keep Lucas six volt lights for the sake of originality, when unobtrusive twelve volt conversions or vastly improved six volt lamps are available, are wearing smoked, rather than rose-tinted, glasses.

Despite the criticisms made in the last few paragraphs, I greatly enjoyed riding the Gold Flash, and came away feeling that it possessed a great charm. I can readily understand why it became a standard, large capacity workhorse, and it must have been ideally suited to the needs of developing countries, where poor roads would have limited speeds to the bike's best range, and ease of maintenance would have been a big bonus. BSA proudly boasted that they made the most popular motorcycles in the world, but I don't think — in this case at least — that it was the popularity engendered by charisma. The Gold Flash is essentially a pre-war machine, and it sums up the supposed virtues of pre-war English folk: understatement, kindliness and a willingness to play the game without an overwhelming desire to win. Like them, it was doomed to extinction in the modern world.

Specification

ENGINE

Type	ohv parallel twin
Bore x stroke	70 x 84mm
Capacity	646cc
Compression ratio	7.25:1
Carburation	1⅛in Amal
BHP @ rpm	34 @ 5750
Electrical	6v 60w dynamo, magneto

TRANSMISSION

Primary drive	duplex chain
Clutch	multiplate, wet
Gearbox	4 speed

CYCLE PARTS

Frame	duplex tubular
Suspension (front)	telescopic
(rear)	swinging arm, Girling units
Wheels (front)	3.25 x 19in
(rear)	3.50 x 19in
Brakes (front)	8in sls
(rear)	7in sls
Wheelbase	56in
Seat height	30in
Ground clearance	6in
Dry weight	430lb
Fuel capacity	4gal

PERFORMANCE

Top speed	104mph (see text)
0-60mph	10secs
Fuel consumption	60mpg
OWNER	Maurice Belcher, Oxford

Swinging on a Star

'YES', I thought, 'yes, how terribly, terribly English.' Above me the sun broke out from behind a bank of clouds which, only seconds before, had been probing my Aviakit waxed cotton with lances of cold rain, while from a wood somewhere to my right a cuckoo hiccupped its repetitive song. All around, the verdant Cambridgeshire countryside seemed to sigh with bucolic contentment and on the roadside a BSA A7 pinged and clicked as it cooled down. 'The sweetest twin ever made' is how someone — probably Bruce Main-Smith — described it, and I had to admit he was not far wrong.

The original A7 was produced under Bert Hopwood's aegis, although the basic layout of the engine unit has been attributed to Val Page, and Edward Turner is known to have done some work on it during his wartime stint with BSA. When hostilities ceased, Herbert Perkins and David Munro completed the concept for Hopwood, and the bike was launched in September 1946.

It was not the first parallel twin the factory had designed, for before the war there had been prototypes of a sporty overhead-cam 500, and a more workaday, but very tidy, 350. The A7 provided something of a compromise between these two, and the basic layout endured until the A50/A65 unit construction engines were launched (and even then they were very similar under the skin).

The initial version of the A7 lasted until 1950, when the basic motor was revamped, enlarged and launched as the 650cc A10. Shortly after, the bore and stroke of this mark two engine were reduced to slightly squarer proportions than the first 500, and a new A7 emerged. This is probably the secret of the model's sweetness, for it is normal practice to enlarge an existing unit rather than scale down a new (or newish) one. By strengthening the twin for greater capacity, then putting less strain on it the engine was given a great margin of safety. Only a few mechanical parts were interchangeable with the earlier twin, though the cycle parts were the same.

The machine continued in its basic form until 1950, when the swinging-arm frame was made standard on all models. An Amal Monobloc replaced the old Type 6 carburettor, and a sports model was launched. Dubbed the Shooting Star, it featured an alloy cylinder head in place of the iron one, and a 7.25:1 compression ratio. A road test of the new model recorded a top speed of 93mph, with peak power of 32bhp being delivered at 6,250rpm. This apparently remained the same for the rest of the bike's model life, although the compression ratio was upped again in 1958, to 8:1. The A7 was dropped in 1962, replaced by the A50.

The machine tested here is, I admit immediately, a hybrid. Neville Cross, its owner and builder, acquired a '59 A7 in boxes, paying £50 for the privilege of taking it out of someone's garage. When he found the camshaft was useless, and that a new one would cost £16 (quite a sum in 1977, especially for an obsolete heap) he almost sold the lot again. However, a couple of months later he found a 1960 Shooting Star for £45 and between the two he has built up a very nice Shooting Star specification A7.

This was the first twin he had ever owned, being more of an AMC singles man (his BSA shares the garage with a 1966 G80 short-stroke Matchless and a 1960 AJS 16MS first registered in the name of 'The Chief Constable, Cambridgeshire Constabulary') and he is still not entirely sure of it. He likes it, right enough, but somehow the unhurried thump of a heavyweight single gets into the blood.

Despite the rain, an easy prod on the kickstart brought the motor to life and after a few seconds idling it was ready to ride away. The first thing to impress me — once again — was the immensely wide handlebar which BSA fitted to the A-range. Not only do these inevitably lead to the rider billowing in the wind at speed, they also — in my case — caused a sharp pain in the ribs every time the bike hit a pothole.

And hit is the right word. Neville has swapped the rear damper units for some he believes are off a B44, and they are very, very hard. Likewise, the front forks seem greatly oversprung, though they are in standard trim. Combined with the thinly padded, narrow seat this makes a bike which is not very comfortable to ride over bad roads.

Lovers of the marque or model should not throw down the magazine at this point and claim gross bias, total ineptitude and lack of intestinal fortitude in the rider, for that is — with one further exception — the limit of my criticism. And fair enough, the rear units *are* non-standard.

To compensate for the harsh ride, there is very little vibration from the engine, which provides a level of performance good enough to keep the rider interested, without being exactly spine-snapping. The BSA gearbox is well-known for its smooth action, and this one was no exception. With plenty of low power available from the long-stroke twin, acceleration in the first two gears was brisk, while third should be — according to road tests published in the fifties — good for 84mph. Top gear felt rather low on this example, but this appears to be common with standard BSA boxes — Neville's is stamped STD,

Right: Surely one of the best-known outlines in motorcycling, BSA's parallel twin sits pretty in a sturdy duplex frame. The gearbox is one of the best.

Above: A slight weep from the chaincase inspection cover was all that marred this unit. Single carb was the only option.

and as far as he is aware it contains the correct ratios. The performance in the first three speeds is consistent with a correctly cogged 'box, and the lowness of top merely emphasises — once the rider is accustomed to it — the good top-end characteristics of the engine.

Not a unit that needs to be thrashed to its 6,250rpm peak power output, the A7 nevertheless delivers the goods through its usable rev range, cleanly and crisply. Naturally some of this is down to Neville Cross's ability to tune the motor, which, although he says he is no engineer, places him towards the top end of the competence scale. Having only one carburettor to set — there never was a twin-carb option — undoubtedly helps smooth running.

Something else which compensates for the level of suspension comfort is the handling, which is superb. A previous encounter with a machine fitted with BSA's A-range frame left me less than convinced of its merits as a bend swinger, but, as Neville said to me while we were chatting about the bike, 'It's almost as though it wants to go round for you.' Despite his love for AMC singles, and their reputation for fine handling, he is prepared to rate the BSA a notch above his AJS and Matchless in the roadholding department.

The steering is precise and stable at all speeds, and there is no trace of wallow or pitch (the stiff suspension must make some difference here). Compared with a Triumph of the same vintage, the BSA offered a much more reassuring ride, and my experience with this one explains just why the TriBsa was second only to the Triton in specials builders' pop charts.

It is always difficult to know how far to judge a whole production run from one example. If the bike is in fairly standard condition, then basics such as engine performance and handling may be fairly assessed, assuming the owner has maintained and tuned all the relevant parts. One of the most difficult areas is braking. The trouble is that a rider soon gets used to the deficiencies of a bike's brakes, and makes allowances for them on the road. Unless something terrible happens, this state of affairs is likely to continue until the linings reach the end of their life, or the cable snaps, or whatever. Rarely does an owner voluntarily dismantle and try to improve something which works to his or her satisfaction.

I know from my own experience just how much difference a new set of linings, or even a new cable can make to a brake's efficiency, so I now hesitate to condemn the A7's front brake wholesale. I was warned about it before starting off, the owner admits to not having looked at it, and I cannot believe that any factory would issue a bike with such a puny device as standard. The rear brake, by contrast, worked extremely well, and as it

is only seven inches in diameter, as opposed to the front's eight, there was undoubtedly something wrong with this example. Not even the dreaded cable operation impeded the back stopper's performance, though it did lack something in feel, leading to a slight skid on some loose gravel as I attempted to come to a graceful halt.

In his column this month Peter Watson offers some thoughts on the value of originality. As he says, people have been modifying bikes in the interests of better running ever since the first motorised bicycle rolled out of the first workshop. The clutch of this A7 is a perfect example of the unseen modification, because it is actually a Triumph component, adopted to facilitate easier adjustment. Light and progressive in action, it complements the gearbox perfectly, to make one of the best drive trains I have ever used.

Looking at the bike as the cuckoo sang from that wood, it seemed very low and small. The seat height is a reasonable 30in, and the Shooting Star weighs in at 416lb dry, 9lb lighter than the standard model. Neville has finished the tinware in the attractive polychromatic green BSA

used for the sporting 500 twin from 1955 onwards, using a Carplan aerosol, available from most car accessory shops, and a reasonable match for the original shade.

The paintwork is actually one area he would treat differently if asked to do the job all over again. Scraping off the original, so diligently applied by Armoury Road, was a long and tedious task, using up gallons of paintstripper and sheets of abrasive paper of all types and grades. Wiring proved a little easier, as he adapted a loom stripped out of an old Ford. The colour coding is all wrong, of course, but it is consistent. Not having examined the system closely all I can say is that it works perfectly, and looks the part, having that slightly ropey appearance which so suits British bikes.

After riding the A7 through some of the weather which made this April the wettest since meteorological records began — and the sunny intervals — I have no hesitation in endorsing that 'sweetest twin' tag. With more forgiving suspension, narrower bars and — in this instance — a better front brake, the A7 could be a bike for all seasons. Especially the English spring.

Above: The details may not be accurate, but those bars are achingly wide.

Right: The Shooting Star can be swung through bends with great confidence thanks to a stiff frame and good steering geometry.

Above left: Front brake on this example was hopeless. The forks were harsh, and tended to top out.

Above centre: Rear brake worked well, though cable operation reduced the feel.

Above: Low and compact, BSA's A7 gained a well-earned reputation as the company's nicest twin.

Specification

ENGINE
Type ....ohv parallel twin
Bore x stroke ....66 x 72.6mm
Capacity..497cc
Compression ratio 7.25:1
Carburation ....1in Amal Monobloc
Bhp @ rpm ....32 @ 6,250
Electrical ....Lucas magneto, 6v dynamo
TRANSMISSION
Primary drive ....single-row chain
Clutch................................wet, multiplate
Gearbox ....4 speed
CYCLE PARTS
Frame ....duplex cradle
Suspension (front) ....telescopic fork
     (rear) ....swinging-arm
Wheels (front)................................3.25 x 19in
     (rear)..............................3.50 x 19in
Brakes (front)..............................8in sls drum
     (rear)..............................7in sls drum
Wheelbase 56in
Seat height..............................30in
Ground clearance 6in
Dry weight................................416lb
Fuel capacity 4gal
PERFORMANCE
Top speed..............................93mph
0-60mph 7.5sec
Fuel consumption 64mpg
OWNER ....Neville Cross, Histon, Cambs.

THE STAR TWIN THAT DIDN'T WIN THE MAUDE'S!

THERE is nothing very special about Ray Meggett's BSA Star Twin, as he readily admits, but that's what makes it interesting. Does that sound confused? Very well then, it is confused, but by casting back to 1952 we can find a reasonable explanation. In that year, or probably a bit before, BSA decided that the Maudes Trophy, the award given for the best test of reliability organised by a factory, should be reclaimed from Meriden. The idea was quite simple—to run three Star Twins, taken from a normal production batch, for 5,000 miles around Europe, and include in that mileage the International Six Days Trial.

The riders chosen obviously had to be capable of holding their own in international competition, and to make sure that BSA's name was not besmirched Fred Rist (who came out of competition retirement), Brian Martin and Norman Vanhouse were put up to the job. The ACU was the observing body, and on its behalf the late John McNulty selected the three stock machines from Small Heath, and accompanied the riders to ensure fair play all the way.

Suffice it to say that the bikes and their riders took all the punishment offered by such a rigorious test and covered the 4,958 miles with need of no more than a few replacement bulbs and a couple of welds on the petrol tanks. BSA was duly awarded the Maudes Trophy and the three Star Twins passed into obscurity until Norman Vanhouse's was discovered and restored from its 'chopperised' state.

This is what makes Ray's bike special. Still no clearer? Well, his *could* have been one of the three selected, for it was made in the same production year as the Maudes machines, and it is therefore of exactly the same stock (as they would say of

a thoroughbred horse) as them.

DEE 392 was rescued from a small holding (Ray seems to have a penchant for rustic locations—he also has a BSA Gold Star found in a garden shed), and bought for the princely sum of £17.50 from an owner who had no idea what it was or what was wrong with it. The engine appeared to be seized solid, the wheels, exhaust pipes and silencer were too far gone to be salvageable, and the rest of the machine was in a generally delapidated condition, as you would expect.

However, on getting it home, Ray discovered that the engine would not turn over simply because the kickstart ratchet was jammed. The rest of the engine was perfect, with standard size bores and crankshaft. As he says, "I wasted my time stripping the engine, but I had to do it as I didn't know what state it was in." All the oil had drained from the tank into the crankcase, which must have helped preserve

LEFT: THE lining on the tank is not quite right, but the owner did it himself before discovering the correct proportions. The engine was in perfect condition.

A handsome beast from either side, Ray Meggett's Star Twin is a good example of what the budget restorer can achieve. A sound basis helps, of course.

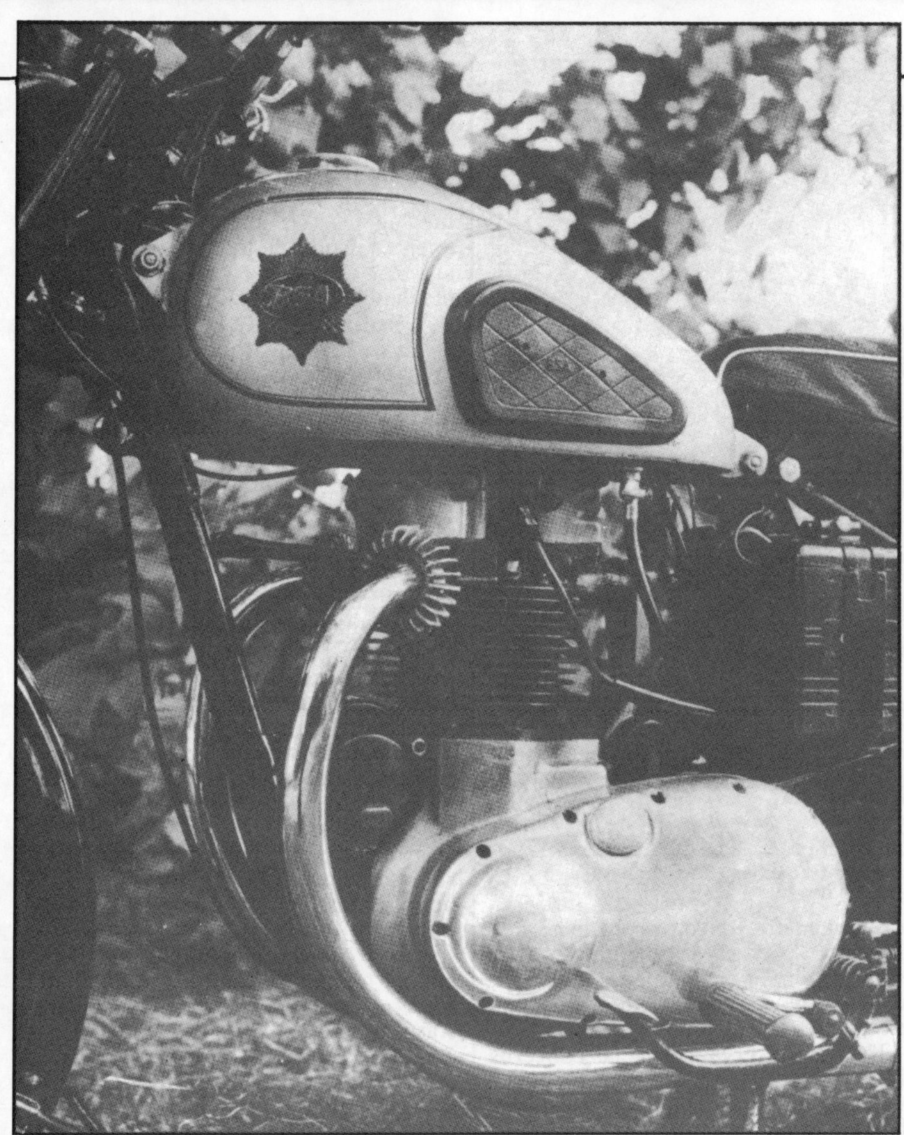

the bottom end, and when he started it up for the first time it ran sweet as a nut, with the original spark plugs (cleaned up of course) and all.

In fact, the only parts that Ray had to find were wheel rims, which he acquired from a breaker's yard, and the exhaust system. Silencers came from a local shop which was on the point of changing its allegiance from British motor cycles to those from "another place", and the pipes were obtained from Bruces of Birmingham. On the subject of the latter, Ray points out that he was foolish enough to discard the original pipes before he had located replacements, thus leaving himself without a pattern. Fortunately he was able to buy some off the shelf, but had the worst transpired he could have had some bent to shape by a specialist—had he but known the shape!

Some parts are not original, and he is quick to point them out. The handlebar and levers are later than 1952, although he still has the rusty remains of the components found with the machine, and he may refurbish them. The rear lamp is larger than it should be because the correct one is now illegal (though the one fitted does look-out of place); and some of the paintwork detail is wrong. However, when you consider that the whole job (including purchase price) was done

LEFT: THE serial number proclaims the Star Twin as one of those which *might* have been selected for the Maudes Trophy. HC stamping indicates a 7:1 compression ratio.

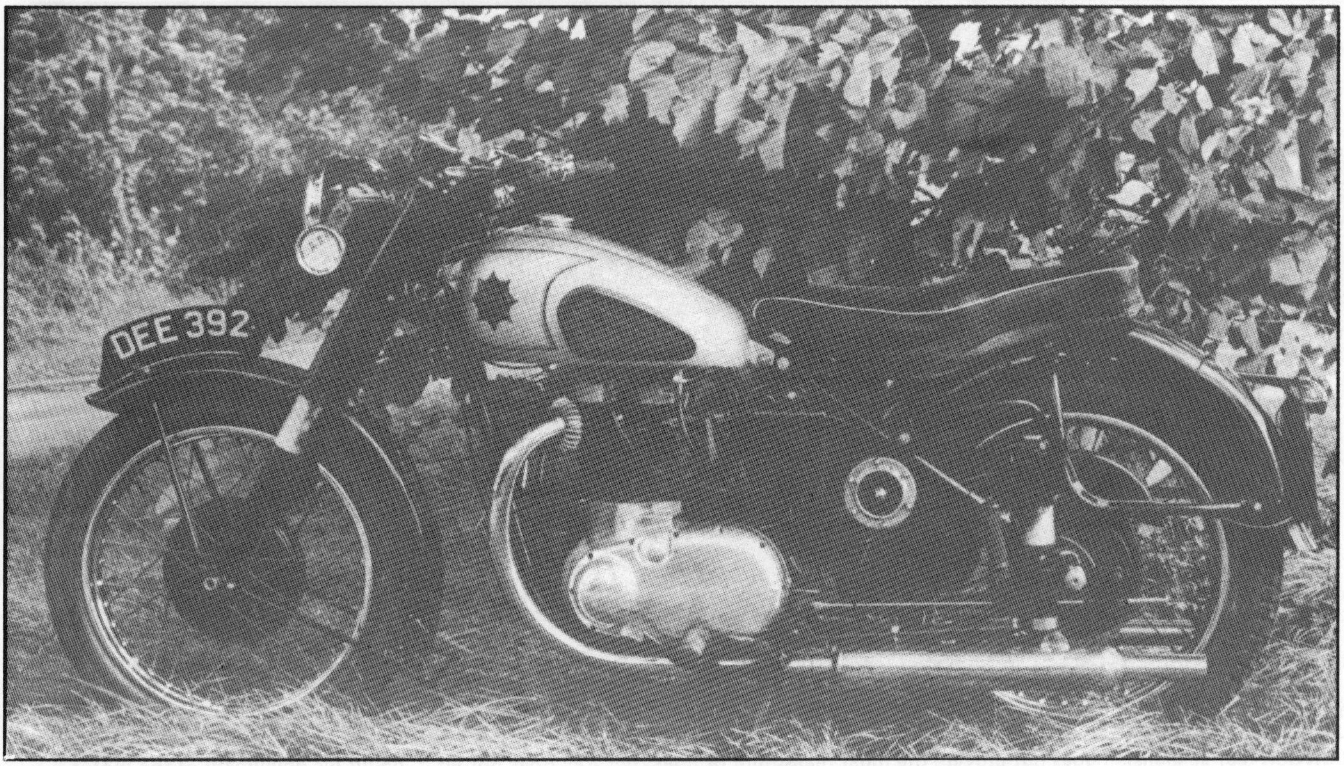

IN frequent use, the machine has covered 8000 trouble-free miles. Ray often goes to work on it, which makes a nice start and finish to the day.

for less than £100—and not so very long ago—it must be admitted that Mr Meggett has done capitally well.

He is not one to hide his handiwork away, and uses the Star Twin for everyday transport, having covered some 8,000 miles since the restoration, with no sign of trouble. The as-found dynamo and voltage regulator, and the magneto have all functioned perfectly which says something for the enduring quality of some Lucas parts, however much the detractors may sneer and scoff.

The only reservation he has concerns the handling. With a plunger frame, suspension movement is limited, and the rear wheel spindle is not clamped as rigidly as it is in some other designs. Ray illustrates this with a story about a Vincent-owning friend of his who came over for a run to a vintage race meeting at Cadwell Park. Working very hard, Ray managed to keep up the agreed 60 mph-top-whack run over to Cadwell by the back roads, and on the way back they swapped machines.

"Well," says Ray, "I started off at 60 mph, then I had to drop to 55, then 50, and I was still way ahead of him. When we got back to my place he said 'How did you keep up with me going over?', 'With great difficulty', I replied. 'I'm not surprised', he said, 'The first corner we came to, I just threw it into the bend, and it snaked all across the road. Then I backed off and it did it more than ever.' As I told him, the secret with plungers is to keep the power on gently, all the time. Even then it can be a bit rough, and that's how I got the flat on one of the silencers. Hit a pot hole."

Whatever its limitations in the corners, riding the Star Twin makes a nice counterpoint to Ray's Gold Star. It will cruise at 60 or 70 mph, and returns over 60 miles per gallon of two-star. Made in the days of pool petrol, the Star Twin was a high compression job (as shown by the HC stamped beneath the engine number), but by today's standards 7:1 does not seem excessive. With no particular starting routine to follow, and no need to slip the clutch in slow traffic, the Star Twin provides a nice relaxing run. Just the thing to take on a 5,000 mile trip around the continent.

PLUNGER rear suspension does not provide the most reassuring of rides, but Ray does not let it inhibit his enjoyment of the motor cycle's relaxed nature.

RAY Megget's 1952 Star Twin – which didn't win the Maudes.

T hese days most Classic bikes are at least as good as new, and lots of them are better. So to come across a BSA Star Twin in condition typical of the time when we spoke of 'motorbikes' and used the things for transport was a nice change. Not that I have anything but admiration for a well restored machine, but just the same it was refreshing.

The bike has a pleasing patina of age and use, but its owner Brenton Howard is as keen on BSAs as anyone I've ever met. He bought his first Star Twin in 1951, when it was two years old. He paid Claude Rye, of Fulham, £212 for it. This was 25 'bob' more than a new one would have cost, but he couldn't get a new one. There was an 18 month waiting list, and anyway the twin carb model that he wanted had been dropped in 1949.

It had a bore and stroke of 62mm x 82mm, and a capacity of 495cc, while the later single carburettor version which came out in 1950, and was dropped for 1955, had a shorter stroke of 72.6mm, and a bore of 66mm.

The Star Twin was developed from the BSA A7, the firm's first postwar twin, officially attributed to Herbert Perkins. In fact, a similar engine had been designed before the war, by Val Page, and Edward Turner had a hand in it before going back to Triumphs. Nevertheless, Perkins got the credit for designing the A7, and he deserved a lot of it. It was a very nice machine, the founder of a family.

He sorted out the engine, and got it right first time, give or take a few irritating drawbacks. The BSA twin unit, regardless of capacity, remained basically the same for 27 years, and if the family became a little decadent towards the end, well, that was hardly Herbert's fault.

The Star Twins had a high compression ratio, comparatively speaking, and high compression engines had 'HC' stamped upon the crankcase. In this case high meant 7.0:1, and that was high, as 72 octane petrol, aptly known as 'Pool', was the only fuel available. This may explain why, with 31 bhp, the Star Twin was no more powerful, and certainly no faster, than its single carburettor parent which compressed its dreary diet at 6.6:1. And also may explain why the twin carb model was short lived.

In a contemporary road test, which if it was set to music would become a hymn of praise, 84mph was claimed as the top speed. The tester had the grace to say that if the throttle was snapped open then the

AS BIKES USED TO BE

Peter Dobson
rides a pleasant BSA
Star Twin

engine 'pinked', and vibration could be felt at handlebars and footrests above 70mph, but in every other way the reader gets the strong impression that the bike was perfect. Brent says that the performance data is accurate enough, but the test does not entirely mirror his experience in other ways, though a lot of what was said is true.

Take the forks for example. The tester wrote that they had "... a very long soft movement (approximately 7 in) which, whether the model is upright or heeled over almost to the limit of tyre adhesion, smooths out road irregularities in the most satisfactory manner. Round the static load position, the movement of the fork is extremely light so that care is taken of even the most minor road ripples. Even at high speed there was never any trace of jarring, and the fork never bottomed". He doesn't ❯❯

AS BIKES USED TO BE

tell you that they had a tendency to 'top', but apart from that he was absolutely right. At the time Small Heath's telescopics were the best there were.

Even bearing in mind that he rode a new machine, and that rear springing was still something of a luxury in 1949, he is equally selective when he talks about the rear suspension. "It earned full marks" he wrote. ". . . It was unobtrusive — apparent only by the marked absence of wheel hop". As far as hopping goes that could very well be true, but he forgot to mention that at over 60mph on bumpy roads the Star Twin has a tendency to weave. This isn't caused by wear (though that doesn't help stability), but by the lack of damping. The only damping for the springs is provided by the grease inside the plunger boxes, and that is mainly there to lubricate. In terms of comfort if not

Above: The new front rim shows the correct finish of chrome and silver enamel. Dobson claims the BSA forks were 'the best there were in 1949'.

Left: Peter Dobson rates the Star Twin as a practical, honest, mildly sporting classic.

Neat and tidy - 'a pleasing patina of age and use.'

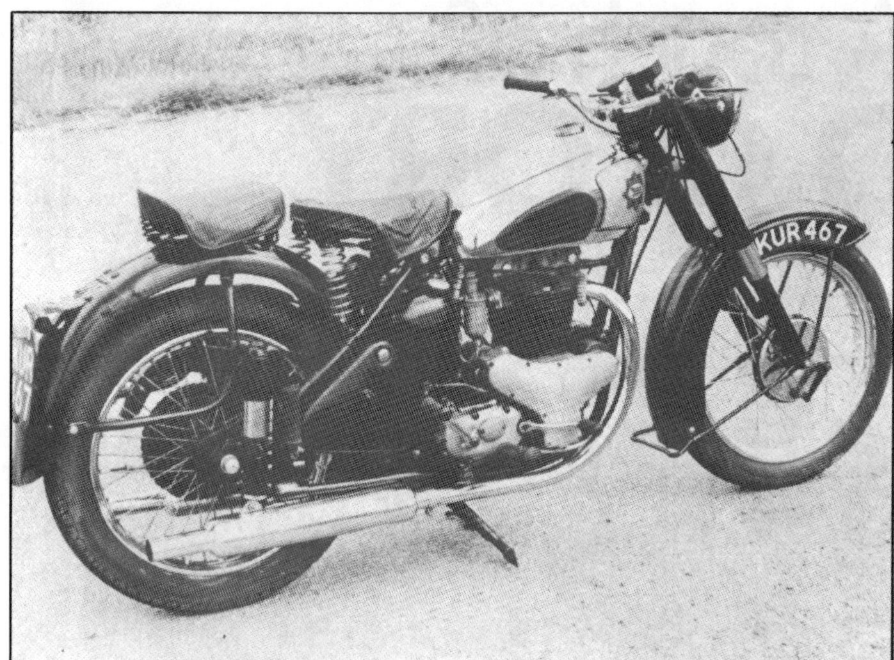

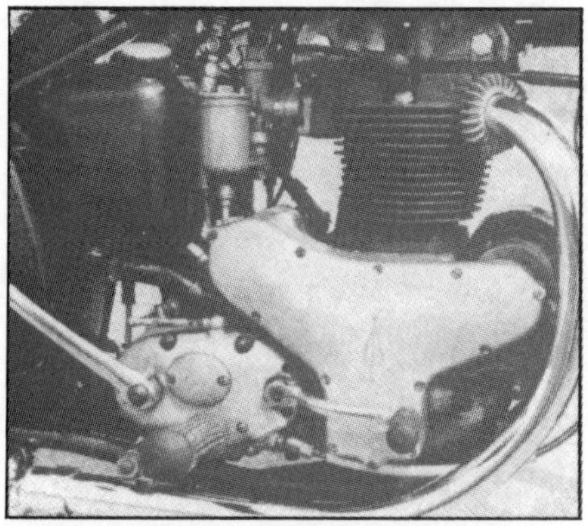

'The works' - 66mm x 72.6mm, 495cc twin, Engine No. ZA7S 1424 confirms it as a 1949 model.

handling, the plunger frame is better than a rigid one, but retaining the sprung saddle was a good idea.

Regarding the vibration that the tester mentioned, Brent went everywhere at 70mph on his first Star Twin, and while at that speed very little in the way of tremors from the engine reached the rider's hands or feet they reached the petrol tank alright. That item used to split at the back seam, and he regularly bought new tanks.

That apart, the engine is a vice free unit, noted for its durability. Brent covered 150,000 miles on his 1949 model, with one major overhaul. He lived on it. Used it for the run to work, as general transport to the pub, the shops, to road race meetings, and for such long distance trials events as the National Rally, the Lands End, the Exeter, the Derbyshire, and the Sunbeam 200. In the Jubilee Year National Rally of 1953 he won the manufacturers award. Later on he put a Watsonian Windsor lightweight sidecar on the BSA, and when he wasn't using that for social and domestic purposes, took the sidecar body off and put a platform in its place, using the outfit to transport his Francis Barnett trials bike to events.

"It ended up with a 21 in front wheel; standard sidecar gearing, and a Gold Star wide ratio trials cluster in the gearbox. When I sold it, it was knackered".

He parted with the BSA in 1958, and gave up bikes for all the usual reasons, but in 1984 the bug began to bite again and for old time's sake, as much as anything, he started looking for another BSA Star Twin. He discovered that things hadn't changed, Star Twins were hard to find. "I saw several advertised, but when I rang and asked about twin carburettors, and the valanced mudguard at the front there was usually a silence, and of course they weren't 1949 Star Twins.

"In the end I found one up in Newcastle. I phoned the bloke on Christmas Day, and two days afterwards we were on our way to pick it up with the car and trailer. My wife went with me as she hadn't seen much of the north of England, and she still hasn't seen much of it! It was very foggy and we couldn't see a thing.

"The bike was in a reasonable state. The bloke had run into a car with it, so I had to buy a new front rim, and have that painted and re-lined. The carburettor slides were different, but he had tried to file the cutaways to match. Apart from that it wasn't bad. He'd bought the bike in Portsmouth and ridden it home to Newcastle, and then restored it, to a point.

"It was in a right old state, judging by the sum he'd spent which was around £350, but most of that went on the bike's appearance. It cost him £110 to have the tank repaired and painted. On the more fundamental side he had to buy a camshaft, three camshaft bushes, and a crankshaft bearing, but that was about it.

"We spent the morning with the BSA in rural Hertfordshire. For me it was a case of 'You've read the roadtest! Now try out the bike', and it was interesting to learn just how much of what was written on the subject almost 40 years ago still apppliedto a machine with an unrecorded, but certainly substantial, mileage.

"Engine starting is very easy indeed" the man had said. "And because of the leverage of the kick-starter pedal and its gearing, only slight physical effort is required . . . Provided that the throttle was opened only the merest fraction, starting was certain at the second kick if the engine was cold, and first kick if it was hot". I wouldn't disagree with that, nor with the statement that . . . "Mechanically, the engine was reasonably quiet. After a cold start there was a fair amount of piston slap and noise from the valves. This decreased, of course, after the engine was hot."

He also said, quite rightly, that ". . . clean, sweet, gear changes were not too certain," and that selecting bottom gear when stationary with the engine idling wasn't possible without a crunch.

Brent said his first Star Twin had a brief vibration period at 50 mph which the 1940s tester also found, whereas this tester found that Brent's current bike is smooth right up to 70. Smooth that is by parallel twin standards. You can feel the presence of the engine all the time. The roadtest said that the exhaust note was an ". . . unobtrusive hum" but this became a pleasing snarl if I wrung its neck a bit. There was no pinking with modern fuel. The so-called high compression is really rather low these days, making for flexibility.

The riding position isn't bad for somebody who's 6ft 3in, but a great deal better for a rider who stands only 5ft 10in. The unladen 31in saddle height was somewhat on the high side in 1949, but the handlebars are also rather high which gives a nice position for admiring views — not very good for press-on motor cycling!

The clutch is very light in operation, as the roadtest said, and that combined with a 12ft turning circle, close to that provided on the trials bikes of the day, meant that full lock, feet-up turns were easy. Especially as there was no danger whatever of one's thumbs being pinned and crushed against the tank.

My main complaint was the ridiculous amount of effort needed when I came to haul it on the centre stand. Like those of several other British manufacturers the centre stand is diabolical. The roadtest mentions a lifting handle fitted just above the nearside seat stay to ". . . facilitate the operating of the centre stand" but it doesn't mention that 15 stone of bone and muscle would still be straining its guts to get it on the stand at all. And at 385lb, dry, Star Twins are not particularly heavy.

Other than that muscle building exercise, and the weaving above 60mph, which I didn't care for much, I liked the BSA Star Twin as a practical, honest, mildly sporting Classic though *The Motor Cycle* tester's last remark that "The Star Twin is a machine to make a wide appeal . . . to all those who want high cruising speed and handling that is as good as the best available today" is sadly out of date. But then I don't suppose the bloke had ever seen a stream of lorries, nose to tail, doing 80 mph in a cloud of spray. Things have changed since 1949, and not always for the better.

A touch of
OLD GLORY

NOT every motor cyclist dreams of owning an ultra-modern example of mass-produced technology. In fact a growing number of enthusiasts are discovering the joys of renovating and maintaining an older machine, many of which are still available at reasonable prices.

While the chances of finding a veteran (pre-1915) or vintage (1915 to 1930) machine are increasingly remote, and while even post-vintage (1930 to 1945) seem available only at extremely high cost, there are still many post-war bikes waiting to be "discovered".

The type of machine you can obtain will obviously be governed by your pocket, for even if the initial purchase price is low, proper restoration can be costly. Your own experience will also count. There's nothing worse than getting a bike half-finished then having to get someone else to complete the job for you, or leave the bike to

MARK YATES tells how he brought back the sparkle to a big BSA twin.

Top: The good old days. Above: the immaculate A10 that's the subject of this feature.

deteriorate. The ideal first machine is either one you already have knowledge of, or one that's easy to work on, like a BSA A10/A7 or a Triumph twin.

Of the two, my first choice would be the BSA twin, as this is a bike that can still be found relatively cheaply, and the spares are quite easy to get. The Triumph tends to be a bit dearer. When choosing a bike, don't be put off too much by a generally tatty condition, or by non-runners. These things bring down the cost considerably. The main thing is that the bike is as original as possible and also complete, as some of the parts may be unobtainable and it is handy to have a pattern to work from. This also applies to the paint work.

A first essential is join one of the many one-make owners' clubs up and down the country, as a lot now hold a stock of spares for sale. Their members can also help assist with any historical or technical queries.

OLD GLORY

When picking a machine, check that the frame and forks are serviceable, as these in particular can be expensive to replace. Also check the tyre size and condition, as older tyres might be unobtainable.

It is not advisable to buy a dismantled machine, as there might be another reason why it was not assembled, apart from the owner's "I've just not got round to it", like an unobtainable part.

Assuming the bike is complete, you need a manual, a pile of old newspapers, some assorted boxes, a pen, note pad and a camera with both black and white and colour film, then follow these steps:

1. Wash the complete machine down with Jizer or Gunk, making a thorough job under the engine and mudguards. Also drain out the engine and gearbox oil. It is handy to have a paraffin bath as well, as this is a lot cheaper than degreasants, and works just as well in most places.

2. With a camera loaded with colour film, take pictures of the complete machine, preferably with each one overlapping the next. It would also help if some were taken from different angles. Pay particular attention to the parts you might later have difficulty assembling. If the machine still has its original paintwork, it should also have its transfers. Don't forget to take close-ups of these as they will probably be hard to get. After taking the photos, try to take the transfers off the machine, or you can stick a bit of tape marked out in quarter-inch measurements alongside the transfer, and when the film is processed ask the shop to print one to scale so you can either get a transfer printed or get someone to paint a copy of the photo on to the finished bike.

3. Check over the machine to see if the mudguards, exhaust pipe, petrol tank, or frame have to be replaced. Also check whether any other bits have to be changed, as it will save scratching around later.

4. Place the boxes around the workshop and start to dismantle the bike into its component parts, i.e. engine, gearbox, etc. While doing this, put in the boxes all the parts that have got to be sent away. On the B.S.A. The nut and bolts were either plated with nickel or chrome, so these had to be sorted as they were taken off the machine. As you do this, make sketches of where the nuts and bolts come from, as it aids the rebuild. With the parts that are to be painted make two separate piles — the bits that are to be either bead or shot-blasted, and those that will be cleaned with paint remover. Remember to clean thoroughly all the parts that are to be sent out as the bead blaster will not work through grease. The same applies with plating and if the surface to be plated is not absolutely smooth, the finished part will be covered in ripples and the plating will not have a very long life.

5. Send off all parts you can as soon as possible, not forgetting to make note of everything you send, no matter how small. The small bits are the easiest to lose and the hardest to replace.

6. Start to strip the engine, making certain that there are some permanent means to retime the engine, both the spark and the valves. If not, try to put some on before you go any further. Again, as you are taking the engine to pieces, take photos (black and

The A10 in its present condition. A later owner decided that "Gold Star" colours looked best. Original restoration was black.

white will suffice at this stage) and keep doing sketches, as these will aid reassembly. The memory can fade after a few weeks.

7. Next come the wheels, and on the BSA it was possible to have the rims painted to match the bike, consisting of a line about 1½ inches wide.

It is very important to take photos and make accurate drawings of the spoke pattern. Whoever replaces the wheels must have an accurate record to work from, and this job is best left to the expert. It you want to do it yourself, practise on a spare wheel first.

There was a very good article on wheel building by Dave Walker in the March, 1977, issue of MCM. When stripping the wheel, try to leave at least one spoke from each side in place to aid the search for new spokes.

8. You should now have at least one box to take to the platers. Make sure you get a receipt for the amount of parts, as this may save a later disagreement. This also applies to the parts to be enamelled. After they have been blasted, they start to draw the moisture from the air, so they must be covered with a primer, and must not be touched with bare hands, as the natural acids in sweat can cause oxidation after a couple of hours.

If there is still rust on some of the parts it can be killed either by taking them to an engineering firm and asking for them to be put in acid for a couple of hours, or by using a rust-eating gel. If the petrol tank is a soldered type, warn the enamellers first. It could split in the enamel oven if they are not forewarned.

9. It's now time to start on the longest and slowest part of the restoration, the engine. This has to be stripped and all the parts checked for wear or age.

The A10 BSA has been called old-fashioned and underpowered, but was one of the easiest engines I've worked on. The model also has a lot of gutsy low down pulling power — but yes, it is possibly outdated. It's a machine not many people have restored to original condition. It's the only one I have seen, although I would imagine there must be quite a few others.

This bike cost the grand sum of £150 to buy in running condition. It was quite clean

The well-loved power unit was solid and unburstable.

and had passed the M.O.T., when the owner decided to make the bike even better by restoring it.

Sensibly he tried to get all the parts before starting to strip the bike down, as this was his transport to work. Our paths crossed when he was trying to trace some tank badges as I walked into his office. Sadly, I could not help him at that time, but he invited me to give him a hand on the strip down, which went according to the plan I had laid out. This model is quite similar to the 500cc A7. The only special tool necessary is a push-rod comb, but the owner had worked on three or four B.S.A. twins, so was experienced enough not to need it.

Other items you will need are valve spring compressor, grinding paste and chain rivet extractor. An extractor for the centre of the clutch is helpful but isn't always needed. We also used a puller for the front forks. As well as the listed tools, it is advisable to have a comprehensive tool kit including sockets, open-ended spanners and ring spanners, in both A.F. and B.S.F./Whit and the usual pliers, screwdrivers and hide mallet. Hammers are not needed.

The engine strip can be made much easier if there is a handbook and workshop manual close to hand. All through the strip,

For leisurely touring, the A10 has a lot going for it. Brakes have improved since its heyday, though.

The BSA turns heads wherever it's parked.

keep alert for bits that need sending out or replacing.

When taking the head off, loosen the bolts in sequence to try to lessen distortion. The same applies to nuts which hold the barrel on the crankcase, although to a lesser degree. When the barrels are off do not forget to stuff rags into the crank opening, because the con-rods are prone to hitting the crank cases, and the circlips can fall into the opening.

The pistons are then removed. Don't throw the circlips away unless you have already got new ones, as you may need them for a pattern.

The timing cover can then be removed, taking note of where the screws come from as there are three sizes. All the timing wheels on this bike are marked, but check that they are legible. One of the cam wheels has a cork washer on it that's part of the crankcase breather, and it must be in good condition, so try to keep it complete so at least you have a pattern. The dynamo drive should not be tight, so a light tap should loosen it. The oil pump must be pulled out with the pump drive as this is a tight fit.

The primary drive is now ready to be removed. Don't forget to take note of the screws. It is advisable to replace these with

socket head screws on the rebuild, but this would disqualify it from the concours class. Small things like this lose hard-earned points in these competitions, so the type of screws depend on what you are going to use the bike for.

If the clutch centre is stiff it might be possible to hire a puller from your local British bike dealer. To remove the shock absorber, it might be necessary to make up a special 'C' spanner. I used one from a cycle tool kit. Once the inner primary drive cover is off, the bolts on the crankcase can be removed, but try not to take all off one side at once as this can cause leaks because of warped crankcases. Now you will have eased the crankshaft out of the cases, and you will be able to see if the main bearings need replacing.

When the bushes and the bearings have been removed it is possible to recondition the cases. This can be done in two ways. You can take them to be blasted. This will make them look as if they have just come out of the sandcasts as original, and will be expensive. But this method takes metal off and if done too often will weaken them. You can also clean them by filling a small bath with boiling water and putting the previously warmed crankcases into it. This should make the crankcase look as good as new. It will help if you repeat the operation, washing them clear in paraffin in between. The gearbox can also be treated in this way.

To dismantle the gearbox, unscrew the four nuts and the three screws round the rim of the cover, but do not remove the screw and nut that are not on the edge as these do not prevent its removal. The cover is then taken off complete with kickstart, gearchange and clutch lever The gearchange can be dismantled by removing the lever and circlip. If the claw is not in good condition it should be replaced.

When the gearbox has been dismantled, clean in the previously stated method, making sure that all the bearings are first taken out. Check the gear teeth for wear and replace any parts that do not look 100 per cent.

By this time you should have some of the parts back from the plater's or enameller's so you can start assembling the frame components, like the swinging arm engine plates and front forks.

Then you can fit the handlebars and levers, front and rear wheels and mudguards.

Now you should have the engine, gearbox, primary drive, petrol and oil tanks and seat and lights left. You should also have a pile of clean, dry, soft, fluff-free cloth.

When your engine has been rebuilt, fit it back into the frame, making sure you do not scratch the paintwork. Then comes the gearbox, but do not tighten the bolts up at this point, the bottom rearward one is the pivot point for the drive chains. The primary chain inner case is next (hopefully all the bits and pieces are still there). Fit the rear chain and adjust it, then fit the primary drive chain, adjust this and check the rear chain, then fit the rest of the clutch and engine shock absorber. The outer primary chaincase can now be fitted.

Next the electrics can be connected. It is essential to have good wiring, and I consider it worthwhile to renew the wiring harness. It's just as easy to put a new harness on as an old one.

The cables can also be fitted at this time.

All we now have left are the tank and seat. The transfers should not be fitted yet, but the tank can be lined. The reason the transfers are left is because the oil tank on the BSA is not vertical, so it's best to leave it until the tank is on the bike.

As soon as the bike is finished, you'll want to take it out on to the road. But, remember, it will start to deteriorate immediately. Keeping paint work immaculate can be a problem. You will need a very soft "Tac-cloth" that works without scratching.

If you intend using the bike regularly, the best method is first to use hot, soapy water, then to rinse in clean hot water and wipe dry. Then use a Tac-cloth or similar at night when the bike is not in use. It also helps if the storeroom is kept fairly warm.

Useful addresses:—
Suppliers of mudguards, silencers, badges etc., Armours Products, 145 Malvern Rd., Bournemouth (0202-579409); suppliers of parts, Hamrax, Ladbroke Grove, London W10 5AD (01-969 5389); Honor Oak Motorcycles, 29 Honor Oak Park, Forest Hill, London (01-291 1272); Brian Verrall and Co., 20 Tooting Bec Road, London SW17 (01-672 1144); Mark Yates, 41 High St., Spalding, Lincs; Marque histories, Roy Harper and Co, (Mail Order), 35 Gunter Grove, Kings Road, London (01-352 4744).

The cost of the restoration of the BSA A10 was as follows:

Motorcycle purchase	£150.00
Tank badges (pair)	£4.00
Transfers (2 BSA, I oil level)	£1.70
New bearings	£8.00
Headlight rim (chrome)	£3.00
Wheel rims (the pair)	£14.00
Speedometer cable	£2.00
Gasket set	£2.00
Stove enamelling	£15.00
Chrome plating	£15.00
Nickel plating	£2.50
Shot blasting	£12.95
total outlay approx	£230.15
total time taken	4 weeks
total hours actual work	106 Hrs.
approx. value of complete restored machine	£450.00